Trends In
European Social Policy

Essays in memory of Malcolm Mead

Edited by

Jeff Kenner, LLB, LLM (London)
Lecturer in Law, University of Leicester

Dartmouth
Aldershot • Brookfield USA • Singapore • Sydney

Published by
Dartmouth Publishing Company Limited
Gower House
Croft Road
Aldershot
Hants GU11 3HR
England

Dartmouth Publishing Company
Old Post Road
Brookfield
Vermont 05036
USA

British Library Cataloguing in Publication Data
Trends in European Social Policy: Essays
in memory of Malcolm Mead
    I. Kenner, Jeff
    341.763

ISBN 1 85521 704 X

Printed and bound in Great Britain by Ipswich Book Co. Ltd., Ipswich, Suffolk

Contents

Preface

European social policy is entering a new and uncertain phase as the millennium nears. The publication of the European Commission's *White Paper on European Social Policy*, in July 1994, coinciding with the full implementation of the Maastricht Social Policy Agreement in fourteen Member States of the enlarged European Union, exempting the United Kingdom for the time being, provides a new and timely challenge to the Union's policy makers.

For the first time there is Community legal machinery capable of giving practical effect to a significant number of outstanding social policy objectives encompassing many of the subject areas analysed in this volume, notably promoting worker participation, extending equal treatment rights for women and men, and establishing employment rights for part-time workers. However, the expansion of the Community's competence to act must be understood in the context of the changing nature of the European labour market and the consequential shift in social policy priorities away from traditional employment protection measures and towards a pro-active strategy intended to create jobs, improve vocational skills and integrate marginalised groups into the workforce.

By selecting a range of contributions on current social policy themes this publication seeks to provide an opportunity for political scientists and lawyers, and anyone with an interest in the European "social dimension" and labour law, to study a number of individualised topics which reflect the sheer breadth and diversity of this expanding field of policy development.

Each of the contributions, with the exception of the opening chapter written by the author, were originally submitted as part of University of Leicester's Masters programme in European Management and Employment Law.

The contributors include: a Norwegian Government minister, a senior lecturer in industrial relations, a principal officer in the Irish Civil Service, a specialist in the business application of information technology, and a member of the New York bar. In each case they have brought their academic ability and professional experience to bear on an important aspect of European social policy.

Chapter One provides an in-depth analysis of the scope of individual employment law in the European Community and considers the prospects for the development of a "social citizenship" for Community workers. Chapter Two, by Brian Jones, offers a challenging and provocative overview of Community developments on sex equality in pension schemes written from a United States perspective. Chapter Three, by Philip Jones, contains a critical assessment of the impact of the Works Council Directive in the United Kingdom in the context of previous Community proposals for forms of workers' participation.

Chapter Four, by Ingeborg Borgerud, analyses the agreement establishing the European Economic Area and considers, from a Norwegian perspective, the prospects for free movement, without discrimination on the grounds of nationality, for EEA workers. Chapter Five, by Paul Cullen, compares the European Community provisions for equal treatment and working time with long established labour standards on night work for women adopted as protective measures through the International Labour Organisation. He discusses the lessons learnt through the process of resolving this policy conflict. Chapter Six, by Nick Rahtz, highlights the difficulties faced by the Community in adopting legislation to protect part-time and other "atypical" workers both to ensure equality with full-time workers and also to allow for fair competition.

The idea for writing this book as a tribute to Malcolm Mead came spontaneously from Malcolm's fellow postgraduate students and the academic staff at the International Centre for Management, Law and Industrial Relations, based in the Faculty of Law at the University of Leicester.

Malcolm Mead possessed all of the attributes which have helped to make the LL.M./M.A. course in European Management and Employment Law a resounding success. Malcolm was a determined self-achiever who was committed to broadening his knowledge and understanding of European Community law and social policy whilst pursuing an active and prominent professional career.

Many of these attributes were shared by Malcolm's peers, although such is the variety of professional and academic backgrounds represented amongst the contributors to this book, that it would be incorrect to describe Malcolm, or indeed anyone else involved in the course, as typical of the student body as a whole. Malcolm's sudden and unexpected death was a great shock to us all and I am particularly grateful to Christopher Docksey for his fulsome tribute in the foreword to this book.

I would like to thank everyone involved in producing this book, not least the Directors of the International Centre, Professor Alan Neal and Colin Bourn, for their encouragement throughout this project. Thanks are also due to Sue McNaughton and everyone at Dartmouth Publishing for being very supportive and helpful at all times.

I owe a particular debt of gratitude to Susan Thornton and John Williams for the excellent administrative support and secretarial assistance which I have received.

I would like to give special thanks to Jacqueline Abbott for her patience and unstinting support.

Finally, I would like to thank the contributors and all of the current and former students involved in the European Management and Employment Law course from its inception in 1991. Without you this book would not have been possible.

Jeff Kenner
Leicester
February 1995

International Centre for Management, Law and Industrial Relations
Faculty of Law, University of Leicester

LL.M./M.A. in European Management and Employment Law

1992 Student Entry

Niaz S. Alam

Roisin B. Barry

Fiona Bevan

Ingeborg M. Borgerud

Elizabeth Bylund

Patrick Canavan

Jane E. Cleator

Steven B. Clifford

Paul Cullen

Peter Fontes

Antonio Gomez De La Torre

Ragnhild M. Hagen

David J. Hood

Thomas Hui

Philip G. Jones

Brian A. Jones

George T. Lyon

Malcolm Mead

Penny McConnell

Johan Muller

Jane Murphy

Francis Navaratne

Ursula O'Hanlon

Richard A. Powell

Nick Rahtz

Martti O. Reuna

Paolo Ricci

Ian Ritchie

Barbara L. Scully

Christopher A. Short

Richard Tapp

Malcolm Mead

Foreword: A Tribute to Malcolm Mead

Malcolm Mead was a distinguished labour lawyer from Devon who gave the lie to the patronising overtones of the expression "provincial solicitor".

He left his Grammar School in Tiverton at 15 because of illness, but proceeded to study at home for his "A" levels and subsequently for his external law degree. He qualified as a solicitor whilst working for Bevan Ashford, the Tiverton-based firm of which he later became managing partner, and subsequently deepened his academic knowledge of labour law by taking an external Master's degree at Exeter University. As a labour lawyer he was at the same time a practitioner, an author and a judge. As a practitioner he gave advice to employers, employees and trade union clients from all over the country. As an author he is responsible for the successful *Mead on Unfair Dismissal*, which reappeared in its fourth edition in 1992. And as a judge he sat as a highly-regarded part-time Chairman of Industrial Tribunals in Southampton. He combined all these roles with being the managing partner of his firm and studying for an LL.M. in European Management and Employment Law at the University of Leicester.

Malcolm Mead has the unusual distinction of leaving the same memory with those who knew and worked with him in all these roles, regardless of whether they worked above, beside or below him. They all thought he was excellent. When pressed they will explain that he was unusually good at understanding and explaining things, that he was extremely efficient, and that he was unfailingly friendly and helpful. As I know from my own personal experience, he was an effective communicator, and could command any audience, whether in a small group or a large meeting. He had presence, he was inspirational, and he could get things done. One person even felt he was unfairly good because he was so consistently excellent in all he did, but I suspect there was nothing unfair about Malcolm Mead. He had a fine mind and personality, and he made his way by working very hard indeed.

Malcolm Mead died in mid-career in 1993 at the age of 44. It is rare for a practitioner, whether in London or in Devon, to make the name that he already had in his field. We will never know how many cases he would have brought to the House of Lords as a legal adviser or referred to the Court of Justice from his Industrial Tribunal. What we do know is that English law has lost a lawyer with a formidable brain and a practical touch and that Community law has lost the aid of an energetic and determined English lawyer who was methodically preparing himself to contribute to its development.

In preparing this foreword I have been very struck by the fact that the most impressive professional monument that Malcolm Mead has left behind is not his book, or the state of his firm, or the undoubted quality of his judicial pronouncements; it is the warm memory of excellence and admiration retained by all the people who have worked with this remarkable man.

Christopher Docksey
Brussels, 1995

*   Christopher Docksey is a member of the European Commission Legal Service. This tribute is written in a personal capacity.

1. Citizenship and Fundamental Rights: Reshaping the European Social Model

Jeff Kenner

1. INTRODUCTION

As the fifteen Member States of the European Community embark upon a concerted drive for "labour market flexibility" in an increasingly desperate search for the holy grail of employment-intensive growth and competitiveness there is growing equivocation over the future direction of Community social policy. Thus, although the application of the Maastricht Protocol and Social Policy Agreement[1] offers, for the first time, the potential of a widely extended floor of social rights for Community citizens, the European Commission's 1994 Social Policy White Paper merely asserts that:

> Given the solid base of European social legislation that *has already been achieved*, the Commission considers that there is not a need for a wide-ranging programme of new legislative proposals in the coming period.[2]

Instead, after years of frustration arising, not least, from the limitations of the Community's legislative base for social policy measures, there will

---

1.   The Agreement on Social Policy is Annexed to Protocol 14 of the EC Treaty as amended by the Treaty on European Union (TEU) — hereinafter the "Social Policy Agreement" (SPA). The SPA came into effect on 1 November 1993 in 11 Member States, excluding the UK which has opted out under the terms of the Protocol. The application of the SPA was extended to Austria, Finland and Sweden on their accession to the EU on 1 January 1995.

2.   *European Social Policy — A Way Forward for the Union*, COM(94) 333 of 27.7.94 — hereinafter the "Social Policy White Paper" (SPWP), Introduction, para.22. *Author's emphasis.*

be a period of "consolidation" intended to "preserve and develop" the "European social model" during the last quinquennium of the twentieth century.

In order to assess the veracity of the Commission's confident claim in the White Paper it is necessary to trace the historical development of the "European social model" and to ascertain whether the Community's achievements to date genuinely provide a "solid base" of exercisable rights for workers as Union citizens[3] consistent with the Community's overriding task of promoting "a high level of employment and of social protection, the raising of the standard of living and quality of life, and economic and social cohesion among Member States".[4]

This Chapter will examine the scope of substantive individual employment rights under Community law as one central aspect of the widening "social dimension". In each section key elements of Community social policy will be fully explored as a means of determining the nature of Community labour law and identifying areas of weakness where action is required to fill gaps and remedy defects. The impact of the Social Policy Agreement on individual employment rights will be assessed together with its political and legal complexities. In the conclusion there will be a critique of the Social Policy White Paper and a reassessment of the "European social model" based on the need not only for an extension of existing Community legislation in the social policy field, but also, more importantly, calling for a new paradigm of Union citizenship fully embracing fundamental economic and social rights which are tangible, accessible, and capable of enforcement and protection by the courts.

2. WHITHER THE EUROPEAN SOCIAL MODEL?

As a concept, the social policy of the Community remains opaque and almost incapable of precise definition. The Commission's own Social Policy Green Paper opted for the broadest possible approach whereby social policy:

> ...is taken to mean the full range of policies in the social sphere including labour market policies.[5]

3.   "European Union" is an umbrella term which is broader than "European Community" and covers inter-governmental matters which are not within the purview of the Court of Justice. As social policy is featured in the EC Treaty, all references in this Chapter are to the Community with the exception of Union citizenship within the meaning of Article 8 EC.

4.   Article 2 EC as amended by the TEU.

5.   *European Social Policy — Options for the Union*, COM (93) 551 of 17.11.93 — hereinafter the "Green Paper".

To an extent this vagueness is a consequence of the economic imperative that has always driven the Community's social priorities. Enhancing
the rights of workers and eradicating inequalities of wealth and income
among its citizens have never been independent political objectives of
the Community. Indeed many aspects remain outside the competence
even of the fourteen Member States, with the exception of the United
Kingdom, who have agreed to act under the Social Policy Agreement
(SPA). Article 1 of the SPA defines the Community's social policy objectives as:

> ...the promotion of employment, improved living and working
> conditions, proper social protection, dialogue between manage-
> ment and labour, the development of human resources with a
> view to lasting high employment and the combating of exclu-
> sion.

However this apparently more specific definition continues thus:

> To this end the Community and the Member States shall imple-
> ment measures which take account of the diverse forms of na-
> tional practice, in particular in the field of contractual relations,
> and the need to maintain the competitiveness of the Commu-
> nity economy.

Furthermore Article 2(6) of the SPA provides that any Community legislative provisions arising therefrom, and any Community level agreements
by management and labour:

> ...shall not apply to pay, the right of association, the right to strike
> or the right to impose lock-outs.

When the Community acts as fifteen, the option which is always intended
to be chosen in the first instance,[6] the launching of new legislative proposals in the field of labour law will normally have to be justified in so far
as they "...affect the establishment or the functioning of the common
market", under Article 100 EC, requiring unanimity in the Council of
the European Union, and not as internal market measures because Article 100a EC, introduced under the 1987 Single European Act (SEA),
specifically excludes provisions "...relating to the rights and interests of
employed persons". This Chapter will explore later the extent to which

6.   SPWP, Introduction, para. 23. Note that: "However the desire to act as [15] cannot be
     used as an excuse for standing still".

the limitations of Article 100a are mitigated by the availability of Article 118a EC concerning the encouragement of improvements "...especially in the working environment, as regards the health and safety of workers".

From the outset Community social policy has been an adjunct of the overriding market oriented objectives of the Treaty of Rome. A former Director-General for Social Affairs, writing in 1977, explained the rationale for this approach in the following terms:

> The underlying assumption behind the Treaty was that if one could remove all artificial obstacles to the free movement of labour, goods and capital, this would in time ensure the optimum allocation of resources throughout the Community, the optimum rate of economic growth, and thus an optimum social system.[7]

The priorities of growth and competitiveness remain paramount and the Social Policy White Paper (SPWP) must be understood in the context of the Commission's far more influential 1993 Growth White Paper (GWP)[8] which calls for:

> ...a *thoroughgoing reform of the labour market*, with the introduction of greater flexibility in the organisation of work and the distribution of working time, reduced labour costs, a higher level of skills, and pro-active labour market policies.[9]

While the terminology of labour market "flexibility" is more politically acceptable than "deregulation", with its Thatcherite connotations, there is no doubting the change of tone in both White Papers which is far removed from the "social dimension" rhetoric which accompanied the Community "Social Charter".[10] Just three years earlier the Commission had called for "a new, wider declaration and commitment to the basic principles of social justice and opportunity".[11]

The SPWP addresses the debate from another perspective, dispensing with any overt commitment to furthering of social justice and seeks

7.   M. Shanks, " The Social Policy of the European Communities", (1977) 14 C.M.L.Rev. 375.

8.   *Growth, Competitiveness, Employment — The Challenges and Ways Forward into the 21st Century*, Bull. of the E.C., Supp. 6/93 — hereinafter "GWP".

9.   *ibid.*, Chap.8, p.124.

10. The Community Charter of the Fundamental Social Rights of Workers was adopted by eleven Member States, excluding the UK, as a "Solemn Declaration" at the Strasbourg Summit in December 1989.

11. Commission Report on Employment in Europe, 1990.

to complement the GWP by emphasising the perceived areas of consensus among *all* Member States and "social partners" purporting to represent management and labour. From this assumption of consensus, derived in part from an interpretation of the varied responses to the Green Paper,[12] the Commission concludes that:

> ...there are a number of shared values which form the basis of the European social model. These include democracy and individual rights, free collective bargaining, the market economy, equality of opportunity for all and social welfare and solidarity.[13]

According to the technical annex attached to the SPWP:

> Contributions from all sides stress that there is a *European social model*. It is a cornerstone of our society even if the levels of social protection differ from country to country. This model is based on negotiation, solidarity and a high level of social protection.[14]

What then is the future for Community social policy? According to the Commission the "European social model" is almost complete and the only steps to be taken will be to introduce the outstanding items from the Action Programme,[15] to propose a consolidation of labour standards when strictly necessary, to respond positively to any attempts by management and labour to utilise the provisions in the SPA by seeking Community level agreements,[16] and to promote health and safety at the workplace.[17]

Thus Community legislation will be used as a last resort when the Community's objectives cannot be achieved by other means. Whilst this approach is primarily a consequence of the centrifugal tendencies created by the application of the principle of subsidiarity, it also confirms that employment law and social protection are policy areas which will

---

12. In a notable demonstration of transparency the Commission has published a 314 page technical Annex to the SPWP based on 530 written contributions made in response to the Green Paper containing over 7,000 pages of written material. (COM 94 (333) final/2 of 27.7.94, Chap.1, paras.2 & 5).

13. SPWP, Introduction, para.3.

14. Annex to the SPWP, Chap.1 para.12.

15. COM (89) 568 final, 29 November 1989. The second Social Action Programme is contained in the Commission's communication to give effect to the principles embodied in the Community's "Social Charter".

16. Article 4 of the SPA.

17. SPWP, Chap.3, para.5.

remain predominantly in the national domain with Community laws being required to establish "minimum standards" and not total harmonisation.[18]

3. THE EVOLUTION OF THE EUROPEAN SOCIAL MODEL: STAGES OF DEVELOPMENT

In the following sections consideration will be given to the development of Community social policy in the form of the Treaties and labour legislation, from the immediate post-war period through to the EEC Treaty and onwards to the Treaty on European Union (TEU). A full assessment will be made of the pivotal role played by the Court of Justice of the European Communities in ensuring effective protection of individual employment rights. Case law will be considered up to the end of 1994 in order to measure the scope of genuine "achievements" arising from the legislative activity in question.

(i) The Origins of Community Social Policy

An embryonic European social model emerged in the aftermath of the Second World War with a shared desire between the victors and the vanquished of Western Europe for social progress based on the establishment of the welfare state; encompassing education, public health and social services; the achievement of full employment, and the extension of labour standards through the International Labour Organisation (ILO)[19] and the Council of Europe.[20] In this way policy makers sought to overcome the privations of war and to achieve universal and lasting peace through societal harmony based on the principles of social justice and solidarity.[21]

It is indeed no coincidence that in this period the ILO adopted Conventions[22] on freedom of association, the right to organise and equal remuneration. At European level, the Convention for the Protection of Human Rights and Fundamental Freedoms (ECHR), 1950, contained a

18. *ibid.*, Introduction, para.18.

19. The International Labour Organisation (ILO) was founded in 1919 following the Treaty of Versailles and was reformed in 1944 before becoming an autonomous part of the United Nations based in Geneva.

20. Founded as an inter-governmental organisation in 1949.

21. For a fuller explanation see: N. Valticos, "International Sources and Institutional Aspects", Chap.1 of Vol. XV of the *International Encyclopaedia of Comparative Law* (1978), pp. 3-6.

22. Convention Nos. 87 (1948), 98 (1949) and 100 (1951).

broad range of individual rights including freedom of association and the right to organise (Article 11), and the prohibition of forced labour (Article 4). This was later supplemented by the European Social Charter (ESC) of 1961 and its Additional Protocol of 1988, which have been ratified by most EC Member States. The ESC is far more wide-ranging than the ECHR, as a statement of fundamental economic and social rights, and was a considerable influence upon the Community's 1989 "Social Charter". The importance of the ESC as a potential source for the "crystallisation" of fundamental rights which can be upheld by the Court of Justice,[23] will be assessed further in Section 4 of this Chapter.

The Treaty of Paris, establishing the European Coal and Steel Community (ECSC), 1951, was also part of this process of social solidarity and, while it is strictly sectoral in its effects, it is generally considered to have more social content than the later EEC Treaty.[24] However by the time of the Spaak Report, 1956, the rising post-war tide of social reformism had abated, and the Foreign Ministers called only for a "gradual coalescence of social policies" based on removing obstacles to the migration of labour and to distortions to competition.[25] A Joint Committee of Experts of the ECSC and the ILO also concluded that social policy legislation was not a necessary component of the goal of European integration and proposed that any intervention should be minimalist in character.[26]

(ii) *The Principle of Equality and Employment Protection under the EEC Treaty*

(a) *The Economic and Social Objectives of the Treaty of Rome*

The EEC Treaty, signed in Rome by the six ECSC members in 1957, was imbued with the ethos of social minimalism reflecting the prevailing *laissez-faire* economic policies which lasted throughout the late 1950s and the 1960s. The assumption behind the Treaty was that the removal of obstacles to the free movement of labour, goods, services and capital, would inexorably lead to higher growth and rising living standards which would, in turn, uplift all socio-economic groups and therefore benefit the socially disadvantaged. Thus Article 2 EEC proclaimed the Community's task as:

---

23. See O. Kahn-Freund, "The European Social Charter", Chap.10 of *European Law and the Individual"*, Ed. F.G. Jacobs (1976), pp.181-211 at p.197.

24. Shanks, *op.cit.* n.7, at p.375.

25. See B.A. Hepple, "The Crisis in EEC Labour Law", (1987) 16 I.L.J. 77 at pp.77-78.

26. ILO Studies and Reports (New Series) No.46, "Social Aspects of European Collaboration", Geneva, 1956. For a discussion on this point see R. Nielsen and E. Szyszcak, *The Social Dimension of the European Community*, 2nd. Ed. (1993), at pp.16-17.

...establishing a common market and progressively approximat-ing the economic policies of Member States, to promote...an accelerated raising of the standard of living.

The preamble to the EEC Treaty refers to the objectives of "social progress" and the "constant improvement of living and working condi-tions", but the social provisions in the Treaty, Articles 117 *et seq.*, pro-vided no specified legal basis for the enactment of legislation to fulfil these objectives. Thus, prior to the SEA, the Commission had to seek unanimous Council approval for social legislation as common market approximation measures under Article 100 or under Article 235 as ap-propriate measures "necessary to obtain one of the objectives of the Community and this Treaty has not provided the necessary powers". This restricted legal base stunted the development of the Community's social policy with ramifications which continue and have been exacerbated by the exercise of the Council veto by several Member States, not least the United Kingdom after 1979.

(b) Article 48 — Freedom of Movement for Workers

The Community's achievement in progressing towards trans-national free movement for workers by the end of the transitional period is often cited as an exemplar of Community actions fulfilling broader social policy goals. However the purpose of Articles 48-51 is to guarantee free move-ment for workers on the basis of the principle of non-discrimination on the grounds of nationality. This liberates the factors of production as "human capital" within the common market.[27] The measures used to achieve this were principally regulations to ensure equality of treatment in employment and social advantages in the host Member State,[28] and for the co-ordination of social security schemes.[29] The use of legislation in the form of a regulation in these areas which will be "...binding in its entirety and directly applicable in all Member States",[30] is significant and can be contrasted with the mainstream social policy measures of the 1970s where the issuing of directives was usually preferred.

Regulations are indeed appropriate as a means of achieving free movement precisely because they do not involve intervention to raise

---

27. See S. Weatherill & P. Beaumont, *EC Law*, (1993), at pp.481-2.

28. Regulation 1612/68/EEC of 15 October 1968. OJ Sp.Ed. 1968, L 257/2, p.475.

29. Regulation 1408/71/EEC of 14 June 1971 as amended and updated by Regulation 2001/83/EEC of 2 June 1983, OJ L 230, 22.8.83, and subsequently amended between 1985 and 1992 by 11 Regulations.

30. Article 189 EC.

social standards but rather they serve to neutralise living and working conditions as between Community nationals. Therefore while free movement measures may have beneficial social consequences they are not, strictly speaking, instruments of social policy. However this has not prevented the Court of Justice ("the Court") from drawing upon these provisions as a means of benefiting certain groups of workers. For example in *Levin* [31] the Court applied Article 48 to part-time workers on the basis that such employment constitutes for a large number of persons "an effective means of improving their living conditions". Undoubtedly free movement has created job opportunities and more security for transnational workers but the overall effect has been to spread the scope of neutrality of treatment for workers and those seeking employment rather than to enhance social conditions in general.[32]

(c) Article 119 and the Principle of Equality

The principle of equality derived primarily, but not exclusively, from Article 119, extended through legislation, and recognised by the Court of Justice as a fundamental right applying to all nationals of the Member States who are workers under Community law, shines as the beacon of achievement in the field of Community social policy.

Article 119 calls for all Member States to abide by the "...principle that men and women shall receive equal pay for equal work". The scope of Article 119 was examined by the Court in the *Defrenne (no.2)*[33] case and explained in the following terms:

Article 119 pursues a double aim. First, in the light of the different states of development of social legislation in the various member states, the aim... is to avoid a situation in which undertakings established in States which have actually implemented the principle of equal pay suffer a competitive disadvantage in intra-Community competition as compared with undertakings established in States which have not yet eliminated discrimination against women workers as regards pay.

Secondly, this provision forms part of the social objectives of the Community, which is not merely an economic union, but is at the same time intended, by common action to ensure social

31. Case 53/81, *Levin v Staatssecretaris van Justitie* [1982] ECR 1035, para.15.

32. Free movement is considered further in Chapter 4 by Ingeborg Borgerud in the context of the European Economic Area Agreement.

33. Case 43/75, *Defrenne v Sabena (no.2)* [1976] ECR 455, paras.8-10.

progress and seek the constant improvement of the living and working conditions of their peoples...

Within these two paragraphs the Court has intertwined the dual aims which lie at the heart of the Community's treatment of social policy and which have, in trying to determine the relative priority between these objectives, presented the most difficult conundrum for policy makers and labour lawyers alike. In this instance the Court was able to elicit as a primary objective the need to eradicate what has now become known as "social dumping" arising from the undercutting of labour standards.

Furthermore equal pay was also recognised by the Court in *Defrenne (no.2)* as a free standing directly effective right enforceable by individuals, and the obligation applies both vertically and horizontally.[34] Therefore Article 119 provides protection on a higher plane than any directive, including the Equal Treatment Directive,[35] which has been held to be incapable of enforcement between two private parties even if the terms are sufficiently precise and unconditional to be otherwise directly effective, on the grounds that under Article 189 EC the binding nature of a directive exists only in relation to each Member State to which it is addressed and cannot of itself "impose obligations on an individual and that a provision of a directive may not be relied upon as against such a person".[36] This approach has recently been reaffirmed in the field of consumer law.[37]

The result is that where a worker *vis-à-vis* their employer is subject to the laws of a State which has failed to transpose, or incorrectly implemented, a directive, and the employer is not an emanation of the State,[38] they will have to bring an action against the State directly and establish fault on the part of the State in accordance with the test laid down in *Francovich*.[39]

---

34. *ibid.*, at paras.24 and 39.

35. Directive 76/207/EEC of 9 February 1976, on the implementation of the principle of equal treatment for men and women as regards employment, vocational training and promotion and working conditions. OJ 1976 L39/40.

36. Case 152/84, *Marshall v Southampton Area Health Authority* [1986] ECR 723, para.48. On the principle of direct effect see Case 26/62, *Van Gend en Loos v Nederlandse Administratie der Belastingen* [1963] ECR 1.

37. Case C-91/92, *Faccini Dori v Recreb S.r.l*; judgment of 14 July 1994 (nyr), discussed by T. Tridimas, "Horizontal effect of directives: a missed opportunity?", (1994) 19 E.L.Rev. 621.

38. See Case C-188/89, *Foster v British Gas* [1990] ECR I-3313.

39. Cases C-6 & 9/90, *Francovich v Italy* [1991] ECR I-5357, at para.40: three conditions must be fulfilled; (1) the directive should entail the grant of rights to individuals; (2) it should be possible to identify the content of those rights on the basis of the provisions

The greatest significance of the principle of equality is that it goes far wider than Article 119. This Treaty provision "...is part of the *implementation* of the principle; it is not the *source*".[40] In the third *Defrenne* case the Court proclaimed that:

> ...respect for fundamental personal human rights is one of the general principles of Community law...There can be no doubt that the elimination of discrimination based on sex forms part of those fundamental rights.[41]

In *Defrenne (no.2)* the Court had also specifically interpreted the "narrow criterion" of Article 119 in the light of Convention 100 of the ILO which established the principle of equal pay for work of "equal value".[42] Thus while the "equal value" principle was subsequently codified by the Equal Pay Directive[43] it was already implicit within Article 119 according to the Court.

The Court in the *Defrenne* cases chose to give the principle of equality a "special status" as a fundamental right under Community law and this has been applied and extended through supplementary legislation on equal pay and equal treatment, arising from the 1974 Social Action Programme, and later measures under the aegis of the 1989 Social Charter and its Action Programme.[44]

Further judgments of the Court of Justice have broadened the scope and application of the principle of equality to encompass a broad definition of "pay", for the purposes of Article 119, to include sick pay,[45] employers contributions to pension schemes,[46] and occupational pensions.[47] The principle also covers sex discrimination in employment[48] and social

---

of the directive; (3) there must be a causal link between the breach of the State's obligation and the loss and damage suffered by the injured parties. The wider implications of *Francovich* in the employment protection field will be considered later in this section.

40. C. Docksey, "The Principle of Equality Between Women and Men as a Fundamental Right under Community Law", (1991) 20 I.L.J. 258 at p.259.

41. Case 149/77, [1978] ECR 1365, paras.26-27.

42. para. 20. of the judgment.

43. Directive 75/117/EEC of 10 February 1975, OJ 1975 L 45/19.

44. See generally, Docksey *op.cit.* n.40.

45. Case 171/88, *River Kuhn v FWW* [1989] ECR 2743.

46. Case 170/84, *Bilka Kaufhaus v Weber* [1986] ECR 1607.

47. Case C-262/88, *Barber v Guardian Royal Exchange* [1990] ECR I-1889.

48. Directive 76/207/EEC *op.cit.* n.35.

security.[49] The Court has recognised indirect discrimination, albeit subject to the limitation that the alleged discriminatory practice may be
capable of objective justification without reference to the sex of the workers concerned.[50] However dismissal on the grounds of pregnancy has
been held to amount to direct discrimination.[51] The Court has also insisted that an employer must satisfy a burden of proof to show that their
pay systems are transparent[52] but a proposed Directive dealing with the
burden of proof was later blocked by opposition in the Council and is
listed in the White Paper as an outstanding item for action.[53]

Article 6 of the Equal Treatment Directive places an obligation on
Member States to enable all people "who consider themselves wronged
by failure to apply to them the principle of equal treatment...to pursue
their claims by judicial process after possible recourse to other competent authorities". The Court has held in *von Colson* that although Article
6 is not in itself vertically directly effective,[54] in the sense that it could not
be relied upon by individuals to obtain specific compensation where that
is not provided for under national law, it does have "indirect effect" *vis-
á-vis* Member States and their public bodies whereby victims of unlawful
sex discrimination are entitled to financial compensation in full for the
loss and damage suffered and the Member States must put in place such
measures as to guarantee effective judicial protection and to have a real
deterrent effect on the employer.

The rationale for this development can be found in Article 5 EC
which places a duty of solidarity on Member States to "take all appropriate measures...to ensure fulfilment of [Treaty] obligations...or resulting
from actions taken by the institutions of the Community. They shall facilitate the achievement of the Community's tasks". The *von Colson* principle was applied and developed in *Marshall (no.2)* where it was held that
national limits on compensation for unlawful sex discrimination may be
overridden and adequate compensation can include an award of interest.[55] Curtin argues that *Marshall (no. 2)* should be given general application as:

49.   Directive 79/7/EEC of 19 December 1978 on the principle of equal treatment for men
      and women in matters of social security. OJ 1979 L6/24.
50.   Case 96/80, *Jenkins v Kingsgate Ltd.* [1981] ECR 911.
51.   Case C-177/88, *Dekker* [1990] ECR I-3841.
52.   Case 109/88, *Danfoss* [1989] ECR 3199, and *Barber, op.cit.* n.47, at para.33.
53.   OJ 1978 C176. SPWP, Chap.5, para.16.
54.   Case 14/83, *von Colson and Kamann v Land Nordrhein Westfalen* [1984] ECR 1891, para.27.
55.   Case C-271/91, *Marshall (No.2)*, [1994] IRLR 445. See casenote by D. Curtin, (1994) 31
      C.M.L. Rev. 631-652.

...a specific expression of a much more general principle, the right to an effective remedy, which is an obligation inherent to the system of Community law...[56]

Some indication of the wider ramifications empowering national courts to override domestic provisions conflicting with Community laws can be found in the UK case of *ex parte Equal Opportunities Commission*,[57] where the House of Lords found that the national system of redundancy payments for part-time workers was indirectly discriminatory because of the longer qualification periods applicable to part-time workers who were predominantly women. Further the case is important because it established that the EOC had *locus standi* to represent the public interest as a statutory body seeking the elimination of discrimination.[58] This precedent may well provide access to justice for many victims of discrimination in the UK and in other countries where the courts follow suit.[59] *Ex parte EOC* amounts to a significant advance towards the constitutionalisation of Community rights for individuals seeking a right of action and a remedy at national level. The outcome was a rebuff for the UK Government who have been forced with "extreme reluctance" to introduce legislation to comply with the judgment whilst remaining implacably opposed to the proposed part-time workers directive.[60]

The principle of equality is subject to very few exceptions by way of derogation and these have been strictly interpreted by the Court of Justice. For example Article 2(2) of the Equal Treatment Directive contains a derogation where the sex of the worker is the determining factor by reason of the nature of the job. The Court in *Johnston v RUC* [61] restricted the application of this exception to particular duties rather than general activities and held that a general ban against women serving as full-time members of the reserve police force in Northern Ireland was unlawful sex discrimination.

---

56. Curtin, *ibid.*, at p.647. Evidence in the UK is encouraging. According to the *Equal Opportunities Review*, No.54 (March/April 1994), the average payment to ex-service women dismissed because of pregnancy increased from £4,500 before *Marshall (no.2)* to £52,738 afterwards.

57. *R v Secretary of State, ex parte Equal Opportunities Commission* [1994] 1 All ER 910, noted by M. Ross, "The British EOC Case — A Model of Compliance?", (1994) 10 Int.J.Comp.L.L.I.R. 139.

58. Ross, *ibid.*, at p.140.

59. On this point see C. Docksey, "The Impact of European law on UK Remedies", Paper presented in a personal capacity at the Bar Conference, 1 October 1994, at paras.11-14.

60. *The Independent*, 20 December 1994.

61. Case 222/84 [1986] ECR 1651.

Other restrictions on the reach of the principle of equality arise from economic considerations which have influenced the Court to agree with submissions by Member States to limit the temporal effects of its judgments in *Defrenne* and *Barber*,[62] a weakness which has been subject to criticism,[63] and reflects the "tension between the 'economic' and the 'fundamental principle' approaches" of the Court.[64]

The principle of equality has been considered with a mind to brevity in this section and is developed much further elsewhere in this book.[65] Later sections of this Chapter will examine the limited steps taken after 1987 and identify the obstacles that remain. However, it can be confidently asserted, on the basis of the content of the principle as elucidated by the Court, and as set out in the EEC Treaty and directives prior to 1987, that equality is the most developed aspect of the "European social model". Further the emphasis on effective remedies for individuals and the fundamental rights approach of the Court in the field of equality can be seen as a model which needs to be applied to other aspects of social policy guaranteeing rights respected by the ILO and the Council of Europe and infusing them with a supra-national effect for the benefit of all Union citizens.

(d) Employment Protection

Articles 117 and 118 EEC were otiose in the early years of the Community. These provisions are exhortary and of a fairly general character. Article 117 calls for the promotion of "improved working conditions and an improved standard of living for workers, so as to make possible their harmonisation while the improvement is being maintained". Article 118 gives the Commission the task of "promoting close co-operation between Member States in the social field", particularly in matters relating, *inter alia,* to employment, labour law and working conditions, vocational training, prevention of occupational accidents and diseases, the right of association and collective bargaining.

---

62. *Barber* judgment para.45. The interpretation of this judgment has been much debated but one possible interpretation that the ruling is not retrospective, i.e. it cannot be relied upon for any pension entitlement for service before 17 May 1990, has now been codified by Protocol 2 of the EC Treaty. The legality of the "*Barber* Protocol" is considered by T.K. Hervey, Chap.8 of *Legal Issues of the Maastricht Treaty*, Eds. D. O'Keefe and P.M. Twomey (Chancery, 1994) at pp.329-337. Hervey correctly predicts that the Protocol will be followed by the Court.

63. Docksey, *op.cit.* n.40, at pp.274-6.

64. C. McCrudden (Ed.),*Women, Employment and European Equality Law*, London 1987 at pp.184-5.

65. See Chapters 2 & 5 by Brian Jones and Paul Cullen.

The principal reason why these goals did not form the basis for a meaningful programme leading towards a harmonisation of Community social policy was not so much the lack of a specific legal base in the Treaty but the remarkable economic success of the Member States, a sustained low level of unemployment, and the growth of indigenous welfare benefits systems as living standards rose. By the early 1970s, when the first social action programme was envisaged, there was a change of political priorities because as Hepple explains:

> It was only when the boom began to fall apart, when economic integration within the Common Market was visibly failing to protect working and living standards, and when a wave of strikes and wage explosions had swept across Europe, that EEC labour law came to life.[66]

The breadth of the guidelines of the 1974 Programme;[67] full and better employment, better living and working conditions, and greater participation; provided the prospect of a wide-range of legislative activity covering the matters contained in Article 118.[68] However the Programme was knocked off course by the depth of the recession in the mid-1970s and the resulting action was driven by the need to expand the scope of the European Social Fund[69] to alleviate unemployment, which had begun to rise, although only to 4.5% in 1975, a level almost unthinkable today.

Further measures were based on a need for the Community to react to specific economic and industrial circumstances and were directed at employment protection either in the face of mass dismissals,[70] or following changes in the ownership of the employing undertaking,[71] or in the event of corporate insolvency.[72]

---

66. Hepple, *op.cit.* n.25, at p.78.

67. At the Paris Summit, 1972, the Member States declared that they "attached as much importance to vigorous action in the social field as to the achievements of monetary and economic union". The first Social Action Programme was launched following a Council Resolution of 21 January 1974, OJ 1974 C13/1.

68. See generally; Hepple, *op.cit.* n.25, Shanks, *op.cit.* n.7, and A. Arnull, "Integration with a Human Face", (1987) 3 Int.J.Comp.L.L.I.R. 243.

69. Article 123 EEC. For a discussion see J. Kenner, "Economic and Social Cohesion — The Rocky Road Ahead", (1994) LIEI 1, pp. 8-12.

70. Directive 75/129/EEC of 17 February 1975 on collective redundancies, OJ L 48, 22.2.75.

71. Directive 77/187/EEC of 14 February 1977 on safeguarding employees rights in the event of transfers of undertakings, businesses or parts of businesses, OJ L 61, 5.3.77. hereinafter the "Acquired Rights Directive".

72. Directive 80/987/EEC of 20 October 1980 on the protection of employees in the event of the insolvency of their employer, OJ L 283, 20.10.1980.

Before considering these measures in turn it is worth noting that they were each introduced as approximation measures under Article 100 in the form of directives. The use of directives rather than directly applicable regulations, "binding in their entirety" under Article 189, can be seen as symptomatic of a generally cautious and pragmatic approach to social policy. A fierce desire on the part of the Member States, understood and respected by the Commission, to retain some independence of action in relation to both individual and collective labour law is a continuing feature of the "European social model" and has delimited the effects of Community activity. Directives are binding "as to the result to be achieved" but leave to the national authorities "the choice of form and methods".[73] Viewed from a certain perspective the use of directives has to be seen as obvious common sense because of the sheer diversity of social systems in the Member States not least in the variety of methods of "industrial democracy" and the differing forms of the employment relationship. The Court of Justice has recognised the general limitation on the intended scope of these measures. When considering the Acquired Rights Directive in *Daddy's Dance Hall*,[74] the Court noted that the directive:

> ...is intended to achieve only partial harmonisation, essentially by extending the protection guaranteed to workers independently by the laws of the individual Member States to cover the case where an undertaking is transferred. It is not intended to establish a uniform level of protection throughout the Community on the basis of common criteria.

Thus approximation in this context does not mean full harmonisation. This statement would apply equally to the related directives on collective dismissals and insolvency and to a later measure on the contractual information rights of employees.[75] As we can see from the case law on equality, in the preceding section, and on the transfers directive, below, the Court of Justice has, through its application of the principle of direct effect, ensured effective judicial protection of individual rights in relation to the Member States and full implementation of the necessary secondary legislation where the Commission has sought to bring proceedings before the Court under Article 169 EC. This has meant that whereas there has not been strict uniformity or full harmonisation there has,

---

73. Article 189 EC.

74. Case 324/86, *Foreigningen af Arbejdsledere i Danmark v Daddy's Dance Hall A/S* [1988] ECR 739, para. 16.

75. Directive 91/533/EEC of 14 October 1991, OJ L 288, 18.10.91.

nevertheless, been an obligation on the Member States to uphold the minimum standards required to make the directives available as a means of protecting individual employees to the extent that they "must be considered to be mandatory, so that it is not possible to derogate from them in a manner unfavourable to employees".[76]

The Collective Redundancies Directive provides a detailed procedure for dealing with mass dismissals, including public notification and consultation with workers' representatives, to be triggered by the number of workers involved and the timing of the dismissals. A collective redundancy is defined as a "dismissal effected by an employer for one or more reasons not related to the individual workers concerned".[77] The consultation of employees shall involve "at least...ways and means of avoiding collective redundancies or reducing the number of workers affected and mitigating the consequences".[78] While the Directive contains the most advanced form of obligatory employee consultation to arise out of the 1970s legislation it does not amount to full participation and the employer retains his prerogative. The Court held in *Dansk* that the Directive did not affect the employer's freedom to decide whether and when to formulate plans for collective dismissals. The procedural rules only applied where the employer has in fact contemplated redundancies or drawn up a plan for them.[79]

At this stage it is worth noting that the Collective Redundancies Directive has been amended to take into account the changing nature of company organisation, following on from the increasing number of mergers occurring in the Single Market, and local management will no longer be able to argue as an excuse that they are ignorant of redundancy proposals. Instead consultation is to take place "in good time" before everything is signed and settled and when consultation can still be effective.[80] This brings the Directive into line with the Additional Protocol of the ESC but it neither defines the remedies available nor alters the prerogative of the employer, as in *Dansk*, to decide whether redundancies should be foreseen in a given situation. These amendments have been rightly criticised for being somewhat cosmetic and amounting to little more than a rearrangement of the deckchairs.[81]

---

76. *Daddy's Dance Hall, op.cit.* n.74, para.14.

77. Article 1 of Directive 75/129.

78. *ibid.*, Article 2(2).

79. Case 248/83, [1985] ECR 1459, noted in Arnull, *op.cit.* n.68, at p.256.

80. Directive 92/56/EEC of 24 June 1992. OJ L 245, 26.8.92. See C. Bourn, "Amending the Collective Dismissals Directive: A Case of Re-arranging the Deckchairs?", (1993) 9 Int.J.Comp.L.L.I.R. 227 at pp.227-8.

81. Bourn *ibid.*, at pp.241-3.

The appropriateness of the method of consultation proscribed by national law or regulation has been considered most recently in *Commission v UK*.[82] There were two main grounds of complaint concerning the UK's implementing legislation.[83] First, there was no mechanism for designating workers' representatives in the absence of a recognised trade union and second, it was claimed that the system for awarding compensation was inadequate because the UK allowed compensation to be "set off " against other statutory or contractual compensation payable to the employee, reducing the overall amount of compensation. The Court found, *inter alia,* that the UK had breached the Directive by failing to designate workers' representatives where an employer does not agree to do so, and for not providing for effective sanctions in the event of a failure to consult. The Court's primary concern was that the protection provided for in the Directive should not be dependant on the employer's consent. This view was strongly emphasised in the Opinion of Advocate General Van Gerven when he asserted that:

> ...to make the activity of workers' representatives totally dependant on voluntary recognition by employers is incompatible with the protection of workers as apparent from the directives in the light of their objective, structure and wording.[84]

This is an landmark judgment because it is the first time that the Court has insisted upon a change to a national system of workers' representation. However, although *Commission v UK* is a large step forward the Court limited the effects of its judgment by reiterating that the Directive was "not designed to bring about full harmonisation of national systems for the representation of employees in an undertaking".[85] This means "that the UK government will have considerable discretion as to how it brings UK law into line with the Directives...".[86] Nevertheless, the UK will be obliged to provide for a system of consultation which is not dependant upon the employer's consent and this may mean either, the introduction of a statutory right of compulsory trade union recognition, or, that

82. Cases C-382/92 & C-383/92, [1994] IRLR 392, 412. The infringement proceedings also dealt with the UK's implementation of the transfers directive (see below). For a discussion see P. Davies, "A Challenge to Single Channel", (1994) 23 I.L.J 272; G. More, "Community labour law and the protection of employees' rights in the United Kingdom", (1994) 19 E.L.Rev. 660.

83. Part IV of the Employment Protection Act, 1975, now consolidated as ss.188-198 of the Trade Union and Labour Relations Act, 1992.

84. Cases C-382/92 & C-383/92, Opinion of the Advocate General at para.9.

85. Case C-382/92, para. 28 of the judgment.

86. Davies, *op.cit.* n.82, at p.275.

workers' representatives will have to represent all of the employees concerned, implying a requirement to establish a consultative body akin to a works council.[87] This latter interpretation would have very significant implications in the UK in the light of the recent Works Council Directive.[88]

The Acquired Rights Directive is the most substantive piece of Community social legislation from the first Action Programme outside of the equalities field. The preamble to the Directive proclaims that "it is necessary to provide for the protection of employees in the event of a change in employer, in particular, to ensure that their rights are safeguarded", and notes that while differences still remain, as regards the extent of protection afforded to employees, "these differences should be reduced".

Article 3(1) preserves the employees terms and conditions of employment on the date of the transfer. Further the Court has held that dismissals before the date of transfer where the reason for the dismissal was the transfer itself, are void and ineffective in law.[89] However before the employees, or indeed a single employee in certain circumstances,[90] can secure the transfer of these acquired rights a number of procedural hurdles have to be crossed to bring them within the scope of the Directive.

By Article 1(1) the Directive applies to "the transfer of an undertaking, business or part of a business to another employer as a result of a legal transfer or merger" which leads to a change in the employer's identity. Therefore protection depends on the form of merger and will not, for example, cover the acquisition by one company of a controlling shareholding in another, or indeed where the transferor has been adjudged insolvent and the undertaking is deemed to be part of his assets,[91] thus excluding whole areas of corporate activities affecting the position of the employees which were particularly prevalent in the late 1980s.[92]

The Directive is also subject to other limitations. Article 3(3) excludes rights under occupational pension schemes. Furthermore, while the transfer shall not in itself constitute grounds for dismissal by either the

87. *ibid.*, at pp.277-8.

88. Directive 94/45/EC of 22 September 1994. OJ L254/64 of 30.9.94. The Directive is considered in more detail by Philip Jones in Chapter 3.

89. Article 4(1) of the Directive provides that: "The transfer...shall not in itself constitute grounds for dismissal...". See: Case 101/87 *P. Bork International A/S v Foreiningen Arbejdsledere i Danmark* [1988] ECR 3057, and the UK House of Lords case, *Litster v Forth Dry Dock and Engineering Ltd.* [1989] IRLR 161.

90. Case 392/92, *Schmidt v Spar-und Leihkasse* [1994] IRLR 302.

91. Case 135/83, *Abels* [1985] ECR 469.

92. See Arnull, *op.cit.* n.68, at p.249.

transferor or the transferee, the provisions will not "stand in the way of dismissals that may take place for economic, technological or organisational reasons entailing changes in the workforce" (Article 4(1)).

Undoubtedly the most contentious aspect of the Directive has concerned the meaning of the terms "undertaking, business or part of a business". Does this terminology allow for circumstances where a public service is subject to a process of privatisation?; a policy adopted in various forms and in varying degrees in several Member States in the late 1980s, but most enthusiastically in the UK.; or the related activities of "Compulsory Competitive Tendering" or "Market Testing" introduced as a means of restructuring central and local government in the UK?[93]

Recent cases suggest that the Directive will apply to most of these circumstances providing the factual test that a "legal transfer or merger" has taken place is satisfied, taking into account "whether the business was disposed of as a going concern, as would be indicated, *inter alia*, by the fact that its operation was actually continued or resumed by the new employer, with the same or similar activities".[94] This will be a question of fact for the national courts to determine.

The Court, in *Stichting v Bartol*,[95] determined that the Directive could apply where the undertakings were charitable foundations funded by public subsidy. The main factual consideration was whether the unit being transferred retained its identity and the functions performed were carried out or resumed by the new owner with the same or similar activities. In *Rask*,[96] a company had contracted out its canteen service and, although the contractors undertook full operational responsibility, they agreed to employ the existing staff and continued with essentially the same service using the company's facilities. The Court followed *Stichting v Bartol* and concluded that the "retention of identity" test was the decisive criterion although it would be left for the national court to finally determine the matter. A "shopping list" of factors will be taken into account in determining whether there has been a transfer in fact, including, the type of business concerned, whether its tangible assets are transferred, the value of those assets at the time of transfer, the retention of employees and customers, and continuation of similar activities. These are single factors in an overall assessment and cannot be considered in isolation.[97]

---

93. For a full discussion see: B. Napier, CCT, *Market Testing and Employment Rights: The Effects of TUPE and the Acquired Rights Directive*, Institute of Employment Rights, 1993.

94. The factual test was laid down in Case 24/85, *Spijkers v Gebroeders Benedik Abbatoir C.V.* [1986] ECR 1119.

95. Case C-29/91, [1992] ECR I-3189, at para.23.

96. Case C-209/91, *Rask and Christiansen v ISS Kantinservice* [1993] ECR I-5755.

97. *ibid.*, at paras.18-20.

In a subsequent case, *Schmidt*,[98] the Court held that there could also be a transfer where a company contracted out its cleaning service even though only one employee was involved. The fact that there was no transfer of assets did not prevent the transfer taking place because the retention of identity was the decisive overriding fact to be established and there had been a transfer of services. This approach has recently been applied in the UK in *Dines v Initial Health Care Services*,[99] where the Employment Appeal Tribunal has held that the contracting out of a cleaning service at a public hospital was covered by the Directive because it was a self-contained service which had a separate economic identity.[100]

These cases have to be considered alongside *Commission v UK*, the joined cases involving the Collective Redundancies and Acquired Rights Directives.[101] The UK implementation of the Acquired Rights Directive had long been considered defective by the Commission and eventually Article 169 proceedings were brought. The UK responded by bringing the domestic legislation broadly in line with the Directive with the exception of the employee consultation issue where the Court again found against the UK. However many employees will have been denied the protection of the Directive because of its defective implementation prior to 1993,[102] not least because of the original requirement in the statutory regulations excluding employees working for non-profit making undertakings.

One of the most important questions to arise from *Commission v UK* is whether the test in *Francovich*[103] will apply in a case of improper implementation of a directive, rather than complete non-compliance? In *Francovich* the Court may have reacted so adversely because the Italian Government had failed to act despite infringement proceedings brought before the Court three years earlier.[104] The UK may argue that it had sought to correct its error prior to the Article 169 hearing. The Court might apply the arguments of Advocate General Mischo in *Francovich*, who advised first, that a successful Article 169 action should be a precondition for state non-contractual liability and the Member State concerned must have failed to comply with the judgment in accordance with Article 171, secondly, that the judgment on damages should not be retrospec-

---

98. *op.cit.* n.90.

99. [1993] IRLR 321.

100. For a discussion on the implications see John McMullen, "Contracting Out and Market Testing — the Uncertainty Ends?", (1994) 23 ILJ 230.

101. *op.cit.* n.84.

102. TURER came into force on 30 August 1993.

103. *op.cit.* n.39.

104. Case 22/87, *Commission v Italy* [1989] ECR 143.

tive, and thirdly, that the conditions for liability should be the same as for EC institutions under Article 215 EC whereby the breach must consist of a grave and manifest disregard of limits of powers in violation of a sufficiently serious breach of a superior rule of law for the benefit of individuals. A strong case can be put forward for these limitations to be applied to a *Francovich* action where an issue of incorrect implementation rather than non-compliance is under consideration.[105]

Were such arguments to be accepted the outcome would serve to undermine the scope of judicial protection of individual rights, which has already been circumscribed by the Court's finding in *Marshall* that directives are not capable of "horizontal direct effect", individual *qua* individual, not least because the Court decided in *Francovich* that the Insolvency Directive was insufficiently precise and unconditional to be directly effective, an interpretation which enabled the Court to develop the alternative approach of state liability for breach of Community obligations, but which may be held to apply equally to the other employment protection measures introduced in similar terms as market equalisation measures under Article 100 EC. Even if the UK is liable does liability start in 1979, when the Directive should have been implemented, or in 1981, when it was implemented defectively? Undoubtedly there would be immense economic consequences arising from retrospective liability and this may lead the Court to err on the side of caution perhaps applying a temporal limitation as in *Defrenne* and *Barber*.[106] In the view of Advocate General van Gerven, writing in a personal capacity,[107] there is no doubt that the *Francovich* principle applies to partial or incorrect implementation and the compensation payable should correspond to the damage caused. This approach, if followed, would clarify the law and would provide an incentive for Member States to comply with their Community obligations both promptly and precisely.

The trilogy of employment protection directives was completed with the adoption of the Insolvency Directive by which Member States are required to establish "guarantee institutions",[108] where the employer is in a state of insolvency, to ensure "payment of employees' outstanding claims resulting from contracts of employment or employment relation-

---

105. Docksey, *op.cit.* n.59, at paras.55-64. *Francovich, op. cit.* n.39, Advocate General's Opinion paras.74,76 & 87.

106. *op.cit.* ns.33, 41 & 47.

107. W. van Gerven, "Non-contractual liability of Member States, Community Institutions and Individuals for Breaches of Community Law with a View to a Common Law for Europe", (1994) 1 M.J. 6, at pp.16-17 and 31-32.

108. Article 3(1) of Directive 80/987.

ships" and relating to arrears of pay.[109] There has been little litigation before the Court of Justice on the substantive aspects of the Directive, but it did form the basis of *Francovich* following the failure of Italy to comply with its provisions.

From the above discussion it can be seen that the Court has applied the doctrine of effective judicial protection of individual rights drawing upon Article 5 EC in order to ensure that national law is consistent with Community law and that the directives will apply as widely as possible in order to reduce differences in the laws of the Member States. The Court's approach also shows the flexibility of the mechanism of the directive by interpreting the law so as to allow national discretion as to the form and method of implementation whilst ensuring that this is within a framework that ensures provisions that are not less favourable to employees and provide a real deterrent to the employer. In this way laws of the 1970s have been applied to the changing circumstances of the 1990s and the Commission's updating measures have already been anticipated by the Court, and in the case of the proposed revisions to the Acquired Rights Directive, may even be regarded as a retrograde step.[110]

While the approach of the Court in relation to employment protection measures is to be strongly applauded the limited scope of the legislation as a whole must also be appreciated. All three directives deal only with crisis situations in the employment relationship and serve either to provide a limited degree of consultation over collective dismissals, continuity of employment and transfer of acquired rights in certain factual circumstances, and a guaranteed payment to employees in the event of the employer's insolvency. A related later measure on information rights of employees is of limited use and specifically excludes the Commission's original proposal for a proof of employment directive.[111] Further, the employment protection area is devoid of any legislative protection against individual dismissal, a notion which is considered in the SPWP and is currently the subject of a detailed Commission study.[112] The prospects for further legislation in this area will be considered later in this Chapter.

---

109. *ibid.*, Article 5.

110. See COM(94) 300 final of 8 September 1994. The Commission propose to revise the Directive to bring it into line with *Stichting v Bartol* and *Rask*.

111. Directive 91/533/EEC of 14 October 1991 on an employer's obligation to inform employees of the conditions applicable to the contract of employment or the employment relationship. OJ L288, 18.10.91. For a discussion see J. Clark and M. Hall, "The Cinderella Directive? Employee rights to Information about Conditions Applicable to their Contract or Employment Relationship", (1992) 21 I.L.J. 106.

112. SPWP, Chap.3 para.14.

(e) Workers' Participation

The Council Resolution concerning the first Social Action Programme promised "vigorous action" to increase the "involvement of
management and labour in the economic and social decisions of the
Community, and of workers in the life of undertakings", and included a
commitment, *inter alia*, "to facilitate...the conclusion of collective agreements at European level in appropriate fields".[113] The early seeds of what
we have now come to know as the "social dialogue" were planted. Following the establishment of the Standing Committee on Employment in
1970,[114] discussions had begun involving representatives of management
and labour — the "social partners" — ministers for employment or social affairs, and the Commission. The purpose of this policy was clear,
namely, to commit both sides of industry to the overall objectives of Community economic policy. This overriding and essentially optimistic goal
has formed the basis of an evolving strategy which has gradually enmeshed
the social partners into the Community decision making process with as
yet uncertain consequences.

During the 1970s there was much sparring between the members of
the Standing Committee but only a very limited output. A twin strategy
had been launched to achieve harmonisation of company laws based on
obligatory workers' participation on company boards,[115] and, later, a social policy draft directive on procedures for informing and consulting
employees in large national and multinational firms.[116] These proposals
failed to secure a sufficient level of support in the Council due to the
concerted opposition of several Member States.[117] The content of the
worker participation proposals will not be considered further here, not
least because of the discussion of these issues in Chapter 3, but also because they may be seen as seeking to establish *procedural* rather than *substantive* rights for workers, and therefore, it can be argued that their practical utility is ultimately dependant upon the prior existence of a broad
layer of employment protection and equality laws which enable the workers concerned to be consulted and, in certain circumstances, participate

113. *op.cit*. n.67.

114. Council Decision 70/532/EEC of 14 December 1970 (modified in 1972 and 1975).

115. The Draft Fifth Company Law Directive and the European Company Statute (ECS).
The Fifth Directive was originally proposed in 1972, COM (72) 887 final of 27 Septem-
ber 1972 — and later relaunched in COM(90) 629 final of 13 December 1990. The
ECS was initially proposed in 1970, Supp. 8 EEC Bull., and was revived in 1989, OJ
C263/41.

116. The "Vredeling" directive. OJ C287/80.

117. For a discussion see: M. Rood, "Workers' Participation: New Initiatives at European
level", (1992) 8 Int.J.Comp.L.L.I.R. 319.

in decision making in the workplace without the fear of negative consequences.

By early 1994, twenty-five years on from the first company law proposals, the only measures involving a degree of obligatory employee consultation involved very specific situations, collective redundancies and acquired rights, and the provisions in the framework Directive on the health and safety of workers, to provide all necessary information concerning health and safety risks.[118] While these particular steps are important and, in the health and safety field at least, have helped to establish better practice, a comprehensive process for workers' participation remains elusive. In this context the 1994 Works Council Directive,[119] adopted as the first measure under the SPA, represents a significant advancement, albeit with certain limitations, in the process of informing employees about trans-national matters concerning their employment in large enterprises.

(iii) The Single European Act — One Step Forwards, Two Steps Backwards?

(a) Minimum Standards Replace Harmonisation

By the mid-1980s there was a widely acknowledged need to fill the vacuum created by the lack of a follow up to the Action Programme and the continuing limitations of the legal bases for social policy measures in the EEC Treaty. Piecemeal progress in the social field was one factor amongst many contributing to a feeling that the Community needed to be "reawakened" from its slumbering mood of "Euro-pessimism".[120] However, despite the emphasis of the newly appointed President of the Commission, Jacques Delors, on the need for a "European social area" to be established,[121] the motor for the Internal Market programme launched following the publication of the 1985 Single Market White Paper,[122] was deregulation in order to create "an area without internal frontiers in which the free movement of goods, persons, services and capital is ensured...".[123] As Vogel-Polsky later commented:

---

118. Article 10 of Directive 89/391/EEC of 12 June 1989. OJ L183 of 29.6.89. For a discussion see: H. Krieger, "Participation of Employees' Representatives in the Protection of Health and Safety of Workers in Europe", (1990/91) 6 Int.J.Comp.L.L.I.R. 217.

119. Directive 94/45/EC, *op.cit.* n.88.

120. See Weatherill & Beaumont, *op.cit.* n.27, at pp.18-21.

121. Bull. EC /2 (1986) at p.12.

122. COM (85) 310 final of 14.6.85.

123. Article 8a EEC as amended by the SEA, 1987, now Article 7a EC.

The concept of a European Social Area has been abandoned for the present; in its place has been substituted that of the Social Aspect of the Internal Market.[124]

Thus while the SEA provided some new opportunities for a broadening of the scope of social policy, particularly in the health and safety field, it represented a retreat from the goals of the Action Programme which was based on "vigorous action...in order to attain the...improvement of living and working conditions so as to make possible their *harmonisation* while the improvement is being maintained...".[125] The SEA, and the second Social Action Programme, represented a subtle but important change in the priorities of Community social policy, a point noted in the White Paper:

> Since the adoption of the Single European Act, the emphasis has shifted from harmonisation to the adoption of minimum standards...[126]

Before assessing the implications of the Treaty changes enacted in 1987 it is necessary to consider the restraining impact on the development of Community labour law resulting from the policies of Mrs Thatcher's administration in the UK after 1979. This period of "Thatcherism Versus the Social Dimension"[127] culminated with the UK rejecting the Social Charter in 1989, even though it had no binding legal effect, on the basis that it was "more like a socialist charter".[128] Between 1979 and 1990 the UK regularly denounced ILO conventions while falling foul of the ILO Committee of Experts for removing trade union rights at the Government Communications Headquarters.[129] Mrs Thatcher set out her stall most clearly in her notable, perhaps notorious, address in Bruges when she warned that:

> We have not successfully rolled back the frontiers of the state in Britain only to see them re-imposed at European level; with a European super-state exercising a new dominance in Brussels.[130]

---

124. E. Vogel-Polsky, "What Future is There For a Social Europe?", (1990) 19 I.L.J. 65 at p.75.

125. COM (89) 568 *op.cit.* n.15.

126. SPWP, Chap.3, at p.29.

127. See generally, B.A. Hepple, "Social Rights in the European Economic Community: A British Perspective", (1990) 11 Comp.Lab.L.J. 425.

128. House of Commons, *Official Report*, vol.153, col.474 (18.5.89), cited ibid., at p.425.

129. See: K. Ewing, *Britain and the ILO*, Institute of Employment Rights, 1989.

130. Reported in *The Guardian*, 21 September 1988.

The weaknesses of the EEC Treaty provisions on social policy, which were dependant upon unanimity and a generous interpretation, as well as a liberal application, of Articles 100 and 235 as the means of initiating legislation, were cruelly exposed once a single Member State adopted a posture of vehement opposition. The UK's belligerent attitude to Community social policy in the early 1980s led to a considerable shortfall in legislative progress, notably with the proposed legislation on the organisation of working time[131] and on part-time[132] and temporary work.[133] The amendments to the EEC Treaty in the SEA are best understood as a compromise designed, in part, to break the deadlock by adopting a policy approach amounting to a sizeable inflection towards the Thatcherite agenda of "flexible labour markets", as evinced by the deregulatory nature of the Internal Market programme, in return for the introduction of Qualified Majority Voting (QMV), coupled with the co-operation procedure involving the European Parliament, in certain fields, most notably under the health and safety provisions in Article 118a.

While this compromise may have paved the way for limited progress, not least because of the imaginative usage of Article 118a by the Commission and Parliament, and the adoption of the Social Charter, as a means of fulfilling the "social dimension" of the market liberalisation process, the outcome must be regarded as a diminution of the Community's social objectives particularly in those areas most easily identified with mainstream labour law: employment protection, equitable pay, and collective labour rights. These aspects remain peripheral even with the subsequent adoption of the Maastricht SPA by all Member States except the UK.

(b) Legislative Activity under the Single European Act

Following the SEA, Article 100, requiring unanimity, remained as the most explicit legal base for labour legislation for the purposes of market approximation. Faced with the UK's implacable opposition to the general thrust of Community social policy, the Commission has looked to other means for promoting legislation using alternative provisions in the SEA susceptible to QMV.

Article 100a(2), excluding the "rights and interests of employed persons" from internal market approximation provisions, might have been interpreted as an insurmountable obstacle to further progress in the

---

131. Discussed by Hepple, *op.cit.* n.25, at p.81. See Council Resolution in OJ C2/1980 and the Resolution in the European Parliament, C260/1981.

132. OJ C62/1982 as amended, OJ C18/1983.

133. OJ C128/1982 as amended, OJ C133/1984.

labour law field. The provision may also be understood as applying equally to health and safety approximation measures because Article 100a(3) states that: "The Commission, in its proposals...concerning health, safety, environmental protection and consumer protection, will take as a base a high level of protection".

Three possible interpretations of Article 100a(2) have been elaborated by Bercusson.[134] Unanimity is required either:

(1) For proposals concerning *solely* the rights and interests of workers; or

(2) Proposals which *predominantly* effect the rights and interests of employed persons; or

(3) Any proposal which bears *directly, indirectly or in part*, on the rights and interests of employed persons.

The third interpretation would entirely negate any social proposals and indeed many other market approximation measures, for example concerning free movement. Therefore it is more likely that the Court would err towards either of the first two suggested interpretations when considering any legal challenge to the validity of a directive. This question will be put to the test when the Court considers the UK's impending challenge to the Working Time Directive.[135]

Further legal uncertainty has been created by the provisions in Article 118a whereby "Member States shall pay particular attention to encouraging improvements, especially in the working environment, as regards the health and safety of workers, and shall set as their objective the harmonisation of conditions in this area, while maintaining the improvements made". This objective in Article 118a(1) is, however, subject to qualification. Article 118a(2) specifies directives as the means of adopting *"minimum requirements for gradual implementation*, having regard to the conditions and technical rules obtaining in each of the Member States" (*author's emphasis*). At the same time such directives "shall avoid imposing administrative, financial and legal constraints in a way which would hold back the creation and development of small and medium-sized undertakings". Any doubts that Article 118a is designed for minimum standards rather than upward harmonisation are clarified by Article

---

134. B. Bercusson, *Fundamental Social and Economic Rights*, (1989), EUI, Florence 1989, pp.12-14. See also Vogel-Polsky, *op.cit.* n.124, at pp.70-72. For a discussion see Nielsen & Szyszcak, *op.cit.* n.26, at pp.23-26; and B. A. Hepple, "The Implementation of the Community Charter of Fundamental Social Rights", (1990) 53 M.L.R. 643 at pp.647-8.

135. Case C-84/94, *UK v Council*.

118a(3) which states that "provisions adopted pursuant to this Article shall not prevent any Member State from maintaining or introducing more stringent measures for the protection of working conditions compatible with this Treaty".

The resulting confusion can be best demonstrated by the Commission's attempt to relaunch initiatives concerning atypical workers using three different legal bases — Articles 100,[136] 100a(1)[137] and 118a. To date only the health and safety proposal under Article 118a has been successful.[138] The Commission has now been forced, again because of UK opposition, to revert to the SPA as an alternative base for legislation in order to provide equivalent rights for workers in "non-standard employment" by reformulating its original proposals.[139]

A number of conclusions may be drawn from this untidy morass. The first is that, prior to the Maastricht SPA, any explicit provisions for the improvement of working conditions introduced without a health and safety dimension would fall foul of Article 100a(2) and would require unanimous support under Article 100 for adoption. Second, as these were precisely the areas where the UK's opposition had hitherto been most trenchant — employment protection, workers' participation — the prospects in 1987 for substantive progress seemed minimal.[140] Thirdly, even if a creative method could be found for bringing a proposal outside the mainstream health and safety field within the remit of Article 118a, it would have to be denuded of at least some of its potency by the need to accommodate a specific health and safety purpose, to be based on minimum standards requiring only gradual implementation, while allowing small and medium-sized enterprises leeway from restrictive regulation. Fourthly, only directives can be promulgated under Article 118a and these must have regard to the existing conditions in each Member State, an early example of the principle of subsidiarity.

When referring to the "solid base" of legislative achievements in the White Paper the Commission is undoubtedly including three measures which have been adopted under Article 118a despite the protestations

136. Proposal for a Council Directive on contracts and employment relationships other than full-time open-ended contracts (atypical work); working conditions (Article 100). COM (90) 228/1 final of 29.6.90, OJ C 224, 8.9.90.

137. Distortions of competition (Article 100a). COM (90) 228/2 final of 29.6.90, OJ C 224, 8.9.90, Amended proposal COM (90) 533/1 final, OJ C 305, 5.12.90.

138. Directive 91/383/EEC of 25 June 1991, supplementing the measures to encourage improvements in the safety and health at work of workers with a fixed-duration employment relationship or a temporary employment relationship. OJ L206/19, 29.7.91.

139. See SPWP, Chap.3, para.8. Also see Chapter 7 by Nick Rahtz for a full discussion.

140. See Hepple, *op.cit.* n.25, at p.85: "The prospects for a revival of the social action programmes of the 1970s are nil".

of the UK that they fall foul of Article 100a(2). How satisfactory are these measures?, and do they legitimately come within the bounds of Article 118a?

The first adopted measure to test the scope of Article 118a was the Pregnant Workers Directive introduced in 1992 for implementation by October 1994.[141] The source of this Directive was the 1989 Action Programme which contained a commitment to introduce a directive on the protection of pregnant women at work within the Chapter on equal treatment.[142] A directive containing minimum requirements was promised as an alternative to specific measures covering particular health and safety risks concerning, *inter alia,* the dangers for pregnant women associated with visual display units and risks arising from exposure to carcinogens. By placing the proposal in this context the Commission provided the basis for its inclusion as an individual "daughter directive" within the meaning of Article 16(1) of the Framework Directive on the introduction of measures to encourage improvements in the safety and health of workers at work. Further, Article 15 of the Framework Directive provides that particularly sensitive risk groups must be protected against the dangers which specifically affect them. In order to fit the Directive within this structure the Commission had to accentuate in its proposal the protective health and safety goals rather than ask the Council to legislate specifically for the purpose of establishing maternity rights.

A brief examination of the resulting Directive shows that the primary objective is to draw up guidelines concerning health and safety hazards for pregnant workers, and for workers who have recently given birth, or who are breast feeding, with a view to risk assessment for these groups of workers.[143] There is an obligation on the employer to take necessary measures to avoid the exposure of the worker concerned to such risks.[144] Workers may have to be moved or granted leave in accordance with national legislation and practice. There are also limitations on nightwork after childbirth.[145]

The remainder of the Directive grants women positive rights to at least 14 weeks maternity leave, in accordance with national legislation and practice, including at least two weeks leave before and after confine-

---

141. Directive 92/85/EEC of 19 October 1992, on the introduction of measures to encourage improvements in the safety and health of pregnant workers and workers who have recently given birth or are breast feeding (tenth individual Directive within the meaning of Article 16(1) of Directive 89/391/EEC), OJ L 348, 28.11.92.

142. 1989 Action Programme, Part 2, Chap.8.

143. Directive 92/85. Articles 3 & 4.

144. *ibid.*, Article 5.

145. *ibid.*, Article 7.

ment.[146] There is also a right to time-off without loss of pay for ante-natal examinations.[147] Dismissal of the workers concerned is prohibited save in exceptional cases not connected with their condition which are permitted under national legislation and practice and with an obligation on the employer to show written grounds for dismissal.[148] An adequate maternity allowance must be paid guaranteeing income at least equivalent to that which the worker concerned would receive in the event of a break of her activities on grounds connected with her state of health. This will be subject to any national ceiling and also the worker may have to fulfil national conditions of eligibility for such benefits.[149]

Undoubtedly the central provisions of the Directive concerning protection from exposure to risks can be justified within Article 118a and do provide important rights to the workers concerned. However, the position of a worker who refuses to be moved depends on national conditions and it is not clear whether this might constitute grounds for dismissal. By relying so heavily on national legislation and practice, in relation to action arising from the risk assessment, prohibition of dismissal, and employment rights generally, the Directive offers varying levels of protection, albeit subject to the provisions of the Equal Treatment Directive. Further, the positive rights are strictly minimalist in character having been subjected to substantial revision in order to secure wide support in the Council but also with a view to avoiding a legal challenge based on Article 100a(2). After some initial posturing the UK, having abstained in the Council vote, decided not to challenge the validity of the Directive. Despite these inadequacies the SPWP contains no proposal to strengthen the Directive.

Bercusson's intermediate interpretation of Article 100a(2), including measures with *predominant* effects on the rights and interests of employed persons, may be tested in the case of the 1993 Working Time Directive.[150] As Hepple has asked does a directive for the adaptation of working time predominantly affect employees rights and interests?[151] or does it mainly "enable firms to undertake the internal organisation of work and production, which is an important factor in the adaptation of firms to the terms of competition and the improvement of their com-

146. *ibid.*, Article 8.

147. *ibid.*, Article 9.

148. *ibid.*, Article 10.

149. *ibid.*, Article 11.

150. Directive 93/104/EC concerning certain aspects of the organisation of working time, OJ L 307, 13.12.93.

151. Hepple, *op.cit.* n.134, at pp. 647-8.

petitiveness at different levels"?[152] Alternatively the focus of any legal challenge may revolve instead around the narrower issue of whether the Directive falls within Article 118a or not?

The 1989 Action Programme made no mention of a health and safety basis for legislative action on the organisation of working time. Indeed the measure was a hangover from the commitment in the 1974 Programme to a forty hour standard working week and four weeks annual paid holiday. Instead the proposal was presented in the Programme as a central part of the strategy to improve living and working conditions consistent with the objective of labour market flexibility. However both the formal Commission proposal and the adopted Directive relied on Article 118a as the legal base. The justification for this approach is contained in the preamble to the Directive which proclaims that the measure would ensure the safety and health of workers by granting minimum periods of rest, adequate breaks, and, in this context, a maximum limit on weekly working hours.

The Commission's success in steering the Working Time Directive through the Council in the face of vehement opposition by the UK amounted to a commendable achievement but a heavy price was paid because of the need to make concessions to try, unsuccessfully, to accommodate UK objections, whereas other more cosmetic elements of the measure were designed to place the Directive within the health and safety provisions rather than introduce an approximation measure under Article 100 as originally intended.

A cursory read of the Directive might suggest that it substantially augments the rights of Community workers. Member States are expected to take measures to ensure that *every worker* is entitled to:

— a minimum daily rest period of 11 consecutive hours;[153]
— a rest break where the working day is more than 6 hours. The duration will be determined by a collective agreement or national legislation;[154]
— weekly rest amounting to a minimum uninterrupted period of 24 hours;[155]
— an average working time for each seven-day period, including overtime, not exceeding 48 hours "to protect the safety and health of workers";[156]

152. Action Programme, Part 2, Chap.3b.

153. Directive 93/104/EC, *op.cit.* n.150, Article 3.

154. *ibid.*, Article 4.

155. *ibid.*, Article 5.

156. *ibid.*, Article 6.

— paid annual leave of at least four weeks;[157]
— night work not exceeding an average of 8 hours in any 24-hour period.[158]

Other provisions grant night workers a right to a free health assessment and transfer to day work if they suffer from health problems; and allow for an adaptation of work patterns with a view to alleviating monotonous work, especially by allowing for breaks during work time.[159]

A closer examination of the Directive reveals that the exclusions are substantial and include many workers who are subjected to longer than average hours of working. Article 1(3) excludes, *inter alia,* the following sectors of activity from the provisions in the Directive *in toto*: "air, rail, road, sea...and the activities of doctors in training". These might be considered to be precisely the areas where the workers concerned, and the public who rely on their services, are most at risk of hazards to their health and safety arising from overlong work periods. Further, Member States may derogate from the main provisions[160] in the cases of managing executives or other persons with "autonomous decision-making powers".[161]

An array of other derogations exist for workers who have to work at a distance from home, for security and caretaking staff, and in a variety of other fields including, *inter alia,* residential institutions, dock or airport workers, agriculture, media, postal and emergency services, or where there is a "foreseeable surge of activity" in agriculture, tourism or postal services.[162] These derogations amount to the exclusion of a significant proportion of the workforce, covering whole sectors, from the protection of a whole or a substantial part of the provisions of the Directive.

The Directive carries a sting in its tail when it reaches the final provisions.[163] Not only is there a generous three year period for implementation,[164] but the provision for maximum weekly working time can be deferred by a Member State for a further seven years until 2003, in return for alternative provisions which merely prevent an employer from forcing the employee to work more than 48 hours per week without his agreement.

157. *ibid.*, Article 7.

158. *ibid.*, Article 8(1).

159. *ibid.*, Articles 9(1) and 13.

160. *ibid.*, Articles 3,4,5,6,8 or 16 (reference periods).

161. *ibid.*, Article 17(1).

162. *ibid.*, Article 17(2.1). These derogations are from Articles 3,4,5,8, and 16.

163. *ibid.*, Article 18.

164. The implementation date is 23 November 1996.

The result is a decidedly weak piece of legislation which satisfied neither the main supporters of attempts to legislate in this field, notably Parliament, nor its principal detractor, the UK, which, having abstained in the Council vote, has lodged Article 173 proceedings with the Court of Justice for judicial review in order to seek to have the Directive annulled, and will not implement the measure until the case has been decided.[165]

What has been achieved by the Directive? At best it represents a hesitant first step towards establishing minimum requirements concerning working time arrangements. Alternatively, the Directive can be viewed as being so severely compromised by exclusions, derogations, and delaying provisions, that any positive effect is likely to be so substantially diluted as to render it almost nugatory. A legal challenge may, perversely, present the Court with an opportunity to extend the scope of Article 118a while delimiting Article 100a(2). This may encourage the Commission to be bolder with future proposals and for other Member States to make fewer concessions to the UK in the future. A more satisfactory approach would be to resort directly to the SPA and recognise that working time and related matters are not primarily health and safety issues. Higher standards can then be established in 14 Member States pending the eventual return of the UK to the fold.

In the meantime there is a vacuum to be filled and, following an outcry in Parliament, the Commission has now proposed to "complement the existing Directive to cover all employees" while encouraging flexibility once minimum requirements are established. Consultations are proceeding with sectors excluded by the Directive and the matter will be put forward first to the social partners and, if they do not reach agreement during 1995, proposals for a Directive based on Article 118a will be considered.[166]

A third Directive on the protection of young workers[167] can be criticised on similar grounds. The Young Workers Directive is based on a range of commitments in the Social Charter including the introduction of a minimum employment age of 15 subject to derogations for "certain light work".[168] The Action Programme envisaged that there would be a proposal as a health and safety measure containing this limitation and also restricting the working hours of young people under 18.[169] The key

165. *op.cit.* n.135.

166. SPWP, Chap.3 para.9.

167. Directive 94/33/EC of 22 June 1994, OJ L 216, 20.8.94.

168. Social Charter, point 20.

169. Action Programme Part 2, Chap.11. and COM (94) 88 final of 30.3.94

provisions of the Directive ban child labour under 15, subject to certain exceptions including "light work", cultural or similar activities, and vocational training.[170] There are also periods of daily, weekly, and annual rest, and limitations on working time stipulated for children under 15 and adolescents under 18, and a ban on night work by adolescents.[171]

The Young Workers Directive is due for implementation by 22 June 1996. Article 17, containing the final provisions, includes a significant, indeed unique, concession to the demands of the UK. In a departure from all previous precedent concerning social legislation outside the Maastricht SPA, there is a specific derogation for the UK in allowing a further four year period after the implementation date during which time the UK can refrain from complying with the provisions concerning working time for schoolchildren, the working time of adolescents, and night work for adolescents.[172] While there may be different cultural traditions in certain Member States, not least the British tradition of employing schoolchildren to deliver newspapers, there can be no justification for singling out a Member State for special treatment and thereby denying the children and adolescents affected the health and safety protection that the Directive is designed to afford.

This retrospective social opt-out, albeit in the form of a delaying mechanism, from the provisions of a binding Directive applying to a pre-Maastricht Treaty provision, represents a serious threat to the homogeneity of the existing body of Community social laws and it establishes a precedent which should not be repeated. Further there are grounds for arguing that this specific national derogation is inconsistent with Article 189 EC whereby a directive shall be binding "upon each Member State to which it is addressed". The Treaty does not allow any explicit grounds for exemptions of this kind in individual directives. Indeed the Court of Justice has repeatedly warned of the dangers of inconsistencies in the Community legal order which may jeopardise the attainment of the objectives of the Treaty enunciated in Article 5 and give rise to prohibited discrimination under Article 7 EEC/Article 6 EC. In a case against the UK in 1979 the Court justified strict uniformity of application thus:

> For a State unilaterally to break, according to its own conception of national interest, the equilibrium between the advantages and obligations flowing from its adherence to the Community brings into question the equality of Member States before Com-

---

170. Directive 94/33/EC, *op.cit.* n.167, Articles 4 & 5.

171. *ibid.*, Articles 8,9,10,11 & 12.

172. *ibid.*, Article 17(1)(b) allowing for derogations from Articles 8(1)(b),8(2),9(1)(b) and 9(2) respectively.

munity law and creates discrimination at the expense of their nationals. This failure in the duty of solidarity...strikes at the very root of the Community legal order.[173]

Although the UK's action may have been sanctioned by the other Member States and there is no direct challenge to the Community's supremacy, the effect of specific national derogations leads to precisely the same result. A similar argument could arise over the legitimacy of the Maastricht Protocol and SPA but, unlike the Young Workers Directive, these provisions form an integral part of the Treaty.[174] An Article 177 reference on the UK derogation from the Directive would be a worthwhile test of this question.

All remaining directives adopted under Article 118a stem directly from the Framework Directive 89/391 on health and safety at the workplace. The objective of community legislation in this field is to provide a set of minimum standards which will ensure an adequate level of protection against work accidents and occupational diseases and facilitate free movement of workers.[175] The Framework Directive is a programmatic measure laying down general principles regarding employers' obligations and responsibilities for the safety and health protection of workers, and defines the procedures for the information, training, consultation and participation of workers. In addition the Framework Directive acts as a catalyst for individual horizontal "daughter" directives intended to cover a maximum number of risks covering all workers in a specific area of activity and thus avoiding fragmented legislation. Sixteen horizontal directives had been adopted by the end of 1993 covering a broad range of measures under five headings: chemical agents, information, work equipment, working conditions, and physical agents.[176]

The importance of Community action in the area of health and safety for the protection of workers cannot be understated. The Commission has noted that of 120 million Community workers almost 10 million are victims of work accidents or occupational diseases each year at an estimated annual cost of ECU 26 billion.[177] While the achievements thus far are laudable it must be questioned whether the pace of progress based, under Article 118a, on minimum requirements and gradual implementation, is sufficiently responsive to the needs of workers in a rapidly chang-

173. Case 128/78, *Commission v United Kingdom* [1979] ECR 419 at para.12 of the judgment.

174. This point is considered later in this section.

175. COM (93) 560 of 19 November 1993. General framework for action in the field of safety, hygiene and health protection at work (1994-2000), at p.5.

176. *ibid.*, at pp.7-8 and Annex.

177. *ibid.*, p.1. The figure in ECUs is based on 1991 prices.

ing environment at work where workers are in increasing danger of being subjected to new risks. Further, the exception for small and medium-sized enterprises should be reviewed if it proves over time to have endangered certain groups of workers concentrated in particular sectors. The use of directives ensures maximum flexibility enabling the Commission to propose new measures when necessary. Five further outstanding directives are identified in the SPWP.[178] This programme of activity needs to be continued but the time has arrived for a renewed emphasis on the varying national standards of implementation, monitoring and enforcement of Community health and safety standards.[179] The SPWP notes that as of 30 June 1994 five Member States had failed to transpose the Framework Directive,[180] while only France had implemented all of the health and safety directives in force. There is an important commitment in the SPWP to pursue infringement proceedings under Article 169 EC where necessary and to encourage complaints through the new European Ombudsman. In order to raise national standards there is also a need for the European Agency for Health and Safety at Work, based in Bilbao, to become fully operational.[181]

(iv) The Social Charter, Subsidiarity, Social Dialogue and Soft Law

A variety of legislative and non-legislative techniques have been pursued to underpin the drive for the Community's "social dimension" in recent years. In order to circumvent the need for unanimity required to enact binding legislation outside the nebulous field of health and safety, and to fulfil the desire to make progress on a range of social policy goals not clearly brought within the Community's competence after the SEA, the Commission has proposed a range of initiatives which can be described as "soft laws" of an influential but non-binding character, while the Council has adopted its own resolutions and other purely declaratory statements of intent. The constitutionalisation of the principle of subsidiarity in Article 3b of the amended EC Treaty raises the prospect of a further move in this direction with soft law being used as a ready

178. Draft Directives on health and safety for activities in the transport sector, OJ C 271, 16.10.93; physical agents, OJ C77, 18.3.93; chemical agents, OJ C 165, 16.6.93; travel conditions of workers with motor disabilities, OJ C 15, 21.1.92; and work equipment (modification) COM(94) 56 final of 14.3.94.

179. For an argument in favour of stronger enforcement see generally: R. Baldwin, Ch.8. of *Harmonization and Hazard: regulating Workplace Health and Safety in the European Community*, Eds. R. Baldwin & T. Daintith (Graham & Trotman, 1992).

180. Germany, Greece, Spain, Italy and Luxembourg. See SPWP, Chap.10, pp.63-66.

181. A Council Regulation setting up the Agency has now been adopted. Regulation 2062/94 of 18 July 1994, OJ L 216, 20.8.94.

alternative to binding legislative norms, an approach which is further encouraged in the SPWP. Ensuing Community instruments have created a degree of fluidity in the composition of social policy and the implications of this development will now be examined.

(a) *Soft Law — Form and Effect*

Soft law emanating from the Community institutions is multifaceted and serves diverse purposes. From the Community's inception soft law has existed as an established feature of the system of decision making, both in the forms sanctioned by Article 189 EC, as Council recommendations and opinions which "shall have no binding force", and in a variety of other forms unspecified in the Treaties, including communications and memoranda, issued by the Commission, and Council resolutions. Snyder describes soft laws as:

> ...rules of conduct which, in principle, have no legally binding force but which nevertheless may have practical effects.[182]

An immediate issue concerns the precise nature of these "effects". Are there legal consequences arising from the interpretation of soft laws by the Court of Justice and the national courts?

Article 164 EC places an obligation on the Court of Justice to "ensure that in the interpretation and application of this Treaty the law is observed". In *Grimaldi*[183] the Court held, when considering the status of a recommendation, that:

> ...it must be stressed that [non-legally binding measures] cannot therefore be regarded as having no legal effect. The national courts are bound to take recommendations into consideration in order to decide disputes submitted to them, in particular where they cast light on the interpretation of national measures adopted in order to implement them or where they are designed to supplement binding Community provisions.

This approach by the Court raises the prospect of developing the notion of indirect effect of directives by using non-binding measures as aids to interpretation where national provisions are vague or uncertain in or-

---

182. F. Snyder, "The Effectiveness of European Community Law: Institutions, Processes, Tools and Techniques", (1993) 56 M.L.R. 19 at p.32.

183. Case C-322/88, *Grimaldi v Fonds des Maladies Professionelles* [1989] ECR 4407, discussed by A. Arnull (1990) 15 E.L.Rev. 318. See also Case C-188/91, *Deutsche Shell AG v Hauptzollamt Hamburg-Hamburg* [1993] ECR I-363.

der to ensure conformity with other binding Community laws and the objectives of the EC Treaty.[184] In this way there is the potential for soft law to be converted into hard law at national level where the courts are prepared to accept this form of Community guidance.

The potential interpretative effects of soft laws will now be illustrated by an analysis of three recent Community initiatives.

The first measure for consideration is the Commission Recommendation and Code of Practice on Sexual Harassment[185] following on from an earlier Council Resolution.[186] This is a good example of what McCrudden has described as a "hybrid" between legislation and litigation "devised as much to influence national court and ECJ interpretations of existing legal provisions as to influence Member States to adopt new legal provisions or new practices".[187] The Commission Recommendation is intended to address the issue of unwanted conduct, sexual or otherwise, based on sex affecting the dignity of women and men at work and the preamble declares that such conduct is:

> ...unacceptable and may, in certain circumstances, be contrary to the principle of equal treatment within the meaning...of Directive 76/207...on the implementation of the principle of equal treatment for men and women as regards access to employment, vocational training and promotion, and working conditions, a view supported by case-law in certain Member States.

Thus the Commission's Recommendation provides further elaboration of an existing binding Community provision as a means of encouragement and guidance for national courts seeking to interpret national rules in line with Community laws in order to give them maximum "useful effect".[188]

184. The leading case is Case C-106/89, *Marleasing SA v La Comercial Internacional de Alimentacion SA* [1990] ECR I-4135. See C. Docksey & B. Fitzpatrick, "The duty of national courts to interpret provisions of national law in accordance with Community law", (1991) 20 I.L.J. 113.

185. Commission Recommendation of 27 November 1991 on the protection of the dignity of women and men at work, OJ C27/4, 4.2.92., noted by M. Rubinstein (1992) 21 I.L.J. 70. Also see: C. McCrudden, "The Effectiveness of European Equality Law: National Mechanisms for Enforcing Gender Equality Law in the Light of European Requirements", (1993) 13 O.J.L.S. 320 at pp.362-365.

186. Council Resolution of 29 May 1990 on the protection of the dignity of women and men at work, OJ C 157/3, 27.6.90.

187. McCrudden, *op.cit.* n.185, at p.362. Other examples cited are: Council Recommendation on Childcare, 92/241/EEC, OJ L 123/92, 31.3.92, and Council Recommendation on the promotion of positive action for women, 84/635/EEC, OJ L 331/34, 19.12.84.

188. For cases before the Court of Justice see: Case 41/74, *Van Duyn v Home Office* [1974] ECR 1337 and Case 51/76, *Nederlandse Ondernemingen* [1977] ECR 113.

In Britain, the Code of Practice has been cited before the Employment Appeal Tribunal (EAT). Early signs were encouraging following the advice given by the EAT in *Wadman v Carpenter Farrer Partnership*,[189] where it was held that Industrial Tribunals determining cases of sexual discrimination may use the Code for interpretative assistance. In a subsequent case concerning a display of "pin-ups" in the workplace, however, the EAT found that, as both men and women might object, the overall effect was neutral.[190] While such an approach might reflect a welcome awareness of the degrading nature of these displays for both women and men, the outcome prevents the complainant from seeking any possible recourse under the Equal Treatment Directive or the national implementing legislation.

While the Code may be of assistance to the courts and the social partners, the main force of the Recommendation is directed at the Member States exhorting them to take action to promote awareness of sexual harassment. Article 1 defines conduct as unacceptable where it is "unwanted, unreasonable and offensive to the recipient" and where a person's rejection of such conduct may be used explicitly or implicitly as the basis for any employment related decision. Conduct is as also unacceptable where it creates an intimidating, hostile or humiliating working environment for the recipient. Member States are urged, in Articles 2,3 and 4, to implement the Code in the public sector and to encourage its implementation in the private sector. The Code is also intended to be used in collective bargaining between the social partners. The Code itself is based on experience and best practice in the Member States and therefore seeks to put in place methods of preventing such conduct, encouraging the recipients to come forward, and dealing with their complaints both sympathetically and effectively.

Evidence to date suggests that the Recommendation and Code are having a galvanising effect on at least some Member States. In Belgium a decree now forces employers to ensure that employees are aware that sexual harassment of a verbal, non-verbal and physical nature, is forbidden, to provide support to victims, to set up a complaints procedure, and to establish disciplinary sanctions for offenders.[191] In France the legislation is even stronger. The amended Labour Code provides statutory protection to victims and witnesses of "the abuse of authority at work in sexual matters" and also grants them a right to a legal remedy if they suffer discrimination in employment as a result. In addition the Penal Code has been amended to make sexual harassment a criminal offence.

189. [1993] IRLR 373.

190. *Stewart v Cleveland Guest (Engineering) Ltd.* [1994] IRLR 440.

191. Decree of 18 September 1992. For fuller details see Issue 227 of the *European Industrial Relations Review* at pp.12-13.

A number of conclusions can be drawn from these developments. The use of a Recommendation and the accompanying Code has arguably prompted some Member States to act unilaterally to improve standards rather than to wait for a Community level measure offering only minimum requirements. Thus the resulting national legislation may be much stronger as a result. Further, in certain circumstances, the national courts can draw upon the Equal Treatment Directive and apply it to unacceptable sexual harassment where it causes unlawful sex discrimination outlawed by the Directive.

While such developments can be seen as positive it can equally be argued that many Member States will only pay lip-service to this measure. The Commission will have no power to bring infringement proceedings and the obligation to act will rest with the national courts rather than the Court of Justice. Equally in certain jurisdictions the courts may be disinclined to interpret soft law purposively and there may not be any guiding national legislation which adds to the provisions in the Equal Treatment Directive. There is a danger that there will be inaction in precisely those Member States where, for societal reasons, such behaviour is most prevalent and awareness is at the lowest level. Rubinstein notes that the Commission has decided that "it was necessary to test the adequacy of existing national remedies in the courts before a new Directive could be considered".[192] The absence of any proposal in the SPWP indicates that this process is still ongoing and it is to be hoped that a more concrete measure will be brought forward in due course.

Similar conclusions may be drawn about the Commission's recently published Memorandum on Equal Pay for Work of Equal Value.[193] This Memorandum contains no formal proposals and simply serves as a summary of existing case law together with comparisons of national law and practice in this area. This is quite disappointing not least because the Memorandum was based on extensive research and intended to provide a fillip to the national courts when interpreting national provisions and ensuring compliance with Community law.

The Memorandum echoes the Green Paper on Social Policy which notes that women are more likely to be in low paid and insecure jobs and have lower levels of labour market participation than men.[194] While the Memorandum makes a number of positive suggestions, for example proposing changes in evaluation practices which take greater account of attributes more often found in jobs where women predominate, in the

192. Rubinstein, *op.cit.* n.185, at p.70.

193. Issued on 30 June 1994 and noted by T. Gill (1994) 23 I.L.J. 359. For a critique see: J. Rubery, Chap.8 of *Economic Policy Making and the European Union*, pp.43-50, F. Brouwer, V. Lintner, and M. Newman eds., (Federal Trust, London, 1994).

194. Green Paper, p. 25.

absence of any formal proposals it is difficult to see many tangible benefits arising. Gill notes that the comparative survey suggesting the desirability of intra-industry comparisons may act as a spur in those countries where the law is silent on the question.[195] At best the Memorandum will act as an additional tool to reinforce existing national provisions to give effect to Article 119 and the Equal Pay Directive. An accompanying Code of Practice has been discussed at Community level for over a year but it has still not been adopted.

The above measures both relate to existing Community Directives, in whole or in part, and, in the case of the Equal Pay Memorandum to a specific Treaty provision. By contrast the Commission Opinion on an equitable wage[196] is based solely on the provisions in Article 118 concerning "close co-operation between the Member States in the social field" without specifically mentioning pay. To a degree this is remedied by point 5 of the Social Charter which proclaims that all employment shall be fairly remunerated and workers should be assured of an equitable wage sufficient to enable them to have a decent standard of living while acknowledging that wage-setting is a matter for the Member States and the social partners. Therefore the Commission admits in the preamble to the Opinion that it is merely asserting the fact that low pay is an "important problem for a significant proportion of the working population".

The concept of an "equitable wage" for workers is defined in the Opinion as:

> ...a reward for work done which in the context of the society in which they live and work is fair and sufficient to enable them to have a decent standard of living.[197]

All operational definitions are left to national, regional or sectoral levels and Member States are encouraged to take measures to establish negotiated minima and include anti-discrimination measures to ensure fair treatment. In order to provide a further justification for straying into the area of wages the Commission's Opinion draws upon the commitment of the Community to reinforcing economic and social cohesion noting in the preamble that:

> the persistence of very low wage levels raises problems of equity and social cohesion which could be harmful to the effectiveness of the economy in the long term.

195. Gill, *op.cit.* n.193, at p.362. The countries cited are Germany, Italy and Greece.

196. COM(93) 388 final of 1 September 1993.

197. Point 1 of the Opinion.

There is no explicit reference in the Opinion to Article 130a EC, concerning the goal of social cohesion, and an opportunity was missed to provide an additional justification for a policy position based on social justice, by directly linking the broad objectives of Article 118 with Article 130a. Such linkage has considerable potential as Ross has noted:

> The combination of a constitutionalised principle of cohesion and national judicial convergence in response to Article 5 obligations could breathe fresh life into social policy at a time when consensual legislation may be off the political agenda.[198]

This Opinion is, at least in part, a laudable statement, but it is doubtful if it has any legal significance because there is no clear linkage to other binding Community legislation and it must be questionable whether it will assist low paid workers in a practical sense. Even though the notion of an equitable wage has been under discussion for several years the UK has been able to abolish all of its sectoral wage setting machinery outside of agriculture,[199] while Spain has cut its minimum wage. Further it can be argued that the ambiguous statement in the Opinion that measures should not have "a negative impact on job creation" represents an implicit acceptance of the statistically unproven Thatcherite ideological position justifying low pay and allowing for "social dumping" as in the "Hoover affair" in 1993.[200] Indeed, it is submitted that the exclusion of pay from the coverage of Article 2(6) of the SPA, and the absence of any follow up proposals in the SPWP, suggests that the Commission's aim for "a level playing field of common minimum standards" is incapable of genuine fulfilment. The two areas which are, almost certainly, of greatest importance to the Community worker, pay and job security, appear to fall outside Community competence.

These three examples, amongst the myriad of soft law provisions introduced after the adoption of the Social Charter, show that soft law measures can be of limited use where they can be allied to existing binding provisions subject to interpretation by the national courts. Further they may encourage improvements in national law and practice. However, soft laws, although they may serve as a useful supplement to exist-

198. Ross, *op.cit.* n.57, at p.143.

199. See Issue 29 of the *New Review of the Low Pay Unit* (Sept./Oct. 1994) at pp.8-12. This survey examines evidence which suggests that a minimum wage in the UK would not have harmful effects on employment or on competitive advantage, and would help alleviate poverty.

200. Hoover moved a large plant from France to Scotland ostensibly on the grounds of the lower costs of employment prevailing in the UK. *Financial Times*, 10 February 1993, "Hoover relocation as part of a general trend".

ing provisions to help national implementation, cannot amount to a satisfactory substitute for binding legislation designed to ensure a fair and
genuine platform of exercisable rights available to the Community worker
as envisaged by the Social Charter.

(b)   The Community Social Charter and the 1989 Action Programme

Published in the form of a Council "Solemn Declaration" and a Commission Communication, the Community Social Charter and its Action
Programme are perhaps the most obvious examples of aspirational soft
law in the social policy field. These instruments fit very neatly into Snyder's
explanation for the inclination of Community institutions to resort to
soft law as:

> ...in part a predictable feature of administrative development, in
> part a comprehensible response to institutional inertia, and in
> part a questionable attempt to circumvent or avoid the implica-
> tions of failures to reach political agreement.[201]

The Commission's 1993 Green Paper explained the rationale for the
Social Charter thus:

> It expressed the political will that the completion of the internal
> market should not be achieved without taking the "social dimen-
> sion" into account.[202]

Applying Snyder's reasoning the adoption of the Charter can be seen as
political recognition of the slow pace of progress in the social policy
field and an attempt to escape from the straight-jacket imposed by the
limited legislative base in the Treaties compounded by the UK's persist-
ent obduracy. However, the true status of the Charter can be gleaned
from the Commission's Second Report on its application which begins:

> The Charter, as a European act, merely states and notes the rights
> which were the subject of deliberations in the European Coun-
> cil in Strasbourg in December 1989. In itself, it has no effect on
> the existing legal situation.[203]

---

201. F. Snyder, *Soft Law and Institutional Practice in the European Community*, EUI Working
    Paper LAW No. 93/5, at p.3. (EUI, Florence 1993).

202. Green Paper, p.10.

203. COM(92) 562 final of 23 December 1992.

Moreover, it can be argued that to describe the Council's declaration as a "Charter" is a misnomer which not only confuses this document with the European Social Charter (ESC), but also gives it a false status by seeking to elevate a simple statement of objectives, many of which cannot be realised by legislative means at Community level and fall outside the jurisdiction of the Court of Justice. This can be illustrated by reference to the twelve fundamental social rights listed in the Charter:

- freedom of movement;
- freedom to choose and engage in an occupation and fair remuneration;
- improvement of living and working conditions;
- social protection;
- freedom of association and collective bargaining;
- vocational training;
- equal treatment for men and women;
- information, consultation and participation for workers;
- health protection and safety at the workplace;
- protection of children and adolescents;
- rights of the elderly to a decent standard of living;
- rights of the disabled to improve their social and professional integration.

An examination of these headings reveals that there are several areas where existing avowed Community rights are simply restated including, *inter alia,* free movement and equal treatment. Other listed rights, for example those concerning the elderly and disabled, whilst desirable, would appear to fall outside Community competence and are therefore entirely dependant upon action at Member State level. Among the remaining areas, worker participation and improvements in living and working conditions were, prior to the SPA, only capable of being achieved through legislative means either by unanimity or by the most imaginative use of Article 118a, with all the limitations that this latter avenue entails.

Thus while the Action Programme is intended to be more tangible, the implementation of the Charter is a matter for the Member States alone. Article 27 of the Charter states that:

> It is more particularly the responsibility of the Member States in accordance with national practices, notably through legislative measures or collective agreements, to guarantee the fundamental social rights in this Charter and to implement the social measures indispensable to the smooth operation of the internal market as part of a strategy of economic and social cohesion.

This delegation of responsibility to the Member States might be viewed as the application of practical subsidiarity. In the context of the Community, subsidiarity is best understood as a desire to ensure the effectiveness of Community action, where it is agreed that such action is necessary at all, by placing responsibility for achieving the Community's objectives at the level closest to the citizen, which may be interpreted as at Member State level or, in countries where there is a developed system of regional government, at a more localised level. The preamble to the Social Charter avers to the principle of subsidiarity and, while it places the primary responsibility for implementation on the Member States or their constituent parts, there is also a residual obligation on the Community to act "within the limits of its powers". However, unlike under the second paragraph of Article 3b EC,[204] which constitutionalises the principle of subsidiarity, there is no specific obligation on the Community institutions to act where the objectives of the Charter cannot be "sufficiently achieved" by the Member States alone and can "by reason of the scale and effects of the proposed action, be better achieved by the Community".

The weakness of a Charter issued as soft law was swiftly recognised by the European Parliament which called for its adoption by way of a binding legislative instrument.[205] The Economic and Social Committee, in an influential Opinion, issued before the adoption of the Charter, had sought to establish the Charter as a basic guarantee of social rights drawing directly upon the ESC, the ECHR, and ILO Conventions.[206] The Committee also presented a far broader range of fundamental rights by including, *inter alia*, the right to work, the right to organise and bargain collectively, and the right to protection in the event of individual dismissal. The first draft of the Charter was far closer to this Opinion regarding social rights as free-standing, rather than being an aspect of the internal market, and calling for the development of the social rights of citizens, but the final version was significantly weakened in scope.[207] Moreover, each of these rights is already guaranteed by the ESC and its Additional Protocol, making the ESC not only a stronger document than the Community Charter, but also subject to the supervision of a Committee of Experts.[208]

---

204. As amended by the TEU.

205. See Resolutions of 15.3.89, OJ C96, 17.4.89, and of 14.9.89, OJ C120, 16.5.89.

206. CES 270/89 of 22.2.89 and contained in *Social Europe* 1/90, pp.83-90.

207. See B. Bercusson, "The European Community's Charter of Fundamental Social Rights of Workers", (1990) 35 M.L.R. 624.

208. See Hepple, *op.cit.* n.134, at pp.644-5, and also A. Jaspers and L. Betten (eds.) *25 Years European Social Charter* (Deventer, Kluwer 1988).

The Committee's Opinion is of continuing relevance because it envisages "fundamental values" in terms of social rights for all Community citizens enshrined in Community legislation.[209] Viewed with the benefit of hindsight the rather patchy progress of individual Community legislative initiatives, both in terms of outstanding items and the diluted strength of many of the measures actually adopted, points to the considerable potential of this alternative approach as a means of developing the nascent concept of Community citizenship. This theme will be revisited in the concluding section of this Chapter.

Notwithstanding the inherent weaknesses of the Social Charter the ensuing implementation of the Action Programme renewed the momentum of Community social policy and was regarded by Nielsen and Szyszcak as signalling "the end of a decade of pessimism that the embryonic social policy law of the original Treaty...would never develop".[210] This more optimistic view was shared by the Commission and borne out by the 1993 Green Paper which pointed to all 47 initiatives announced in the Action Programme having been presented by the Commission with 16 of the 29 measures requiring Council approval having been adopted.[211] The ensuing White Paper notes that 21 of these proposals were intended to be directives, mainly using Article 118a, 13 of which had been adopted.[212]

This presentation of results suggests that the Action Programme has given a meaningful gloss to the aspirations of the Charter. Certainly more has been achieved than many commentators thought possible, most particularly in the health and safety field, but on scratching beneath the surface there is revealed a catalogue of measures which have yet to be approved by the Council, most significantly the proposals concerning non-standard and posted workers, and a series of half-baked directives which will require substantial enhancement, not least the Working Time Directive. In addition many important aspects of the Charter have been dealt with by programmatic decisions, as in the case of the Helios programme for the disabled,[213] or the soft law measures considered earlier. Overall the Charter can be seen as a useful temporary vehicle for achieving limited progress during a difficult period leading up to the SPA and the presentation of the SPWP.

---

209. CES 270/89, *op.cit.* n.206, at p.83.

210. Nielsen & Szyszcak, *op.cit.* n.26, at p.15.

211. Green Paper, p.10.

212. SPWP, Chap.3, para.2.

213. Decision 93/136 EEC of 25 February 1993, OJ L 56, 9.3.93.

(c) Subsidiarity — A Wrong Turn for Social Policy?

The scope for Community action post-Maastricht is set out in Article 3b EC, which states that:

> The Community shall act within the limits of the powers conferred upon it by this Treaty and of the objectives assigned to it therein.

> In areas which do not fall within its exclusive competence, the Community shall take action, in accordance with the principle of subsidiarity, only if and in so far as the objectives of the proposed action cannot be sufficiently achieved by the Member States and can therefore, by reason of the scale and effects of the proposed action, be better achieved by the Community.

> Any action by the Community shall not go beyond what is necessary to achieve the objectives of this Treaty.

Interpretation of this elusive concept, described by Lord Wedderburn as a principle of "feline inscrutability and political subtlety",[214] will ultimately be a matter for the Court of Justice. The Court will have to decide whether or not the measure falls within the Community's exclusive jurisdiction and thereby determine when there are grounds under Article 173 EC to annul the act by reason of lack of competence. Hartley notes that there are so many imponderables that it will "almost always be possible for the Court, if it wishes, to find grounds for upholding the measure".[215] After all the Court has traditionally been integrationist by nature seeking, in the words of Judge Mancini to:

> ... 'constitutionalise' the Treaty, that is to fashion a constitutional framework for a federal-type structure in Europe.[216]

However Judge Mancini was writing at a time when judicial activism in the Court of Justice had reached its high water-mark and more recent judicial pronouncements have suggested a more cautious approach, lim-

---

214. Lord Wedderburn, "The Social Charter in Britain — Labour Law and Labour Courts?", (1991) 54 M.L.R. 1 at p.14.

215. See T.C. Hartley, *The Foundations of European Community Law*, 3rd Edition, Clarendon Law Series, 1994 at p.139. *cf.* Temple Lang *op.cit.* n.334, at p.458.

216. F. Mancini, "The Making of a Constitution for Europe", (1989) 26 C.M.L. Rev. 595.

iting the scope of the *Barber* decision on pensions,[217] and rejecting the arguments put forward for the "horizontal direct effect" of directives.[218] The Court may be reluctant, as a matter of policy, to intervene between the Community institutions and the Member States and yet the Court is best placed to determine the scope of the principle because of its avowed independence and its ability to apply general principles of law, including proportionality, in appropriate cases.[219] In any case the Court is likely to be guided by the Council and Commission pronouncements on the matter which will, in turn, dictate the content and subject-matter of both proposed and enacted legislation.[220]

The conclusions of the Edinburgh European Council in December 1992 noted that the implementation of Article 3b should respect a number of basic principles. These will encompass the maintenance in full of the *acquis communautaire*, recognition of the primacy of Community law,[221] and confirmation that the principle will be subject to the control of the Court of Justice. As a general rule the "more specific the nature of the Treaty requirement the less scope exists for applying subsidiarity".[222]

The Council's guidelines provide that subsidiarity is a condition for any Community action and the Council must be satisfied both that the objectives of the proposed action cannot be sufficiently achieved by Member States alone and they can be better achieved by Community action which must produce "clear benefits". Harmonisation legislation should only be introduced where necessary to achieve the Treaty's objectives and consideration should be given to setting minimum standards not just in those areas specified by the Treaty. Any decision in favour of Community action should take into account, *inter alia*, trans-national aspects, the need to avoid distortion of competition, and to strengthen economic and social cohesion. The guidelines also seek to minimise burdens at all levels and all measures should "leave as much scope for national decisions as possible".[223]

217. See Case C-152/91, *Neath v Hugh Steeper Ltd*, (nyr) and Case C-200/91, *Coloroll Pension Trustees Ltd v Russell and Others*, (nyr).

218. *Dori, op.cit.* n.37.

219. See, for example, Case 181/84, *Man (Sugar) v IBAP* [1985] ECR 2889.

220. See Annex 1 to Part A of the Conclusions of the Presidency, at the European Council in Edinburgh, 11-12 December 1992 (EC Bull. 12/92, pp.25-6), and Commission report to the Council on the adaptation of Community Legislation to the Subsidiarity Principle, COM(93) 545 final of 24 November 1993.

221. In full compliance with Article 5 EC and consistent with the principle in Article F(3) of the TEU, according to which the Union shall provide itself with the means necessary to attain its objectives and carry through its policies.

222. Council Conclusions, I. Basic Principles.

223. *ibid.*, Council Conclusions II. Guidelines, 3rd para. point 3.

Significantly the Council has given notice of a decisive shift towards soft laws declaring that:

> Other things being equal, directives should be preferred to regulations and framework directives to detailed measures. Non-binding measures such as recommendations should be preferred *where appropriate*. Consideration should also be given *where appropriate* to the use of voluntary codes of conduct [and]...preference in choosing the type of Community action should be given to encourage co-operation between Member States, coordinating national action or complementing, supplementing or supporting such action.[224]

The Commission will ask itself three questions in each case before proposing legislation in any form:

- What is the Community dimension of the problem?
- What is the most effective solution, given the means available to the Community and to Member States?
- What is the real added value of common action compared with isolated action by the Member States?

Subsidiarity is viewed by the Commission as a means of regulating the exercise of powers and justifying their use in a particular case. This can have both an expansive and limiting effect on Community action. However the Commission has undertaken to include a full justification in each of its proposals, to withdraw or revise pending proposals, and to review existing legislation. The Commission proposes a hierarchy of Community norms to be examined at the 1996 inter-governmental Conference.[225]

The Commission identifies social policy as a field where rules are to be simplified and draws from the Council's conclusions at Edinburgh which refer to the directives based on Article 118a being "too recent to warrant re-examination". Instead they will be supplemented by full implementation of the Social Charter whilst simplifying and codifying older regulations on the free movement of workers.[226] Social policy is specifically excluded from those areas where rules and regulations are to be repealed.

---

224. *ibid.*, points 5 & 6. *Author's emphasis.*

225. Commission Report to the Council, pp.1-7.

226. *ibid.*, p.18.

How will the principle of subsidiarity impact on Community social policy? The easiest answer is that there will be no change because subsidiarity was already built into the Social Charter and the legislation arising predominantly from Article 118a is already based on minimum standards and now clearly falls within the field of "shared competence" a designation which is also now accurate outside of the health and safety area following the upgrading of social policy in Article 2(1) of the SPA. This provides for "directives" containing "minimum requirements for gradual implementation" while the role of the Community is to "support and complement" the activities of the signatory Member States in the social policy fields as set out in the SPA.

While, from an integrationist perspective, social policy may have fared relatively well under these criteria, any optimism must be tempered by the fact that social legislation is much less developed than other areas, notably competition and free movement. Moreover, the base of minimum standards, has often been set, as in the case of the Pregnancy Directive, at too low a level, or, as in the example of the Working Time Directive, with too many exclusions making for an uneven "floor" of rights. Therefore subsidiarity may ultimately mean that the adoption of the SPA may not be the motor for social policy integration hoped for by some and feared by others.

In future social policy measures will be limited to directives, where minimum standards are necessary, and further soft law in other areas where such action is deemed appropriate. Council "decisions" based on agreements between management and labour will be another option and the scope, status and potential of these measures will be considered in the next section. Any criticisms of the White Paper have to be placed in the context of the limitations which arise from the subsidiary dimension to each problem.

(d) Social Dialogue — A Means to an End?

While corporatism has been on the wane throughout the Community during the last decade, the notion of establishing social consensus as a means of achieving Community norms, and thereby by-passing the cumbersome legislative machinery, has become increasingly attractive to all of the "social actors" as a dynamic idea consistent with the principle of subsidiarity, bringing decision making closer to the workplace realities and allowing for variations to suit national collective bargaining practices.

Article 118b EC, inserted by the Single European Act, began to concretise this process by declaring that:

The Commission shall endeavour to develop the dialogue between management and labour at European level which could, if the two sides consider it desirable, lead to relations based on agreement.

This provision does not appear to provide a direct means for binding agreements to be adopted between the social partners at Community level although it carries with it the implication that the Commission might propose legislation consistent with any agreements between "management and labour" possibly in the form of Framework Agreements to be implemented at national level.[227]

The Commission has championed social dialogue convening summit meetings between the social partners, first at *Val Duchesse* in 1985, in order to bring the process to fruition. However progress has been hampered from the outset by differences of approach between the social partners. Thus while the ETUC[228] view social dialogue as a means to an end, developing and strengthening, rather than replacing, existing Community legislation, UNICE[229] regard dialogue as an end in itself, seeking to agree minimum requirements in relatively uncontentious areas, concerning health and safety at work and non-discrimination, but declining to negotiate collective agreements which may be converted into binding Community laws.[230] The result was a stalemate with nine vacuous Joint Opinions being adopted between 1986 and 1992 on subjects mainly relating to vocational training, new technology, and adaptability of the labour market.[231]

Whilst these Joint Opinions may be worthwhile statements of best practice they are purely declaratory and cannot even be described as soft laws because they have not been taken any further by the Community institutions. In the Action Programme social dialogue was regarded as an important means of securing implementation at national level and as an additional method of fulfilling the goals of recommendations and opinions which are otherwise non-binding. Thus for example part 4 of the Opinion on an equitable wage declares that the social partners are invited to:

...examine what contribution they can make to ensuring the right of every worker to an equitable minimum wage.

227. This is suggested as a way forward in the Green Paper at p.63.

228. European Trade Union Confederation.

229. Union of Industries of the European Community.

230. See Annex I of the Green Paper, p.85.

231. Listed in Annex IV of the Green Paper, p.100.

While it may be too early to provide a precise evaluation of the worth of such statements even the Commission has been forced to concede that social dialogue has been "slow to mature".[232]

However, although Community-wide social dialogue is in incipient form, it is regarded by the Community institutions, and the signatories of the SPA, as an alternative method of legislating through collective agreements capable of implementation at national and sectoral level. This is a practice well established through the ILO and the ESC[233] but it has yet to take firm roots at Community level despite the inclusion of provisions in individual directives allowing implementation by collective agreements[234] and recognition of this method by the Court of Justice.[235]

Not least amongst the problems is the representativeness of the parties to such "agreements", the status of any decisions arising from them, and the means of implementation and enforceability. At the heart of the debate lies a deeper question: are the parties involved in collective bargaining or simply structured Community-level dialogue? The inclusion of additional provisions in the SPA, designed to give new impetus to this process, will now be considered, alongside the Protocol and Agreement as a whole, to try to determine some answers to these questions.

(v) The Social Policy Protocol and Agreement: Widening without Deepening?

History appeared to repeat itself when the UK refused to sign the proposed "Social Chapter" at Maastricht in December 1991, which would have amended Articles 117-122 EEC. The outcome left the existing social policy provisions essentially unaltered[236] whilst attaching to the amended EC Treaty a supplementary Social Policy Protocol, number 14,

---

232. Green Paper, p.61.

233. ILO Conventions Nos. 100, 101, 106, 111, 171, 172. Article 35(1) of the ESC. For discussion on this point see A. Adinolfi, "The Implementation of Social Policy Directives Through Collective Agreements" (1988) 25 C.M.L. Rev. 291.

234. See for example Article 9(1) of Directive 91/533/EEC on employee information and Article 2(1) of Directive 92/56/EEC on collective redundancies.

235. In Case 143/83, *Commission v Denmark* [1985] ECR 427 at pp.434-5, the Court held that "Member states may leave the implementation of the principle of equal pay in the first instance to representatives of management and labour". Bercusson has argued that national legislation is only required as a back up where the collective agreement is inadequate: See B. Bercusson, "The Dynamic of European Labour Law after Maastricht", (1994) 23 I.L.J. 1 at pp.16-17.

236. Apart from an amendment to Article 118a allowing for legislation to be adopted in accordance with the cooperation procedure with the Parliament, Article 189 EC. Articles 123 *et seq.* concerning the European Social Fund, education, vocational training and youth, contains enhancements and new Community competences.

agreed by all the Member States, allowing eleven Member States to "adopt among themselves" an annexed Agreement (SPA) "without prejudice" to the social provisions in the Treaty which form an "integral part" of the *acquis*. The substantive social provisions are contained in the SPA and two separate Declarations.[237]

The decision of the eleven to adopt the SPA was a pragmatic, but bold, action recognising that progress in social policy could only be achieved if the UK was left behind, for a temporary but undetermined period, and on the basis that this novel method was the only way to attempt to fill "the wide gap between the powers available under the current legal bases and the ambitions set out in the Charter".[238]

Whilst the motivation for proceeding with the Protocol route was understandable the legal and practical consequences created by this decision are immense and, as yet, have not begun to unravel. First, irrespective of the legal status of the SPA, the exclusion of the UK, or more accurately the decision of the eleven to proceed alone and enter legally uncharted waters, violated the essential unity of application of the Treaty as provided for by Article 227 EC.[239] Curtin has quite properly criticised the SPA as "fundamentally disintegrative" leading to a "hijacking" of the *acquis* based on an assumption that Member States may selectively apply "bits and pieces".[240] However the alternative was to stand still and allow one to dictate to eleven.

(a) Legal Status of the Protocol and Agreement

Although some initial uncertainty was expressed the legal status of the Protocol now seems clear.[241] By virtue of Article 239 EC which states that Protocols annexed to the Treaty "by *common accord* of the Member States shall form an *integral part thereof*",[242] the Protocol cannot be separated from the remainder of the Treaty and is a lawful Treaty amend-

237. Therefore the Agreement supplements rather than replaces Articles 117-122. For a contrary view see M. Weiss, "The Significance of Maastricht for European Community Social Policy", (1992) 8 Int.J.Comp.L.L.I.R. 3 at p.6.

238. Working Document submitted to the Intergovernmental Conference on Political Union, SEC(91) 500 of 30 March 1991, p.84.

239. Article 227 provides that "The Treaty shall apply to...", and then lists all Member States.

240. D. Curtin, "The Constitutional Structure of the Union: A Europe of Bits and Pieces", (1993) 30 C.M.L.Rev. 17 at p.57.

241. In support of this view see Curtin, *ibid.*, at pp.53-4; P. Watson, "Social Policy After Maastricht", (1993) 30 C.M.L.Rev. 481 at pp.489-91; E.A. Whiteford, "Social Policy After Maastricht", (1993) E.L.Rev 202 at pp.203-4; *cf.* C. Barnard, "A Social policy for Europe: Politicians 1:0 Lawyers", (1992) 8 Int.J.Comp.L.L.I.R. 15 at pp.18-21.

242. *Emphasis added.*

ment adopted by common accord of the twelve at a conference of the Member States in accordance with the procedure laid down in Article 236 EEC. As the Protocol is integrated within the EC Treaty it therefore adds to the *acquis* and was part of the Accession Treaties for Austria, Finland and Norway, creating a 14-1 balance among the Member States.[243]

For the purposes of this Chapter the critical question concerns the status of the Agreement and, to a lesser degree, the Declarations, as these contain the essential basis for new legislation by Council "directives" and "decisions" arising from agreements between management and labour. Is this merely an inter-governmental agreement relying upon the Member States to adapt their national laws in accordance with "directives" falling outside the ambit of Article 189 EC and also beyond the jurisdiction of the Court of Justice? There are no clear answers for as the Commission have noted: "This situation has never occurred in the Community before"![244]

Curtin[245] argues that the SPA is not Community law at all but operates as an extra-Community agreement and the "directives" referred to in Article 2(2) of the SPA are not synonymous with directives under Article 189 EC. The Protocol makes it clear that the eleven have agreed to act "among themselves" and the SPA applies "as far as they are concerned". Otherwise the provisions would have been amendments to the Treaty with a Protocol suspending the UKs voting rights as in the case of Protocol 10 on Economic and Monetary Union.[246] Curtin accepts that the Court of Justice may have jurisdiction to deal with violations of the SPA and Article 177 references because the Protocol authorises the eleven to "have recourse to the institutions, procedures and mechanisms of the Treaty".

Watson[247] by contrast, argues that the SPA is not excisable from the Protocol on the basis that it was annexed to the Protocol, itself a part of the Treaty. Watson contends that the contrast with Protocol 10 is simply too indirect, whereas the inconsistencies represent poor drafting.[248] The

---

243. From 1 January 1995. Both the Protocol and the SPA would have to be amended in this way if the UK were to join. See Whiteford, *op.cit.* n.241, at p.204, *cf.* Weiss, *op.cit.* n.237, at p.3. Bercusson argues that it will only be necessary for the UK to "adhere" to the SPA, not to the Protocol: Bercusson, *op.cit.* n.235, at p.5.

244. Commission Communication concerning the application of the Agreement on Social Policy, COM(93) 600 of 14 December 1993 at p.1 of the summary.

245. Curtin, *op.cit.* n.240, at pp.55-60. See also E. Vogel-Polsky, *Evaluation of the Social Provisions of the Treaty on European Union.* Report prepared for the European Parliament. DOC EN/CM/202155 at pp.3-5.

246. See Point 7 of Protocol 10.

247. Watson, *op.cit.* n.241, at pp.491-4. See also Bercusson *op.cit.* n.235, at pp.7-9. Bercusson contends that the Court may decide that the agreement applies to the UK, pp.6-7, *cf.* B. Fitzpatrick, "Community Social Law after Maastricht" (1992) I.L.J. 199 at p.203.

248. See U. Everling, "Reflections on the structure of the European Union", (1992) 29 C.M.L.Rev. 1053.

references in the Protocol to the Community institutions and directives and indeed to "Community action", in Articles 3 and 4 of the SPA, would have no meaning if the SPA is only inter-governmental. In addition, the implementation of the SPA is founded upon the *acquis* and must therefore be the basis for binding Community laws applying to the 14 following enlargement.

Although the *acquis* has always been based on the assumption of uniformity in the Community legal order this does not necessarily prevent the SPA being interpreted as a temporary derogation to ensure that the slower partner can join the more integrated States as soon as possible.[249] The example of the Young Workers Directive also suggests that such two-speed development may be lawful if undesirable.

The Commission, perhaps overstating the case, regard the SPA as "soundly based in law" and consider the Community nature of measures taken under the SPA as "beyond doubt". Social policy is therefore subject to two free-standing but complementary legal frames of reference. The Commission regard a directive adopted under the SPA as "territorial" and not applicable in the territory of the UK. However a UK national, or a subsidiary of a UK company, based in another Member State, will be subject to its provisions.[250]

On balance these latter arguments are more convincing and it follows that any directives issued under the SPA will be binding in accordance with Article 189 EC and subject to the supervision of the Court of Justice under Article L of the TEU. The status of the Declarations is less certain but they may be indivisible from the Agreement because they are attached to it and are separate from other Declarations attached to the EC Treaty which were adopted as the Final Acts of the Conference.

(b)   The Social Policy Agreement as a Basis for Legislative Action

Undoubtedly the utmost significance of the SPA lies with the fact that for the first time there exists an independent legal basis for a wide range of Community social legislation. The scope of the objectives in Article 1 are also wider than under Article 117 and the amended Article 2 EC.[251] However the SPA is strictly minimalist in its approach and because it is supplementary to the Treaty it can only be activated after attempts to legislate among the 15, and thereby secure uniformity, have been exhausted. This is the intention behind the Protocol's declared

249. *cf.* Whiteford, *op.cit.* n.241, at pp.212-220, who argues that the SPA could be challenged *via* an Article 177 reference.

250. COM(93) 600, at paras.7 & 8.

251. Article 2 EC refers to a "high level of employment and social protection", but no longer refers to "an accelerated raising of the standard of living".

aim that the SPA is "without prejudice" to the existing social policy provisions under the Treaty. For this reason the Commission now has to introduce all social policy proposals, other than Article 118a measures, through this circuitous route causing delay although not necessarily a dilution of the text to accommodate the UK.[252] Additional delay will arise from the Commission's obligation in Articles 3(2) and 3(3) to initially consult the representatives of management and labour before submitting any proposals and to consult them again on the content. Article 3(4) will allow them up to nine months to reach their own agreement under the provisions in Article 4. The implications of this procedure will be considered presently.

The minimalist and temporary nature of the SPA can be inferred from its specific objective, in the preamble, to "implement the 1989 Social Charter". While this may be a laudable aim, the initial emphasis will be on action at Member State level whereby through Article 5 of the SPA the Commission "shall encourage co-operation between the Member States and facilitate the coordination of their action in all policy fields". This approach chimes with the overriding Community principle of subsidiarity and the practical consequences flow from the Commission's Green Paper which avers to programmatic action rather than legislation as the norm although soft laws may follow to provide encouragement where necessary with binding legislation remaining only as an instrument of last resort.[253]

Article 2(1) and (2) contain the bases for new legislation which the Council *may* adopt by QMV in the form of directives to support and complement the activities of the Member States. This legislation will be subject to the co-operation procedure with Parliament. The directives will consist of only "minimum requirements for gradual implementation". More stringent requirements will be a matter for individual Member States.

A directive can be implemented at national level by the social partners so long as it is transposed in accordance with Article 189 EC and the Member States are required to take any necessary measure to "guarantee the results imposed by that directive" (Article 2(4)).

Directives must take into account the need to "maintain the competitiveness of the Community economy" and avoid imposing constraints holding back the creation and development of small and medium-sized

252. The UK will not take part in the any deliberations and the adoption of Commission proposals by the Council under the SPA (Protocol, Point 2). Neither the acts nor the administrative costs incurred are applicable to the UK (Protocol, Point 2 para.3). This will not prevent UK appointed officials at the Commission and MEPs being involved — see Watson, *op.cit.* n.241, at pp.504-5, Barnard, *op.cit.* n.241, at pp.27-8.

253. Green Paper, p.10 and p.50.

enterprises.

The directives will be in the following fields:

— improvement in particular of the working environment to protect workers' health and safety;
— working conditions;
— information and consultation of workers;
— equality between men and women with regard to labour market
opportunities and treatment at work;
— integration of persons excluded from the labour market.

Article 2(3) lists additional areas where the Council must act unanimously
and Parliament will only be consulted. The type of measure is not specified and this will allow for soft law in the form of recommendations and
opinions. These areas are:

— social security and social protection of workers;
— protection of workers where their employment contract is terminated;
— representation and collective defence of the interests of workers
and employers, including co-determination, subject to the exclusion of pay, the right of association, the right to strike and the
right to impose lock outs in Article 2(6);
— conditions of employment for third-country nationals legally
residing in Community territory;
— financial contributions for promotion of employment and job-
creation.

A number of observations can be made about the legislative potential of
these provisions.

1) The role of the Commission will be critical in determining the
scope of any proposals which potentially could go well beyond
the Social Charter Action Programme if Article 2(3) in particular is fully utilised. In its Communication on the application of
the SPA the Commission are cautious and merely indicate that
the procedure will be dynamic and decided on a case by case
basis with a review each year in the annual report to be issued in
accordance with Article 7. The Commission express a desire to
ensure that all workers throughout the Community benefit from
a proposed measure but present no clear idea of how this ambition might be fulfilled.[254]

254. COM(93) 600 at paras.2 & 8.

There may also be some overlap between the areas listed in Article 2 giving the Commission a pretext for using the fields requiring QMV. For example one area under consideration by the Commission is the right to payment of wages on public holidays and during illness.[255] This could be justified as relating to "working conditions" under Article 2(2) rather than "social protection" under Article 2(3) even though a significant proportion of the costs would have to be met by the Member States depending upon their social security system. Although the Council may wish to change the legal base the Court is likely to back the legislative procedure which allows co-operation with Parliament.[256]

2) A cursory examination of the wording in Article 2(2) is sufficient to show that it corresponds in form with Article 118a EC which also specifies the adoption of directives and contains identical "minimum requirements" provisions. There is a real danger that in the mood of post-Maastricht caution, which emanates throughout the SPWP, the measures proposed will be strictly limited allowing for considerable national variations notwithstanding the absence of the UK from the final deliberations. Much will depend on the degree to which the Commission is prepared to firm up its proposals once it has failed to secure unanimous support under the primary social policy provisions. Subsidiarity will also limit the Commission's room for manoeuvre in these circumstances and may lead to a choice being made to wait to see if the social partners wish to initiate alternative proposals.[257] The Commission's mettle will be tested when it resubmits its proposals on posted workers and non-standard workers.[258] The probability is that unless a "level playing field" is introduced in these areas the tendency towards social dumping will increase with standards actually worsening at national level.[259]

3) Article 2(4) would appear to guarantee the intended results of a directive even where it is implemented nationally by an agree-

255. SPWP, Chap.3, para.13(iv).

256. See Cases C-65/90 and C-295/90, *European Parliament v Council* [1992] ECR I-4593 and I-4193 respectively.

257. For discussion: see Bercusson, *op.cit.* n.235, at pp.13-15, and Watson, *op.cit.* n.241, at pp.494-8. The Commission regard the SPA as a dual form of subsidiarity regarding regulation at Community and national level and a choice between a legislative approach and an agreements-based approach — COM(93) 600 at para.6(c).

258. See Section 4 of this Chapter.

259. See Watson, *op.cit.* n.241, at pp.511-3.

ment between the social partners by placing a continuing obligation on the Member States to take any necessary measure "at any time" to ensure that the minimum requirements are met. The Commission note that the measures will "take account of the diverse forms of national practices, in particular in the field of contractual relations".[260] While such provisions are not new in individual directives this is the first time that there has been a general provision of this kind and the Commission will need to carefully monitor the quality of these agreements.[261] Monitoring will be particularly important in countries where agreements cannot be legally extended to all workers, including those not covered by collective agreements, *erga omnes*, and would be impossible under current UK law, were the UK to sign up to the SPA, because collective agreements are not legally binding unless incorporated into individual contracts of employment.[262]

4) Despite the exclusions of pay and collective labour law, the provisions in Article 2(3) would appear to offer the greatest scope for extending Community law to new areas which have previously been strictly within the national sphere. The attitude of the 14 will be tested now that the UK is no longer a convenient foil for more widely felt resistance to Community social policy initiatives. The areas requiring unanimity include matters which are paramount to Community workers fearful about job security and seeking, at the very least, to maintain their working conditions in a world of "labour market flexibility". The inclusion of measures concerning third-country nationals "legally resident" in the Community is a potentially important advance raising fundamental issues concerning the notion of Union citizenship which will be explored further in the final section of this Chapter.

5) Although the SPA offers a vital escape hatch for the Commission and the 14, it is important that procedures under the mainstream Treaty provisions are fully exhausted and imaginative use of Article 118a should still be permissible in certain, albeit limited, circumstances. The Community has been presented with a poisoned chalice. Qualitative aspects of social policy proposals may have to be sacrificed in order to benefit all Union citizens, in-

260. COM(93) 600 at para.45.

261. This point is acknowledged in the White Paper at Chap. X, para.6.

262. Section 179 Trade Union and Labour Relations (Consolidation) Act, 1992.

cluding 26 million workers resident in the UK, many of whom are not UK nationals.[263] The alternative will be to deny those Union citizens their full rights under the Treaty and, by excluding the UK, to produce legislation which is not only inconsistent but would also cut across the Community principles of non-discrimination and undistorted competition.[264]

This dilemma may well face the Commission when deciding how to proceed with the proposed amendments to the Acquired Rights Directive should the UK decline to support the changes.[265] There is the prospect of the original version of the Directive continuing to apply in the UK whilst an amended variety operates in the territory of the other 14 Member States. Such differential treatment should be avoided and, were the Community to decide to proceed along these lines, an Article 177 reference on the compatibility of national provisions with Community law on this point would present the Court with a difficult choice. The Court would be most reluctant to go against a political agreement so painfully cobbled together and therefore may have to resort to another avenue to provide a remedy for the individual. Union citizenship, as a dynamic concept, may offer the Court an integrationist solution in such circumstances.

(c)   Article 6 — An Exercise in Futility?

Perhaps the most incongruous provisions in the SPA are those found in Article 6. The first two sections repeat in essence the wording of Article 119 EC on the principle of equal pay. While this may have been intended as a statement of policy continuity in this area it may equally be interpreted as a demonstrable example of the poor drafting which pervades the SPA and its practical effect is nugatory.

Article 6(3) complicates matters further by allowing Member States to maintain or adopt "measures providing for specific advantages in order to make it easier for women to pursue a vocational activity or prevent or compensate for disadvantages in their professional careers". Whilst

---

263. For full statistics on employment levels in each Member State see the Commission's 1994 Report on Employment in Europe, COM(94) 381 final of 14 September 1994 at p.184.

264. For a further discussion on this point see Barnard, *op.cit.* n.241, at pp.21-22, and Fitzpatrick, *op.cit.* n.247, at p.203.

265. Somewhat ironically, the UK is broadly in favour of the revision, a prospect which may lead the other Member States to reconsider their support: See *Employment Department Consultation Document* on the proposal to revise the Acquired Rights Directive, 1994, at paras.22-27.

Article 6(3) does not allow for Community legislation to positively discriminate in favour of women, it may be interpreted as being inconsistent with the Equal Treatment Directive even though it is undoubtedly intended as an encouragement to Member States to improve the rights of women by enhancing educational grants, making more places available on vocational training and retraining courses, and meeting child care costs without any threat of a Community sanction.

Article 6(3) appears to expand Article 2(4) of the Equal Treatment Directive which permits Member States to take measures to remove "existing inequalities which affect women's opportunities...". This could easily be taken out of context because there is no reference to other parts of the Directive which contextualise such measures within the general principle of non discrimination on the grounds of sex and instead Article 6(3) links this provision to equal pay rather than equal treatment. Article 6(3) is a recipe for confusion leading Curtin to suggest that the Court of Justice should interpret it according to the Community norm and should not allow such a liberal interpretation of positive discrimination.[266] The case law of the Court on equal treatment suggests that Member States will move cautiously and will only take positive action of a specific rather than general nature in areas where inequalities can actually be shown to exist.[267] Therefore Article 6 as a whole adds up to little more than a rather misleading restatement of core aspects of Community equalities law.

(d) Articles 3 and 4 — Collective Bargaining or Shadow Boxing?

The most innovative aspect of the SPA is the introduction of procedural mechanisms which may be capable of converting social dialogue into binding Community laws. Article 3 provides for what amounts to a right of pre-emption for "management and labour" covering all Commission proposals, while, under Article 4, the social partners have power to conclude agreements which are, of their own volition, to be implemented through national procedures or, where the substance relates to the areas in Article 2, to be adopted as Council "decisions" on a proposal from the Commission. However there is a qualification in a separate Declaration attached to the SPA which provides that there is no implied obligation on Member States to "apply the agreements directly or to work out rules for their transposition, nor...to amend legislation in force to

---

266. Curtin, *op.cit.* n.240, p.61.

267. Case 312/86, *Commission v France* [1988] ECR 6315. See also Council Recommendation 84/635/EEC of 13 December 1984 on the promotion of positive action for women, OJ L 331, 19.12.84. For comment see Whiteford, *op.cit.* n.241, at pp.206-7.

facilitate their implementation".

Unquestionably these provisions are a significant advance on the nascent process arising from Article 118b. However questions remain as to either whether they are capable, as Bercusson has suggested, of generating a form of Community-level collective bargaining as a primary instrument for extending and implementing fundamental social and economic rights in the Community?[268] or does such a notion amount to, as Fitzpatrick concludes, "an idea before its time" by giving powers to organisations with neither bargaining experience nor political and industrial legitimacy, which it would have been better to leave to develop naturally, without a legislative capacity, until the practice has firmly taken root?[269]

Article 3(1) places an obligation on the Commission to promote social dialogue and to provide balanced support for the parties. Further, under Articles 3(2) and 3(3), the Commission shall consult the social partners both before submitting proposals on the future direction of Community action, and on the content of any subsequent draft legislation. The parties will then have nine months, or longer by joint agreement of the social partners and the Commission, to reach contractual relations or agreements which are capable, under Article 4(2), of being implemented as Council decisions.

For the purposes of this discussion the importance of the process lies with the facilitative role of the Commission and the attitude of the social partners themselves to create a climate whereby agreements can be reached which are capable of strengthening the rights of employees under Community law.

Bercusson has put the case for a special Community body to provide facilities at Member State level for mediation, conciliation and arbitration, with a Community Tribunal operating to enforce guaranteed minimum standards.[270] The Declaration attached to the SPA would appear to prevent this option and the Commission has come up with a much more limited proposal for a European training centre for industrial relations and other measures to raise awareness about European level social dialogue with a view to extending it to national level. Furthermore there is a proposal to institutionalise social dialogue by re-examining the mandate and composition of the Standing Employment Committee.[271]

Additional Community initiatives are necessary if social dialogue is to develop into a form of collective bargaining, as an alternative to regu-

---

268. B. Bercusson, *Fundamental Social and Economic Rights,* in the EUI Report on Human Rights in the European Community, EUI Florence, 1989.

269. Fitzpatrick, *op.cit.* n.247, at p.212.

270. Bercusson, *op.cit.* n.134, at pp.18-19, 37-39, 40-43.

271. SPWP, Chap.8, paras.7-10.

lation, operating as a more flexible instrument capable of creating consensus.[272] However early evidence suggests that, as far as the outcome of social dialogue is concerned, management and labour are not on the same wavelength. Whereas the ETUC seek a wide range of legislation to ensure an upward convergence of social standards, UNICE, while not excluding further legislation, seek specifically to exclude directives on the protection of workers which would "prohibit flexibility" and prefer to evaluate existing legislation before any extension or revision. The Commission admits that there is dissent over the level of minimum standards to be set, the range of issues to be covered, and the pace of legislation.[273] While there may be an element of posturing from either side, the difference in perception remains so large that the prospects for binding agreements to emerge from this process would appear to be very slim.

This difference of approach was exemplified by the first real test of the new procedures when the social partners failed to agree on a non-binding provision for the establishment of trans-national works councils. While the unions were not prepared to settle for anything short of binding legislation, the employers organisations were anticipating that the proposal would not achieve the required level of support even with QMV under Article 2(2). In the event the Commission pressed ahead with the proposal and a Council Directive was subsequently adopted.[274]

This experience offers a salutary lesson for all of the players in the process of social dialogue. From the Commission's perspective this was a proposal which appeared to be perfectly designed for a Community-level agreement. The establishment of works councils is intended to be entirely consensual with maximum flexibility and the resulting "rights" are procedural and trans-national in character. Therefore there is no element of harmonisation involved although pressure is exerted through the existence of a technical annex providing for subsidiary requirements, in the absence of voluntary agreement, governing rules for the establishment, composition and competence of the works council.

The unions will have observed that they have achieved more by waiting for the Commission to act and this will reinforce their preference for binding legislation particularly in areas of substantive employment protection where there is no indication of any rapport with the employers. However it would be incorrect to describe this as a "collective bargaining" triumph for the unions because, unlike under national or sectoral

272. *ibid.*, Chap.8, para.2. Bercusson (1990) *op.cit.* n.207, at p.634., argues that social dialogue "stipulates a relationship between collective bargaining and law which assumes a multiplicity of forms within the Member States and is extremely flexible in its application".

273. Technical Annex to the SPWP, Introduction, paras.18-23. and 78-85.

274. Directive 94/45/EC. See further Chap.3 by Philip Jones.

bargaining, the ETUC has no direct means to coerce concessions out of employers at Community level, and they are therefore reliant on the stance taken by the Commission.[275]

From the employer's perspective the Commission's attitude suggests that, while they may have to compromise more in future, there will be little point in conceding too much ground when lobbying at Member State level may be more effective.[276] Further, any concessions by the employers will be regarded by the unions as an indication that more can be achieved through the traditional legislative route.

An indication of the future direction of social dialogue can be found in the Commission's Communication on the application of the SPA. The attitude of the social partners to legislation will be one of the Commission's considerations when deciding whether to follow the main EC Treaty route or to use the SPA.[277] Where the social partners fail to conclude an agreement the Commission will examine whether legislation will be appropriate on a case by case basis.[278] The extent to which agreement is likely depends on the existence of consensus between the parties and this will, in turn, be influenced by the composition of "management and labour" for the purposes of consultation and dialogue.

The Commission have sought to address the issue of representativeness of the parties by extending the number of organisations involved beyond the "big three" (ETUC, UNICE and CEEP[279]) and including a number of cross-border and sectoral bodies. Moreover, although the Commission is conscious of the practical problems arising from having a "multiplicity of actors" they have rejected the idea of an umbrella liaison committee.[280] Out of 29 listed groups meeting the Commission's criteria,[281] amongst the most controversial is the European Association of Craft, Small and Medium-Sized Enterprises (UEAPME), an organisation which

275. See A. Jacobs, "Social Europe in Delay", (1990) 6 Int.J.Comp.L.L.I.R. 26.

276. For example, UNICE will have looked to the submissions from the Netherlands in response to the Green Paper in the technical Annex to the SPWP. Introduction, para. 18.

277. COM (93) 600 at para.8.

278. *ibid.*, at para.34.

279. European Trades Union Confederation (ETUC); Union of Industrial and Employers' Confederations of Europe (UNICE); and the European Centre of Enterprises and Public participation (CEEP).

280. COM(93) 600 at para.26.

281. *ibid.*, at para.24. The criteria are that the organisations should be cross industry or relate to specific sectors and be organised at European level; be an integral part of the Member States' social partner structures with the capacity to negotiate agreements; and which are representative of all Member States as far as is possible; and have adequate structures to ensure effective participation in the consultative process.

according to Rhodes is "even less sympathetic" to the social dialogue than UNICE leading to a "high risk of paralysis".[282] UEAPME will seek to emphasise Article 2(2) whereby all directives "shall avoid imposing administrative, financial and legal constraints in a way which would hold back the creation of small and medium-sized enterprises". A strict application of this provision would lead to heavily diluted legislation, more soft law, and widespread derogations.

The practicalities are daunting. The Commission notes that the social partners concerned will be those who agree to negotiate with one another and the form of agreement is entirely in the hands of the respective organisations.[283] However the European confederations of management and labour are not necessarily best suited to reach such agreements not least because of the disparities between national bargaining structures and extension procedures.[284] There is no explanation as to how the parties will bargain and by what voting method they will reach an agreement. There is no structure for balancing the parties or allowing for majority voting. The whole process is dependant on an assumption of consensus. The limited proposals on social dialogue from the Commission in the SPWP suggest that there is little prospect of agreement within nine months from such a diverse group of actors in the absence of adequate but streamlined collective bargaining structures. Even where an agreement is reached the Commission appears suspicious of the representative status of the parties and this may be a factor in determining the legality of any agreement.[285]

Another question addressed in the Communication is the content of any agreement. Although the SPA is silent on the point, the Commission maintain that Community action cannot go beyond the areas covered in the Commission's proposal. Further the Commission emphasises its duty as the guardian of the Treaties and will evaluate any agreement to ensure that each clause is consistent with Community law.[286]

The Commission's approach reflects a desire not to relinquish its sole right of initiation under the EC Treaty and to redress the apparent shift in power away from the Commission and Parliament to the social

---

282. M. Rhodes, "The Social Dimension After Maastricht: Setting a New Agenda for the Labour Market", (1993) 9 Int.J.Comp.L.L.I.R. 297.

283. COM (93) 600 at para.31.

284. See B.A. Hepple, *European Social Dialogue — Alibi or Opportunity?*, Institute of Employment Rights, 1993, pp.28-30.

285. COM(93) 600 at para.39.

286. *ibid.*, at para.39. This approach is backed up by case law. See Case C-184/89, *Nimz v Freie und Hansestadt Hamburg* [1991] ECR I-297, discussed by Szyszczak in Chap. 20 of *Legal Issues of the Maastricht Treaty*, (1994) *op.cit.* n.62, at pp.319-20.

partners and the Council.[287] However the approach adopted might circumvent the parties room for manoeuvre even when adequate bargaining structures eventually emerge. Are the parties limited to areas covered by the SPA or can they rely on general Treaty objectives which are wider in scope and might allow for an agreement on a minimum wage, with regional differentiation, which could be regarded as essential to achieve the goal of economic and social cohesion but would be outlawed by a strict interpretation of Article 2(6) of the SPA? Surely pay is an area which is expressly suitable for collective bargaining, and yet is apparently excluded, while other areas of social policy, notably equalities and non-standard workers, are included even though it can be argued that these are subjects where the social partners are least representative.

There is also concern about the need for the process to be democratic and to continue to involve the Parliament and the Economic and Social Committee.

Otherwise the social dialogue route would become an avenue for the Council to adopt "decisions" whilst by-passing the normal institutional consultation.[288]

Even if all of these hurdles are crossed there must be doubt about the status of any "decisions" reached by the Council on the basis of agreements between management and labour. Article 4(2) provides that the social partners' agreements *"shall be implemented...by a Council decision on a proposal from the Commission"*.[289] This suggests that there is little, if any, discretion, but the Commission Communication states that the text of the agreement, while it forms the basis of any binding provisions, will only be annexed to the decision and, where the Council decides not to implement the agreement, the Commission will have to consider whether a "legislative instrument" in the area would be appropriate.[290] This would appear to provide an opportunity to block or delay progress in certain areas for subsidiarity reasons or by a restrictive interpretation of the scope of Articles 2(2) and 2(3).

An alternative option would be for the Council to adopt soft law as Article 4(2) can be interpreted as meaning decisions in the form of any recognised instrument rather than binding "decisions" for the purposes of Article 189 EC. Once again this would appear to be poor drafting because directives are the chosen tool of the Member States for the purposes of implementing legislation arising from the SPA and the use of "decision" in this context simply reflects the desire to have a choice of

---

287. See Weiss, *op.cit*. n.237, at pp.11-12.

288. See Fitzpatrick, *op.cit*. n.247, at p.208.

289. *Author's emphasis*.

290. COM(93) 600 at paras.41-2.

instruments *for* decision.[291] Therefore there is every likelihood of agreements of the social partners being adopted only as codes of conduct within the scope of binding Framework Directives introduced through mainstream legislative means.

The application of Articles 3 and 4 of the SPA is subject to too many uncertain factors to determine their scope at this stage. A great deal will depend on the strategy of the Commission. Bercusson argues that if the Commission adopts a positive approach to set a higher social policy standard there will be additional motivation on the social partners to "bargain in the shadow of the law".[292] The timing of proposals will be crucial because there may be a prospect of three procedures all operating in tandem: legislative proposals under the EC Treaty; social dialogue consistent with Article 118b; and simultaneous proposals using the Agreement. Until such time as the structures for representative social consultations are fully operational, and in the absence of the "new dynamic" which Bercusson seeks, there is every possibility that social dialogue will amount to no more than "shadow boxing" between the parties which will only serve to obfuscate the direction of Community social policy whilst diminishing the content and slowing the frequency of Community legislation.

4.   CONCLUSION — A WAY FORWARD FOR THE UNION?

(i)   *The Social Policy White Paper*

With the adoption of the Maastricht SPA, despite all of its complexity, there is capacity for substantive progress in the field of Community social policy and labour law. However, the widening of legislative competence does not, in itself, amount to a fresh legislative programme. Nevertheless, the Social Policy Green Paper gave a firm indication that the objectives of the "Social Charter" would be pursued "...by exploiting to the full the possibilities offered by the Social Agreement of the Maastricht Treaty".[293]

Despite this clear statement of intent the Green Paper is, in essence, a defensive document published in the face of economic adversity. The Commission's starting point is to assert that the next stage of social policy "cannot be based on the idea that social progress must go into retreat in

---

291. Bercusson, *op.cit.* n.235, at p.28, suggests that one indication is the Danish version which is *ved en afgorelse*, literally "arriving at a decision".

292. *ibid.*, at pp.21-22.

293. Green Paper, p.60.

order for economic competitiveness to recover".[294] The Social Policy White Paper (SPWP), while it follows the basic premise of the Green Paper, regarding legislation as only one of a range of social instruments at the disposal of the Community,[295] is even more cautious, relying instead on the "solid base" of the Community's existing achievements and the need for a more effective application of Community law through proper implementation of directives and enforcement of Community obligations.[296] As far as legislative action is concerned, this will be limited, where it passes the subsidiarity test, to the completion of the Action Programme, a consolidation of labour standards, and the promotion of health and safety.[297]

(a) The Growth White Paper and "Labour Market Flexibility"

Those seeking an explanation for the Commission's paucity of ambition in the SPWP need look no further than its counterpart, the Growth White Paper (GWP). As the Community seeks to find a solution to endemic unemployment, both structural and cyclical, with over 18 million unemployed,[298] there is an increasing emphasis on the dichotomy between the relatively high living standards of those in full-time standard employment and the ever worsening position of the "socially excluded" afflicted by, *inter alia*, long-term unemployment, the impact of industrial change, and the breakdown of family structures.[299] The result has been a shift in the equilibrium of Community social policy away from traditional employment protection measures and in favour of policies designed to create employment, specifically temporary and part-time jobs, intended, at least in part, to increase the participation of women in the labour force and to provide new opportunities for young people. The Commission admits that there is "no miracle cure",[300] despite the plethora of economic theories which abound, and there is a real danger that the underlying tension between the need to create more jobs and protect

---

294. *ibid.*, p.7. For a discussion see J. Kenner, "European Social Policy — New Directions", (1994) 10 Int.J.Comp.L.L.I.R. 56.

295. *ibid.*, p.50.

296. SPWP, Chap.10.

297. SPWP, Chap.3.

298. Source: COM (94) 381 final issued on 14.9.94. "Employment in Europe 1994" at p.9.

299. See the Council Resolution on social exclusion, OJ C 277, 31.10.89., the Commission Communication, COM (92) 542 final of 23.12.92: "Towards a Europe of Solidarity: Intensifying the fight against social exclusion, fostering integration", and the Economic and Social Committee's Opinion, OJ C352, 30.12.93.

300. Growth White Paper, *op.cit.* n.8, p.9.

existing labour standards will be resolved in favour of the former even if these jobs are low-skilled and poorly paid.

Whilst unemployment was cited as the "one and only reason" for the GWP,[301] there is an underlying assumption that relatively high European social standards have damaged competitiveness and thereby contributed towards unemployment. The Commission point to a shrinking economy, with growth down from around 4% to 2.5% a year, falling investment, and a decline in competitiveness in relation to the USA and Japan over twenty years.[302] In turn, increases in unemployment have led to spiralling public debt threatening the austere convergence criteria which are essential for stage 3 of Economic and Monetary Union (EMU) by 1997 or 1999, as required by Articles 102-109 EC.[303] The Commission's Annual Economic Report for 1995 indicates that average growth rates of 3%-3.5% would still leave 7% of the work force, 11 million people, without jobs by 2000 without further remedial action being taken.[304]

Thus while the Commission do not call directly for a dilution of social standards there is a degree of "doublespeak" because improved flexibility connotes the removal of "excessive rigidities resulting from regulation". The Commission cites deregulation in the UK and the Netherlands, as well as Spanish labour market reforms restricting rights on redundancy protection and dismissals, all with a brush of approval.[305] The dangers of this approach have been recognised by Parliament which has warned that "seeking to imitate the sweatshop economies of some newly industrialising nations...[does not provide]...a basis for growth or competitiveness in Europe".[306]

The agenda of deregulation is subsuming Community social policy. Despite the adoption of the SPA there is no independent case put forward in the SPWP for labour standards as a separate arm of a dynamic Community policy which provides an input into European competitiveness. Viewed from this perspective raising labour standards can, as Deakin and Wilkinson argue, interact with economic integration "to produce a continuous upward movement in social and economic outcomes".[307] Oth-

---

301. *ibid.*

302. *ibid.*

303. By 1993 the average public debt for the EC as a whole was 5.7% compared to the 3% required for EMU convergence, *EC Annual Economic Report* (1993).

304. Source: Income Data Services (IDS), Bulletin No. 397, January 1995, at p.3.

305. Bull. of the EU. Supp. 2/94 at p.117.

306. European Parliament Resolution on the broad guidelines of the economic policies of the Member States and of the Community, [Document A3-0384/93] at para.15.

30 . See S. Deakin & F. Wilkinson, "Rights vs Efficiency? The Economic Case for Transnational Labour Standards", (1994) 23 I.L.J. 289 at p.308.

erwise "subservience to the process of market integration fatally hinders the development of a rationale for Community action in the social policy field".[308]

In the absence of either an adjustment to the EMU criteria, or of further increases in the Community's social funds to boost cohesion, the minimalist approach to the "social dimension" in the SPWP is unremarkable. By seeking to "reconcile" high social standards with the overriding objectives in the GWP, as underpinned by the macroeconomic guidelines, the SPWP treads a careful path by promoting a series of relatively uncontentious measures which have even gained some support from the UK Government.[309]

(b) Legislative Proposals under Consideration

In addition to the Works Councils Directive, the SPWP lists four outstanding health and safety proposals,[310] and other draft measures concerning:[311] posting of workers; non-standard employment — working conditions; and distortions of competition.

Although the Commission gave the "highest possible priority"[312] to bringing these proposals to a successful conclusion there has followed the familiar process of gradually watered down measures being presented before the Council designed to secure the support of the UK. By December 1994 the Commission, frustrated by UK opposition, decided to utilise the SPA by determining to publish fresh proposals and consulting the social partners. The Social Affairs Commissioner, Padraig Flynn, has promised that the new proposal on part-time workers will be based on part-time workers being granted exactly the same rights as full-time workers.[313] However, it is highly unlikely that the proposal will be "inderogable" given the prevailing emphasis on "labour market flexibility", the limita-

---

308. P.L. Davies, "The emergence of European labour law", in W.E.J. McCarthy (ed.) *Legal Intervention in Industrial Relations: Gains and Losses* (Blackwell, 1992) at p.346. Cited by Deakin & Wilkinson, *ibid.*, at p.289.

309. See the UK *Employment Department* consultation document on the proposed amendments to the Acquired Rights Directive.

310. SPWP, Chap.3, para.18.

311. *ibid.*, Chap.3, para.3.

312. *ibid.*

313. Europe Information Service (EIS), Bulletin on European Social Policy No. 47, December 1994, at pp.12-13. The SPWP describes the rights of part-time workers as "broadly-equivalent" under the original draft (SPWP, Chap.3, para.8). The revised proposal will be restricted to part-time work, as a first step, and will also take account of the ILO Convention on part-time work of June 1994. For further discussion on non-standard or "atypical" employment see Chapter 6 by Nick Rahtz.

tions concerning small and medium-sized enterprises, and the incremental provisions in Article 2(2) of the SPA, when compared with the unfettered nature of Article 100 EC.[314]

The draft directive on posted workers is a labour market equalisation measure under Article 100a dealing with a loophole in the existing free movement provisions.[315] Concern has increased since the Court's judgment in *Rush Portuguesa* where a company was allowed to use its own Portuguese workers, exempted at the time from Article 48 under the transitional provisions in the Accession Agreement, to carry out temporary sub-contracted work in France on the grounds that this approach was consistent with Article 59 on the free movement of services.[316] This raises the spectre of companies deliberately setting up subsidiaries in central and eastern Europe to bring in low cost labour substantially undercutting the cost of hiring workers locally.

The draft directive seeks to establish a core of minimum standards to protect workers temporarily based in another Member State. However, rights to minimum paid holidays and minimum rates of pay will not apply to contracts of less than one month.[317] Several Member States have expressed reservations, notably Portugal, the UK and Greece, but the proposal may yet succeed because of the strong support of the new Member States who wish to protect their wage and social protection structures. This could weigh the Council in favour under the revised QMV formula.[318] In the meantime France has pressed ahead with its own legislation which is almost identical to the provisions of the draft directive.[319] It remains to be seen whether pre-emptive implementation will become a habit as the relatively poorer southern Member States struggle to match their social ambitions with the economic demands required for convergence. As the SPWP notes any Community measures should not "over stretch" the economically weaker states and not prevent the stronger states from implementing higher standards.[320] The outcome may be a further bifurcation of social policy which will undermine cohesion.

A number of other possible measures to arise from the SPWP will be in the form of "framework" directives. These will allow for maximum

314. Inderogable rights have been defined as labour standards where contracting out is legally ineffective. See Lord Wedderburn, "Inderogability, collective agreements, and Community Law", (1992) 21 I.L.J. 245.

315. COM(93) 225 final of 16.6.93.

316. Case C-113/89, *Rush Portuguesa v ONI* [1990] ECR I-1417.

317. Originally three months: COM(91) 230 of 17.6.91.

318. See EIS Bulletin No. 48, January 1995, at pp.3-4. Council Decision 95/C1/01 amends the QMV votes required to block a proposal. OJ C1 of 1.1.95.

319. IDS Bulletin, January 1995, at pp.18-19.

320. SPWP, Introduction, para.17.

flexibility of implementation, with encouragement given to the social partners to develop them further at national and Community level. Compared with the detailed legislation of the past, laws will be lighter and adaptable to suit the diversity of different Member States.[321]

Thus the Commission proposes to withdraw the draft directive on parental leave, rather than further modify the proposal to meet UK objections, and reformulate the notion within a framework directive to aid the reconciliation of professional and family life, including career breaks such as parental leave, in order to gradually encourage the development of new societal models which facilitate the full integration of women in the labour market. The framework will be designed to "encourage competitive solutions in a changing world".[322] Therefore a draft directive originally designed to provide employment protection during parental leave has been subtly converted into a labour market proposal consistent with the flexibility agenda. While this may still lead to parental leave rights these will be within a framework which will allow for further deregulation.

An additional aspect of the SPWP is the Commission's attempts to meet at least some of the demands of Parliament. In a Resolution of March 1994 Parliament has deplored the weakness of its role in the legislative process of the whole social sphere and expressed regret over the limited impact of social policy even under the SPA.[323] Parliament complains of "...unacceptable derogations, a lack of coherence and too low a level of social protection".[324] Parliament calls for substantial strengthening of the powers of the Community in the social area and demands to be increasingly involved in the legislative process after the 1996 intergovernmental conference.

Parliament has been particularly critical of the Working Time Directive and in response the Commission has given a commitment to make proposals to extend the Directive to cover all employees. However this will start with consultation with the social partners covering a limited number of the excluded sectors only resulting in a Directive under Article 118a if no agreement is reached during 1995. By using Article 118a there is a danger of relatively limited progress as the price to be paid for maintaining the measure within mainstream EC Treaty social policy. A stronger measure under the SPA to cover all workers with a higher minimum standard might be preferable on the basis that the UK could ad-

---

321. Green Paper, p.50.

322. SPWP, Chap.3, para.8.

323. European Parliament Resolution on the new social dimension of the Treaty on European Union, A3-0091/94, OJ C77/30 of 14.3.94.

324. *ibid.*, para.6.

here later as the UK will, in any event, be able to defer its responsibilities under the existing Directive.

Other proposals put forward as part of the consultation exercise and listed in the SPWP include, *inter alia*: [325]

- protection against individual dismissal;

- protection of the privacy of workers in particular with regard to the processing, collection and disclosure of workers' data;

- prohibiting discrimination against workers who uphold their rights or who refuse to perform unlawful tasks;

- rights to payment of wages on public holidays and during illness;

- prohibiting discrimination on the grounds of race, religion, age or disability;

- a measure to take steps to combat the "informal economy".

From this list the Commission propose to address illegal work by linking the issue to illegal immigration. In the areas of individual dismissal and privacy there will be detailed studies with results to be published during 1995. Any further legislation will be considered after a joint hearing with Parliament. The Commission will concentrate instead on the adaptation of existing labour law and ensuring that directives are correctly transposed.

Undoubtedly the need to secure the transposition of directives is important, with five Member States at an implementation level of 70% or less,[326] but the Commission provide no good reason why new legislation cannot be introduced at the same time, nor is there an explanation for such caution when each of these suggestions is consistent with the aspirations of the Social Charter.

For example, instead of putting forward a proposal on equal treatment to combat discrimination on the grounds of race, religion, age, and disability, the Commission merely propose an amendment of the Treaties "at the next opportunity".[327] The original Equal Treatment Di-

---

325. SPWP, Chap.3, paras.13-16.

326. Netherlands, Greece, Spain, Italy, Luxembourg. The UK and Portugal have the best record with a 92% transposition rate. See SPWP, Chap.10, Table 1.

327. SPWP, Chap.6, para.27.

rective, to outlaw gender discrimination, was introduced under Article 235 EC in 1976. Such action might be permissible again because Article 235 remains as a legislative base but its use will be extremely rare because it may be seen as being incompatible with the principle of subsidiarity. Such an approach is counter to an "effects" argument for active subsidiarity which would empower the Commission to act to secure an overriding Community objective.[328] On this basis the Commission have missed an opportunity to act for an indefinite period in an area which should be central to any strategy to combat social exclusion and promote economic and social cohesion and solidarity consistent with the Community's designated tasks and activities in Articles 2 and 3 EC.

Elsewhere the SPWP relies on soft law to supplement existing instruments. For example a "code of good practice to encourage model employers" is proposed in the fields of disability and racial discrimination,[329] while a code of practice on equal pay for work of equal value is to be introduced as a follow up to the recent Memorandum.[330] Other suggestions, including positive action for women, and addressing the conditions of employment of third-country nationals, are to be left to the social partners in the first instance to stimulate their involvement.[331]

The SPWP is a disappointing document by comparison with the Green Paper, which raised fundamental issues about full employment, the welfare state and social justice. Social policy will be allowed to drift at a time when workers need greater employment protection against the heightened threat of unfair dismissal, reductions in pay and working conditions, and the casualisation of the labour market. There is little evidence that these challenges to the "European social model" can be adequately met by the limited measures on offer in the SPWP. There has been a lost opportunity to fully test the scope of the SPA, including, for example, bringing proposals under Article 2(3) to provide full free movement rights to third-country nationals legally resident in the Member States.

In the absence of a renewed legislative action programme to strengthen existing legislation and convert soft law into binding instruments, there is an increasing need for a new approach concentrating on

---

328. A group of experts from several Member States have published a draft directive entitled "the starting line" modelled on Directive 76/207. Bindman has noted that the Commission believe that such a directive could be challenged before the Court on the grounds of lack of competence. The draft has been endorsed by Parliament and has also been promoted as a Treaty Amendment for 1996 by the same group. G. Bindman, "The Starting Point", (1995) 145 N.L.J. 62.

329. *ibid.*, Chap.6, para.23. & Chap.4, para.24.

330. *ibid.*, Chap.5, para.9.

331. *ibid.*, Chap.8, para.11.

achieving normative rights for Community workers through the dynamic concept of Union citizenship buttressed by fundamental rights derived from international labour standards. These areas will now be addressed.

(ii) Citizenship and Fundamental Rights — An Alternative Model

The European Parliament and the Economic and Social Committee, along with the ETUC, have called, in their responses to the Green Paper, for the establishment of fundamental social rights for citizens as a constitutional element of the European Union. The SPWP rather airily suggests that: "Doubtless this vital issue will be considered in the context of future revisions of the Treaties".[332] This is a rather pious aspiration given the current impasse on social policy in the Council, and, although the eleven have adopted a Resolution under the SPA to press ahead with legislation to establish minimum social standards,[333] there is little immediate prospect for progress either through the traditional legislative route, or by utilising the SPA provisions and involving the social partners.

An alternative approach would be for the Court of Justice through its jurisprudence to constitutionalise the fundamental social rights of Union citizens through an extension of the existing *acquis* on the basis of a dynamic Community concept of citizenship forming a central part of a common code of fundamental values, to be drawn from international Treaties and the constitutions of the Member States, and to be uniformly applied for the benefit of all Union citizens.

Although the Treaty of Rome was not designed as a formal constitution it has been constitutionalised by the Court in order to make Community law more effective, to impose safeguards on the exercise of the Community's powers, and to protect individual rights. These constitutional law principles are mostly found in the judgments of the Court rather than in the Treaty itself.[334] As the Court declared in *Les Verts*[335] the Community:

> ...is based on the rule of law...neither its Member States nor its institutions can avoid a review of the question whether measures adopted by them are in conformity with the basic constitutional charter, the Treaty.

---

332. SPWP. "The Next Steps", para.2.

333. EIS Bulletin, December 1994, pp.14-15.

334. See J. Temple Lang, "The development of European Community constitutional law", (1991) 25 *International Lawyer* 455 at p.457. See also Mancini *op.cit.* n.216.

335. Case 294/83, *Les Verts v Parliament* [1986] ECR 1339 at 1365.

Therefore the ability of the Court to develop the Community's constitution dynamically will be driven by the scope of the Community's powers under the Treaty. This can be illustrated by considering the Court's application of a conception of fundamental rights as a general principle of law.

Ever since *Defrenne* Community social policy has been inculcated with notions of fundamental human rights.[336] Thus where there is a direct Treaty principle, as in the case of equal pay under Article 119, the Court has been able to apply fundamental rights directly to give full effect to the rights of the individual as an integral part of Community law.

However, even with the adoption of the Social Charter based largely on ILO Conventions and the ESC of the Council of Europe, the Court has been hesitant about extending international Treaty obligations and directly incorporating them into Community law. The lack of a clear legal base for social policy and employment rights, except under the provisions of the SPA, has perpetuated this problem. Where the Court has applied fundamental rights the rationale has been expediency rather than any moral imperative.[337] The Court has used fundamental rights as a means of interpreting the Community's objectives and not *vice versa*. As Mancini has explained:

> The Court does not have to go looking for maximum, minimum or average standards. The yardstick by which it measures the approaches adopted by the various legal systems derives from the spirit of the Treaty and from the requirements of a Community which is in the process of being built up.[338]

The most explicit statement of the Court's approach can be found in *ERT*[339] which concerned Article 10 of the ECHR which provides for the right of freedom of expression. The Court observed that:

> fundamental rights form an integral part of the general principles of law observance of which is ensured by the Court. For this purpose the Court proceeds from the constitutional principles common to the member states and from pointers in interna-

---

336. *Defrenne v Sabena (no.3), op.cit.* n.41.

337. Hartley *op.cit.* n.215, at p.163.

338. F. Mancini, "Safeguarding Human Rights: The Role of the Court of Justice of the European Communities", John Hopkins University, Bologna, Occasional Paper 62, March 1990. Cited by Hartley *ibid.*

339. Case C-260/89, *ERT* [1991] ECR I-2925 at paras.41-2 of the judgment.

tional instruments concerning the protection of human rights in which the member states have co-operated or to which they have adhered...Measures incompatible with the protection of fundamental rights thus recognised and safeguarded cannot be accepted in the Community.

Thus the ECHR in particular will guide the Court in determining the scope of Community law, but the Court in *ERT* added that where national law violates international Treaties the Court will only have jurisdiction where such national legislation is within the ambit of the EC Treaty.

Many of the fundamental rights in the ESC, which are of an economic and social character, are in areas where the Community has left the development of policy to the Member States and, even though there is an overlap with the aspirations of the Community Social Charter, the ESC is far wider and more detailed in content.[340] These include the right to just conditions of work; the right to fair remuneration; the right to organise; and the right to bargain collectively.[341] Where the Court has cited the ESC, as in *Blaziot v Belgium*,[342] it has been dealing with areas already governed by the Treaty.

Although the preamble to the SEA referred to both the ESC and the ECHR and recognised "freedom, equality and social justice", the TEU, whilst stating that the Union "shall respect fundamental rights" only refers to the ECHR in Article F.2. The Member States declined to take the opportunity to incorporate fundamental rights into the EC Treaty because of the fear of a "Bill of Rights by the backdoor"[343] and Article F.2 is specifically excluded from the areas which are justiciable by the Court.[344] In some respects this is not an undesirable outcome because the ECHR has been a mixed blessing for workers seeking to assert their employment rights.[345]

Those seeking an amendment to the Treaty to directly incorporate the ESC and the ECHR, and thereby indirectly give a supranational effect to the ILO Conventions on which the employment rights are largely

340. See Memorandum by Prof. B.A. Hepple to the House of Lords Select Committee on the European Communities, Session 1992-93, 3rd Report: *Human rights re-examined.*

341. Articles 2,4,5 & 6 respectively.

342. Case 24/86 [1988] ECR 379. The Court referred to Article 10 of the ESC concerning the right to vocational training.

343. See P.M. Twomey, Chap.8, *Legal Issues of the Maastricht Treaty*, *op.cit.* n.62, at p.123.

344. Article L of the Final Provisions, Title VII of the TEU.

345. For a critique see: K. Ewing, *A Bill of Rights for Britain?*, (1991) Institute of Employment Rights.

based, are unlikely to succeed in the present political climate. Such a proposal would be anathema not only to opponents of an integrationist social policy in the UK but also to Member States with a dualist tradition. Further, while the Court of Justice is still by nature the most integrationist of the Community institutions it is unlikely to extend its jurisprudence on fundamental rights any further despite the call by Advocate General Jacobs in *Konstantinidis*[346] for a Community worker to be entitled to assume that:

> ...wherever he goes to earn his living in the European Community, he will be treated in accordance with a common code of fundamental values, in particular those laid down in the European Convention on Human Rights. In other words, he is entitled to say '*civis europeus sum*' and to invoke that status in order to oppose any violation of his fundamental rights.

The constitutionalisation of the concept of Union citizenship as a fundamental principle of Community law in Articles 8-8e EC by the TEU, resting alongside the principles of non-discrimination and free movement in the Treaty hierarchy of enshrined values, provides a basis for the Court to develop Advocate General Jacobs' approach without the need to rely on the interpretation of fundamental rights provisions in international Treaties. Rather, citizenship can be used as a means of bringing fundamental rights within the Community's ambit because citizenship is "essentially dynamic in nature"[347] and is therefore capable of being developed by the Court as a constitutional guarantee of social rights for workers as citizens.

Union citizenship is complementary to national citizenship and not independent of it, but the Community meaning of citizenship is capable of developing as a broader concept which extends beyond ties which are commonly associated with the nation-state and cultural bonding. Thus the objective in Article B of the TEU is to "strengthen the protection of rights and interests of the nationals of the Member States through the introduction of a citizenship of the Union". This aim is constitutionalised within the Community legal order by Article 8 EC whereby citizenship is bestowed on every person holding the nationality of a Member State. Article 8(2) provides that citizens of the Union "shall enjoy the rights conferred by this Treaty and shall be subject to the duties imposed thereby".

The specific rights in Article 8a-d are rather limited and include a right of free movement and residence; a right to vote and stand as a

346. Case C-168/91, *Konstantinidis v Altensteig-Standesamt* [1993] 3 CMLR 401 at p.420.

347. COM(93) 702 final of 21.12.93. Commission report on citizenship of the Union, p.2.

candidate in municipal and European elections in the state where the union citizen resides; a right to diplomatic or consular protection in the territory of a third-country; and a right to petition the European Parliament and apply to the Community Ombudsman. The dynamic potential of citizenship can be gleaned from Article 8e which provides for the adoption of measures to "strengthen or add to the rights in this Part, which it shall recommend to the Member States for adoption in accordance with their respective constitutional requirements".

Three immediate points are worthy of note. First, there is no possibility of weakening citizenship. The concept can only be expanded even if the use of "recommend" may suggest a soft law inclination among the Treaty signatories. Second, although citizenship is dependant on nationality, and thereby excludes many legally resident nationals of third-countries, this discrepancy may be narrowed by the adoption of measures to give rights to these groups, including utilising the provisions in Article 2(3) of the SPA, which may eventually lead to the full inclusion of third-country nationals indirectly into Union citizenship in the interests both of furthering the Single Market and achieving social cohesion.[348] The exclusive wording of Article 8 requires a Treaty amendment to achieve such a change by more direct means. Third, although the specific areas do not include social rights, Article 8 is silent on the scope of citizenship giving the Court every reason to perform its well established role of filling the gaps through an integrationist approach which might cover social welfare, housing, and a right of association by drawing upon fundamental rights as a general principle of Community law. There is every prospect of a *sui generis* form of citizenship developing which embraces a multiplicity of rights of a civil, social and political character consistent with the Community's task of building solidarity.[349]

Support for the argument that Community citizenship extends beyond the national sphere can be found in a memorandum submitted by Spain in advance of the Maastricht deliberations.[350] Spain called for a third sphere of rights and duties which is personal and indivisible in nature and extends beyond the national and Community spheres. This form of political citizenship will be exercised and safeguarded specifically within the boundaries of the Union. The memorandum recommended that citizenship rights should include, *inter alia*, full political participation and environmental and social rights. While the Spanish

---

348. There are between 8 and 13 million third-country nationals in the EU according to different estimates. For a discussion see D. O'Keefe, Chap.6 of *Legal Issues of the Maastricht Treaty, op.cit.* n.62, at pp.104-6.

349. See E. Meehan, *Citizenship and the European Community*, Sage, 1993. *cf.* R. Aron, "Is multinational citizenship possible?", (1974) 41 *Social Research* 638.

350. *Towards a European citizenship*. Council Doc. SN 3940/90 of 24.9.90.

approach is far removed from the final Treaty provisions adopted there is the potential for the concept of Union citizenship to grow from its current embryonic form into a fundamental principle of Community law which will be malleable in the hands of the Court.

A number of basic citizenship guarantees could be developed in the field of social policy and employment rights which could be included as part of a package of rights to strengthen the Union model of citizenship and to bring the Union's political ideals closer to the citizen. The Civil Liberties Committee of Parliament has suggested a right to work as an integral part of social citizenship.[351] Other proposals include an industrial citizenship,[352] providing for democracy and a right of representation at the workplace, and specific citizenship rights for women.[353] The concept of citizenship is also capable of being applied to protect workers facing discrimination in their employment on the grounds of race, religion, age, sexuality or disability. A general guarantee of fair treatment for Union citizens in employment would provide a basis for rights concerning equitable pay, redundancy rights and dismissal protection, data privacy, and a prohibition of discrimination against workers who uphold their rights.

For Union citizenship to develop beyond the formatively narrow confines of Article 8 EC requires a quantum leap which will allow for what Twomey has described as a "symmetry between the status of citizenship and the enjoyment of what are framed as citizen's rights".[354] Union citizenship is an essentially integrative concept capable of development by the Community institutions and the Court as a means of protecting and enhancing individual rights in a framework which is consistent with fundamental human rights. Undoubtedly progress will be incremental and the Court will wish to balance any activism with the need to maintain legal certainty.[355] There will also be a need for the Court to carry the support of national courts by defining the principles of Union citizenship in a consensual manner.

European social policy has a history cluttered with unfinished business and unfulfilled ambition. Ever since the Community sought to adopt a "human face" by embarking upon legislative social action programmes progress towards the establishment of a floor of substantive and legally

351. PE Doc. 174.605, 10.1.94.

352. See J. Grahl & P. Teague, "Economic Citizenship in the New Europe", (1994) 65 *Political Quarterly* 379 at pp.379-80, and Lord Wedderburn (ed.), *Labour Law and Industrial Relations*, Clarendon Press, 1983.

353. See U. Vogel, "Is citizenship gender-specific?", in U. Vogel & M. Moran (eds.), *The Frontiers of Citizenship*, Macmillan, 1991.

354. P.M. Twomey, Chap.7 in *European Citizenship*, E.A. Marias (ed.), EIPA, 1994, at p.119.

355. See generally: A. Arnull, "Judging the New Europe", (1994) 19 E.L.Rev. 3.

enforceable rights for workers has been severely hampered by the twin obstacles of vacillating political leadership and the restricted legal basis for legislative action in the Treaties. The result is a mishmash of social measures comprising binding regulations and directives, often circumscribed by important derogations limiting their scope and effectiveness, and "soft laws"; including influential recommendations and indicative codes of practice. Several manifest gaps remain from outstanding business in the action programmes themselves, and in other important areas which are subject to domestic labour law provisions and reflected in international labour standards. Union citizenship provides an opportunity to fill these gaps by developing the social rights of workers as citizens buttressed by the allied principles of non-discrimination and fundamental rights. In this way social citizenship rights may evolve as free-standing rights which are not dependant solely on the goal of economic integration, but instead reflect a direct political link between the citizens of the Member States and the emergent Union. As Robert Schuman once declared:

> Europe will not be made at once according to a single plan. It will be built through concrete achievements which first create a *de facto* solidarity.[356]

---

356. Declaration of Robert Schuman, Documents on International Affairs, 1949-50, pp.315-17. Cited by E.A. Marias, Chap.1 of *European Citizenship*, *op.cit.* n.62, at p.19.

2. Sex Equality in Pension Schemes

Brian Jones

1. INTRODUCTION

This chapter will analyse the concept of equality in pension provisions with particular reference to Article 119 of the Treaty of Rome[1] requiring that Member States "maintain the application of the principle that men and women should receive equal pay for equal work."

It will apply that principle to different types of pension scheme; develop the conflicts between those applications; discuss the ways in which pension schemes reflect differences in life expectancy at different ages; and, highlight the problems arising from sex-related differences in life expectancy. The discussion will draw heavily on American experience, reflecting both the writer's American consulting actuarial practice and his belief that this experience contains many warnings to others. Throughout this paper and in the legislation under discussion, sex-egalitarianism is a given: what that means is the issue.

The paper will focus primarily on funded pensions of the type found in the United Kingdom and in the U.S. and Canada. Nevertheless, much although not all of the discussion will be relevant to other types of pension scheme. It originally reflected the state of the law as of 16 August 1993, in particular, the Advocate General's Opinion in the *Coloroll* case,[2]

---

1. 5 Mar. 1957 Gr. Brit. T.S. No. 1 (Cmd. 5179-II), 298 U.N.T.S. 3 (1958). Unqualified references to the "Treaty" or "Articles" in this paper will refer to this Treaty, as amended by the Single European Act, O.J. 1987 L 169/19, (as opposed to those establishing the Coal and Steel Community and Euratom). Unqualified references to the Community will, similarly, refer to the European Economic Community. The new "Treaty on European Union", (Office of Official Pub'ns of the E.C., Luxembourg, 1990), amending the three original treaties will be referred to simply as Maastricht.

2. *infra*, n.179.

but not the judgment of the European Court of Justice, and has been revised to reflect the judgment in the *Neath*[3] case.

2. PROVIDING FOR RETIREMENT

In simpler times, providing for the relatively small number of people who survived into old age was generally left to the individuals themselves or their (extended) families. Often an employer such as a farmer would maintain a fortunate superannuated employee on some form of reduced or light duty, which might be considered a form of retirement provision.

Sometimes then, and more often now, employers recognise(d) an obligation to provide retirement income for former employees without expecting current services. However, such recognition is of value only if the employee feels reasonably confident that the employer will be there, and will be willing and able to deliver on his commitments at a retirement date which may be far in the future. Even if the employer allocates funds to meet these future obligations, there may be no guarantee that this allocation will be continued nor, if difficulties arise, that creditors of the employer will not be able to reach the funds before they can be applied for retirement purposes. Hence the trend in many countries towards more formal advance funding of retirement obligations.

Perhaps the simplest form of employer-funded retirement arrangement would be one under which each employee received directly from his employer a special supplement to his salary which might take the form of a percentage of salary or a flat periodic payment of a fixed number of currency units independent of salary. The employee might be encouraged to save these supplements for retirement but could hardly, as a practical matter, be required to do so. The most obvious drawback to such a simple, indeed simplistic, arrangement would be that now it would be the employer who would have no assurance that any such special supplements would in fact be saved, invested and eventually applied to retirement needs. There would, as noted above, be no practical way to require such application. Even if the employee did save the funds, his taxable income would be increased by both the amount of the payments and the earnings on the funds as they were invested. As a result, he would have additional income tax to pay and could, at best, be expected to save the net after-tax amount remaining from the supplements, plus the net investment earnings on the account. As the account built up, it would be exposed to claims of the employee's creditors; also, in many countries, an employee who became unemployed or disabled might have to expend much of his accumulated account for his and his family's sup-

3.   *infra*, n.193.

port before becoming entitled to social welfare benefits.

In response to such problems, certain basic features are present in funded retirement schemes in most countries. Most important for our purposes are the following:

- the assets of the scheme are segregated from the general assets of the employer and held by an independent stakeholder — often an insurance company or, in the common-law countries, a trustee;

- these segregated assets are insulated from the claims of creditors of both employer and employee and have no effect on social welfare eligibility, at least until benefits actually commence;

- the employer receives a tax deduction for contributions made to the scheme; but,

- the employee is not taxed on those contributions nor on investment earnings as they are received and only has taxable income when he retires and begins to receive benefits; and, finally,

- when the employee is eventually taxed on benefits as paid out, he is likely to be in a lower tax bracket.

Governments generally impose conditions and limitations on retirement schemes before granting these tax deferrals and concessions.[4]

German schemes also have some special characteristics which depart from the above standard pattern. Many use a "Book Reserve" approach under which amounts are allocated to pension expense, are deductible for tax purposes, but are, nevertheless, retained within the organisation; essentially this arrangement reduces to a conventional funded scheme with its assets invested back into the sponsoring enterprise. Other employers establish *Pensionkassen*[5] or, in the case of smaller

4. New Zealand recently enacted a variation on the above pattern under which there is no immediate loss of tax revenue but the scheme is eventually subsidized. As Daykin, the British Government Actuary, puts it:

"the tax incentives for employer-sponsored occupational schemes have ... been turned on their head. Instead of contributions to approved schemes being tax-deductible and investment in schemes free of tax there is now no concession on tax-deductibility of contributions and investment income is subject to tax. However, the benefits payable from the scheme are free of tax in the hands of the recipient." "Analysis of Methods of Financing Income for Retirement." International Social Security Association, International Conference on the Application of Methods of Quantitative Analysis to Social Security, Bristol, 11-14 November 1990, C Daykin, Reporter.

5. Separate pension funds, subject to elaborate regulation which makes the approach impractical for all but the largest employers.

employers, purchase pensions from an insurance company.[6] In the latter two situations, there is also a tax to the employee when the contribution is made but at a lower, almost nominal, rate, and the payout is not taxed.

3. Types of Funded Scheme

Funded retirement schemes come in two basic incarnations: Defined Benefit and Defined Contribution. A full statement of the difference between these approaches is essential to our discussion; failure to appreciate the distinction is responsible for much confusion, particularly in the basic definition of equality used to evaluate pension issues.

(i) Defined Benefit (D.B.)

In a defined benefit scheme, a benefit objective is established: two percent of final average salary per year of service would be a typical formula, giving exactly half pay (25 years x 2% = 50% of salary) to a retiree with 25 years of service. Conceptually, determining the contributions required to provide these benefits is the next step in the process. In reality, of course, the benefit formula is established only after complex actuarial calculations projecting the level of employer contributions required to support the anticipated benefits, which benefits are not known in advance and can only be estimated.[7] Periodically, new actuarial valuations are made to update the projections and to establish new recommended contribution levels for the future.

The true cost of a D.B. scheme is not finally known until the last pension cheque is paid and the fund is closed. Until then the sponsoring employer bears the risk of financial or demographic experience unfavourable to the scheme. Any such adverse experience will cause costs to increase above, sometimes far above, those projected and, in extreme cases, may cause the scheme to fail.[8] Conversely, favourable experience can result in lower employer costs as the scheme ages.

6.   These and other German variations are described in more detail for English speaking readers in *Financing Pensions in Germany,* (Frankfurt: William M. Mercer - M.P.A. GmbH, 1985).

7.   These cost projections are based on a number of actuarial assumptions: economic assumptions of investment return and salary increases, both heavily influenced by expected inflation; and, demographic assumptions concerning future rates of mortality, disability, withdrawal, *etc,* amongst participating employees.

8.   "Failure" of a D.B. scheme can result from two radically different causes: unfavourable experience, particularly losses in the assets due to investment losses or even diversion, on the one hand; and, on the other, commitments — generally to provide benefits attributable to service before the scheme is established — for which the necessary funds

(ii) Defined Contribution (D.C.)

A defined contribution scheme, on the other hand, has, as the name implies, a contribution formula fixing the employer's contribution, usually as a percentage of salary for each participating employee. These contributions are deposited into one or more accounts for the benefit of the particular employee; the employer's commitment is essentially limited to making the required contributions; and, when the employee eventually retires, the benefit is simply what can be provided from the account. The benefit/risk of favourable/adverse experience is, therefore, entirely on the employee, except to the extent that he can establish a breach of fiduciary duty[9] leading to losses in the assets of the scheme.

(iii) A Note on Terminology

In Canada and the U.S., D.C. retirement "plans" (never "schemes") may be either "Money Purchase" pension plans with fixed formula contributions or "Profit-Sharing" plans with varying contributions. The term "pension" is usually applied to all plans other than profit-sharing. Outside North America, "pension" is often synonymous with defined benefit. This paper does not need to draw any significant distinctions between the money purchase and the profit-sharing approaches; "pension" and "retirement" are therefore used interchangeably.

References to pension or retirement "provisions" generally focus on the actual payments received by employees — usually, but not necessar-

---

have not been accumulated before the scheme is wound up. The second possibility does not, generally, imply misfeasance on the part of the plan sponsor; merely, in most cases, the sponsor's inability to complete a funding program begun in good faith. The writer has developed this point in a Guest Editorial in Tax Notes, Washington D.C., Vol. 38, No. 3, 289 (1988).

One of the worst features of the coverage of the Maxwell situation is that this distinction was not even alluded to, presumably because it was not understood by the commentators; for example, a recent editorial in the *Financial Times* of 7 June 1993 entitled, ironically enough, "Maxwell: keeping the issue in sight", concluded:

"What is really needed is a demonstration that ... vulnerable members of pension schemes, can look for powerful and reliable protection."

While this is undoubtedly correct as to the security of the assets, it remained unclear to what extent the assets of the schemes would have covered the benefit entitlement had there been no asset loss. The omission was finally remedied by a letter to the editor from the Chairman of the MGN Trustees, published on 10 June 1993, stating that the schemes were actually in actuarial surplus but noting, however, that, for reasons beyond the scope of this paper, this did not guarantee that there would be a surplus on winding up.

9. Where national law permits, schemes often specify gross negligence or misfeasance as the standard. This was typically the case in the U.S. before the Employee Retirement Security Act of 1974.

ily, from funded schemes. In addition, "eligibility" rather than "access" is the preferred term in North America for provisions defining conditions for entry into membership and for receiving benefits as a retiree or "early leaver" / terminating employee.

4. EQUALITY AS A GENERAL PROPOSITION

Equality has inspired an enormous output of scholarly analysis[10] and this paper does not aspire to expand that analysis. It will, however, draw on it in order to put some of the narrow pension issues in context.

Westen[11] reviews much of this output and gives a comprehensive treatment of the issues from Aristotle to the latest current developments. He takes a rigorous analytical approach and also discusses the rhetorical uses of the term. Most important from our point of view, he distinguishes between the purely "descriptive" notion of equality implicit in, for example, mathematical equality, describing things as they *are*; and the more complex notion of "prescriptive equality", involving an opinion of things as they allegedly *should be*.

Descriptive equality is not the same thing as identity; indeed, it only has meaning if we apply it to two things which are not identical, for purposes of comparison.[12] The key is the element of comparison, which necessarily involves a yardstick such as weight or length. Westen draws a sharp distinction between ordinary descriptive equalities and mathematical equality where "we have no trouble understanding the *concept* of equality that underlies them"[13] *(emphasis in the original)*. It may be that the distinction is less clear cut than it appears and that the major difference is that in mathematical equalities the yardstick is built into the mathematical treatment in a way which is less apparent outside mathematics.[14] This

---

10. Westen (following note) states at 285:

   "This volume…is one of 30 to 40 books about equality that can be expected to be published in English this year…It will, if added to the card catalog of the Sterling Memorial Library at Yale University, join ..26 entries under the subject heading 'equality.'"

11. *Speaking of Equality* (Princeton Univ. Press, 1991).

12. *id*. at 13.

13. *id*. at 42.

14. For example, in the following assertions:

   • the total number of players on the Manchester United championship team and the Rochdale Elementary School team is 22;

   • there are 11 on the Manchester team;

   • which means there must also be 11 on the Rochdale team; and,

   • therefore, Manchester United and Rochdale are equal;

suggests that when the term "equality" is used in other than a mathematical way, the yardstick should be made as explicit as possible as often as possible.

Westen summarises the elements of descriptive and mathematical equality to give the following definition:

(1) the relationship that obtains among two or more entities, whether tangible or intangible,

(2) that have been jointly measured and compared by reference to a common standard of measurement,

(3) and that, though not identical by all measures of their dimensions to the extent that they consist of more than one dimension,

(4) are nevertheless indistinguishable by reference to the *relevant standard of measurement*.[15] *(emphasis supplied)*

Prescriptive equality, on the other hand, deals in a world of "should" and "ought to be" rather than "is". Westen points out that the four elements noted above as forming the definition of descriptive and mathematical equalities, also apply to prescriptive equalities.[16] However, the major difference is that the standard used in item (2) is itself prescriptive. It has, therefore, the measurer's view of the ultimately desirable result embedded in it: when we establish the standard of measurement, often knowing in advance where it will be applied, we must, to a large extent, pre-judge (literally) the issue.

it requires some minimal thought to qualify the conclusion so that it is not seen to assert that the teams are equal in ability or transfer value.

It would be a valid, although clearly trivial, piece of algebra to restate this sequence as follows:

- let t = the total number of players on the Manchester United and Rochdale Elementary School teams, m = the number of Manchester players and r = the number of Rochdale school players;

- we are given that $t = 22$ and $m = 11$;

- then, since we know that $t = m + r$, it is clear by substitution and subtraction that $r = 11$; and,

- therefore, $m = r$;

but no inference would typically be drawn from the last equation that the two teams are equal in any respect other than pure headcount — simply, it appears, because the mathematical symbols have built into them their limited meaning as measures of, in this case, headcount. It might be more accurate to say that we, the readers, have that limited meaning embedded in our heads.

15. Westen, *supra*, n.11, at 52. This relevant standard of measurement ("R.S.M.") is an important concept to which we will refer frequently.

16. *id*. at 62.

We will examine prescriptive equality without, it is hoped, losing any generality by looking at examples in the field of sex equality, specifically employee benefits but not, at this stage, pensions.

Consider the Ruritanian legislature enacting rules for the newly introduced concept of employer-provided benefits.[17] Ruritania is a conventional modern state: it disagrees with the Greeks and Romans in disapproving of slavery; it disapproves of all forms of prejudice; and, most important for our purposes, it disagrees with Victorian patriarchs and other earlier generations in proclaiming equal rights for women (who provide about half the votes which elect it). All of these assumptions — and they are clearly assumptions, not universally shared,[18] which should be made explicit if they are to be part of the ground rules — will have a major impact on the legislation which Ruritania adopts.

The first measure which is passed provides for a minimum of two weeks vacation to full-time employees. It merely codifies an almost universal practice which, it is generally agreed, pays for itself in improved employee relations and increased productivity. There is virtually no opposition.

One of the measures which Ruritania considers next is a maternity leave bill under which pregnant females are permitted time off work at the time of confinement, and re-employment rights after delivery. This is also passed without significant opposition; the time off is without pay and there is, therefore, no significant employer cost. Then comes a proposal to offer comparable time off to people, male or female, who are adopting children. There is discussion of the fact that the formalities of adoption can be scheduled in advance, often at weekends, but the measure is passed, one of the supporting arguments being that it is a clear proclamation that the society regards adoption as an important institution. Ruritanian law already gives equal rights to adopted and natural children.

Now the fathers' lobby demands that fathers also receive time off when a natural child is born and, as a result of some rather timidly expressed doubts whether the amount of time off given to fathers should be as extensive as that to mothers, the measure is passed, but fathers are granted only half as many days as mothers.[19]

17. Avoiding, thereby, the difficult issues of retroactivity when existing practice is changed.

18. This is especially true historically. Here and throughout this paper, it could even be conceded, without invalidating its conclusions, that, "it is unclear whether our egalitarianism is the result of the revelation of men's (*sic*) equality or whether it is just what we happen to like today", A. Bloom, "Justice: John Rawls versus the Tradition of Political Philosophy", *Giants and Dwarfs*, p 315 at 317 (New York: Simon and Schuster, 1990).

19. The opposition points out that in the U.S. under the Family and Medical Leave Act of 1993, there is no difference between the rights of fathers, mothers and adoptive parents to maternity/paternity leave.

Next, the Employers' Federation of Ruritania demands that employers be given the right, in carefully defined dire emergencies only, to require a recipient of such paternal rights to come into the workplace for a maximum of three hours on one or two of his time-off days, to be designated by the employer. This is passed for one year on a trial basis despite strong objections, and only after a provision is inserted requiring that the employee receive two full days' pay for any such emergency.

So far, we see debatable but generally reasonable legislation reflecting typical political compromises. Now the Gender Fairness League of Ruritania raises objections[20] that men and women are not being treated equally. First, says the League, the U.S. is right in saying that it is sex discrimination to give less time off to men than to women "just because they are men". Second, it is similarly discriminatory not to subject females to the same limited employer recall rights as males. Therefore, it argues, women who are minutes from delivery or have just delivered should be subject to the same recall obligations as their husbands if the employer has a qualifying emergency; men and women simply must receive equal treatment. The first demand is accepted, unwisely in this writer's opinion, after a good deal of debate. The second is laughed out of court. It is submitted that no reasonable observer, whatever he may think of the recall concept as applied to males in the first place, could defend the second demand.

Why are both demands not instantly accepted once the speeches or briefs proclaim that men and women are equal, and that both new rules must, therefore, be repealed or declared unconstitutional since they are discriminatory on their face?

Westen follows his three-part technical analysis with a one-chapter Part Four entitled "The Rhetoric of Equality".[21] His emphasis on the rhetorical aspect is a fitting close and his questions are essentially a counterpoint to what has been discussed here. He asks:

- Why do arguments for equality put opposing arguments "on the defensive"?

- Why is it that "to our ears inequality has the ring of injustice, unfairness, and discrimination"?

- What is it that gives arguments about equality their "tremendous emotive force"?[22]

20. From the back benches, if Ruritania follows the Westminster model; in court, if it is more americanised.

21. Westen, *supra*, n.11, at 255.

22. *id.* at 256 *(citations omitted).*

A partial answer to these questions, it is suggested, is that the use of the term "equality" gives a presumption of all the favourable attributes listed, without the need to demonstrate that they actually apply. That presumption puts the ball in the opposite court and the opponent on the defensive; he will not proclaim or admit opposition to equality and he must, therefore, indulge in an argument about definitions, meanings, *etc*, which a skilful opponent can present as evasion.

Reverting to our Ruritanian example, we see that the League has given itself the benefit of a favourable presumption by stating its arguments as defence of "equality", and this presumption has ruled in our first example (as it did in the U.S. when comparable legislation was originally introduced). It did not, however, determine the issue in the second case because the demand was so egregious. In both examples, the prescriptive nature of the yardstick means that the analysis is stated as:

(i)   here is the definition of equality (not "*a* proposed definition which should be examined carefully before proceeding");

(ii) X is unequal (not "unequal using, it must be born in mind, our special definition");

(iii) therefore, X is bad and must cease forthwith [step (i) is often omitted altogether].

Stripped to its essentials, the underlying argument reduces, in each case, to:

we think X is bad and it must, therefore, cease forthwith,

a far less compelling formulation!

When X is the relatively less important, certainly less emotionally charged, issue of whether a new father should receive a lesser period of time off than a new mother, there is little inclination on the part of the pundits to make the kind of analysis we have attempted above and to fight the good fight even in the face of accusations of standing against "equality"; there is also likely to be very little public reaction. On the other hand, when the issue is a proposal to drag mothers from their beds in the delivery room and send them back to work, the pundits will, one hopes, make the analysis and fight for it; also, far more important, the public will react. The public will say simply that the League, despite its general record of watching out for and fighting against abuses, has gone too far this time; it has taken it into its head to demand, using fancy arguments which seem silly, something which is clearly unacceptable. It will insist, as a matter of common sense, on far more consideration to women who delivered a few minutes ago than to their husbands who may be close by and closely involved, but need not even be in the neighbourhood.[23] The public's formulation of the issue is, to this writer, at least as accurate as, and probably far more acute than, the earlier more intellectual one. In any event, it is clear that the League's proposal cannot stand. The key element, it is suggested, is that equality was being used by the League not as an analytical tool but simply as a rhetorical device, and there came a point, but only concerning the second demand, at which the audience caught on to that fact. It did not, however, catch on with respect to the first, not particularly egregious, demand. The task for an opponent of demands which are clothed in the rhetoric of equality is, therefore, either to demonstrate that they are egregious or, if he believes them to be merely mistaken, to try to strip away the aura which has been given to them simply by (mis)using the rhetoric of equality.

A fifth factor, to be added to Westen's four,[24] should also be considered: when we are dealing with future contingent benefits and their associated probabilities, the R.S.M. must be applied at the appropriate time. Consider a parent giving lottery tickets to his children. He decides that each child will receive one ticket, *i.e.* the R.S.M. is to be simply status as his child. Equality is achieved therefore, by this definition, provided that the lottery drawing has not taken place, or at least the result is not known, at the time of the distribution. Otherwise, equality disappears. If all tickets are losers, there is only a kind of null equality since the distributed tickets are all worthless; if one ticket is known to be a winner, then clearly one individual is being favoured.

5. EQUALITY AS A PRINCIPLE OF COMMUNITY LAW

Arnull[25] and Docksey[26] both describe the way in which the European Court of Justice (the "Court" or "E.C.J.") has established equality between men and women as a basic principle underlying Community law. The latter's opening paragraph describes it as: "a constitutional code, which controls both national provisions on equality and *even other Community provisions.*" *(emphasis supplied)*

---

23. And, if they are, may well be in the neighbourhood pub.

24. *supra* n.15.

25. *The General Principles of E.E.C. Law and the Individual*, (Leicester: The University Press, 1990).

26. "The Principle of Equality between Men and Women as a Fundamental Right under Community Law", 20 I.L.J. 258 (1991).

These descriptions are based on such cases as the Second *Defrenne* case, holding that "the principle of equal pay forms part of the foundation of the Community",[27] and the Third *Defrenne* case, holding that:

> respect for fundamental ... human rights is one of the general principles of Community law ... elimination of discrimination based on sex forms part of those fundamental rights.[28]

Docksey concludes from these statements that there is a "general and fundamental right of equality in Community law" and, more aggressively, that "Article 119, though it undoubtedly enjoys that status, is part of the *implementation* of that principle; it is not the *source*."[29] *(emphasis in the original)*. He also asserts that:

> (c)ommon lawyers must face up to the implications of a clear constitutional right which they must respect, even in the face of an inconsistent Act of Parliament.[30]

With respect to Irish lawyers practising Community law, also American observers and those from Commonwealth federal states, the observation does not hold. Even limiting it to English lawyers and recognising that judicial review of primary legislation is new to them, it still seems that the Court's approach may sometimes be stranger to civil lawyers than to their common-law brethren. The "Common-law Bill of Rights" announced by *Nold*[31] seems aptly named: it represents the cobbling together of an innovative approach in response to a new challenge.[32]

---

27. Case 43/76, *Defrenne* v. *SABENA* [1976] E.C.R. 455, 472.

28. Case 149/77, *Defrenne* v. *SABENA* [1978] E.C.R. 1365, 1378.

29. Docksey, *supra*, n.26 at 259.

30. *id*. at 264.

31. Case 4/73, *Nold* v. *Commission*, [1974] E.C.R. 491. In this case, the German *Bundesgerichtshof*, the Federal Court of Justice, had held that Community legislation when applied to a German citizen was subject to German constitutional guarantees. Faced with this "brutal blow, a blow jeopardising not only the supremacy but the very independence of Community law" (Mancini, *infra* n.113, at 609) the Court laid its prestige on the line. It established a "common law" (this term appears in Hartley, *infra* n.113) Bill of Rights for the Community drawing its inspiration from, but not necessarily incorporating every specific provision of, international conventions adopted by the Member States, and their constitutions.

32. It would be hard to find a case which fits better, Holmes's description of the common law:

    "What has been said will explain the failure of all theories which consider the law only from its formal side, whether they attempt to deduce the *corpus* from *a priori* postulate

One of the major critics of the Court's activism has been Rasmussen,[33] who describes the Court's approach as one of giving "preference to teleology over text";[34] a failing, if it is a failing, perhaps more common among common-law judges. Whilst, as suggested *supra*, Cappelletti may have the better of the argument with Rasmussen, it is, nevertheless, very desirable that judicial restraint not be forgotten and Rasmussen's warnings not dismissed. It is suggested that this is especially so where a court, be it the U.S. Supreme Court or the European Court of Justice, finds itself in the position of delivering the final word (short, of course, of a constitutional/ Treaty amendment) in an area which is peculiarly within the province of another specialised profession. It is not suggested that where judicial review gives the last word to the highest court,[35] it is in any way illegitimate for the court to pronounce that last word. It is suggested, however, that a court should be extremely careful about setting as the highest standard of accounting procedure, engineering specifications, actuarial analysis, *etc*, something which the relevant experts find internally inconsistent, unacceptable or even laughable.

Another area where Rasmussen's warnings may be salutary is with respect to Article 164 providing that the Court "shall ensure that in the interpretation and application of this Treaty the law is observed." This can be argued to imply an independent (of the Treaty) source of law, as can Article 173;[36] it can equally be argued, however, that the intent is to cover Regulations, Directives, *etc*, issued under the Treaty. Article 215

...or logical cohesion...It is forever adopting new principles from life...It will become entirely consistent only when it ceases to grow." *(emphasis in the original)*, *The Common Law*, (Boston: Little, Brown and Company, M.DeW. Howe, Editor, 1963) at 32.

33. H. Rasmussen, *On Law and Policy in the European Court of Justice. A Comparative Study in Judicial Policymaking*, (Boston: Nijhoff, 1986); and, "Between Self Restraint and Activism: a Judicial Policy for the European Court", 13 E.L. Rev. 28 (1988). See, however, M. Cappelletti, "Is the European Court of Justice 'Running Wild'?", 12 E.L. Rev. 3 (1987), for a powerful critique of Rasmussen's analysis.

34. "Between Self Restraint...", *supra*, at 31.

35. Article 174 clearly does give the last word to the E.C.J. It provides unambiguously that the Court has the authority to review and declare "void" actions of the Community institutions. In the United States, by contrast, *Marbury* v. *Madison*, 5 U.S.(1 Cranch) 131 (1803), was required to extend the power of the U.S. Supreme Court, to declaring Federal legislation void as conflicting substantively with the U.S. Constitution, as opposed to beyond federal jurisdiction. Although it is certainly a minority view, there is a very respectable and well argued body of opinion that the full reach of *Marbury* has no basis in the Constitution. Perhaps the best exposition of the view that the U.S.S.C. did not have the right under the Constitution to review the acts of the other branches on grounds other than *ultra vires*, is by Learned Hand, late Chief Judge of the 2nd Circuit Court of Appeal, in the 1958 O.W. Holmes lectures at Harvard [*The Bill of Rights* (Harvard University Press, 1958)]. These lectures only questioned the logical and historical basis of *Marbury*, not its now well established basis in U.S. law.

36. Also the earlier Docksey quotations.

imposes obligations on the Community with respect to its own non-contractual liability, measured by the "general provisions common to the laws of Member States", and *Nold*[37] drew on those sources to formulate one of the most important concepts of Community law — but only when faced with a major challenge to the whole structure of that law. Even then, the "Common-law Bill of Rights" was based on sources permeating the Treaty but not in any sense independent of it. One danger of an analysis assuming independent sources is that it could suggest that the Court stands, to some extent, over the Treaty. This view might even suggest a power in the Court to hold a Treaty provision invalid by reference to some higher outside source of law.

In arguing against the view that the American Federal Courts could extend their own, inconsistent, common law into an area where State common-law rules were already in place, Holmes wrote:

> The Common Law is not a brooding omnipresence in the sky but the articulate voice of some Sovereign or quasi-sovereign that can be identified...[38]

Nor is any reason apparent to construct a larger "brooding omnipresence" even higher in the European sky, thus elevating the Court above its actual status as a creature of the Treaty. The notion of equality as a fundamental legal principle in the Community should, therefore, be handled with great care. This is especially so when the Court employs it to deal with a highly technical area where, unlike the situation in *Nold*, Community legislation is in place and there is no overriding need to exercise judicial creativity to fill a void and to lay down new policy. Without such care, there may indeed be a danger of the Court, in Rasmussen's phrase, "running wild." It is comforting to note, however, that, as Docksey points out, the Court's judgment in the Third *Defrenne* case[39] states that:

> the principle of equality, albeit a...fundamental right, applies at national level only as and when it is embodied in specific Community or national legislation [and when] only Article 119 was in force, no remedy existed with regard to matters...outside 'pay'.[40]

37. *supra*, n.31.

38. Dissenting in *Southern Pacific Co.* v. *Jensen*, 244 U.S. 205 (1917); a view eventually adopted by the Supreme Court in *Erie R.R.* v. *Tompkins*, 304 U.S. 64 (1938), overruling a long line of cases to the contrary.

39. *supra*, n.28.

40. Docksey, *supra*, n.26, at 260.

6. EQUALITY OF ACCESS TO PENSION SCHEMES

Consider a provision in a pension scheme under which only male or only female employees may participate. Such an access requirement would be so obviously outrageous by contemporary standards that it would not be seriously considered, and it is raised here largely to be dismissed. However, even such an apparently open-and-shut violation raises a conceptual issue: if there were an identifiable section of a community which had much lower life expectancy than the norm, no member of which had ever lived beyond age 50, would it be equal treatment to include them in a retirement scheme providing benefits payable only at age 65 — even to treat the cost of this scheme as part of their package in union bargaining?[41]

With respect to benefits at normal retirement, sex distinct provisions — often an age 65 requirement for males and 60 for females — are the pattern in many of the Member States and were common in North America some years ago; comparable five-year differences for early retirement are/were also common. Such unequal access provisions are typically not defended with any great conviction by the commentators and will certainly not be defended here. They are, it is suggested, no more than hangovers of obsolete social attitudes, especially with regard to single people.[42]

Equalisation of access conditions does not, it appears, raise fundamental conceptual problems.[43] It would clearly be unconscionable to deflate the pension expectations of a women who is on the verge of retiring on full pension at, say, age 60 and to tell her that she must either work an additional five years or be reclassified as an early, rather than normal,

---

41. If no cure for AIDS is found and if its incidence increases, this kind of issue may not be entirely academic. It would arise primarily in D.B. schemes since in D.C. schemes, the employee's account is usually payable to him or his beneficiary in the event of early death or termination of employment (except that a short service early leaver may not be fully vested and may, therefore, forfeit all or part of his entitlement depending on the provisions of the scheme and the national law governing vesting of benefits). This unpleasant prospect illustrates that a slavish pursuit of "equality" may not always be equitable or desirable. The fine sounding word alone does not automatically confer merit; rather, the real effects must be examined.

42. With respect to married couples, it is well known that in the average couple, the husband tends to be three to five years older than his wife, but it is hard to argue that this justifies an expensive pattern of favouring all working females, married and unmarried, by permitting unreduced early retirement benefits at a younger age than that for males.

43. There is, however, a great difference between favouring equal access as a policy matter, on the one hand; and, on the other, asserting that Member States should be prohibited from continuing to do so even for a limited period or, *a fortiori*, that Article 119 already contains such a prohibition.

retiree with a consequent reduction of the order of one-third to one-half in her pension amount. There are, nevertheless, serious problems of retroactivity, raising possibilities of large financial exposures.

7. EQUALITY IN THE D.C. PENSION CONTEXT

We will examine the concept of equality — non-discrimination in North American parlance — as applied to contributions/benefits (as opposed to access) under defined contribution pension schemes, by first constructing a simplified model of how a D.C. scheme works and then applying that model to three leading American cases, two of which are, to this writer's chagrin, cited frequently with respect if not awe in Europe.

(i) A Simplified Model D.C. Scheme

A typical D.C. pension scheme might provide a contribution to each participant's account of, say, 10% of salary. An employee with a salary of 2,000 units per month participating in such a scheme for 20 years would, if he continued at the same salary, generate 48,000 units of contribution. Ignoring interest, he would, therefore, have that amount in his account at retirement. This could obviously be taken as a lump-sum payout at retirement. Alternatively, if taken down over a period, it would give 800 units per month for a five-year period or 400 per month over 10 years, if interest earnings are still ignored. Clearly, as the payout period goes up, the amount which can be paid goes down and, if we were to attempt to pay out 1,000 per month for more than four years, the assets would run out and the scheme would fail. It would, perhaps, be more accurate to say that the attempt was absurd. D.C. schemes, since their pay-out to each participant is determined entirely by the amount in his account, cannot, under our definition, "fail" although they can prove woefully inadequate, especially for older employees with limited periods of coverage. As we have seen,[44] the same is not true of D.B. schemes where lack of funds can mean that a scheme is unable to deliver the anticipated ("defined") benefits.

Without changing the concept, but introducing investment earnings and salary increases in order to give a more realistic picture, we can calculate that our participant would accumulate a total account, in round numbers of approximately 130,000 units; this assumes salary increases of 4% per year from a starting level of 2,000 units per month; investment earnings of 6% per year;[45] and monthly contributions. The simplest form

44. *supra*, n.8.

45. The absolute value of these two rates is less significant than the "spread" between them. This particular combination anticipates, perhaps optimistically, continuing relatively

of retirement benefit would again be a payment, in lump-sum form, of the full account as of the end of the 20-year accumulation period. It is important to note, indeed much of the argument of the paper revolves around, the simple fact that this accumulation is a function of only the units deposited and the investment earnings over the 20-year period. It does not reflect the employee's age, whether 60, 65 or for that matter 45, at the end of the period; nor, whether the employee is male or female.[46] Until we think in terms of monthly benefits payable for life, which we have carefully avoided so far, issues of equality hardly arise. Our admittedly over-simplified model avoids any possibility of unequal treatment as between different employees.

We can take a further step towards a more realistic and recognisable pension scheme, still without losing this basic equality of treatment and, thus, reaching equality issues. This next step is to apply the lump-sum accumulation calculated above to provide periodic monthly income for a fixed period of, say, 15 years. The resulting pension would be just under 1,100 units per month. This calculation is based on the same investment yield of 6% used earlier.[47] It also assumes — this is admittedly, but only temporarily, artificial — that the monthly payment stops after 15 years, even if the employee, now a retiree, is still alive; also, that if he dies earlier, payments will continue until the end of the period, presumably to a beneficiary usually determined, subject to the rules of the scheme, by the employee. Our model scheme is now looking rather more like a real pension; it has not yet come all the way into the real world but will do so eventually.

(ii) The Effect of Life Expectancy

We will focus first on issues arising because of the age of the participants in our model D.C. retirement scheme under which we have, so far, provided only a fixed 15-year payout.

Let us assume that in the population of participating employees, the average retiree is age 65 and his life expectancy at retirement is 15 years. He would typically expect to receive a monthly retirement allowance for his lifetime.[48] We will refer back to this typical retiree later and will call

low inflation affecting both yields and salary progression. It also has the virtue that it produces numbers which do not seem totally unreal to a current reader as do calculations involving high projected inflation.

46. The use of male pronouns being, of course, purely for convenience.

47. With no cost-of-living or other increases in the monthly benefits.

48. Basic actuarial mathematics demonstrates that the value of a monthly pension for life to a pensioner with a life expectancy of 15 years is not identical to that of a pension for a fixed period equal to the expectancy [see, for example, C.W. Jordan, *Life Contingen-*

him M65. Let us further assume that working next to our retiree is another employee whose work history — service, salary, *etc* — is identical. The only difference between these two employees is that the second is age 60 and not 65. We will refer to him as M60. If this employee retires, his accumulated account will be the same as the first retiree's but his expectancy will be a little under 20 years;[49] we will assume 19. This means that if his account is paid to him over that longer period, the monthly instalments which can be provided will necessarily be smaller at about 950 units per month; alternatively, if he were to receive the same pension as M65, it is equally clear that the cost to the employer would have been about 15% higher. This will be true whether the benefit payments are made directly by the pension scheme or, as is more common in D.C. schemes, by purchase of an annuity from a life insurance company.[50]

So far in this discussion, there has been no explicit statement whether the two employees discussed above were male or female. Let us now assume that both were male. Let us further assume that the next employee to come up for retirement is a 65-year-old female whom we will refer to as F65. It is a standard actuarial rule of thumb that female annuitants have mortality rates roughly equal to those of males five years younger.[51] This means that F65 has a life expectancy of 19 and can, on the average, expect to collect payments for about the same period as M60.[52]

cies (Chicago: Society of Actuaries, 2nd Ed. 1967) at 173], but for our purposes the difference will be ignored and we will, with some loss of precision, and at the risk of some pain to any actuarial reader who passes this way, assume that the 65-year-old retiree introduced above can take benefits in the form of a monthly pension for life of the same 1,100 units calculated above.

49. The intuitive figure of exactly 20 (15 at age 65 plus another 5 for the 5 years down to age 60) is, like so many intuitively obvious answers, incorrect because of the probabilities of death between 60 and 65.

50. If an insurance company assumes responsibility for the lifetime payouts, it is clear that that company will set its purchase rates based on its expected payout not for each particular individual but for the group of which he is a member. It would be absurd to suggest that life insurance companies be required to charge the same premium for annuities to 25-year-olds, 90-year-olds, and anyone in between; clearly the life insurance industry could not survive if such a requirement were imposed. To the best of the author's knowledge, no serious commentator has ever made such a suggestion but, as we will see shortly, there has been no dearth of such suggestions — arguably in the statutes, clearly in the decisions, and even in serious commentary — when the perceived inequity was due to sex and not age.

51. Some studies show a value closer to 6 years. See, for example, H.R. Greenlee & A.D. Kee, "The 1971 Group Annuity Mortality Table", *Transactions of the Society of Actuaries*, Vol. XXIII, 569 (Chicago, 1971).

52. More precisely, and this point will apply repeatedly though it will not be restated *ad nauseam*, a large population of such 65-year-old females should produce the same mortality experience as a large group of 60-year-old males, and a retirement scheme which

It seems elementary, if not self-evident, that monthly benefits to M65, M60 and F65 under our model D.C. plan must, if equal contributions flow in for each over the same period, be approximately 1,100, 950 and 950 respectively if the accumulations at their respective retirement ages are to support their benefits. On the other hand, if their benefits are to be equalised, the employer must be prepared to contribute approximately 15% more for M60 and F65 than for M65.

(iii) Three Leading U.S. Cases

The issues arising out of the above model have been considered in three major American cases all construing the provision of Title VII of the Civil Rights Act of 1964,[53] making it unlawful "to discriminate against any individual with respect to his compensation, terms, conditions, or privileges of employment, because of such individual's race, colour, religion, sex, or national origin."[54]

The courts' stated approach to this very general language is one of straightforward statutory interpretation.[55] Nevertheless, in reading the major cases, it is hard to avoid the feeling that one is witnessing something closer to traditional constitutional construction. The courts certainly reach out to set broad policies in a way which seems inappropriate in construing an ordinary statute open to frequent amendment. A notable example of this broad brush approach, as we will see later, is where the U.S. Supreme Court quotes at length a principal sponsor of the statute and then rejects his comments out of hand.

(a) Manhart

City of Los Angeles, Department of Water and Power v. *Manhart*[56] involved a D.B. scheme providing equal benefits, financed by a combination of employer and employee contributions, to male and female employees with the same employment history, but requiring different employee contributions depending on sex. At its simplest, the employee contribu-

is large enough to ride out fluctuations, or a life insurance company selling annuities, can reasonably treat them the same; in fact, the insurance company must do so if it is to avoid unreasonably subsidising one group of policyholders at the expense of another.

53.   §§ 700 *et seq.*, 42 U.S.C. §§ 2000e *et seq.*

54.   § 703 (a)(1) as amended, 42 U.S.C. § 2000e-2(a)(1).

55.   *Manhart, infra* at 709, states that, "the language and purposes of the statute command …"; also, under *Norris, infra* at 1074, "(w)hat we, if sitting as legislators, might consider wise legislative policy is irrelevant to our task. Nor…do we have…any constitutional challenge."

56.   435 U.S. 702 (1978), on remand 577 F.2d. (9th Cir. 1978), appeal after remand 652 F.2d 904 (9th Cir. 1981), judgment vacated 461 U.S. 951 (1983).

tory portion of the scheme can be viewed as one requiring our F65 to contribute a larger amount to what was essentially an employee-paid D.C. portion of the scheme, than would have been contributed by a similarly situated male. (We shall discuss the D.B. aspects of the scheme later).

The Court's opinion gave a very convincing, at least to this reader, recital of the reasons why this requirement was obviously equitable but then held it unlawful anyway. It started by noting, correctly, the demonstrated fact that women as a class live longer than men, also that in this case the differential was based not just on general statistics but also on the Department's own experience studies, and that on this basis women employees were required to make contributions 15%[57] higher than those of men.

Justice Stevens, for the Court, analogised to various "'stereotyped' differences" as possible grounds for variances in insurance-type benefits, such as "flabby" versus "fit" and the highly emotive factor of race.[58] The nub of the *Manhart* opinion is the statement that: "Congress has decided that *classifications* based on sex, like those based on national origin or race, are unlawful".[59] *(emphasis supplied)*

This, however, is not what Congress seems to have said in either the statute or the legislative history. It did, as we saw above, prohibit "*discriminat(ion)*...because of...*sex*". *(emphasis supplied)* The issue, in terms of our model, remains whether the Court's prescription — treating F65, demonstrably virtually identical to M60 for pension purposes, as functionally equivalent to M65 instead — was the real "discrimination". It is submitted that such treatment is self-evidently unfavourable to either M60 or F65 since, in reality, they are hardly distinguishable for pension purposes but they are being treated radically differently. As we will show, the differences flow in different directions for different benefits and options.

At one point, discussing the legislative history, the opinion quotes[60] and then casually dismisses (the characterisation is from the dissent,[61] not from the writer), the following statement, on the floor of the Senate, of Senator Humphrey,[62] floor manager of the bill which became the Civil

---

57. The precise figure was 14.84%; this paper will round to 15% to tie in conveniently to the round numbers of the earlier model.

58. The former, of course, is extensively used in individual life insurance underwriting but generally not in group insurance; reflecting the latter is forbidden in most jurisdictions.

59. At 709 and repeated in *Norris, infra*, at 1084.

60. At 713.

61. At 727.

62. One of the best known American defenders of minority rights in the last half century.

Rights Act. In response to a question whether "similar differences (to those of Social Security) of treatment in industrial benefit plans, including early retirement options for women, may continue in operation under this bill…":

> Senator Humphrey responded unequivocally: "Yes. That point was made unmistakably clear earlier today by the adoption of the Bennet amendment; so there can be no doubt about it." *(citations omitted)*

This is immediately brushed off as an "isolated comment." The usual American practice is to pay rather more attention to such legislative history. While this colloquy clearly dealt with differences in access conditions, it covers, *a fortiori*, the actuarial issues in *Manhart*. This part of the opinion seems, therefore, to represent a clear substitution of the Supreme Court's policy view for the legislative intent underlying the statute.

Having thus dismissed long-standing pension practice, actuarial science, and the legislative branch, the Court added, the not very prophetic language:

> we do *not* suggest that the statute was *intended to revolutionise the insurance and pension industries*. All that is at issue today is a requirement that men and women make unequal contributions to an employer-operated pension plan. Nothing in our holding implies that it would be unlawful for an employer to set aside equal retirement contributions for each employee and let each retiree purchase the largest benefit his or her accumulated contributions could command in the open market"[63] *(emphasis supplied)*

We shall frequently refer back to the above italicised language.

Essentially F65 could, under the *Manhart* analysis, receive a smaller periodic payout from her own contributions than M65 — presumably, though this is not stated explicitly, directly from the scheme, and certainly by taking her account to an insurance company and purchasing

---

63. At 718. However, with the exception of a limited group of deferred profit-sharing schemes, all U.S. schemes which are "qualified" under the Internal Revenue Code ("I.R.C."), 26 U.S.C. (as, in practice, all but a few "Top-Hat" schemes must be), are required to provide annuity options directly; they may, but need not, provide lump-sum payouts; and, if they do, must under I.R.C. § 401(a)(11), require spousal consent if the participant is married.

an annuity.[64] She could not, however, be required to contribute 15% more than M65 in order to equalise benefits at retirement. This result seems defensible *as policy*,[65] especially if it were clear from the facts of a particular case, or seemed likely, that the higher contribution would deter a woman from participating in the scheme; this was not the case here, however, since participation in the Los Angeles scheme was compulsory.[66]

(b) Spirt

Spirt v. *TIAA-CREF*,[67] in the Second Circuit Court of Appeals, took a further step by requiring that balances accumulated in a D.C. scheme be applied to produce equal amounts of monthly income for male and female retirees of the same age. The Court quoted earlier language from *Manhart* that "Title VII's 'focus on the individual is unambiguous'", *(citation omitted)*[68] and held that to treat the complaining employee as merely a member of a class — the class of longer living females — was impermissible. The Second Circuit asserted that:

> [e]very federal court that has considered the issue has found that no significant difference exists between unequal contributions for equal [benefit] payments and equal contributions for unequal payments.[69] *(citations[70] omitted)*

It did not reject, distinguish or even discuss the *Manhart* language quoted above promising not to "revolutionise the insurance or pension industries",[71] nor the remainder of the quotation endorsing equal contribu-

---

64. Depending on national law, taking a lump sum settlement and purchasing an annuity outside the scheme may have adverse tax consequences, usually an acceleration of tax on the value of the whole payout rather than taxation of monthly installments as received.

65. Whether it was compelled by the statute is much more debatable.

66. The Court did not consider whether a female employee could be given the *option* of contributing more in order to increase her accumulation at retirement, thereby equalising her monthly benefits with those of a similarly situated male. It might, of course, be argued that fairness to men would then require that they too be given an option: to contribute less and receive correspondingly less.

67. 691 F.2d 1054 (2d Cir. 1982), judgment vacated 463 U.S. 1223 (1983) on remand 735 F.2d 23 (2d Cir. 1984).

68. 691 F.2d at 1060.

69. *id* at 1061

70. All below the Supreme Court level but including *Norris*, n.73, *infra*, in the 9th Circuit, before it reached the Supreme Court.

71. *Manhart* was, of course, a Supreme Court case.

tions for unequal benefits.[72]

(c) Norris

In *Arizona Governing Committee for Tax Deferred Annuity and Compensation Plans* v. *Norris*,[73] the Supreme Court dealt with the issue raised in *Spirt*: unequal benefits resulting from the use of sex-differentiated mortality tables to convert D.C. accumulations at retirement into lifelong monthly benefits. It quoted again language used in *Manhart* that:

> [a]ctuarial studies could unquestionably identify differences in life expectancy based on race or national origin, as well as sex.[74]

perhaps its strongest argument and certainly its most emotive, and essentially endorsed *Spirt*.

In its footnote 4, well known in U.S. pension circles as the "blending" footnote, Justice O'Connor's concurring opinion instructed the actuarial profession as follows:

> I would require employers to use longevity tables that reflect the average longevity of all their workers;[75]

Probably meaning only those participating in the particular scheme, although this is not entirely clear. Thus, if a male is a participant in a predominantly female scheme, he is to be treated as if he were female too; similarly, a female with an identical service history but in a scheme which is predominantly male, is to be treated as if she were male. The much promised focus on the individual is not apparent.

The O'Connor opinion stressed that when annuities were purchased from life insurance companies for Department employees, those annuities were effectively being provided by the employer:

---

72. The opinion also gives, 691 F.2d at 1066 *et seq*, some of the prior history of the case showing a rather undignified tug-of-war between the New York State Insurance Department (under the McCarran - Ferguson Act, 15 U.S.C. § 1011 *et seq.*, the regulation of insurance is generally a matter for State law) and the Equal Employment Opportunity Commission. The relatively new E.E.O.C., getting into a new area, was seeking to impose "unisex" annuity rates, over the objection of a Department, with about a century of insurance experience behind it, which was apparently reluctant to be "revolutionized".

73. 463 U.S. 1073 (1983), appeal after remand 796 F.2d 1119 (9th Cir. 1986).

74. Justice Marshall's concurring opinion, four other justices concurring, at 1083.

75. *Norris, supra*, n.73, at 1111.

76. *id*. at 1109.

In the situation at issue here, the employer has used third-party insurance companies to administer the plan, but the plan remains essentially a 'privileg[e] of employment,' and thus covered by Title VII.[76]

This language was presumably intended to finesse the commitment not to "revolutionise...insurance" to which we have repeatedly referred and to suggest that the scheme and not the insurers were being "revolutionised". The dissent declined the finesse and belaboured the majority with that commitment. It pointed out that the case could be expected to move employers away from life annuities to lump-sum or fixed period payouts and concluded:

> Explicit sexual classifications, to be sure, require close examination but they are not automatically invalid. *(footnote omitted)* Sex-based mortality tables reflect objective actuarial experience. Because their use does not entail *discrimination in any normal understanding of that term*,[77] a court should hesitate to invalidate this long-approved practice on the basis of *its own policy judgment*.

Congress may choose to forbid the use of any sexual classifications in insurance, but nothing suggests that it intended to do so in Title VII. And certainly the policy underlying Title VII provides *no warrant for extending the reach of the statute* beyond Congress's intent.[78] *(emphasis supplied)*

Unfortunately, the O'Connor "swing" vote went the other way and actuarial science went down by the narrowest possible vote of 5:4.

With respect to retroactivity, the four dissenters persuaded O'Connor, producing a 5:4 split in the other direction. She found[79] three standard criteria[80] satisfied:

(1) "a new principle of law...not clearly foreshadowed";

(2) "the goal [future compliance] in no way requires retroactivity"; and,

(3) "retroactive application would impose inequitable results".

---

77. Original footnote 9. "Indeed, if employers and insurance carriers offer annuities based on unisex mortality tables, men *as a class* will receive less aggregate benefits than similarly situated women" *(emphasis supplied)*.

78. *Norris, supra*, n.73, at 1105.

79. At 1109.

80. *cf. Chevron Oil Co.* v. *Huson*, 404 U.S. 97, 105-109 (1971).

Whatever one may think of O'Connor's logic on the basic issue, it is undeniable that her "blending" approach helped to contain the prospective damage of *Norris*, and that her vote on retroactivity avoided financial chaos.

(iv) Manhart, Spirt and Norris: The Common Thread

In all three of the above cases the main, indeed the only, basic argument is the demand for fairness to individuals rather than fairness to classes, combined with a naked assertion that race and sex, not to mention flab, are really comparable. This argument is unsatisfactory, not least because the differences other than sex quoted in the opinions, are not all-or-nothing "binary"[81] differences; rather, they are differences of degree measurable only on a continuous scale. Flabby grades into fit and all attempts to define members of a "race", from the Nürnberg laws to apartheid, have rightly become a laughing stock. On the other hand, sex differences are, Carnaby Street notwithstanding, cut and dried. It is also significant that status *at and after retirement* is the main determinant of ultimate pension cost. It does not follow from the fact that if an individual is fit, flabby or a smoker today, that will be the case at retirement; as to sex (and, concededly, race) it does.

It is noteworthy that despite the announced intention of merely construing the statute, the flabby/fit discussion is clearly a policy argument not relevant to the statute under examination. The *Manhart* Court was, in effect, telling insurance underwriters (inaccurately) how they actually conduct their business — also, advising them (unwisely) on how they should do so. It stated that:

> [t]reating different classes of risks as though they were the same for purposes of group insurance is a common practice that has never been considered inherently unfair.[82]

Precisely so. And the choice of whether to identify and recognise different groups for underwriting purposes has always been left to the underwriter's business judgment, exercised by weighing the business benefits, the cost, and the practical limitations of doing so. Data must be grouped in order to develop meaningful statistics:

> Because there is little valid basis for rating separately most individual insureds, and because the expense of attempting such a separate determination far exceeds any possible advantage in

81. See Westen *supra* n.11, at 16.

82. *Manhart, supra,* n.56, at 710.

terms of fairness, ratemaking practice requires that insureds be grouped in a manner that reflects *essential* differences in actual or probable loss costs and expense.[83] *(emphasis in the original)*

However,

The finer we classify our data the nearer we approach homogeneity, but the smaller the amount of data in each group. What we gain in homogeneity we lose in credibility of our loss experience.[84]

Nothing in this balancing, which is almost second nature to anyone involved in underwriting risks of any kind, suggests a rationale for deliberately closing one's eyes to significant, easily identifiable characteristics of a proposed insured or group of proposed insureds.

In underwriting one individual, it is practical, indeed essential for any decent-sized risk, to analyse medical and other individual data — including flab — in order to place that individual in the appropriate risk class; for a large group it is often not cost effective to do so for all members, although it may well be appropriate in, say, group life insurance, to individually underwrite some of the largest risks. This is not true as to sex:[85] it is very easy and virtually cost free to establish the kind of differentiation which occurred in *Manhart*.[86]

The basic fallacy in the Supreme Court's analysis is that it ignores the fact that when an individual participates in a risk sharing enterprise, he does so as, *and only as,* a member of a class.[87] To treat a purchaser of

83.   C.A. Kulp & J.W. Hall, *Casualty Insurance*, (New York: The Ronald Press, 4th Ed. 1968) at 778.

84.   L.H. Longley-Cook, "Notes on Some Actuarial Problems of Property Insurance", *Fire Insurance Rate Making and Kindred Problems*, (New York: Casualty Actuarial Society, 1960) at 89.

85.   If this were not so, the Los Angeles Department and most other employers might well have done, voluntarily and for common-sense reasons, what the Department was eventually forced to do in *Norris*. It would not have engaged in a lengthy and expensive struggle on behalf of what it considered, based on professional actuarial and other advice, to be sound business practice.

86.   For this reason, the remainder of the Supreme Court's paragraph:

"To insure the flabby and the fit as though they were equivalent risks may be more common than treating men and women alike; but nothing more than habit makes one 'subsidy' seem less fair than the other." *(footnotes omitted)*

is not just incorrect; it is unsupported and insupportable.

87.   Even when Lloyd's of London insures such well known "one-off" risks as Betty Grable's legs, the underwriters will only do so if they have a large number of risks in the same experience pool. To take such a single risk alone without such pooling, rather than a collection of them, however disparate, would be pure gambling, not underwriting.

fire or life insurance or a member of a pension scheme as anything other than a member of a class leads immediately to absurd results.

Would anyone seriously argue that if 500 people purchase fire insurance and only one house burns down during the policy period, 499 people have been swindled?[88] If we ignore, using our Supreme Court blinkers, the fact that they have voluntarily avoided risk (it might be more accurate to say shared or pooled risk) by becoming members of the class of policyholders, and we focus on them simply as individuals who have sustained no loss but have had premiums taken from them "for nothing", that absurd result is compelled.

Should a focus on individuals lead to the conclusion that owners of wooden houses should not be charged a larger premium than owners of brick houses on the ground that some individuals' wooden houses do not in fact burn down, but some brick ones do?

Closer to home, should a D.C. retirement scheme covering the U.S. Supreme Court give equal lifetime benefits from the same accumulations to the Justices and to their young clerks on the theory that some Justices retiring at 65 or 70 years of age have lived a further 15 years, while some of their clerks leaving before age 30 have lasted fewer than that? Under *Manhart*, of course, "the statute's focus on the individual is unambiguous."[89]

To ask such questions is to answer them, but this did not inhibit the Supreme Court from saying:

> Even if the statutory language were less clear, the *basic policy* of the statute requires that we focus on fairness to individuals rather than fairness to classes.[90] *(emphasis supplied)*

However, one of the basic requirements of a fairness/equality test is an R.S.M.[91] and that standard must be applied *before* the outcomes are known when we are dealing with contingent events involving probabilities. The equality issue then becomes nothing more and nothing less than: were the *individuals* placed in the right *class*?

It is not suggested that the Supreme Court would actually endorse the above absurd results. However, it is submitted that when the analysis

---

88. Such an analysis would lead to a premium, to be refunded to all except those policyholders who incur claims, equal to the anticipated cost of a full claim, plus expenses and less anticipated investment earnings to the extent they were not also refunded to non-claimants — a novel actuarial approach to say the least, making nonsense of the whole concept of insurance/risk sharing.

89. *Manhart, supra*, n.56, at 708.

90. *id.* at 709.

91. *supra*, n.15.

mutatis mutandis supports them, it should be viewed very sceptically. It is recognised that the business of the law is often to draw a line at a point in a continuous spectrum and say that conduct on one side is prohibited while that on the other side is not. The line, once drawn as it must be, can always be attacked by taking two close cases on either side of the line and charging arbitrariness and inconsistency because the results conflict; this is an occupational hazard for judges and lawyers. However, the Supreme Court's argument of comparing sex differences to the far removed issue of "race" (whatever that means), which carries a subliminal accusation of racism against defenders of sex differentiation of the kind discussed here, is even more misleading at the other extreme: it compares two radically different items with only a superficial resemblance. It is indefensible to suggest that the conduct of the sponsors of the schemes in our three cases was closer to racial discrimination than to the recognition of age as a major, indeed the most fundamental, variable which must be reflected in the design of retirement schemes; also of life insurance and health and disability insurance. This is a textbook example of the illegitimate use of Westen's "Semantic Bias in Favor of Equality",[92] resulting in unfair distortion of the majority, indeed the generally accepted, actuarial position.

It is hardly more defensible to graft onto Congressional support for civil rights, an intent to treat actuarially based recognition of sex differences as closer to racial discrimination than to simple recognition that providing a lifetime benefit to a youngster is likely, though not certain, to prove more expensive than providing the same benefit to that youngster's grandparent; also that this is certain, not just likely, where large groups are concerned.[93] This is especially so when one of the leaders of that

---

92. *supra*, n.11, at 274.

93. Perhaps the best way to illustrate the problem with the Supreme Court's race-based analysis is to visualise a hypothetical benevolent English sovereign, enraptured by the *Norris* analysis, issuing decrees on pensions shortly after 1066. (The reader is respectfully reminded that he cannot, by definition, argue with the facts of a hypothetical.) No doubt those decrees would have forbidden any discrimination in benefits, contributions and options (a) between Normans and Saxons and (b) between males and females. It is submitted that provision (a) would have proved merely an intelligent anticipation, and perhaps acceleration, of future developments, the increasing fuzziness of the distinction between Normans and Saxons and its eventual disappearance; also, that despite initial grumbling, opposition would have quickly faded. Provision (b), on the other hand, would not have proved intelligent and opposition would not have faded; female retirees would have continued for centuries to be better off avoiding expensive, inequitable and unscientifically calculated settlement options; in effect, they would have been denied these options except at indefensible prices.

All of this is not to deny that the modern equivalent of provision (b) above may conceivably prove to be an intelligent anticipation; how soon, if at all, is another question. The Supreme Court could be correct that women's exposure to tobacco and work-related stress may equalise 21st (or 22nd or 23rd) century mortality rates but this is at

Congress expressly disavows any such intent and no other member contradicts.[94]

Actuaries given their mathematical training, frequently analyse issues by means of *reductio ad absurdum*, a technique which is, unfortunately, under-utilised in the law. *Norris*, especially the famous footnote 4,
offers a textbook opportunity to apply the method. As noted earlier, this
footnote recommends that each employer use "longevity tables" based
on the make up of *its own* actual workforce which, in terms of our model,
means that if an M65 happens to work for a company where the workforce
is almost entirely female, he will be treated just as if he were female.[95]
Conversely, if F65 happens to work for an almost entirely male company,
she will be treated just as if she were male. This means that each will be
unreasonably subsidised or, depending on the form of benefit, unreasonably penalised by being treated not equally, but rather unequally as if
(s)he were a member of the opposite sex living in a rational world. This
may be a triumph for the new concept of unisex; if so, its rationale es-
capes this writer and most actuaries.[96]

8. EQUALITY IN THE D.B. CONTEXT

It is important to recognise that in all of the above discussion of the
American statute and decisions, the R.S.M. has been simply the contri-

best uncertain. Should the phenomenon actually occur, the actuarial profession is likely
to be the first to discover it. As yet, there seems to be nothing to report.

Studies by a major U.S. Life Insurance Company for the period 1965-70 have been
provided to the writer, on a basis which unfortunately does not allow direct attribution,
showing that there was no detectible difference between the mortality of female primary annuitants, who were all in the labour force, and female beneficiaries, most but
not all of whom were not. The study also mentions that "a [then] recent study of Rail-
road Retirement Board beneficiaries shows slightly *longer* life expectancies at all ages
60 and over for female retired employees than for wives and widows of male retired
employees." (emphasis supplied). A more recent published study also showed differences by sex between actively employed people over the period 1970-74, somewhat
higher than those shown for the general population in U.S. Life Tables 1959/61 - 1969/
71, E.A. Lew & L. Garfinkel, "Differences in Mortality and Longevity by Sex, Smoking
Habits and Health Status", *Transactions of the Society of Actuaries*, Vol. XXXIX, p. 107
(1987).

94. See *supra*.

95. Even *Spirt* acknowledges that:

"(a)n inequity might also arise if a group were so female dominated that retroactive use
of unisex tables would cause a substantial reduction even of unspecified benefit levels
of males." 735 F.2d 23, 28.

Partial inequities are not discussed; for example, the corresponding 50% inequity in a
conventional employer with an evenly divided workforce.

96. At the risk of an excess of mathematical terminology, Q.E.D!

butions flowing into the account of each participating employee. We noted that there is general acceptance that in a D.C. scheme with equal contributions, M65 and M60 will eventually receive different monthly benefits if their benefits are paid as monthly annuities on an actuarial basis. Even when the American F65's monthly benefits were forced into an artificial equality with those of M65 rather than those of M60, this was done by what we argued was a distortion of the calculations — not by forcing the allocation of higher contributions to her account. Indeed, we saw in *Manhart* that unequal contributions were anathema when paid directly by the employee and it now seems equally clear in the U.S. that such unequal contributions would also be anathema if paid by an employer into a conventional D.C. account. Yet the U.S. cases give no hint of an objection to the fact that in *Manhart* the lifetime monthly benefit amount was the same for both male and female employees although there was clear recognition that the benefits paid to female employees were significantly more expensive to the employer than those of males.[97]

In dealing with defined benefit schemes, this implicit definition of equality as equal inflow of contributions is largely abandoned. The focus becomes one on equality of benefits flowing out of the scheme at retirement; more precisely, on the monthly benefit rate of outflow. In virtually all D.B. schemes employees such as M65 and F65 will receive the same monthly benefits at retirement age. If benefit outflow is adopted as the standard, this necessarily means that the employer contributions required to support F65's benefits will be about 15% higher than those for M65. Some D.B. schemes may also grant unreduced early retirement benefits, *i.e.* may give M60 the same monthly benefit as M65, again requiring an increase in contribution to the same level as for F65.[98] Other D.B. benefit formulae give rise to such variances in cost. Here also, benefits may seem equitable when the examination focuses on them as benefits, but the associated costs often seem anomalous if the scheme is viewed through D.C. spectacles.

If this basic change to benefit outflow as the standard used to define equality (the R.S.M.) is not acceptable, there is simply no way in which defined benefit schemes can be accepted as equitable. Either this new R.S.M. must be applied to analyse equality under D.B. schemes, and the old focus on contributions must be dropped; or, the whole D.B. concept must be rejected as incapable, by definition, of producing anything acceptable as equality. This is, perhaps, the only fundamental policy deci-

97. Equal benefits to F60 as to M65 — no longer found in North America but still, as we have noted, common in some of the Member States — are obviously even more costly.

98. In most countries military pensions are granted on this basis and the same is often true of other uniformed personnel such as police and fire-fighters. Such benefits based on service alone are often referred to as "service pensions".

sion on sex equality in the pension area which has to be faced.[99] The heated debate in our three U.S. cases — and, as we shall see later, in the European cases and in the commentary — does not deal with this fundamental issue; it bogs down in what are really just minor secondary consequences[100] of an unspoken and unexamined assumption that equal monthly benefits should be permitted.

If this alternative standard is accepted, the *necessary* consequence is that the total cost of employing an older worker covered by a D.B. scheme will exceed that of his otherwise identical younger counterpart simply because the cost of providing his D.B. pension is higher.[101] This does not mean that we have inequality *under our definition*: as we noted in Section IV *supra*, our selection of the R.S.M. used to define equality has, since we knew in advance where it would be applied, pre-judged the issue of equality favourably to the D.B. design.

Similarly, the cost of a female employee will be higher than that of her male counterpart, otherwise identical in all respects including age; the cost of her D.B. pension will exceed that of the male[102] simply because she has a higher life expectancy but this does not mean that equality is lost, unless we establish a different R.S.M., such as cost inflow, which defines it away.

In *Manhart*[103] the Los Angeles Department had, in effect, established as its R.S.M. for measurement of differences in treatment *between individuals of the same age*, cost inflow; but had maintained benefit outflow as the standard for age differences. By these definitions, it had achieved equality and the necessary consequence was a difference in benefits by sex at each age. Its policy decision was to subsidise older employees by contributing more for them but to do so, it would say, in a way which subsidised older males and older females "equally." Its implicit definition of equality — its R.S.M. — seems clearly within the realm of reason and is, therefore, an area where, in the words of the *Norris* dissent, "a court should hesitate to invalidate (a) long-approved practice on the basis of its own policy judgment,"[104] especially, perhaps, a 5:4 policy judg-

99. In a Community context it amounts to a decision whether Article 119's "equal(ity of) pay" does or does not demand equality of contribution inflow as the only acceptable R.S.M.

100. Usually involving cash-outs and other optional forms of benefit.

101. As is the cost of some other employee benefits such as life or health insurance if the same benefits are provided to all, or a broad range of, ages.

102. The unisex gyrations which we will discuss in detail later do not affect this basic fact. They simply make nonsense of some of its secondary consequences.

103. *supra*, n.56.

104. *supra*, n.73.

ment.[105]

The earlier discussion of *Manhart* focused on the employee contributions and treated them as essentially a separate D.C. scheme, noting at the time that this was not the full story. In fact, the scheme was D.B., financed by contributions from employer and employees. Benefits at retirement, therefore, cost about 15% more for females than males, which was the rationale for requiring 15% higher contributions from female employees. When the Court eliminated the higher female employee contributions, the extra cost of their benefits did not magically vaporise; an additional piece of the overall cost was simply transferred from the female participants to the employer.[106]

The thrust of the three U.S. cases discussed above was greatly expanded in I.R.C. § 401(a)(25)[107] requiring all option factors to be in the plan document and limiting amendment. The Internal Revenue Service insists, citing our three cases, that these factors be unisex although as yet the requirement appears in neither the parts of the I.R.C. dealing with pensions, nor in the associated Treasury Regulations.[108]

Although the cases dealt primarily with D.C. schemes, the main effects of these new requirements were on D.B. schemes. Most dramatic was the requirement that lump-sum settlements of D.B. benefits be based on sex-neutral factors. In terms of our model plan, this means that if

105. Once again the above discussion is oversimplified in that it ignores the fact that D.B. schemes are not typically funded by means of deposits to individual accounts. In reality, a variety of actuarial techniques are used to balance contributions or ranges of contribution with the total benefit outflow and, as the assets of the scheme build up, they are treated as a single pool dedicated to providing all benefits.

   The discussion could be made technically purer by substituting "the marginal long-term increase in the cost of the scheme attributable to individual x's participation" or similar language for "x's cost".

106. For a benefit costing, say, 100,000 units at retirement for a male and 115,000 for a similarly situated female, the employer's accumulated cost (contributions accumulated at interest) would be 80,000 for the male (100,000 less, say, 20,000 from the employee) and 92,000 for the female (115,000 less 23,000). The effect of *Manhart* would be to change the cost to the employer, at retirement, of the female employee to 95,000 (the same 115,000 less only 20,000 from the employee). Assuming that the concept of the D.B. scheme is accepted and equity is defined in terms of outflow, there is no fundamental objection to this, indeed it is the cost and benefit pattern which most employers choose for contributory schemes. However, to *impose* it on a scheme which the employer adopted voluntarily in the first place, is clearly more dubious. Discussion of pension matters often becomes more down to earth when it is recalled that not maintaining any scheme at all, is always an option.

107. Which codified the requirement of Revenue Ruling 79-90, 1979-1 C.B. 156, that a D.B. scheme must spell out the actuarial assumptions used to compute optional forms of benefit "in a way that precludes employer discretion."

108. Although the actuarial tables appearing in Treas. Reg. § 1.72-4 *et seq.* dealing with annuity and other periodic payments, including those from retirement plans, are unisex.

M65 and F65 are entitled to the same monthly benefit under a D.B. scheme and F65's benefits have, therefore, been funded by larger contributions leading to a larger build up of assets to provide her benefits, F65 must, nevertheless, receive exactly the same lump-sum settlement as M65 if both elect to cash out. F65's cash-out will, therefore, produce a windfall to the scheme of the order of our recurring 15%.[109] When a woman elects a lump-sum "cash out" from a D.B. scheme, she generally does so because she prefers to provide her own benefits, making her own investment decisions, and she is willing to take[110] the risk of "outliving her expectancy." Because her expectancy is higher than that of an otherwise identical male, she needs more funds to do so than he would; more funds will have been accumulated in the scheme for her;[111] therefore, taking those extra funds away from her is absurd on its face. It is apparent that the public perception of the new requirements as being generally favourable to female employees is incorrect in this instance. The same is true of many other optional forms of benefit.[112]

9. Pension Benefits Under the EC Treaty

This paper argued earlier that the U.S. Supreme Court's approach to the Civil Rights Act of 1964 was, despite its protestations, more akin to

109. Or, under the "blending" approach of the O'Connor footnote, *supra* n.75, there will be an attempt to neutralise the effect on the scheme by robbing Paulette to a lesser extent and paying the resulting smaller windfall to Peter rather than to the scheme.

110. Or, perhaps, to insure against.

111. It is assumed that the scheme is well funded since, if it is not, cash outs will probably not be offered.

112. A clear example is the situation of a retiree who wishes to elect a reduction in his/her pension to provide a survivor pension to a spouse, *i.e.* to trade each 1,000 units of monthly benefit for a reduced benefit such as 800 units to him/her with 800 continuing to the spouse under a "100% survivor option" or about 888 with a 444 continuation under a 50% option (actual reduction factors depend on the actual age combinations). For the typical M65 retiree/F62 spouse combination, the reduction in M65's pension should be much greater than would apply to a F65 retiree/M62 spouse situation because the probabilities of payout to a survivor are vastly different; nevertheless, the new U.S. rules require that an identical factor be used for each. The M65/F62 combination must be heavily subsidised to the detriment of the scheme; F65/M62 must be gouged to the benefit of the scheme; or, the baby must be divided. In practice, this will not be the result. M65s will take their equitable, subsidised or partially subsidised "blended" factors. F65s who are not wealthy enough to have sophisticated financial advice may well take unfavourable survivor options under their pension schemes; those who are wealthy or lucky enough to be well advised, will take their full pensions from the scheme and will purchase life insurance to provide survivor benefits from an insurance company on a sex-differentiated basis reflecting the actual risk. Note 147, *infra*, describes an actual example of such "anti-selection". (At the time of writing, the first half of the Supreme Court's commitment not to "revolutionize the insurance and pension industries" remains good as to life insurance purchased outside pension schemes).

constitutional analysis than to conventional statutory construction. The relevant part of the Treaty, unlike the American statute, is a relatively short statement of a general principle and not subject to frequent amendment and fine tuning. Whether the Treaty should be viewed as a constitution is beyond the scope of this paper;[113] there is, however, little question that it is closer than is the U.S. Civil Rights Act. It is legitimate, therefore, for the E.C.J. to approach its task of construing Article 119 in a more constitutional and policy oriented way. It should obviously begin its analysis by looking to the intent of its founding fathers to the extent that that intent can be determined, but it can be expected that the farther it is from the drafting of the Treaty the more likely it is to develop results which would surprise the drafters.[114]

Even though the American analysis may, therefore, be more apposite to European cases than it was when first applied at home, this paper will continue to argue that taken as a statement of policy it remains fundamentally unsound — no less, and perhaps more so, than when treated as statutory construction.

(i) Article 119 in General

As noted at the outset, Article 119 mandates equal pay for men and women; it defines the term "pay" to include:

> salary and any other consideration, whether in cash or in kind, which the worker receives, directly or indirectly, from his employer.

The Court has had no difficulty in holding that this Article meets all the requirements for "direct effect" of the *Van Gend en Loos* case;[115] that is, that it is sufficiently precise that it "must be interpreted as producing direct effects and creating individual rights which national courts must protect"[116] without waiting for national implementing legislation. It has

---

113. See, G.F. Mancini, "The Making of a Constitution for Europe", 26 C.M.L. Rev. 595 (1989) and T.C. Hartley, "Federalism, Courts and Legal Systems: The Emerging Constitution of the European Community", 34 Am.J.Comp. Law 229 (1986).

114. Not an unusual situation. As Felix Frankfurter remarked in his landmark book on the Interstate Commerce Clause (U.S. Constitution, Article 1, Section 8), referring to Marshall's use of the clause:

"It was an audacious doctrine which, one may be sure, would hardly have been publicly avowed in support of the adoption of the Constitution", F. Frankfurter, *The Commerce Clause*, (Quadrangle, 1964) at 19.

115. Case 96/80, *Jenkins* v. *Kingsgate (Clothing Productions) Ltd.*, [1981] E.C.R. 911.

116. Case 26/62, *Van Gend & Loos* v. *Nederlandse Administratie der Belastingen*, [1963] E.C.R. 1, 12.

also extended the reach of the Article broadly, even beyond conventional fringe benefits to such areas as travel concessions to former employees which were not contractual obligations of the employer.[117]

(ii) Pensions as "Pay"

Given this broad reach, there seems very little doubt that an employer's pension commitments would similarly fall under Article 119 and numerous cases have so held.[118] However, the Article itself gives no indication whether only the simplest of our measures of equality for pension purposes — equality of contribution inflow — is acceptable as the measure of equal pay, or whether equality of inflow or equality of benefit outflow are equally acceptable. As shown earlier, it is typically impossible to satisfy both yardsticks at the same time. This situation cries out for secondary legislation under Article 119, preferably a directive.[119]

(iii) The Four Directives

Four major directives have substantially expanded the reach of Community equalities law but without, unfortunately, providing or even laying a foundation for, the basic guidance suggested above.

(a) The First "Equal Pay" Directive

Directive 75/117/EEC[120] expanded the concept of equal pay to embrace equal pay for work of equal value. This major expansion of the reach of Article 119 followed, as the commentary on Article 119 in the Common Market Reporter points out, Article 2(1) of the International Labour Organisation Convention[121] which did cover work of equal value. In *Worringham*[122] the Court approved this expansion saying:

---

117. Case 12/81, *Garland* v. *British Railways Ltd.* [1982] E.C.R. 359.

118. For example, Case 170/84, *Bilka-Kaufhaus* v. *Weber von Hartz*, [1986] E.C.R. 1607, citing numerous other cases.

119. It seems sensible to specify in such secondary legislation that benefit outflow generally be the yardstick for D.C. schemes and contribution inflow for D.C. with some exceptions for special types of scheme such as "target plans" which are beyond the scope of this paper. In the U.S. failure to do so has led to great difficulty in the recently proposed, then final, then reproposed Treasury Regulation (in the American sense of that term) § 1.401(a)(4).

120. O.J. 1975 L 45/19, which takes as its legal basis Article 100, providing for "the approximation of...law, regulation or administrative action in Member States...affect(ing)...the common market."

121. No. 100, 1951, U.N.T.S. Vol 165, 303.

122. Case 69/80, [1981] E.C.R. 767, 790.

> [a]lthough Article 1 of the directive explains that the concept of 'same work' contained in the first paragraph of Article 119…includes cases of 'work to which equal value can be attributed', it in no way affects the concept of 'pay' contained in the second paragraph … but refers by implication to that concept.

This broad approval was not, as we shall see, forthcoming for less expansive Community legislation.

(b)   The Second "Equal Treatment" Directive

Directive 76/207/EEC[123] established the principle of equal treatment of men and women with respect to: access to employment, vocational training, dismissal, *etc.* Its Article 2(2) makes explicit that Member States may make exclusions where sex is a "determining factor".[124]

(c)   The Third "Social Security" Directive

Directive 79/7/EEC[125] is directed towards equality under governmental social security schemes. Its Article 7(1) permits the maintenance of different pensionable ages for men and women but Article 9 requires Member States to:

> inform the Commission of their reasons for maintaining any existing provisions on the matters referred to in Article 7(1) and of the possibilities of reviewing them at a later date.

— about as broad a hint as can be imagined of the drafters' view on the issue. This directive does not reach other actuarial unisex issues, which is not surprising since optional forms of benefit are not an issue in most governmental schemes.[126] However, in the first paragraph of its judgment in the recent *Van Cant*[127] case, the Court invalidated, citing Articles 4(1) and 7(1) of the Third Directive, Belgian legislation "which permits male and female workers to retire at identical ages [while] maintaining

---

123. O.J. 1976 L 39/40.

124. Which would effectively silence the Gender Fairness League of Ruritania's worst excesses.

125. O.J. 1979 L 6/24.

126. Particularly lump-sum cash outs and joint and survivor options. The former are, of course, not available at all; the latter are typically given automatically to married couples, without any actuarial reduction in the primary annuitant's benefit.

127. Case 154/92, *Van Cant v. Rijksdienst voor pensloenen*, nyr. Provisional English translation, O.J. 1993 C 204/10.

in the method for calculating the pension a difference depending on sex, such difference being linked to the difference ... under the previous legislation;" also a broad hint, it appears, that the Court is not sympathetic to the delays which the Third Directive permits. Apparently once a Member State has begun to equalise, no half measures will be allowed.

(d) The Fourth "Occupational Scheme" Directive

Directive 86/378/EEC[128] provides guidance in the area of employer sponsored schemes not covered by the Third Directive. In fact, its Article 9, permitting deferral of equal pensionable ages until equal ages are introduced in statutory schemes or required by a directive, was clearly designed to avoid inconsistencies between the acceptance in the Third Directive of sex-distinct pensionable ages in governmental schemes and the treatment of the same issue in occupational schemes covering the same workforce. This directive also permitted, in its Article 6, sex distinct benefits flowing out of D.C. schemes as a result of using distinct actuarial factors and the use of different levels of *employer* contributions, also in D.C. schemes, in order to equalise benefit outflow.

(e) Direct Effect of Directives

The *Van Gend en Loos*[129] case which announced the principle of direct effect of Treaty provisions was not an equalities case, but one of the leading cases on direct effect of directives was: *Marshall*[130] which held that a woman could not be compulsorily retired at a younger age than would have applied to a similarly situated man. The Court held that:

> a directive may not of itself impose obligations on an individual ...[but]...where a person involved in legal proceedings is able to rely on a directive as against the state he may do so regardless of the capacity in which the latter is acting, whether employer or public authority. In either case it is necessary to prevent the state from taking advantage of its own failure to comply with Community law.[131]

This Estoppel view of direct effect gives rise to great difficulties in identifying "the state" for these purposes, causing such unnecessary prob-

128. O.J. 1986 L 225/40.

129. *supra*, n.116.

130. Case 152/84, *Marshall v. Southampton and South-West Hants. Area Health Authority*, [1986] E.C.R. 723.

131. *id.* at 749.

lems as those arising from privatisation.

A better approach might be to allow the rationale of *Francovich*,[132] which awarded compensatory damages against the Italian State for the detriment suffered by the plaintiff resulting from a failure to implement a directive, to subsume *Marshall* and similar cases.This would mean treating Mrs. Marshall's claim as one against the British Government for the same kind of damages recovered in *Francovich*, without reference to the question of whether the Authority was or was not an organ of the State. Mrs. Marshall, presumably, would not care whether her cheque came from London or Southampton although the Authority's budget director might.[133]

(iv) The Basic Pension Issue under Article 119

It seems clear that when otherwise identical male and female employees receive equal credits to their accounts under a D.C. retirement scheme, those credits can be viewed as deferred pay satisfying Article 119 with ease. However, as shown earlier, there is a fundamental decision to be made whether equal periodic benefit payouts to our M65 and F65 under a D.B. scheme with their attendant variances in the contributions required to support them (also, under "service" schemes, equal payouts to M65 and M60), can be considered equitable. M65 v. F65 is clearly an Article 119 issue. M65 v. M60 raises issues of fairness but not Treaty issues; as before, it is raised here primarily for the light it sheds on sex-equality issues. The Court could conceivably have taken a very hard line; measured equality only by contribution inflow for Article 119 purposes; and effectively required that all European retirement schemes be D.C. with equal contributions, *i.e.* required that the R.S.M. for equality among M65, F65, M60 and all other employees be equal contribution inflows.[134]

It would be logical to so reject D.B. schemes as inherently unfair and, in effect, to demand that all retirement schemes be D.C. but, in the European context where many pension arrangements are not pre-funded, this should logically lead to a flat prohibition on any kind of salary

---

132. Case 6/90, *Francovich v. Italy*, [1991] E.C.R. I-5357.

133. This approach also is more likely to hold the line against the pernicious doctrine of horizontal direct effect which could punish an innocent third party, usually an employer, for the failure of the state to implement a directive even though he had no means of knowing of its existence. It seems that such an injured party would then have as strong a claim against the state as Mrs Francovich. There seems no sensible reason to have him involved at all.

134. It is hoped that the Court would not then follow the U.S. Supreme Court by requiring artificially equalised annuity purchase rates (*i.e.* equality of outflow) between M65 and F65 and prohibiting recognition of the essential identity, for pension purposes,between F65 and M60, thus immediately discarding its insistence on equity.

continuation for retirees, including arrangements which are not pre-funded. Half-pay at retirement for a typical long-service retiree is either inherently unfair to other workers or it is not. If it is, then to provide it by means of a pre-funded arrangement or directly must be equally unacceptable, and an employer who does the second must be deterred since; in both cases, the payment is in consideration of earlier services and, therefore, "pay" under Article 119. If defined benefits are not to be provided in an unfunded situation, the question arises: what is? Payouts based on some kind of hypothetical D.C. accumulation of contributions which never actually took place? If so, on what assumptions?[135]

Recognising that Article 119 deals only with sex and not age, the Court could require that the *cost* of our M65's and F65's benefits be equalised; that is, that F65s receive 15% lower monthly benefits based on equal contributions, but equal lump-sum cashouts. This would implicitly assume — without, it is submitted, any logical compulsion to do so — that the objective of the exercise[136] is to treat F65 equally with M65 (with contributions as the R.S.M.), and not equally with M60. This even though, as we have demonstrated at length, F65 and M60 are far closer from a pension point of view, especially in a D.C. or a "service pension"[137] context where M60's benefits are not subject to actuarial reduction because of age.

It is submitted that the most equitable, and also the least disruptive, approach would be to treat equality of *benefit outflow* as an acceptable, but not necessarily the only, R.S.M.[138] to determine equality under Article 119. This seems an ideal area for a directive under that Article and/or an explicit endorsement of the approach by the Court. Logically, this should imply, absent gyrations of the *Spirt* and *Norris* type, higher employer contributions and lump-sum settlements for females.

(v) European Commentary

However unsatisfactory the logic of our three American cases may be, it is undeniable that they have greatly influenced European commentators. Unfortunately, none of these commentators discuss the use of benefit outflow as a standard of equality.

Curtin[139] draws heavily on *Manhart* and *Norris* in her discussion of

135. Again, we have a classic *reductio ad absurdum* demonstrating, it is suggested, that an R.S.M. based on benefit outflow cannot, in practice, be totally rejected.

136. More precisely, the legal requirement which a plan sponsor must observe in establishing his objectives.

137. See n.98 *supra*.

138. Making it the only standard would, of course, outlaw D.C. schemes.

139. "Occupational Pension Schemes and Article 119: Beyond the Fringe?" [1987] C.M.L. Rev 216.

the unisex issue — the main focus of her article. A weakness of her analysis is that she fails to differentiate between: *(a)* areas, primarily "equal
access," where different treatment of males and females is a hangover of
obsolete social attitudes;[140] and *(b)* areas where differences reflect well
established differences in the cost of providing benefits based on an analysis of the expectancies and probabilities. For example, she decries the
fact that: "not only may there be differential treatment in the availability
of ... an allocation or surrender option ... but *the terms are frequently calculated on an actuarial basis*" *(emphasis supplied)*; as opposed, presumably, to
some kind of real basis apparent only to her.[141]

A second problem is that, like the U.S. Supreme Court, she fails to
appreciate that there is no inequity in the different benefits actually paid
to members of a properly selected class because their *actual* experience
falls above or below the *expected* results for the class (each individual's
experience always does). There can be gross inequities when classes with
radically different expected results are forced into combination.[142] Again,
we must apply a coherent R.S.M. and we must apply it at the appropriate
time: before the event, if probabilities are involved.

Curtin's argument that "men do not subsidize women more under
such [mortality] tables than short-lived men can now be said to subsidize
long-lived men. Is not the eventuality implicit in any insurance arrangement that some participants will obtain more than others for the
same contributions?"[143] is simply wrong. The argument is incoherent:
the second sentence is true but it does not support the assertion of the
first. The fallacy is obvious to anyone trained in decision making under
uncertainty, be (s)he statistician, actuary or bookmaker, and it comes
down to misuse of the term "subsidy". Short-lived pensioners do not *subsidise* long-lived; they simply begin their benefit payouts at the same time
and on the same terms, but eventually develop less satisfactory outcomes;

140. At the risk of undue repetition, this writer agrees with her *as a matter of policy* on unequal pensionable ages in all types of scheme, even though it will clearly be some time
before equalisation comes to pass; but has serious reservations about the notion that
the Treaty can properly be interpreted to foreclose the opposite view.

141. One must wonder whether, had her focus been on the Billingsgate market rather than
the pension market, she would have made a similar distinction between fishmonger-
established prices and some separate reality, divorced from unreal distinctions introduced by specialists in fish — insisting eventually, perhaps, on averaging out the price
of caviar and catfish roe.

142. An obvious example is the hypothetical U.S.S.C. retirement scheme dealt with *supra*.
Even if it is established, after the fact, that old Justice X did outlive young clerk Y, it
would still have been inequitable to combine the classes of Justices and clerks. The
judgment as to equity must be made when the classifications are made and not after
the fact, when the actual experience of each individual is known — for the same reason
that the bookmaker establishes his odds before the race and not after.

143. *supra,* n.139, at 228.

this means, in effect, that they *lose* to the more fortunate people.[144] In exactly the same way, losers at the racetrack do not, in any meaningful sense of the word, subsidise winners; they simply lose to them.[145] It is only if the odds at which they place their bets are unscientific — when evaluated before the race — that any subsidy occurs. The U.S. Supreme Court's contribution to the pension world, applauded by Curtin,[146] has simply been to make the odds unscientific and thus inadvertently to introduce real, honest-to-goodness subsidies (often flowing in the opposite direction from that intended[147]). Finally, Curtin repeats the error of the U.S. Supreme Court in failing to distinguish between characteristics measured on a binary scale and those which reflect a continuous spectrum.[148]

Ellis[149] repeats many of the above errors with respect to pension actuarial issues. Like Curtin, she does not deal with the fundamental issue of a benefit-based R.S.M. for D.B. schemes. Without any such foundation and without discussing its legal basis, she makes a harsh attack on the Fourth Directive[150] as "mere secondary legislation" which "*purports* to contain exceptions which, in light of the *Barber* decision are *all* now of very dubious validity." *(emphasis supplied)*[151] She categorically denounces (the full quote is at the end of this paragraph), without specifying whether she is discussing D.C. or D.B. schemes, all unequal employer contributions.[152] This is indefensible. With respect to virtually all D.B. schemes, it

---

144. The pension scheme is only an intermediary which exists for the purpose of pooling experience for classes of retirees; it channels funds accumulated on the basis of expectancies, to provide actual benefits to both the short-lived "losers" and the long-lived "winners", knowing, in advance, that there will be such, *but not knowing who they will be* (unless, of course, the U.S.S.C. has stacked the deck).

145. The bookmaker, provided that he is really making book, *i.e.* balancing his book scientifically and not gambling for his own account, is also just an intermediary.

146. And, as we shall see on page , by the Advocate General in *Coloroll*.

147. For example, one of the New York City employees most closely involved in arguing for the city in the case of *Women in City Government United et al. v. City of New York et al.*, 75 Civ. 2868 (MJL), told the writer recently that he was the recipient of such an artificial subsidy. His pension was inflated by well over 10% as a result of a settlement which conceded the unisex issue after *Norris* came down. When he retired later, he was well aware of his opportunity for anti-selection and elected a 100% Joint and Survivor option; he confirms that had his wife been the primary annuitant, she would never have considered J&S options. (Note 112, *supra*, gives an explanation of these options).

148. See n.81, *supra*.

149. E. Ellis, *European Community Sex Equality Law*, (Oxford Univ. Press, 1991).

150. *supra*, n.128.

151. At 55.

152. At 57.

is a simple fact that today contributions must be unequal by sex.[153] In D.C. schemes which as Ellis seems to overlook is the context of the passage she discusses, it is also demonstrably incorrect. It seems inconceivable that Article 119 could be held to prohibit even a D.C. scheme with unequal contributions designed to produce identical benefits to males and females *with no other optional provisions*; such a scheme would produce benefits to each sex which were identical in all respects.

With a clarifying but non-distorting addition, Ellis's statement that: "an employer [providing identical benefits by] paying a higher contribution for a woman employee is in effect discriminating against an equivalently placed male employee", simply collapses. The alleged problem does not exist, unless and until optional forms introduce what we called earlier "minor secondary consequences".

This paper does not suggest that government should abdicate completely in this area and give the sponsors of schemes, or their actuaries or other pension professionals, a completely free hand. It does maintain, however, that government should be cautious about overriding professional judgment, especially when the results of doing so have been shown in the U.S. to be illogical, sometimes to the point of absurdity. As a leading actuary has noted:[154]

> Classification systems used by insurance organisations have always been considered a matter on which the public has a legitimate interest. Government has given insurance regulators the responsibility to see that insurance pricing is adequate but not exorbitant, and that it is not *unfairly discriminatory*. Because the principle of homogeneity of risk is sometimes in direct conflict with public *perceptions* of fairness or justice, classification systems used by insurance organisations have been under considerable attack in recent years.

> Part of the reason is that the civil rights movement has effectively outlawed discrimination in many areas, especially th[ose] based on race, sex, national origin, religion — sometimes age, sexual preference, or handicaps. The distinction between unfair discrimination and [other] discrimination is unclear at best, so *the classification of insurance risks by such variables as age or sex becomes suspect, and may require elaborate justification. On the other hand,*

---

153. As we saw in n.93, *supra*, that fact can be masked but will not change except perhaps, and even this seems doubtful, in the distant future.

154. C.L. Trowbridge, *Fundamental Concepts of Actuarial Science*, (Washington: Actuarial Education and Research Fund, 1989).

the ignoring of any significant underwriting variable, on the grounds of public acceptance, leads to dangers of subsidisation,[155] *when demonstrably poor risks are pooled with good.*[156] *(emphasis supplied).*

Subsidisation of male recipients of lump-sum pension distributions at the expense of similarly situated females seems a textbook example of the dangers to which Trowbridge is pointing. The windfalls to schemes or "robbing Peter to pay Paulette" which we saw *supra* show the result of cavalier imposition of fine-sounding but unscientific social engineering.

(vi) The Barber Case and its effect on the Directives

Despite its status as perhaps the Court's leading pension case to date, *Barber* v. *Guardian Royal Exchange Assurance Group*[157] was actually a rather narrow holding. It was a referral under Article 177[158] and concerned a male employee made compulsorily redundant at an age which did not entitle him to the immediate pension which he would have received had he been a female. The case focused on the "access" issue of entitlement to the pension, not on the higher value of the hypothetical female's benefits.

Barber repeated that Article 119 has direct effect and held, *inter alia*, that:

> 3. It is contrary to Article 119 of the Treaty for a man made compulsorily redundant to be entitled to claim only a deferred pension payable at the normal retirement age when a woman in the same position is entitled to an immediate retirement pen-

155. Here, it is gratifying to see, in the true sense of the word.

156. Trowbridge, *supra*, at 60.

157. Case 262/88, [1990] E.C.R. 1889.

158. Article 177 gives a procedure, not unusual in the Civil Law, under which a lower court may seek guidance on a preliminary question by referring that issue to a higher court for clarification, suspending its own proceedings until the question is resolved. It provides:

"The Court...shall have jurisdiction to give preliminary rulings concerning:

(a) the interpretation of this Treaty; ...

Where such a question is raised before any court or tribunal of a Member State, that court or tribunal *may*, if it considers that a decision on the question is necessary to enable it to give judgment, request the Court...to give a ruling thereon.

Where any such question is raised in a case pending before a court or tribunal ... against whose decision there is no judicial remedy under national law, that court or tribunal *shall* bring the matter before the Court..." *(emphasis supplied)*

and is the major mechanism of the Treaty to ensure its consistent interpretation in the courts of the Member States.

sion as a result of the application of an age condition that varies according to sex...;

Thus the Member States did not have the power under Article 119 to permit sex-based differences in pension age under *occupational* pension schemes and, by implication, that such power was not to be found elsewhere in or under the Treaty. This analysis raises problems as to the status of directives which have broad implications well beyond pensions or equalities; for example, in the Third and Fourth Directives, particularly in light of their legal bases.

The Third Directive provides in its Article 7, that with respect to their *statutory* social security schemes:

> [t]his directive shall be without prejudice to the right of Member States to exclude from its scope:
> (a) the determination of pensionable age for the purpose of granting old-age and retirement pensions and *the possible consequences thereof for other benefits*; (emphasis supplied)

The Fourth Directive provides in its Article 9, that with respect to *occupational* schemes:

> Member States may defer compulsory application of the principle of equal treatment with regard to:
> (a) determination of pensionable age for purpose of granting old-age or retirement pensions, and the possible implications for other benefits:
> — either until the date on which equality is achieved in statutory schemes,
> — or, at the latest, until such equality is required by a directive.

In combination, therefore, the two directives provide that the Member States shall have such power as to each type of scheme.

The distinction between statutory and occupational schemes is not as clear-cut as it appears at first blush. Daykin notes that:[159]

> The level of pension provided by social security schemes varies from basic subsistence provision in some cases to 80% or so replacement of income while in employment...where the basic state pension is low, or where it is only payable to those on low in-

---

159. n.4, *supra*, at 73.

comes, there is a very real need for supplementary provision. This is provided by a variety of mixes of supplementary statutory schemes, employer-sponsored schemes and personal pensions.

In Switzerland and Finland employers are obliged to provide schemes to supplement the basic state pension. These must satisfy certain criteria and *can be viewed as quasi-statutory arrangements operated through employers as agents. (emphasis supplied)*

The "contracted out" scheme at issue in *Barber*, as the opinion makes clear, duplicated part of the statutory benefit (as such a scheme is required to do) and also provided benefits over and above that minimum level, making it, perhaps, semi-quasi-statutory.

The language of the judgment immediately following the portion quoted above, states explicitly that the result holds even as to "an age condition that varies according to sex in the same way as is provided for by the national statutory scheme" — which seems dubious with respect to this scheme which was designed to mesh with a statutory social security scheme containing unequal pensionable ages, and indefensible with respect to one designed only to duplicate the statutory benefits without any additional features. Essentially, with respect to the second kind of plan, the "contracting out" provisions of national law may well require the difference to appear but *Barber* invalidates that law. Without questioning the superiority of Community Law where a clear conflict with national law arises, it is at least arguable that this is an overreach, in the absence of some definitive indication that the Community provisions were intended to reach that result, *i.e.* that there really is a conflict.

The above argument does not deny that had the Fourth Directive simply blessed different pensionable ages without reference to differences in the underlying statutory schemes, there would have been a major issue as to conflict with Article 119,[160] especially if it had been issued under that Article, but this was not the case. The Fourth Directive was a serious attempt to steer a consistent path between the conflicting notions of: the Member States' right, clearly recognised in the Third Directive, to establish such differences in access requirements in their statutory schemes; the obvious overlap of occupational and statutory schemes, and the resulting impact of one on the other; and, finally, the effect of Article 119 on these differences in occupational schemes.

The Third and Fourth Directives each take as their legal basis Article 235 of the Treaty. This means that when they were adopted this was done in the belief: first, that permitting sex-based differences in pensionable age under both statutory and occupational schemes was "nec-

---

160. The conclusions of this paper would not have changed although the analysis might have been a little harder.

essary to attain ... one of the objectives of the Community";[161] and, second, that the Treaty "has not provided the necessary powers" (which seems clear). Having so decided, the Council proceeded to "take the appropriate measures" by issuing the two Directives, with all the formalities for which Article 235 calls.

Clearly a Directive issued under Article 119 would have been secondary legislation dependent on that Article and the Court's holding that Article 119 is directly effective and prohibits sex-based differences in pensionable age, would have invalidated it. However, since the directives are not grounded on Article 119 but take as their legal bases Article 235, they represent the grant of a new power not previously spelled out in the Treaty: the power to discriminate between the sexes in this narrow area.[162] This may not be sound policy but that is not the issue which was before the Court. It is difficult to reconcile the harsh treatment of these two directives' legislative development in the penumbra of Article 119, with the endorsement in *Worringham*[163] of that of the First Directive. Rasmussen[164] might find such a reconciliation less difficult.

What the Court seems to have done is not just to invalidate parts of two humble Directives but, rather, to undermine a key element of the Treaty: the ability granted by Article 235[165] virtually[166] to amend the Treaty by adding powers to fill perceived gaps.[167]

In addition, it is important to recognise that directives in general, by definition,[168] and these four Directives in particular, are addressed to the Member States; they prescribe, as they should, general approaches to the areas which they cover, leaving details of implementation to those States. The principle of subsidiarity, with its new Maastricht underpinning,[169] would seem to suggest that maximum flexibility of approach be

161. An incorrect assessment, in this writer's opinion, but one which was made by all the parties entitled to act or opine under Article 235 — which does not, of course, include the Court.

162. Louis refers to such legislation as "Derived" rather than secondary legislation. J-V Louis, *The Community Legal Order*, (Office of Official Pub'ns of the E.C., Luxembourg, 1990).

163. *supra*, n.122.

164. *supra*, n.33.

165. And perhaps the rather narrower grant of Article 100, see n.120, *supra*.

166. "Virtually" because Article 235 could clearly not be used to override a Treaty provision, the procedure for a true amendment being in Article 236.

167. There is a serious question whether including this broad ability in the Treaty in the first place was wise; also, whether its use has been excessive or even cavalier; but, as long as it is not misused for purposes other than to fill in gaps, these do not seem to be questions for the Court.

168. Article 189, third paragraph.

169. Maastricht Preamble, final "Resolved" clause at p 4; and, new Article 3b, added to the Treaty by Maastricht Article G(5) at p 13.

left in national hands. At the very least, this may be desirable in the early years so that the Member States can experiment with different definitions and approaches. Some may even adopt the Curtin/U.S. Supreme Court approach to pension matters. If so, it is suggested that drawbacks of that approach are likely to emerge as experience develops and more rational approaches eventually find favour. If, of course, the alleged merits of that approach do, in fact, appear, pressure will develop to adopt it in all Member States. The writer is sufficiently confident of his analysis to let experience so decide and sees such room for competing approaches as a plus.

(vii) Issues remaining after Barber

The first question left unanswered by *Barber* is its effect on the Fourth Directive (and the knock-on effect on similar directives issued under Article 235 which is a question of significance far beyond pensions and equality). Is it torpedoed as invalidly conflicting with Article 119 or does it, at least, have a large hole where its Article 9(a) has been "voided",[170] as Docksey suggests?[171] If so, much sensible flexibility has been destroyed. Most optimistically, has it only sustained superficial damage which can be patched by either a reconsideration by the Court of what has been argued here to be an overreach, or even by a Protocol.[172]

Retroactivity of *Barber* also raises complex and interesting issues, as did the U.S. cases discussed earlier. Once again, important general principles with wide implications are being developed in the area of equalities law. It seems clear that both the Court and the U.S. Supreme Court recognise that it is virtually impossible to apply certain decisions with full retroactive effect without violating the principle of legal certainty.[173] It would, however, be even more indefensible to use this as a reason to shrink from a major decision. The only practical approach is to limit retroactivity in a situation like *Barber.* On this basis, *Barber* follows *Norris* and declines to give retroactive effect to its decision on pensionable age to litigants who had not made their claims before the decision but it is not clear just what this means; for example, whether it applies to benefits commencing in the future but based on pre-*Barber* service. The *Coloroll* and related cases, currently before the Court, can be expected to resolve much of the confusion, on the lines, one hopes, suggested by

170. In the Article 174 sense.

171. *supra*, n.26, at 263.

172. Such as that in Maastricht "Concerning Article 119, limiting retroactivity under Occupational Schemes".

173. S. Honeyball & J. Shaw, "Sex, Law and the Retiring Man", [1991] E.L. Rev. 47.

Hudson:[174] confining the effect of the decision to benefits attributable to service after the date of the decision.

(viii) The Coloroll Case

In *Coloroll*,[175] six series of questions were referred to the Court under Article 177[176] by the Chancery Division of the (English) High Court of Justice. Five of these, in turn, contained a number of related and alternative questions.

The first question related to the liability of scheme trustees *vis-à-vis* employers, and the rights of dependants and other beneficiaries *vis-à-vis* employees and the mechanics of equalisation. The second and third sought to clarify issues of retroactivity for both regular and contracted-out schemes. The fourth and fifth dealt with sex specific actuarial tables as applied to both benefits and employer and employee contributions. The sixth and final question asked whether a scheme which was always single-sex, should be treated as if it had a member of the other sex.[177]

Coloroll was combined with three other cases: one Dutch, one German and one English from the Leeds Industrial Tribunal.[178]

The Advocate General opens his opinion[179] with the statement that his two most important issues are retroactivity and sex-related actuarial tables.[180] Following and citing Honeyball and Shaw,[181] he lists[182] four possible interpretations of *Barber* as to retroactivity:

---

174. "Some reflection on the implications of the *Barber* decision", [1992] E.L. Rev. 163, 168.

175. Case 200/91 *Coloroll Pension Trustees Ltd* v. *Russell, Mangham and Others,* (not yet decided by the E.C.J.).

176. *supra,* n.158.

177. This question invites a double *reductio ad absurdum*. If the Court imposes unisex treatment on a single-sex scheme, thus catering to non-existent hypothetical members, the absurdity is clear; if it does not, a single-sex scheme, sensibly administered as such with the Court's blessing, will be turned upside down if a single member of the other sex is ever introduced.

178. Illustrating the fact that many Article 177 referrals, including some leading cases, come from relatively low levels of the Member State legal systems.

179. Opinion of Mr. Advocate General van Gerven, delivered on 28 April 1993 (provisional text).

180. In that order, even though the first issue, however significant financially, is only transitional.

181. *supra,* n.173; and, in fact, significantly improving their formulation since they refer, at page 56, to "pensions in respect of contributions" for the various periods; the Advocate General's references to benefits *accruing* is better because, as we saw in n.105, *supra,* there is no direct relationship between contributions to a D.B. scheme and a particular participant's benefit.

182. At para 10.

- covering only workers who entered schemes post-*Barber*;
- covering only benefits accrued post-*Barber*;
- covering all benefits payable or paid post-*Barber*, whenever accrued; and,
- covering all payments made post-*Barber*, including those to pre-*Barber* retirees.

Alternative 1 is dismissed as of no benefit to current participants; alternative 3 as unfair in its radically different treatment of those close to but on different sides of the cut-off; and, alternative 4 as unreasonable costly and disruptive. Adoption of alternative 2 is recommended. The opinion notes that this will be the result under Maastricht, assuming ratification.[183] It is hard to disagree with any of these conclusions assuming, of course, that no reconsideration of *Barber* is contemplated. One gap in the analysis is its failure to clarify how increases in pre-*Barber* accruals attributable to post-*Barber* salary increases should be treated.[184]

With respect to actuarial factors the Advocate General cites Curtin and also the *Manhart* and *Norris* cases — and falls into the same logical traps. Perhaps the clearest example is his statement that:

I could for instance imagine that factors having a direct impact on the life expectancy of a specific individual, such as risks asso-

183. Under the Protocol described in n.172, *supra*.

184. A numerical example may help to clarify this issue. Assume that a female participates in the D.B. scheme with which we opened our discussion of this type of scheme in the introduction, which provides a benefit of 2% of final average salary for each year of service. Assume further that the scheme specifies a retirement age of 65 for males and 60 for females pre-*Barber* and 65 for both post-*Barber* and that our participant entered at age 35, was 50 with a final average salary of 10,000 units per month in 1990 when *Barber* came down, and retires at 60 with a final average salary of 16,000/month. Her benefit at 60 can be viewed in three pieces (two straightforward and one more problematic):

A. 30% (2% for each year from age 35 to 50) of 10,000 equaling 3,000 units per month, all clearly pre-*Barber* and, therefore, payable at 60; plus,

B. 20% (2% for each year 50 to 60) of 16,000 equaling 3,200/month all accrued post-*Barber* and, therefore, payable at 65 or, if paid at age 60, reduced actuarially by about one-third to approximately 2,000; together with a third piece, conceptually between A and C,

C. 30% (the same percentage as in A) of 6,000 (16,000 less 10,000) equalling 1,800/mo, which represents the effect on the pre-*Barber* accrual of the subsequent salary increases.

Note: A + B + C, before reflecting any actuarial reductions, add to 8,000 which is 50% (2% for each year from 35 to 60) of 16,000; confirming the arithmetic.

The Advocate General does not make clear whether piece B does or does not suffer an actuarial reduction. The cleanest approach is not to apply the reduction, but this should be made explicit.

ciated with a particular occupation, smoking, eating or drinking habits and so forth, would be taken into account, if this is technically possible, in order to justify individual differences in contributions and/or benefits. As regards differences in average life expectancy between men and women, the situation is different, however. These differences bear no relation to the life expectancy of a specific individual and are thus irrelevant for the calculation of the contributions and/or benefits which may be ascribed to that individual.[185]

The distinction which this passage purports to draw is, quite literally, meaningless. As we saw earlier, the facts are exactly opposite to the Advocate General's statement: all of the factors he lists affect life expectancy but with one exception they are difficult to incorporate into the underwriting of large groups, though not of individuals; only sex, the one factor he seeks to suppress, is binary and, therefore, easy to identify and to reflect in pricing. It is trivially true, as Curtin and the Advocate General[186] point out, that some men live longer than some women of the same age. Neither, however, draws any meaningful conclusion from this fact. There is none to be drawn: it is equally true, and equally uninformative, that some smokers outlive otherwise identical non-smokers.[187]

The concept of expectancy, which each uses so cavalierly, only has meaning if the individual is viewed as a member of a class. Isolated individuals simply do not have expectancies until they are identified with an appropriate group. People of the same age, people with the same smoking habits, people in the same state of health, people in the same or similar occupation *and people of the same sex* are categories which actuaries have found, over the years to be most useful. Viewed purely as individuals, without any regard to similar people from whose experience one can derive meaningful averages and statistics, individuals have only individual life *spans* which can be measured only after the fact.

At no point does the Advocate General define an R.S.M. to use in analysing this issue: neither explicitly, as could be expected, nor implicitly.[188] He does not even consider whether equality of benefits is a valid definition of equality for pension purposes, which means that he does

185. At para 36.

186. At para 35.

187. Indeed, with some searching, one could find a terminally ill patient who had outlived his own grandchild, but no rational underwriter would, on that ground, sell life insurance to the class of terminally ill grandparents at lower rates than to their grandchildren.

188. Although the D.B./D.C. distinction itself is mentioned but not developed in his footnote 38.

not discuss the basic issue of male/female equality in pension plans: whether it is legitimate for an employer to spend something of the order of 15% more to support the benefits of his female employees *simply because they are females* than he spends on the males. Instead, like Curtin and Ellis, he focuses on secondary, almost trivial, side-effects of an unstated assumption that it is:[189] lump-sum and other optional settlements.

His ultimate result, therefore, is that he is endorsing, without any satisfactory analysis, a situation where more funds are committed to the average female than to the average male since the former will collect benefits for a longer period. If, however, a female should elect certain forms of benefit, some or all of those extra funds will be withheld. We saw earlier that statements of prescriptive equality often reduce to, "we think X is bad and it must, therefore, cease forthwith." This seems to be the case here with X as recognition of the admitted fact of sex-distinct mortality.

It is clear — so clear that citations are hard to find — that *Stare Decisis* is not recognised by the E.C.J.; if it were, the *"Acte Claire"* doctrine[190] would never have been needed. That doctrine permits, but does not require, a court of a Member State, despite the mandatory language of the final paragraph of the Article, to decide an Article 177 issue itself, rather than referring, where the Court has already created a substantial body of case law. The doctrine presupposes that national courts may refer an issue identical or similar to one previously referred and appears to contemplate repeated rulings on the same issue by the Court; it is clearly far removed from the Common Law's approach to case law. The gap is illustrated by such cases as *Technische Universität Munchen* v. *Hauptzollamt Munchen-Mitte*,[191] an Article 177 referral from the *Bundesfinanzhof* in which the Court was asked in an Article 177 referral to reconsider prior rulings in the area of the Common Customs Tariff. It did so, holding Commission Decision 83/348[192] invalid.

This might have been an instance where there was reason to be grateful that we are operating under this approach and not under the more usual common-law rules. It is clear from Article 177 that an English court, or a court or tribunal of any other Member State, which wishes to do so

---

189. An assumption which we have recommended for D.B. schemes, but which is far from self evident.

190. Announced in Case 28/62, *Da Costa en Schaake et al* v. *Nederlandse Belastingadministrate*, [1963] E.C.R. 31, as to "materially identical" issues; expanded in Case 283/81 *C.I.L.F.I.T.* v. *Minister of Health*, [1982] E.C.R. 3415, to situations involving the same point of law "even though the questions at issue are not strictly identical".

191. Case 269/909, [1991] E.C.R. I-5469.

192. O.J. 1983 L 188/32.

is free to refer the unisex issue to Luxembourg again. This means that a *Coloroll* result which follows the Advocate General may qualify for *Acte Claire* treatment, might have given rise to a binding precedent within the national system according to that system's rules, but would still have been less final than a typical common-law precedent. A well-reasoned request for reconsideration or, perhaps more likely, a case which illustrates a particularly absurd result of the unisex analysis, might well have brought about a reconsideration of the type seen in *Technische Universität*.

Fortunately this analysis may not be necessary. The Advocate General's opinion will almost certainly not carry the day since it is flatly opposed to the Court's judgment in the following case which was decided after that opinion was delivered, but the judgment in *Coloroll* was still pending.

(ix) The Neath Case

In *Neath*,[193] an Article 177 reference by the Leeds Industrial Tribunal (U.K.), the Court was again asked to consider the issue of retroactivity under *Barber* and again made clear[194] that "by virtue of the *Barber* judgment the direct effect of Article 119...may be relied on...only in the case of benefits *payable in respect of...* service subsequent to 17 May 1990 subject to the [usual] exception...". *(emphasis supplied)* This issue now seems firmly resolved.

The second issue in the case concerned, and the related questions of the tribunal were limited to, lump-sum settlements. Mr. Neath contended, correctly, that had he been a woman of the same age, the actuarially calculated capital value corresponding to his annuity payment would have been higher and, therefore, the payment to him if he elected a lump-sum settlement, or the transfer value payable to a transferee plan, would have been more liberal. Therefore, it was claimed, his lump-sum entitlement should be increased.

In Part (b) of the judgment, the Court rejected this claim. It described Defined Benefit schemes[195] in general and the fact that such plans require employer contributions which "vary over time, so as to cover the balance [not provided by employee contributions] of the cost of the pensions promised"[196] and stated that "(t)he fact that women live *on average* longer than men is one of the actuarial factors taken into account

---

193. Case 152/91 *David Neath v. Hugh Steeper Ltd.* (Judgment of the Court, 22 December 1993, nyr).

194. In para 18.

195. The scheme at issue provided a benefit of one-sixtieth of final average salary for each year of service.

196. At para 22.

in determining how the scheme…is to be funded" *(emphasis supplied).* Most important, it noted[197] that "the employer's commitment to his employees concerns the payment, at a given moment in time, of a periodic pension…[which]… commitment does not necessarily have to do with the funding arrangements chosen to secure the periodic payment of the pensions, which thus remain outside the scope of application of Article 119. This is a clear affirmation that the R.S.M. to be used in measuring equality under a D.B. scheme may properly be taken as benefit outflow, and in the following paragraph the Court explicitly rejects any suggestion that employer contributions must be the same.

Therefore, concluded the Court,[198] "(i)t follows that … inequality of employers' contributions paid under defined-benefit schemes, which is due to the use of actuarial factors differing according to sex, is not struck at by Article 119…[and]…(t)hat conclusion *necessarily* extends to…conversion…into…a capital sum and the transfer of pension rights, the value of which can be determined *only* by reference to the funding arrangements chosen". *(emphasis supplied)*

Thus the Court adopted for purposes of lump-sums paid directly to the employee or to a transferee scheme, the approach advocated earlier in this paper. In addition, its recognition of the fact that unequal employer contributions by sex are part and parcel of the very concept of D.B. schemes and its analysis of unequal payments under certain (lump-sum) options as being an inevitable result of that fact, mean that other optional forms of payout which are sex-distinct but equal in actuarial value, seem to be similarly endorsed; in particular, joint-and-survivor periodic payments.

In light of this extremely satisfactory analysis and result, it is almost churlish to criticise the minutiae of the Court's language; nevertheless, the words "necessarily" and "only" italicised above may open the analysis to attack. It is certainly true — as the Court, in happy contrast to the United States Supreme Court, recognises — that the operative fact in D.B. schemes is that employer contributions are necessarily affected by sex. However, it would have been possible for the Court to mandate lump-sum payouts which were artificially equalised by sex as the U.S.S.C. has done, thus obliging actuaries to calculate funding levels reflecting such artificial constraints. This would typically have been done by estimating the probabilities of the various elections or, particularly in the smaller plans where such averages would be practically meaningless, by simply assuming that the most expensive election would be elected. In the United States, as noted earlier,[199] IRC §401(a)(25) requires that options be com-

197. At para 30.

198. In paras 32 and 33.

199. See n.107, *supra.*

puted "in a way which precludes employer discretion"[200] so that the actuarial factors used for options cannot be precisely aligned with the funding assumptions. Thus the above problem arises to a limited extent with
respect to lump-sum even before the requirement that the factors be
sex-neutral is reached. As demonstrated earlier, major policy errors have
been made in the U.S., but the fact that the American pension scene
reflects serious anomalies rather than collapse shows that it is an over-
statement to say that "capital sum and transfer...value(s) can be determined *only* by reference to the funding arrangements chosen." A better
formulation might be that imposing capital sum and transfer values which
did not properly reflect the underlying funding arrangements would
have seriously distorted those arrangements, as it has in the U.S.

In the United Kingdom, much more effort is made to keep transfer
and other lump-sum value consistent with funding assumptions to avoid
strain on the scheme assets and inequities between participants who leave
schemes and those who remain.[201] This means that the Court's formulation is much less open to criticism in a U.K. context than it would have
been in the U.S. Nevertheless, it would be useful to tighten the language
in future cases, including perhaps *Coloroll*.

10. The Irish Legislation: A Model

The First Report of the (Irish) National Pension Board[202] was published
in 1987. It laid the foundations of the subsequent Irish legislation[203] dealing comprehensively with the whole area of pensions.

The new Act's § 69 is of particular interest in this discussion; it epito-
mises the broad, flexible approach to equitable recognition of sex which
this paper advocates and is recommended as a model for other Member
States. *A fortiori*, it is recommended as an approach which the Court
should approve as satisfying the requirements of, and under, the Treaty
including, but not limited to, Article 119.

Sub-section (1) reads as follows:

---

200. And, by the same token, precludes the use of actuarial expertise to ensure equity between the terminating employee and the scheme, *i.e.* the remaining participants.

201. See, for example, Guidance Note GN11, "Retirement Benefit Schemes — Transfer Values", Members' Handbook, (London: Institute of Actuaries, 1993) p D/51. This Guidance Note is mandatory in the United Kingdom. A detailed discussion of the reach of
this and other GNs is beyond the scope of this paper; however, each such note contains
a section listing the Legislation and Authority on which it is based.

202. The Stationery Office, Dublin, 1987.

203. The Pensions Act, 1990.

69.— (1) In determining whether a scheme complies with the principle of equal treatment under *section 66,* account shall not be taken of —

(a) any difference, on the basis of sex of members, in the levels of contributions which the employer makes, to the extent that the difference is for the purpose of removing or limiting differences, as between men and women in the amount or value of benefits provided under a defined contribution scheme,

(b) any difference, on the basis of sex, in the amount or value of benefits provided under a defined contribution scheme to the extent that the difference is justifiable on actuarial grounds,

(c) any special treatment for the benefit of women to whom *section 72(1)* relates,

(d) any difference of treatment in relation to benefits for a deceased member's surviving spouse or other dependants,

(e) any difference of treatment in relation to any optional provisions available.

Since this chapter supports the Irish legislation as a model for other countries, and at the very minimum as an approach which the Court should support, we will examine its provisions and compare them with the American results and with the Occupational Scheme Directive, once again basing the discussion largely on our model.

Paragraph (a), following the Directive, permits but does not require, an employer to contribute to the accounts of female participants in D.C. schemes, the additional 15% required to produce equal monthly outflows for them. This necessarily implies that the scheme, not just an outside insurance company, would use different purchase rates to convert lump-sum accumulations to monthly income reflecting the fact that lifetime benefits to F65 cost more than those to M65. It would also mean that when employees elected lump-sum payouts, the accumulated amounts would be higher for females. There is no suggestion that in a contributory scheme, higher *employee* contributions could be required for females along the lines of the *Manhart* scheme. This is not an unreasonable result since such higher contributions, could[204] be construed as an unequal condition of access in violation of *Barber*. If so, then it would become necessary for an Irish court to construe the statute as not permitting them.[205] The writer would prefer, as this paper has noted repeat-

204. Absent an option, of the type discussed earlier in n.66, *supra*, for females to contribute less and receive less.

205. Article 29, 4, 3° of the Irish Constitution confirming the supremacy of Community law.

edly, contributions as the usual criterion for equality in a D.C. scheme. Nevertheless, it seems reasonable (but not acceptable under *Neath*[206]) to leave that choice with the employer and to the employees who may endorse it directly through collective bargaining or, arguably, by remaining in employment.

Paragraph (b) is a simple recognition of the fact that equal contributions to a D.C. scheme must, in a rational world, produce equal lump-sum payout to M65 and F65 but unequal monthly payouts — just as they do for M65 and M60. The writer applauds this realism and common sense; additional supporting arguments would be overkill.

Paragraph (c) merely permits special maternity benefits to women, eliminating the need to justify special treatment of mothers by verbal gymnastics[207] of the type found in *General Electric Co.* v. *Gilbert*[208] which held that maternity benefits did not violate Title VII of the Civil Rights Act[209] even though they were payable only to females.

Paragraph (d) reflects such obvious equities as the fact that a death beneficiary's benefit may also reflect sex, giving better or worse benefits to members of one or the other sex depending on the cost of a particular benefit.

Paragraph (e) recognises that if M65 and F65 elect certain optional benefits, the cost of those benefits will vary depending on the age and sex of the employee and, if applicable, of the dependant or other beneficiary. It will not be necessary to reflect age but ignore sex as it now is in the U.S. It is a substantial step forward in clarity from, but is not inconsistent with, the directive.[210]

This legislation clearly recognises the sex differences which exist in the real world, as does (did) the Fourth Directive. It does not attempt to sweep them under the rug; rather it highlights them and enables the employer, or the employer and the union in collective bargaining situations, to decide on a definition of equality — inflow or outflow, or in certain cases a combination of the two — as the R.S.M. and then to accept the actuarial consequences of that choice.

---

206. n.193 *supra*, para 31.

207. "The two groups of potential recipients which [an earlier] case concerned were pregnant women and non-pregnant persons. 'While the first group is exclusively female, the second includes members of both sexes.'"

208. 429 U.S. 125 (1972).

209. n.54, *supra*.

210. It avoids the artificial windfalls of n.109, *supra*.

11. CONCLUSION

We have focused on two radically different areas of application of Article 119 to pension issues: first, areas of plan design, such as access to membership and age requirements for benefit eligibility, where existing different treatment of men and women is simply a hangover of old social attitudes and changes can be made without difficulty subject only to serious but temporary problems of retroactivity; and then, at more length, on the more challenging areas where existing differences of treatment reflect not attitudes of society which can be changed but facts of nature, the external world, which cannot. The prime such fact is that women live longer than men *now*, a situation which is unlikely to change overnight, if it changes at all; and present indications are that it will not.

With respect to access, this paper agrees with the commentators and cases that, as a matter of policy, sex-related differences in access conditions are incompatible with modern notions of equality; also that Article 119 can hardly be read to endorse them prospectively. However, the E.C.J.'s refusal to accept Community derived legislation under Article 235 permitting a transitional period, seems to be an overreach. The same can be said of the U.S. Supreme Court's refusal to accept the broader reach of the legislative history under the American Civil Rights Act.

In most countries equal access has often not been the rule in the past so that when it is imposed, complete retroactivity is not practical: it would mean enhancement, often at great expense, of pensions accrued (and, in many cases, already paid for by the employer) based on service in earlier years; pensions now in pay status; and, conceivably, subject to statutes of limitation, benefit amounts already distributed. U.S. case law has already adopted prospective application of the new standard. Community cases, in particular the Advocate General's *Coloroll* opinion, are pointing in the same direction. We noted that some refinement of the definition of "prospective application" will be required.

We have demonstrated that the concept of equality is straightforward only if we envision a highly artificial defined contribution scheme, omitting many of the features normally considered essential to a retirement arrangement, and use contribution inflow as our standard. We have seen that age and sex-related differences in life expectancy mean that equality of contribution inflow leads inevitably to unequal benefit outflows. In addition, we have seen that equality in the defined benefit context suggests a completely different formulation of the concept of equality: one which equalises outflow rather than inflow and is extremely favourable to older employees and often, but by no means always, to females. We noted that there are arguments against accepting this concept of equality in the first place but that once it is accepted, difficulties arising from the impossibility of equalising inflow and outflow at the same time, must be faced. We then faced those difficulties with, however, some mathematical shortcuts and simplifications.

We have seen the artificiality of the United States Supreme Court's approach: a negation of well established actuarial principles in the name of a poorly defined, or perhaps it would be more accurate to say a barely defined, concept of equality/non-discrimination which attempts to square the circle by simultaneously equating inflow and outflow. U.S. case-law seems determined to ignore the well established difference between male and female mortality; in effect, to pretend that it does not exist or to repeal it for pension purposes. The law is on a collision course not with actuarial dogma but with reality.[211] We have deprecated European commentary seeking to import that approach and have also noted and applauded some attempts to avoid the traps which the courts have created in the U.S., including especially some heavily criticised EC Directives and recent Irish legislation.

Article 119 does not require that European pension schemes fall into these traps and the European Court of Justice did not interpret it in *Barber* in a way which would raise the same difficulties. Indeed, *Neath* rejects the approach of the American cases and the commentary based on them in favour of a much less destructive approach. It is hoped that this commendable judicial restraint will continue and that European pension arrangements will remain rather more rational than they have become in the U.S. Regrettably, this is not the course suggested by the Advocate General's opinion in *Coloroll* but it seems highly likely that that opinion will be rejected in the final judgment and that the rational of *Neath* will control.

12. Postscript

Just before this book went to press, the long-awaited judgment in *Coloroll* and related cases came down. As noted earlier, a large number of questions were posed to the Court and much analysis and commentary can be expected.[212]

---

211. The situation is reminiscent of the apocryphal (one hopes) story of the Southern state legislature which decided that π should be set equal to exactly 22/7 to "simplify" calculations in that State. It appears that neither the circumferences of circles nor any other scientific phenomena depending on π were transformed.

The best response may be the possibly apocryphal (one hopes not) comment of Galileo after the inquisition forced him to recant: *E pur si muove*, "But it does move", *Oxford Dictionary of Quotations*, (Oxford University Press, 2nd Ed. 1953) p. 212.

212. The *Financial Times* had a headline "Analysts beg time to digest judgment" in its report, 29 September 1994, p 10.

The most dramatic holding, in a related case,[213] holds that "the right to join a scheme falls within the scope of Article 119"; "the limitation of the effects of the *Barber* judgment does not apply [to access]"; and, "the [Maastricht] protocol...does not affect the right to join...".

This will enable women disproportionately affected by the exclusion of part-time employees the right to retroactive benefits, subject, in schemes requiring employee contributions, to retroactive payment of the appropriate contributions. This may have serious financial consequences for employers with substantial numbers of employees affected

With respect to sex-distinct actuarial factors, the basic issue discussed in this paper, the Advocate General's approach was rejected; the principal of *Neath* was resoundingly re-affirmed (using essentially the same words) in paragraphs 76-82; and, it was extended in paragraph 83 to two other forms of pension: joint-and-survivor and reduced early retirement. The key language is in paragraphs 79, 81, 82 & 83:

> in the context of defined-benefit... schemes,...the employer's commitment to his employees concerns the payment...of a periodic pension...However, that commitment does not necessarily have to do with the funding arrangements chosen to secure the periodic payment of the pension, which thus remain outside the scope of Article 119 (paragraph 30).

[Therefore]

> ...inequality of employer's contributions...is not struck at by Article 119 (paragraph 32)

[and]

> this conclusion necessarily extended to...conversion...into a capital sum (paragraph 33)

[and now]

> it must be added...[to] a reversionary pension...and...early retirement (paragraph references are to *Neath*)

In the terms used in this paper, it is clear that the benchmark of equality in a D.B. scheme is now recognised as benefit outflow, and that once that standard has been applied, Article 119 does not "strike at" what we called

213. Case 57/931, *Anna Adriaanje Vroege* v. *NCIV Instituut voor Volkshuisvesting BV, & Stichting Pensionfonds NCIV,* (Judgment of the Court, 28 September 1994, nyr).

"minor secondary consequences of an unspoken and unexamined assumption that equal monthly benefits should be permitted." That assumption is no longer unspoken nor unexamined.

The European Court has, therefore, avoided what were described as the "traps" into which the U.S. Supreme Court has fallen, and it is no longer just a pious hope that "European pension arrangements will remain rather more rational than they have become in the U.S." An interesting issue is now whether *Neath* and *Coloroll* might trigger a reconsideration of the U.S. position; regrettably, this is likely to remain a pious hope.

3. Industrial Democracy: A United Kingdom Perspective on the Works Council Directive

Philip Jones

1. INTRODUCTION

United Kingdom labour law has had a European dimension for 20 years, dating back to the time of UK accession to the European Economic Community in 1973. During those 20 years, the influence of Community law has steadily widened and deepened, a process likened by Lord Denning to an incoming tide flowing into the estuaries of England.[1] This evolutionary process gained a new momentum in 1987, when the coming into force of the Single European Act heralded a new phase of legislative activity on the road towards a possible European Union.

A distinguishing feature of this latter phase has been a renewed emphasis on the social dimension of the Community, a term which encompasses a broad range of economic and social issues, but particularly those relating to matters of employment, health and safety, and the working environment. This emerging emphasis on social issues has exposed a rift in political and socio-economic philosophy between member states. The resultant debate is peculiarly sensitive because it touches upon issues of national sovereignty, political beliefs, economic priorities, social welfare and industrial traditions. Completion of the single market in 1992 has given a new urgency to the labour relations arena, deriving not only from increasing internationalisation of labour markets, but also from the free movement of goods, services and capital between member states.

---

1. *HP Bulmer Ltd* v. *J. Bollinger SA* [1974] 2 All ER 1226 at 1231. He later drew a starker analogy by comparing European law to a "tidal wave bringing down our sea walls and flowing inland ...". See Szyszczak E., "Sovereignty: Crisis, Compliance, Confusion, Complacency" (1990) 15 *European Law Review* 480.

Set against these developments has been a global downturn in economic performance, with attendant rising unemployment and calls for protectionist measures by national governments.

As a consequence of these events, the climate of industrial relations in Europe is changing. The UK, in contrast to other member states, has sought to isolate itself from mainstream Community thought on issues associated with development of the social dimension and pursue instead its own agenda.

Two events, in particular, have epitomised UK hostility to the extension of Community competence in the social sphere. First, was the refusal of the UK government to endorse the 1989 Charter of the Fundamental Social Rights of Workers.[2] Second, and of arguably greater significance, was its rejection of proposed changes to the social policy provisions of the EEC Treaty at Maastricht in 1991. Undeterred, however, by the UK's continued opposition, the remaining eleven member states concluded between themselves an Agreement, annexed to a Protocol of the Maastricht Treaty.[3]

The Social Protocol lays the foundation for a fundamental change in Community labour law. It aims, *inter alia,* to develop the Community's social dimension in three distinct ways: by extending the use of qualified majority voting; by allowing the implementation of directives via collective agreements; and by extending the role of the social partners. To effect these goals, it establishes a new framework for the participation of management and labour in the formulation of proposals in the social policy field.[4] Significantly, the absence of the UK from the signatories to the Protocol injected fresh life into a proposed directive for the establishment of European works councils, to which the UK government had been resolutely opposed.

In October 1993, the Commission agreed to progress the European Works Council Directive under the terms of the Social Protocol, and a consultative process was initiated.[5] By April 1994, however, it was clear that the social partners had failed to reach agreement on the matter, and the Commission thus decided to legislate. The scene is set, therefore, for the creation of what may eventually lead to a European industrial relations framework within which national systems will have to function.

---

2.   COM (89) 568 final, November 1989. Hereafter referred to as the Social Charter.

3.   Treaty on European Union: *Protocol on Social Policy* and its associated *Agreement on Social Policy.* For the purpose of simplicity, the Protocol and the Agreement will be considered in this paper as a single concept, and hereafter referred to as the Social Protocol.

4.   Article 3 Social Policy Agreement.

5.   *European Industrial Relations Review,* No.245 at 18.

This paper addresses some of the central issues arising from this move towards greater regulation of industrial relations within the Community. The theme of the paper is "industrial democracy", a term widely used to refer to participation in industry between the employed and their employers.[6] Community activity in this area will be reviewed, and its place in the broader scheme of Community objectives will be examined. The various forms that participation can take will be discussed. A comparative element will be introduced by reviewing and contrasting traditions and attitudes in other European states. Arguments for and against employee participation will be evaluated against empirical evidence drawn from a sample of European companies. The focus of the discussion will be the European Works Council Directive, which will be assessed on the basis of the 1991 text. Although this text has since undergone some revision, it encapsulates those elements which provoked controversy, and formed the basis of the Directive which finally emerged. The provisions of the Directive will be compared with existing practices. A UK perspective will be developed in the context of the country's historical legacy, its industrial traditions and current political climate. Consideration will be given to the question of whether the UK will be able to sustain its isolationist stance, given the renewed commitment by other member states to greater employment protection and the promotion of workers' rights. Subsequent amendments to the 1991 text of the Directive are summarised in a postscript to the paper.

2. Towards Participation

Community Treaties adopted in the 1950s established only a narrow legal base for the enactment of legislation in the social field. This reflected a belief that social benefits would follow automatically from economic prosperity, which the Community would itself promote. In consequence, social policy constituted only a minor role in the early years of the Community. Such relative inactivity was perhaps obscured by a generally favourable economic climate of industrial growth and high employment: such a climate was of itself conducive to social progress and real income growth.[7]

A move away from this minimalist approach took shape in the 1970s as disparities in economic growth within the Community became increasingly apparent. Environmental concerns gained in prominence and led

6. Budd S. and Jones A., *The European Community: A Guide to the Maze* (Kogan Page, 1991) at 109.

7. See Lintner V. and Mazey S., *The European Community: Economic & Political Aspects* (McGraw-Hill, 1991) at 113.

to a questioning of the hidden costs of economic growth in terms of pollution, low health and safety standards, and quality of life. A more affluent, and better educated, workforce began to argue the case for a greater say in the decision-making process. There was a view that new initiatives were needed to underpin the concept of the Community as a social entity, rather than simply a common market. A consensus began to emerge that economic growth needed to be tempered with, and accompanied by, a more active programme of social reform.

Responding to these pressures, EC heads of state or government affirmed in 1972 the "social dimension" of the Community,[8] an affirmation which took practical form in the launch of a social action programme in 1974.[9] A principal objective of the programme was to increase labour and management involvement in policy making. This was to be attained in two separate, albeit related, ways:

- By progressive involvement of workers or their representatives in the life of undertakings in the Community.[10]

- By promotion of the involvement of management and labour in the economic and social decisions of the Community.[11]

Ironically, adoption of the social action programme coincided with the first oil crisis and the onset of global recession. Unemployment levels rose significantly throughout the Community, with some regions, industries and groups of workers affected particularly badly. Political and economic priorities shifted accordingly. The Commission nevertheless maintained an active interest in promoting various forms of employee participation.

Progress was limited, however, to relatively uncontroversial areas relating to consultation procedures in the event of collective redundancies,[12] and during transfers of undertakings.[13] The legal base in each case was Article 100 EEC, on the grounds that different practices in member states could have a direct effect on the functioning of the common market. Also adopted were provisions in the area of health and safety. The Preamble to the 1978 Action Programme referred to the need for in-

8. Communiqué issued at Paris summit.
9. Council Resolution of 21 January 1974 concerning a social action programme (74/c 13/1).
10. *ibid.*, para. 8.
11. *ibid.*, para. 9.
12. Directive 75/129 EEC.
13. Directive 77/187 EEC.

creased "participation of management and labour in the decisions and initiatives in the field of safety, hygiene and health protection at work".[14] A specific requirement for information and consultation with workers and their representatives on health and safety issues was later provided for in the so-called "framework" Directive 89/391, which called for "balanced participation in accordance with national laws and/or practices".[15]

The Commission attempted to extend the principle of employee involvement into a wider sphere of decision making. The proposed fifth Directive[16] sought to lay down binding rules for public limited companies regarding internal structure and decision-making, and to establish models for worker participation in companies with 1000 or more workers. Proposals were revived for the introduction of a European company statute, with the aim of allowing certain companies to opt out of national legal systems: each organisation would incorporate itself instead as a "European Company" or SE (*Societas Europæa*), subject to Community law.[17] A company so established would be obliged to incorporate elements of worker participation in its statutes.

But such proposals met with opposition from employers and governments, apprehensive about potential cost implications and the political ramifications of such developments. The specific issue of worker participation was nevertheless revived in 1980 by the so-called "Vredeling" proposals.[18] The draft Directive targeted certain companies comprising either a parent company with one or more subsidiaries, or a company with several branches, and which operated in more than one member state. Vredeling proposed the establishment of common board structures and mandatory procedures for informing and consulting employees on company strategy.

Vredeling also encountered opposition. There was a perception that, as with previous participative proposals, the draft Directive was over-prescriptive and insufficiently flexible. In addition, there was a reluctance to impose a common mandatory regime upon divergent national practices. Given this continued lack of success, the Council recommended that worker participation be reconsidered as part of the deliberations on the social dimension of the single market.

The entry into force of the Single European Act in 1987 introduced several changes in the legal bases of social policy. *Inter alia,* it removed

14. Council Resolution of 29 June 1978 on an action programme of the European Communities on safety and health at work (78/c 165/1).
15. Directive 89/391/EEC, Article 1(2).
16. Originally proposed in OJ C 131/72.
17. Bulletin of the European Communities, Supplement 4/75.
18. Originally proposed in OJ C 297/80.

the need for unanimity within the Council on health and safety matters,[19] as it did for provisions relating to "the establishment and functioning of the internal market".[20] Unanimity was retained, however, for provisions relating to "the rights and interests of employed persons".[21] The
Act charged the Commission to "endeavour to develop the dialogue between management and labour at European level".[22] A practical consequence of this new provision was the *Val Duchesse* initiative, held under
the auspices of the Commission, to promote discussion between the two
sides of industry.[23] Early discussions centred on economic policies, and
later ones on issues associated with the introduction of new technology.

The outcome of these discussions has been a series of joint opinions
between, amongst others, UNICE[24] and the ETUC.[25] Overall, the initiative has generally been seen as successful. This, it has been suggested, is
primarily because UNICE is satisfied with the non-binding nature of such
agreements; and because the ETUC perceives the process as being consistent with collective bargaining.[26]

A clearer definition of the Community's "social dimension" emerged
in 1989, when Community heads of state or government, with the exception of the UK, adopted the Social Charter.[27] Its inspiration partly origi-
nated from Conventions of the International Labour Organisation (ILO)
and from the European Social Charter of the Council of Europe.[28] The
Social Charter declared that a common base of employment rights and
objectives should be established throughout the Community. *Inter alia*,
the Charter reiterated the need for employee involvement on health
and safety issues.[29] It also declared that "[i]nformation, consultation and
participation for workers" was to be "developed along appropriate lines,
taking account of the practices in...Member States".[30] Such information,

19. Article 118a EEC.

20. Article 100a EEC.

21. Article 100a(2) EEC.

22. Article 118b EEC.

23. So called after the chateau in Brussels where meetings were held. Kapteyn & Verloren
    van Themaat: *Introduction to the Law of the European Communities after the Coming into Force
    of the Single European Act* (Kluwer, student edition, 1990) at 628.

24. Union of Industrial and Employers' Confederations of Europe.

25. European Trade Union Confederation.

26. Roberts I., *Industrial relations and the European Community* (*Industrial Relations Journal*
    Vol. 23 No.1) at 5.

27. n.2, *supra*.

28. Social Charter preamble, recital 10.

29. Social Charter Title I para. 19.

30. *ibid.*, para. 17.

consultation and participation was perceived to be of particular importance:[31]

- when technological changes affecting working practices were introduced;

- in connection with restructuring, or mergers affecting employment;

- in cases of collective redundancy;

- when transfrontier workers in particular were affected by employment policies pursued by the undertaking where they were employed.

The Charter thus not only developed and consolidated many of the provisions of the EEC Treaty, but revived some of the issues which had previously proved too contentious for EC legislation. Being a declaration, the Charter had of itself no legal force; but it was accompanied by an action programme to implement its main principles, and which lent a new impetus to the area of employee participation.

In 1989 the Commission submitted to the Council a draft Regulation concerning the European Company Statute[32] and a draft Directive on worker participation under that statute.[33] It was proposed that the founders of any new "European Company" would be required to guarantee the right of worker representatives to consultation and information, though they would have one of three models from which to choose. Additionally, provision was to be made for corporate profit sharing, though not at the expense of other forms of participation in corporate strategy.

In the light of reactions to its proposals, the Commission issued an amended document in 1991.[34] The essential elements regarding worker participation, however, remained unchanged. In a consultative document on the revised proposal, the UK government declared that it had "profound reservations" on the participation provisions. These, the government asserted, were incompatible with what it claimed to be the UK's successful, voluntary arrangements.[35]

31. *ibid.*, para. 18.

32. See n.17, *supra*.

33. OJ C 268/89.

34. COM (91) 174 - OJ C 176/91.

35. DTI Consultative Document, *Revised Proposal for a European Company Statute* (Department of Trade and Industry, January 1992) at 2.

In 1990, the Commission focused specifically on the subject of employee participation and submitted a draft Directive on the establishment of European Works Councils in Community-scale undertakings or groups of undertakings.[36] The draft Directive aimed to formalise procedures for informing and consulting employees who worked in such enterprises. Attempts were made within the European Parliament to change its legal base from Article 100 EEC (requiring unanimity) to Article 118a EEC (qualified majority voting), but this was rejected by the Commissioner then responsible.[37] The proposal surfaced again at the first meeting of the Labour and Social Affairs Council under the Danish presidency in April 1993, at which time a majority of member states agreed that the proposed text needed revision.[38]

The UK alone was opposed to the proposal in principle. Re-iterating previous objections, it argued that the proposal fulfilled no proven need, would undermine existing local arrangements, impose costly delays, and discourage inward investment.[39] Such opposition would, under the constraint of Article 100 EEC, effectively block adoption of the proposal. The advent of the Maastricht Treaty, however, opened up an alternative route for the enactment of this seemingly controversial proposal.

Article 2(1) of the Maastricht Social Policy Agreement requires the Community, *inter alia,* to "complement the activities of the Member States" in the field of "information and consultation of workers". By virtue of paragraph (2) of the associated Protocol, such proposals are subject to qualified majority voting, suitably adjusted to reflect exclusion of the UK. Invocation of the Social Protocol thus side-steps UK opposition, allowing legislative progress among the other eleven member states.

Enactment of the draft Directive via this route would clearly establish a firm foothold for the advance of industrial democracy within the Community, though at the expense of consolidating the UK's isolation in an important facet of the social dimension. Given the historical controversy of proposed legislation in this particular field, and the attendant political risks of embarking on the road to a two-speed Social Europe, it is appropriate to consider why the Commission continues to pursue the issue of worker participation with such apparent vigour.

36.   COM (90) 581 final - OJ C 39/91.

37.   *European Industrial Relations Review* No.211 at 2.

38.   *European Industrial Relations Review* No.231 at 2.

39.   Department of Employment, *People Jobs and Progress* (Department of Employment, April 1993) at 16.

3.   THE ECONOMIC RATIONALE

A central tenet of the Commission's argument is that, if the Community is to attain its goal of a unified whole, then that unity must be reflected in the field of industry.[40] Large companies are significant producers of wealth, are often a vehicle for the introduction of new technologies and industrial methods, and they play a strategic role in the economic and social life of the Community. Yet substantial differences currently exist between the various national legal systems within which companies operate. These differences encompass areas such as the power of company directors, the rights of shareholders and employees, and the design of corporate structure. Such differences constitute a barrier to cross-frontier activities and so impede efficient exploitation of opportunities opened up by the single market. Existing strategies to overcome these barriers impose additional and unnecessary costs on industry. Approximation of national laws will go some way to overcoming these obstacles, thus freeing industry to operate fully and effectively across national boundaries.

Greater convergence of laws regulating employee participation will, it is argued, "facilitate the restructuring of enterprises within the Community on an international basis".[41] Such convergence would obviate the need for the complex legal devices currently employed to satisfy divergent national requirements.

More fundamental, perhaps, has been the argument that the single market is not an end in itself, but is simply a means to realising the "essential objective of…constant improvement of living and working conditions" within the Community.[42] Corporate life constitutes a socio-economic nexus, and thus provides a conduit through which social and economic policies may be simultaneously advanced. A broader democratic base within an enterprise also facilitates the pursuit of goals other than purely financial ones, by providing a mechanism for debating issues such as working conditions, environmental concerns and the interests of the consumer.

A further consideration is that the modern era is one of rapid social, economic and technological change. To survive, organisations will frequently have to adapt — often rapidly — to new threats, opportunities and challenges. Ensuing uncertainties, particularly during periods of economic adversity, can impose great strains on industrial relations sys-

---

40. See Part I of *Employee Participation and Company Structure* (Bulletin of the European Communities, Supplement 8/75).

41. *ibid.*, at 8.

42. EEC Preamble, recital 3.

tems, highlighting perceptions of conflicts of interest. Some degree of participation is a *sine qua non* if industrial societies are to retain their democratic character in the face of such pressures. For the Community to have tangible meaning for a large number of its citizens, the legal rights of employees cannot continue to be well developed in some member states but rudimentary in others. Widely differing legal rights could act as a barrier to the free movement of people, itself one of the fundamental freedoms of the Community.[43]

Variations in employee participation practices may also affect the realisation of another key element of the single market, namely freedom of establishment.[44] The logic of the single market requires that the location of an establishment be determined by economic considerations, and not by what has been termed the "national peculiarities" of participation practices.[45] Mergers with other undertakings have, it is claimed, demonstrably been impeded by varying degrees of employee participation.[46]

Henrik Vredeling, whose draft Directive encountered opposition in the 1980s,[47] has observed that the lack of a Community-wide participation framework might serve to frustrate national legislation in that area. Failure to submit proposals in the area of participation might, he suggests, leave the Commission open to the accusation of failure to act, within the meaning of Article 175 EC.[48]

Development of the single market may, however, bring an attendant problem of its own. The problem arises from the growth of multinational companies, which increasingly operate across national boundaries, exploiting discrepancies between national legal systems to their own advantage. The economic impact of such companies is potentially significant, extending to sensitive areas such as domestic economic growth, trade balances or even the value of currencies. Bourn, for example, has observed that enforced devaluation of the pound sterling in September 1992, and other upheavals within the European exchange rate mechanism, partly resulted from multinational companies globally transferring

43.   Kapteyn & Verloren van Themaat, n. 23, *supra* at 355.

44.   Article 52 (2) EC.

45.   Daubler W., "The Employee Participation Directive - A Realistic Utopia?" (1977) 14 *Common Market Law Review* 457 at 463.

46.   *ibid.*

47.   n.18, *supra.*

48.   Blanpain R., Blanquet F., Herman F. and Mouty A., *The Vredeling Proposal: Information & Consultation of Employees in Multinational Companies* (Kluwer, 1983) at 6.

money at short notice for short-term gain.[49] Further, multinationals frequently operate in industries of strategic importance such as telecommunications, high technology and energy. This corporate concentration of economic power makes such companies partially independent of national policies, and thus a potential threat to national sovereignty.

The international dimension of multinationals contrasts with that of trade unions, which are essentially national in scope. Whilst the formation of a suitable trade union counterbalance is not *per se* a Community issue, encouragement of collective agreements at European level[50] is clearly a step in that direction. Harmonisation of labour law to guarantee appropriate employee participation would further redress this apparent imbalance of power.

Despite its prominent role in Community deliberations, the subject of employee participation is not a uniquely Community concern, and initiatives to promote participation should be placed in the context of a more general international debate on the topic. The Organisation for Economic Co-operation and Development (OECD), for example, has long had an interest in the operations of multinational enterprises. In recognition of the substantial economic influence which such enterprises wield, the OECD in 1976 formulated guidelines which multinationals were expected to observe. *Inter alia*, multinationals were enjoined to "[r]espect the right of their employees to...engage in constructive negotiation...with a view to reaching agreement on employment conditions".[51] This objective was to be facilitated by the provision of information and other relevant facilities;[52] and changes which would have "major effects" upon employees were to be communicated with "reasonable notice" so that adverse effects might be mitigated through a process of co-operation.[53]

The guidelines, though jointly issued by OECD governments, are voluntary and have no legal force. Nevertheless, they set a framework for the conduct of multinationals, encouraging a positive attitude to co-operation with, and general disposition towards, employees. They were reviewed and, where necessary, updated in 1979, 1984 and 1991.[54] The

49. Bourn C., "Amending the Collective Dismissals Directive: A Case of Re-arranging the Deckchairs?", (1993) 9 *International Journal of Comparative Labour Law and Industrial Relations* 229.

50. Article 118b EC *cf.* Article 3 of the Maastricht Social Policy Agreement.

51. *OECD Declaration on International Investment and Multinational Enterprises*, 21 June 1976 (Section headed 'Employment and Industrial Relations', para. 1).

52. *ibid.*, paras. 2 & 3.

53. *ibid.*

54. Tergeist P., *The OECD Guidelines - an Analysis* (P+ European Participation Monitor, European Foundation for the Improvement of Living and Working Conditions) No.6, 1993 at 38.

existence of the guidelines has not, however, obviated the need for additional developments in this area. Tergeist, for example, has noted a continuing concern when key decisions affecting a subsidiary are taken elsewhere; when employees have difficulty in accessing the decision-making process; and when information necessary for collective bargaining is unavailable.[55]

Other international bodies have also expressed a view on the subject. In 1988, member states of the Council of Europe issued an Additional Protocol to the European Social Charter which, *inter alia,* guaranteed the right "to be informed and consulted within the undertaking...in accordance with national legislation and practice".[56] Such consultation was to be carried out "in good time" where proposals could substantially affect workers' interests.[57] Further, contracting states were to encourage worker contribution to "the determination and the improvement of the working conditions, work organisation and working environment".[58]

The ILO has classified arguments for greater worker participation under three main headings.[59] Firstly, are what it terms socio-political considerations. Employees, it is argued, have an interest in the functioning of an enterprise which is at least as great as that of shareholders: often more so, since the success or failure of an enterprise can affect much more than just an employee's economic circumstances. In a democratic society, it is inconsistent to eschew democracy within industry whilst advocating it in the wider sphere of public life.

Secondly, economic considerations suggest that there may be efficiency gains by involving workers in the decision-making process. Better utilisation of the knowledge, experience and intelligence of those directly involved in corporate activities can improve industrial productivity. Thirdly, there is an ethical argument that those who contribute to production and services are entitled to have their views taken into account. A younger, better educated, and more critical generation is less willing to accept authority in which it has no share.

In order to respond effectively to external competitive pressures, companies need to cultivate more dynamic, flexible and committed workforces. Greater corporate dialogue between management and labour can help anticipate change, and make adjustment processes both more efficient and more socially acceptable. Industrial democracy, it is claimed, can thus promote better relations between management and

55. *ibid.*, at 37.

56. Additional Protocol to the European Social Charter, Article 2(1).

57. *ibid.*, Article 2(1)(a).

58. *ibid.*, Article 3(1)(a).

59. *Workers' Participation in Decisions within Undertakings* (ILO, Geneva, 1981) Chapter 2.

workers, and contribute to a reduction in potential conflict. Further, a reinforcement of democratic values in commerce helps permeate those values to other levels of society, a point recognised by a 1977 inquiry into industrial democracy within the UK.[60]

Viewed against this general background, therefore, the pursuit of industrial democracy is both a necessary component of the social dimension and a pre-requisite for maintaining social cohesion in the context of the single market. It is properly to be regarded not as a discrete or peripheral measure, but as an essential element in a broad strategy aimed at realising Community objectives.

The question arises, therefore, of what the enactment of the European Works Council Directive might mean, both for the co-signatory eleven and, particularly, for the UK. A key determinant of this will be the national legislative frameworks alongside which the Directive will sit. A specific difficulty for the UK in this respect is rooted in its traditional approach to state regulation of the labour market, a difficulty further compounded by the ideological beliefs and industrial strategy of its present government.

4.   LEGISLATIVE DIVERSITY: THE UK TRADITION

Community member states differ significantly in the degree of state regulation of the labour market and in their attitudes to collective bargaining.

Drawing on material compiled by the Commission, Due *et al* have noted the existence of three main regulatory traditions within Europe.[61] Under what has been termed the "Roman-Germanic" tradition, the state plays a central role in industrial relations, typically establishing a core of basic rights as the cornerstone of national regulation. Detailed labour market legislation covers areas such as the length of the working day, mandatory rest periods and employee representation. Such a system is found in the majority of mainland European states such as Belgium, France, Germany, Greece, Italy, Luxembourg and the Netherlands. In most of these states, collective agreements between the social partners are extended, via legislation, to cover all workers and employers.

In comparison, the Anglo-Irish system of industrial relations has traditionally adopted only a limited role for the state. There has, at least

---

60. *Report of the Committee of Inquiry on Industrial Democracy* (Cmnd. 6706, HMSO, 1977). See n.64, *infra*.

61. Due J., Madsen J. and Jensen C., "The Social Dimension: convergence or diversification of IR in the Single European Market?" (*Industrial Relations Journal*, Vol. 22 No.2) 85 at 90.

until recent years, been very little legislation conferring basic rights, and there has been a tendency to abstain from regulation in the industrial relations arena. Collective agreements apply only to the parties involved: there is no general principle of *erga omnes* extension of such agreements.

The third main European system is that exhibited in the Nordic countries, of which Denmark was the sole Community representative until 1995. Nordic countries typically have strong central employer and union organisations, with many aspects of labour relations governed by central collective agreements. Legislation is very limited in comparison with the Roman-Germanic tradition, but may be initiated at the urging of the social partners. Although there is no general *erga omnes* extension of collective agreements, the high rate of union membership means that the great majority of workers are, in fact, covered by the provisions of such agreements. Worker participation is supported by formal information and consultation rights within companies.

This apparent co-operation and complementarity between state and commerce exhibits a flexible approach to legislative interventionism. Although not historically of major influence within the Community, the Nordic model may become so with the accession of Sweden and Finland as member states from 1 January 1995.

Differences in regulatory systems within the Community are reflected equally in the level at which collective agreements are negotiated, whether at national, regional or company level. And it is against such a general background, therefore, that different models of participatory practices have emerged.

The essential character of UK labour law is generally considered to have been formed in the nineteenth century, when the trade union movement first acquired a legitimate place in British society.[62] The union movement at the time sought not so much for legislation to encourage the development of collective bargaining, but for legislation to provide immunity against common law actions, which would otherwise have rendered illegal the employment of industrial sanctions by workers in the event of dispute. Unlike the case in most other industrial nations, there was a preference for a voluntary approach, rather than regulatory legal intervention. The mainstream European tradition of positive legal rights, albeit subject to conditions and qualifications, did not therefore evolve in the UK.

By the beginning of the twentieth century, unions were well established as collective bargaining organisations: collective agreements were negotiated voluntarily between the parties concerned, though they were not legally enforceable. A policy of collective *laissez-faire* emerged as the

---

62. Davies P. and Freedland M., *Labour Law: Text and Materials* (Weidenfeld and Nicolson. 1979).

dominant philosophy of UK employee relations. Gradually, however, this *laissez-faire* policy was modified by a foray of state interventions, principally on the grounds of health and safety, social stability and social justice.

The onset of the First World War, and consequent state control of strategic industries, heralded a move away from decentralised bargaining arrangements towards a more national focus. This change was consolidated by the findings of the Whitley Committee in 1917, which recommended — partly as a means of stabilising industrial relations — the creation of a number of "industrial councils", consisting of employer and union representatives. The councils were charged with the task of determining wages and conditions, and the promotion of industrial cooperation, productivity and efficiency. During the 1930s the councils largely fell into disuse, but were revived after the Second World War; and the system was extended by the introduction of statutory wages councils for the setting of minimum pay levels in low paid industries.

The first indications of a move to greater state interventionism came in the mid 1960s, with the passing of the Contracts of Employment Act, 1963, and the Redundancy Payments Act, 1965. Davies has interpreted this intervention as an attempt to promote more efficient use of labour, and thus help stem the UK's relative economic decline.[63] Further employment legislation followed in the 1970s, a decade in which the influence of Community law became increasingly apparent.

The issue of statutory provision for employee participation in the UK gained prominence in 1977, with the enquiry of the Bullock Committee into the question of industrial democracy.[64] Although the enquiry was concerned principally with the question of participation in the form of board-level representation, many of the issues raised were equally relevant to participation in the form of works councils. In a contribution to the ensuing debate, Kahn-Freund noted what he called the "fundamental dilemma" that employee participation could too easily metamorphose into negotiation.[65] Further, he contended that corporate and workers' interests might diverge in a way that corporate and shareholder interests could not. It followed, he concluded, that employee representatives might be exposed to a conflict of duties which was "insoluble".[66]

Such views did not go unchallenged. Davies and Wedderburn, for example, questioned the premise that corporate and shareholder inter-

---

63. *ibid.*, at 4.

64. *Report of the Committee of Inquiry on Industrial Democracy* (Cmnd. 6706, HMSO, 1977).

65. Kahn-Freund O., "Industrial Democracy" (1977) 6 *Industrial Law Journal* 65 at 75.

66. *ibid.*, at 77.

ests necessarily coincided.[67] Companies, they argued, had responsibilities other than simply the pursuit of profit: they had to balance the interests of a number of stakeholders — such as customers, employees and society at large. This being so, corporate and shareholder interests were not always identical. A potential conflict of duties was not, therefore, uniquely a characteristic of employee representation.

In the event, the then Labour government failed to implement the Bullock recommendations before their election defeat in 1979; and the incoming Conservative government shelved the proposals.

The coming to power of the Thatcher government in 1979 initiated a fundamental shift in the nature and underlying philosophy of UK labour law. In a radical departure from post-war consensus, the government developed a legislative programme which challenged existing assumptions about the role of trade unions and sought to give precedence to individual, rather than collective, rights. This legislative programme formed part of a broader economic strategy which aimed to reduce burdens on business, "liberalise" the labour market, and thus make industry more competitive. Ironically, this shift in philosophy coincided with, but in many respects ran counter to, the increasing influence of social legislation emanating from the Community.

The Community's legislative activity in the fields of employee rights and participation was generally resisted by the government. Statutory requirements for employee participation would, the government asserted, constitute a drain on corporate resources, would hinder effective decision-making, and undermine direct communication between employers and employees.[68] Formalism and legislation, it concluded, was inconsistent with the UK's voluntarist tradition and would reduce, not enhance, effective employee involvement. Despite the government's stance, however, elements of a participatory framework within the UK had already begun to emerge.

The Health and Safety at Work Act, 1974, for example, had earlier included provision for consultation on health and safety matters, including the establishment of committees with which consultation was to occur. Davies has observed that this approach constituted a "novel" departure for UK labour law, and was at odds with the traditional reluctance to regulate the institutions and procedures of industrial relations.[69] This apparent acceptability of regulation within the area of health and safety has been interpreted by Hepple as a concession to growing environmen-

67. Davies P. and Wedderburn of Charlton, "The Land of Industrial Democracy" (1977) 6 *Industrial Law Journal* at 200.

68. "Employee participation in Europe" (*European Industrial Relations Review*, Report No.4, 1990).

69. Davies P. and Freedland M., n.62, *supra* at 178.

talist concerns. He notes further that a concern for industrial safety is not *per se* inconsistent with the ideology of a deregulated market.[70]

An early Community initiative to have effect in the UK was the Collective Redundancies Directive of 1975,[71] which Davies has identified as the first to have a "substantial impact" on British labour law.[72] The Directive, which required consultation with workers' representatives when an employer was contemplating mass redundancies, was transposed into UK law as the Employment Protection Act, 1975. A further element in the construction of a participatory framework emerged with the enactment of the Acquired Rights Directive in 1977,[73] implemented in the UK as the Transfer of Undertakings (Protection of Employment) Regulations, 1981. But the subtlety of its transposition into UK law well illustrates the less than whole-hearted enthusiasm which such Directives encountered in the UK.

The 1981 Regulations were criticised by Rideout as clearly intended to limit the operation of the Directive: they were, he contended, constructed "so full of holes as to catch very little".[74] The Directive required that employee representatives be informed "in good time" prior to any transfer being carried out, and in any event before employees were affected by the transfer. Consultation with employees, or their representatives, was to be carried out "with a view to seeking agreement".[75] The obligation was thus quite clear.

In contrast, the UK Regulations granted the employer dispensation from the obligation to consult, where it was not reasonably practicable for him to comply. Further, the Regulations required consultation only with recognised trade unions, a restriction nowhere contained in the Directive. Even when consultation was carried out, however, the Regulations did not require them to be undertaken with a view to reaching agreement, as required by the Directive. And the Directive's constraint to provide information "in good time" was transformed into a requirement to do so only "long enough" for consultation to occur. This, Rideout

70. Hepple B., "The Crisis in EEC Labour Law" (1987) 16 *Industrial Law Journal* at 83.

71. Directive 75/129/EEC on the approximation of the laws of the Member States relating the collective redundancies.

72. Davies P. and Freedland M., n.62, *supra*, at 167.

73. Directive 77/187/EEC on the approximation of the laws of the Member States relating to the safeguarding of employees' rights in the event of transfers of undertakings, businesses or parts of businesses.

74. Rideout R., "The Great Transfer of Employee Rights Hoax" (1982) 35 *Current Legal Problems* 233 at 237.

75. Directive 77/187/EEC, Article 6(2).

observes, envisaged a considerably shorter period than the Directive intended.[76]

Whilst the UK government thus ideologically opposed increased participation rights for employees, it nevertheless pursued a related — though qualitatively different — strategy of participation through share ownership schemes, financial participation and workplace-based forms of involvement. The strategy was supported by tax changes designed to encourage profit sharing and performance-related pay. Such a strategy was seen as an alternative route to improved morale and productivity, and would help foster a change in employee attitudes and commitment. It had the perceived advantage of inherent flexibility, and would help mitigate inflationary pressures resulting from traditional wage bargaining.

The spread of financial participation in the UK during the 1980s, however, seems to have had little or no measurable effect on employee ideology. Research suggests that the implementation of such schemes has not resulted in any weakening of existing bargaining arrangements; nor has the strategy had any discernible effect on productivity. The popularity of such schemes arises more from financial opportunism than from strengthened employee commitment.[77] Financial participation has generally been regarded with some suspicion by trade union organisations, which have taken the view that it is not an effective means of influencing corporate decision-making. There is concern, too, about the associated risk to employees, who might have both their working lives and their finances invested in one organisation.

Historical traditions, coupled with the country's recent political climate, have thus conspired to set the UK apart from mainland European experience. Even within mainland Europe, however, member states have evolved a variety of participative models. But the advent of the single market has already — among a number of multinational companies — triggered a move towards a more Community-level approach. If the European Works Council Directive is not to attract widespread opposition, therefore, it needs to proffer a model which shares at least some characteristics both with national traditions and with developing practices. What might these characteristics be?

76. Rideout R., n.74, *supra* at 244.

77. *Financial Participation in Britain: a review*, (P+ European Participation Monitor, European Foundation for the Improvement of Living and Working Conditions) Issue No. 1, at 13 *et seq.*

5. Participation In Practice

(i) European Traditions

Even when the principle of participation is accepted, its mode of implementation may vary. The choice of implementation method may be influenced not only by the objectives of the parties concerned, but also by political, economic, social and cultural factors. The term "participation" may itself be interpreted in a number of ways. A distinction, for example, is sometimes made between "bargaining" (on matters where the interests of employers and employees supposedly differ) and "consultation" on matters of common interest. Both aspects, however, fall under the umbrella of "participation" for the purposes of this paper.

In its simplest form, participation may amount to nothing more than the provision of information to employees on matters of major interest. A more meaningful approach is one in which management both informs and consults employees before a decision is reached. Although an opinion may be sought, however, any decision remains the provenance of management.

The newer democracies of Greece, Portugal and Spain, for example, have works councils (or committees) which are largely informative in nature. Participation, where it exists, tends to be limited to areas such as health and safety, the organisation of production activities and training.[78]

More advanced systems of participation may be found in most other Community member states, where employee participation has evolved to embrace a broader concept of co-decision or co-determination: that is, employer and employee have an equal voice in the decision-making process, and both sides must come to an agreement before initiating change. Mechanisms for such participation range from statutory systems containing detailed provisions, to systems built on national collective agreements with more broadly defined obligations. Typically, the right of co-determination is vested in a works council or similar body, consisting of elected workers' representatives. Such a body might be empowered with certain rights and obligations in their dealings with management and employer. Participation may also extend to worker representation at board level. This may operate simply on a voluntary basis (as in Eire and France) or be established by statutory provision according to the nature and size of the company (as in Denmark and Germany). Depending on the extent of board representation, such systems amount not so much to co-determination as to co-management.

---

78. See Incomes Data Services, *Industrial Relations* (Institute of Personnel Management, 1991).

The Netherlands, for example, is characterised by a high degree of consultation and consensus. Organisations exceeding a threshold size are obliged to establish a works council, meet a minimum number of times per year, and discuss business issues on a specified minimum number of occasions. Consultation between the employer and the works council must allow sufficient time for the council's opinion significantly to influence any decision. Works council agreement is mandatory in areas such as works regulations, remuneration and job evaluation schemes, recruitment, training, dismissal and employee appraisal.

The most formalised participatory system within Western Europe is found in Germany, which operates a highly regulated form of industrial relations.[79] Industrial democracy in Germany is supported by two main elements: a structure of board-level employee representation and a system of statutory works councils at workplace level. This latter element was first established by the Works Council Act of 1920. Following abolition under the Nazi regime, works councils were re-introduced by the Works Constitution Act in 1952, and endowed with additional rights by an amendment to that act in 1972. The legislation was further amended in 1989.

Works Councils consist of employee representatives directly elected by secret ballot by the eligible workforce of an establishment, with the number of representatives determined by the size of the workforce. Representation of distinct employee groups is proportional to their numbers in the workforce. Council members are entitled to relevant training for their roles, and are released with pay for council activities. A company operating several establishments may have several works councils at each location, with a corporate works council consisting of delegates from individual councils.

Works councils are not mandatory, but may be formed in any establishment with at least five eligible employees. Once formed, however, the employer is obliged to recognise them, and meetings must be held at least once a month. Costs associated with operating a works council are the responsibility of the employer, who must also provide accommodation facilities. Members of the company's management, and other defined corporate executives, are excluded from membership. Certain establishments, principally those not of a commercial nature, are covered by separate legislation.

Works councils are separate institutions from trade unions. They represent all employees at a workplace, irrespective of whether or not they are union members. They differ from trade union representation in that they are not principally a bargaining forum: there is an emphasis

79. See Weiss M., *Labour Law and Industrial Relations in the Federal Republic of Germany* (Kluwer, 1987) at 149 *et seq.*

on co-operation for the mutual benefit of employees and the establishment, and council representatives are legally enjoined to abstain from
activities which might imperil industrial peace. Nevertheless, close links
do exist with unions, not least because the majority of council representatives tend to be union members.[80] Communication between works
councils and employees is required at least once a quarter, subject to the
proviso that representatives are bound by obligations of secrecy on matters of commercial sensitivity.

Councils have the right to express opinions on certain issues, and
may initiate proposals in some areas. They have a right to be informed
in good time on matters necessary for the discharge of their duties, and
prior to any decision being taken. They have the right of co-determination on matters such as the period of the working day, payment systems,
holidays and training. Where no agreement is reached, the matter is
decided by an arbitration committee, typically chaired by an independent labour court judge. Co-determination extends also to the introduction of new technology, where consensus is required on projects such as
the installation of some personnel information and corporate data management systems. Councils have power of veto over staff dismissals, which
allows an employee in any disputed case to appeal to the local labour
court. The German model thus endows workers with a relatively high
degree of influence over conditions of employment, working practices
and work organisation.

The French model of industrial democracy shares a number of principles in common with the German model, but differs in some respects.
Works councils (*comités d'entreprise*), legally established in 1945, are mandatory in companies of 50 or more employees. As in Germany, the
number of representatives is determined by the size of the workforce,
albeit according to a different formula. In companies of sufficient size,
councils may be established at any or all of three corporate levels - group
(*comité de groupe*), undertaking (*comités d'entreprise*) and establishment
(*comité d'établissement*). Unlike in Germany, however, works councils are
bipartite, comprising both employee and employer representatives, and
are chaired by a representative of the employer.

The operation of works councils, and associated employee activities,
is funded by the employer through the allocation of a minimum 0.2 per
cent of the gross pay bill. Depending on the size of the undertaking, sub-
committees must be established to address particular areas such as health,
safety and working conditions. In general, the role of works councils is
consultative in nature, though council agreement is mandatory in matters of profit-sharing, organisation of working time, and the establishment of health and safety committees.

80.   *ibid.*, at 152.

Taken across the Community as a whole, the scope of participation is thus something of a continuum, which starts with involvement on employee welfare issues and extends to co-decision on matters of strategic corporate interest.

The prevalence of works councils throughout the Community offers, it is suggested, *prima facie* evidence of a widespread belief in their utility at both corporate and national level. Such an interpretation would seem to be reinforced by the emergence of a trend towards the formation of works councils established at European level.[81] Developments in this area have been encouraged by significant financial assistance. At the instigation of the European Parliament, some 31 million ECU have been allocated to the financing of trans-national meetings of employees working in multinational companies — pending adoption of the European Works Council Directive.[82] There thus exists a source of empirical evidence against which the utility of works councils can be gauged. Analysis of European-wide participation within multinational companies provides both a template for comparison with the Works Council Directive and a yardstick by which to test the validity of views put forward by the UK government. In order to place Community proposals in context, therefore, corporate developments in participation practices will be reviewed.

(ii) European Multinationals

The ubiquity of works councils in mainland Europe provides a bedrock of corporate experience in industrial democracy. Completion of the single market, together with clearly signalled Community objectives in the area, seems to have provided an incentive for a number of multinational companies to address the issue of works councils at European level, in anticipation of Community legislation.

A trend towards this particular form of participation was heralded by Article 118b EEC, as amended by the Single European Act, interpreted by a number of observers as a precursor to the advent of Europe-wide collective bargaining.[83] Moves towards the formation of European level bodies first emerged in the latter half of the 1980s within French companies such as Thomson (a consumer electronics company), BSN (a food and drink producer) and Bull (an information technology manufacturer).

---

81. Gold M. and Hall M., *Report on European-level Information and Consultation in Multinational Companies — An Evaluation of Practice* (European Foundation for the Improvement of Living and Working Conditions, 1992).

82. *European Industrial Relations Review*, No.238 at 15.

83. Kapteyn & Verloren van Themaat: n.23, *supra*, at 631.

All three companies adopted an understandably cautious approach, and established the arrangement for an initial two-year period. Two of the companies (Bull and Thomson) entered into a formal agreement with trade union organisations, whereas BSN implemented an informal agreement via an exchange of letters after preliminary discussions. In each case, the forums were established principally for the purpose of exchanging and receiving information: they were not consultative in nature. In the case of BSN, it was made explicit that the European Committee was not to be a negotiating body, nor was it to encroach upon the activities of representative bodies already extant within the company.[84]

Interestingly, Thomson chose to establish two parallel European-level bodies. One, the "Liaison Committee" (*Comité de liaison*) consisted of management and trade union representatives; in the other, the "European Branch Committee" (*Commission de branche Européene*), trade union representation was replaced by staff representation drawn from existing members of works councils or similar bodies. The two committees, however, were broadly similar in purpose. Bull and BSN established single bodies comprising a mixture of trade union representatives and lay delegates.

These early moves towards European forums were later reinforced by similar developments in other multinationals, some of which were initiated by management and some by trade union organisations. In 1990, for example, the motor manufacturer Volkswagen established a European Volkswagen Group Works Council for the purpose of exchanging information, and the working out of joint positions on an agreed list of issues, where such issues affected two or more national groups. Issues encompassed by the arrangement included: security of employment; developments in group structure; trends in working time and working conditions; rationalisation through the introduction of new technology; work organisation; pay; health, safety and environmental protection; social provision; and policy developments and decisions. Trade union representatives from outside the company, and internal or external advisers, might be invited to meetings. Volkswagen management, whilst adopting a co-operative disposition, did not initially give any commitment to the continuation of the arrangement.

In 1991, employee initiatives at Mercedes Benz, with tacit support from management, led to the introduction of a European forum for the exchange of views. The petro-chemical company Elf Aquitaine reached an agreement with trade union organisations to establish a forum for the purpose of promoting "a constructive social dialogue" at European level, covering a range of "economic, financial and social issues".[85] The

84. Gold M. and Hall M., n.81, *supra,* at 120 *et seq.*

85. *ibid.,* at 103.

agreement was to operate for a trial two-year period.

Such tentative steps towards European-level arrangements have generally continued beyond the period initially agreed and, in some cases, have developed further.[86] The dual structure adopted by Thomson Electronics, for example, was replaced by a single committee comprising both employee and trade union representatives. The trial arrangement in Bull was revamped, and a transition made away from an information-oriented forum towards one more consultative in nature: employee representatives may submit recommendations on issues discussed, to which management must respond within an agreed time scale. Informal arrangements established in 1990 at Volkswagen were replaced in 1992 by formal recognition of their European works council, and providing for information exchanges on agreed topics within a framework of consultation.

Other Community based multinationals have begun to adopt similar strategies. Trade union and employer agreements within the German chemical industry, for example, have paved the way for European-level information exchanges in Bayer, Continental and Hoechst. In France, the banking group Crédit Lyonnais and the hotels group Accor — both with operations in a number of member states — have taken steps to establish European forums.

Such developments have not been confined to Community based multinationals, but have also evolved amongst a broader base of European companies. In 1990, the Swiss food and drink company Nestlé, responding to an approach by the International Union of Foodworkers, held an initial meeting with trade union representatives from each of its operating countries.[87] In the Nordic countries, too, a trend has emerged towards trans-national representation, building on the existing works council system. Ågotnes has observed that such trends imply a refocusing of trade union activity away from industry based structures towards international forms of group-level organisation.[88] Despite the absence of any statutory requirement to do so, instances of voluntary trans-national arrangements are proliferating. In Sweden, the signing of the Co-determination at Work Act, in 1977, secured an institutional foundation for participatory practices, consolidating a long established industrial tradition. Although it is not a uniquely Swedish trend, there seems to be an

86.   See Carley M., *Voluntary Initiatives — an Update* (P+ European Participation Monitor, European Foundation for the Improvement of Living and Working Conditions) No.6 1993 at 14 *et seq*.

87.   Gold M. and Hall M., n.81, *supra*, at 22.

88.   Ågotnes H., *Developments in the Nordic Countries* (P+ European Participation Monitor, European Foundation for the Improvement of Living and Working Conditions) No.6 1993 at 22.

emerging pattern of closer integration between employee participation and business planning.[89] The car manufacturer Volvo, for example, has developed a culture of participation and consultation as an explicit part of its business management strategy.[90]

(iii) An Emergent Model

This growth in multinationals which have established arrangements for — at least — the disclosure of information at European level provides the first glimpse of an embryonic Community level participatory system. A comparison of corporate experiences suggests, despite a number of variations, the emergence of some key themes.

Firstly, there is the issue of the formality of the arrangements. Some practices have been established by formal agreement whilst others have emerged as de *facto* practices given informal management support. Typically, companies initially adopt the latter approach on an experimental basis, without prejudice to future management policy. If successful, the arrangement tends to be established on a more permanent basis with the conclusion of a formal agreement. Secondly, forums thus established tend to be information oriented: that is, their competence is limited to receiving and debating information provided by corporate management. Consultation, as developed and practised through national works councils, has not yet emerged as a common characteristic. Further, discussions are generally confined to group level issues: European forums are seen as complementing, and not supplanting, extant national bodies.

The general pattern seems to be that European forums are bipartite in nature, involving both employer and employee. This is a departure from the German model, where works councils comprise employee representatives alone. The relationship between trade unions and the European forum is an issue of some debate. Employee representatives, if not themselves trade union officials, are often trade union nominees, or those who already represent employees in national bodies. Gold and Hall have suggested that this intersection helps to ensure the acceptability of the European forum to all parties concerned.[91]

There seems to be some variation between corporate practices in the way European forums are run. Some companies, for example, have

89. Cressy P., *Worker Participation: What can we learn from the Swedish Experience?* (P+ European Participation Monitor, European Foundation for the Improvement of Living and Working Conditions) No.3 1992 at 3.

90. Forslin J., *Towards Integration: the Case of Volvo Engine Division* (P+ European Participation Monitor, European Foundation for the Improvement of Living and Working Conditions) No. 3 1992 at 12.

91. Gold M. and Hall M., n.81, *supra*, at 31.

no formal agenda whereas others set the agenda in consultation with forum representatives. Similarly, procedures for recording and disseminating the discussion content of such forums vary between companies. Two common characteristics, however, are that annual meetings seem to be the norm, and the costs of running the forums are paid by the employer. There seems to be no demand for discrete representation of particular employee groups such as part-timers, ethnic minorities or the disabled.

Generally, therefore, across a wide variety of companies both within and outside the Community, the foundations are being laid for what may turn out to be the participatory elements of a European level industrial relations system. Clearly, the Works Council Directive would consolidate, formalise and develop these embryonic arrangements. The essential characteristic of existing arrangements, however, is that they are voluntary in nature, whereas the proposed Directive would introduce the shadow of legislation into this sensitive area. A fundamental question, therefore, must be how the Directive proposes to strike a balance between the imposition of prescriptive legislation on the one hand and the preservation of unfettered corporate freedom on the other.

6.   THE DRAFT EUROPEAN WORKS COUNCIL DIRECTIVE

The Directive[92] fulfils the commitment to worker involvement embodied in the 1989 Social Charter.[93] It takes as its legal base Article 100 EC, which relates to matters which "directly affect the establishment or functioning of the common market". This is consistent with the approach taken on related social legislation enacted in recent years.[94] Such legislation, when enacted through procedures of the EC Treaty, requires unanimity. Invocation of the Maastricht Social Protocol,[95] however, subjects

---

92. The analysis which follows is based on the text published in Com (90) 581 final, OJ C 39 of 15 February 1991. In an attempt to secure wider consensus on the proposal, a revised text was later issued (Com (94) 134 final, 13 April 1994). Significantly, the revision omitted all references to a 'Works Council' and used instead the term 'European Committee'. This change in nomenclature was not sustained, however, and the final revision considered at the Council of Ministers on 22 September 1994 included again the term 'Works Council'. See Postscript, *infra*.

93. Community Charter of the Fundamental Social Rights of Workers, para. 17.

94. For example, Directive 75/129 on Collective redundancies; Directive 77/187 on Transfer of undertakings; Directive 80/987 on Employment protection in the event of employer insolvency; Directive 91/533 on employers' obligations to provide details about the employment relationship.

95. Article 2 Social Policy Agreement.

the field of "information and consultation of workers" to qualified majority voting amongst the co-signatory eleven.

Reflecting, no doubt, the criticisms of the earlier Vredeling proposal[96] the Commission has clearly sought to make the Directive as flexible as possible in its application, thereby minimising its impact on any national participatory systems already in place. The Directive aims not to impose a new structure, but to create a basic mechanism for informing and consulting workers. Its purpose is to "improve the provision of information to and the consultation of employees in Community-scale undertakings and groups of undertakings".[97]

(i) Basic Principles

Organisations to which the Directive will apply are described in some detail. A "Community-scale undertaking" is defined as one having at least 1,000 employees within the Community, including at least 100 people in each of two or more member states.[98] "Community-scale group of undertakings" is defined[99] as a controlling undertaking which has:

- at least 1,000 employees within the Community;

- at least two group undertakings in different member states, each employing 100 or more employees within the Community.

A "controlling undertaking" is defined by reference to certain specified criteria.[100] The formal request to set up a European Works Council may come either from employees, their representatives, or from management.[101] Such a request having once been made, however, it falls to an undertaking's central management to implement the request.[102] Negotiations regarding the setting up of a European works council are conducted between central management and a "special negotiating body".[103] This latter body is to consist either of employee representatives or of employees

---

96. n.18, *supra.*

97. Article 1(1).

98. Article 2(a).

99. Articles 2(b) and 2(c).

100. Article 3.

101. Article 5(3).

102. Article 4(2).

103. Article 5(1).

specifically elected for the purpose.[104] Member states determine for themselves the method by which "representatives of employees or, in the absence thereof, the body of employees…shall appoint or elect [its members]".[105] The composition of the negotiating body is subject to the constraints that:

- Each member state employing 100 or more employees has at least one representative.

- Additional national representation is determined in proportion to the number of employees thus represented.

For negotiation purposes, the negotiating body may be assisted by experts of its own choosing.[106] Expenses relating to negotiations are to be met by the undertaking concerned.[107] Once established, the negotiating body may decide unanimously not to request the setting up of a European Works Council.[108] Should negotiations with central management proceed, however, then one of four possible outcomes may result:

(a) An agreement to establish a European Works Council [109]

Any such agreement must determine:

— the nature and composition of the European Works Council;
— its function and powers;
— the procedures by which it is informed and consulted;
— the place, frequency and duration of council meetings;
— the resources to be allocated to the council.

(b) An agreement not to establish a European Works Council [110]

By written agreement, the negotiating body and central management may jointly decide not to set up such a council. In this event, minimum rights to information and consultation — specified in an Annex to the Directive, and described later in this paper — come into play.

104. *ibid.*
105. Article 5(5).
106. Article 5(3).
107. Article 5(4).
108. Article 5(3).
109. Article 6(1).
110. Article 6(2).

(c) An agreement to apply national legislation [111]

The negotiating body and central management may jointly decide to apply the minimum legislative requirements of the member state in which central management is located. Such minimum requirements must satisfy the minimum requirements specified in an Annex to the Directive.

(d) Failure to agree [112]

If — after one year of the initial request to convene the special negotiating body — no agreement is reached, then minimum national requirements apply as described in the preceding paragraph.

Member states may permit central management to withhold information the release of which could "substantially damage" the interest of the undertakings concerned.[113] Equally, members of a European Works Council are obliged to respect the confidentiality of any information provided to them in confidence.[114]

Members of both the European Works Council and the negotiating body are afforded the same legal protection as is normally enjoyed by employees' representatives in the country of employment.[115] They must be allowed to attend meetings of the negotiating body or the council; and members who are also employees must be guaranteed "full wages" while absent from work in connection with their duties.[116]

Member states are to provide "appropriate remedies" in case of failure to comply with the Directive. In particular, states are to ensure that "adequate procedures" exist by which provisions of the Directive may be enforced at the suit of the European Works Council.[117]

(ii) Minimum Requirements

In cases where the negotiating body and central management decide to rely on national provisions, or when they fail to reach an agreement, then the minimum requirements summarised below apply:

111. Article 7.
112. *ibid.*
113. Article 8(1).
114. Article 8(2).
115. Article 9.
116. *ibid.*
117. Article 10(2).

(a) Competence is to be limited to matters either concerning the undertaking as a whole, or concerning two or more of its establishments in member states.[118]

(b) The European Works Council must consist of at least one representative from each member state where an undertaking has 100 or more employees. It must have not less than 3 and not more than 30 members.[119]

(c) Meetings with central management must occur at least annually. At such meetings, the council will be informed about business, financial and economic issues affecting or relating to the undertaking.[120]

(d) The European Works Council has the right to "timely" consultations on "any management proposal likely to have serious consequences for the interests of the employees of the undertaking".[121]

(e) At least one annual "special meeting" may be held "where necessary" for consultation purposes, when requested by the council.[122]

(f) Council members must inform workers' representatives at establishment or group level of the outcome of meetings with central management. "In the absence" of such representatives, communication is to take place directly with the body of employees.[123]

(g) Operating expenses of the council are to be borne by central management.[124]

Conditions (b) and (e) above do not apply in cases where the negotiating body and central management formally agree not to establish a European Works Council.[125]

118. Annex 1(a).
119. Annex 1(b).
120. Annex 1(c).
121. Annex 1(d).
122. Annex 1(e).
123. Annex 1(f).
124. Annex 1(g).
125. Article 6(2).

7. OBSERVATIONS AND REACTIONS

There are clearly some similarities between the voluntary arrangements described earlier and the requirements of the Directive. A key difference, however, is that existing voluntary arrangements tend to be limited to the provision and discussion of information. The Directive goes beyond that by providing for consultation on any management proposal having "serious consequences" for employees. It is important to note that such consequences must have a trans-national element — that is, a proposal having an effect in one member state alone falls outside the scope of the Directive. Nevertheless, despite this mandatory consultation, the final decision remains the exclusive responsibility of management.

A second important consideration is that the Directive makes no explicit provision for trade union participation, leaving the matter to be decided by the legislation of individual member states. Further, the definition of employee "representatives" may vary from state to state. Trade union representatives from Eire, therefore, could participate in a European Works Council alongside works council members from states such as France and Germany. Such flexibility is reflected, too, in the mode of selection for both the negotiating body and the European Works Council, which will follow national practices.

Also of note is the fact that the Directive follows the German model, in that European Works Councils are to consist of employee representatives alone: they are not to be bipartite forums, as is the case in France. This represents a departure from the emerging pattern of voluntary arrangements, which typically adopt the French model. The practical consequences of this, however, are likely to be minimal, since the function of the council is defined principally in terms of meetings with central management. In contrast, the minimum requirement of an annual meeting is consistent with the voluntary pattern; but the Directive goes further in that it allows at least one additional "special meeting...where necessary" for consultative purposes. Unlike existing voluntary arrangements, European works councillors are obliged to disseminate information either to employee representatives or directly to employees themselves, although the method for doing so is not specified.

Not surprisingly, perhaps, the Directive has attracted much comment. Rood, for example, has taken a generally critical stance, suggesting that the Directive "promises more than it delivers".[126] At a strategic level, Rood criticises the Commission's apparent preoccupation with trans-national

---

126. Rood M., "Workers' Participation: New Initiatives at European Level", (1992) 8 *International Journal of Comparative Labour Law and Industrial Relations* 319 at 330.

companies, noting that such a focus excludes the majority of companies within the Community. By doing so, he argues, the Directive fails to address its declared aim of reducing inequality in the treatment of employees, and hence fails to reduce market distortion. The Directive is "ineffectual" in that — *vis-à-vis* conglomerate companies — it concentrates on decisions by the parent company. It ignores the fact that decisions having unfavourable consequences for employees may be taken by subsidiaries: decisions in which employees might have no say. The right to consultation, he asserts, will rarely be relevant.[127]

The European employers' organisation, UNICE, has also taken the view that the Directive will not achieve its aim.[128] Citing the diversity of company operations within Europe, it argues that no single process can be applied to all companies. Existing practices of information and consultation have evolved in response to particular circumstances, and a single legislative approach is inflexible and harmful. On the basis of a recent study, it suggests that multinationals already inform their employees better than do national organisations, and that the most meaningful communication process occurs between employees and their immediate superior. The tenor of the Directive, it is claimed, is at odds with decentralised management structures. A statutory requirement to inform and consult may result in an inefficient use of resources, constrain management decision-making, and have an adverse effect on competitiveness. UNICE takes the view that the Directive is based on questionable research, and its implementation will impair the performance of European business.[129] Underpinning this perspective seems to be a concern that the proposal is a vehicle for the development of trans-national union structures, and hence for pan-European collective bargaining.

The CBI has echoed these sentiments, contending that the Directive brings "costs without benefits". Mandatory consultation would, it is argued, prove a "substantial drain" on management resources, and would entail protracted "difficult" negotiations against the "threat" of compulsory fall-back procedures.[130] It suggests that the Directive will have a disproportional effect on British companies because the UK labour market is more decentralised than its continental neighbours, and thus less suited to centralised negotiation. It argues, too, that the UK has more multi-union workplaces, which would make application of the Directive in the UK more cumbersome. More fundamentally, the CBI asserts that

127. *ibid.*

128. UNICE, *Thriving on Diversity: Informing and Consulting Employees in Multinational Enterprises* (1993).

129. *ibid.*, at 23.

130. Confederation of British Industry, *Social Europe After Maastricht: Freedom, not license* (CBI, 1992) para. 28.

the continental system of purposive legal interpretation places UK firms at a relative disadvantage, since British courts enforce a literal interpretation of the law. Lest there be any residual doubt about its hostility to the proposals, it denounces the Directive's requirements as "costly and irrelevant charades".[131]

The British Institute of Directors, in a more strategic critique of Community social legislation, takes the view that current economic and political forces point to the need for a change in policy direction.[132] It encourages the application of subsidiarity in social and employment policy, and favours the promotion of individual enterprise over collectivism. In emulation, perhaps, of government initiatives in other areas, it has formulated its own "Charter for a Citizens' Europe".[133] In keeping with the IOD's preference for flexibility, the "Charter" offers no legally enforceable rights, but simply enunciates a set of broad principles and guidelines. Employee involvement would be limited to a "participative role...through financial participation schemes", but without the imposition of any particular system.[134]

Such responses find ready support within the UK government which believes that the Directive would create "damaging" delays in implementing business decisions and impose an unnecessary burden at a time when the Community is struggling to emerge from recession.[135]

The view of employee bodies within Europe is, however, radically different. The ETUC has broadly welcomed the Directive, regarding it as a necessary counterbalance to the centralisation of corporate decision-making which the single market will engender.[136] Policy formulation at European level is perceived as a necessary precondition for action at other levels, if market distortions are to be avoided and social and economic cohesion is to be secured.[137] Subsidiarity, the ETUC observes, necessarily implies action at European level on certain issues. Information and consultation in European-wide companies, it argues, is just such an issue — since no individual member state can effectively tackle a matter which is, by definition, trans-national.[138]

131. *ibid.*, at para. 43.

132. Institute of Directors, *The Future of European Social Policy: IOD Submission to the European Commission* (IOD, 1993).

133. *ibid.*, at 8.

134. *ibid.*, at 10.

135. Forsyth M., (Minister of State at the Department of Employment), *The Future Direction of EC Social Policy* (Paper delivered at CBI conference, London, 14 October 1993).

136. Gold M. and Hall M., n.81, *supra*, at 62.

137. Gabaglio E., *The future direction of EC Social Policy: the ETUC View* (Paper delivered at CBI Conference, London, 14 October 1993) at 6.

138. *ibid.*

Within the UK, the TUC has echoed this interpretation, observing that the Directive exemplifies what it terms the principle of "subsidiarity through collective bargaining".[139] It sees the Directive as the archetype of a new, flexible approach to social legislation which both contributes to economic efficiency and advances social justice. New consultative structures in multinational companies, it argues, are of critical importance to unions as the economic consequences of the single market begin to take effect.[140] Despite this seemingly favourable response, however, the fact remains that the proposal raises issues for the UK regarding both the selection of workplace representatives and the role of trade unions. The relationship of a works council system to collective bargaining as developed in the UK also remains unresolved.

The Commission, meanwhile, seems to regard British reaction as a consequence of the Directive having been "misinterpreted".[141] The flexibility inherent in the Directive is seen as providing the social partners with an opportunity to play a much greater role in developing and implementing policy. Accusations that social legislation has a deleterious effect on business are rejected. National regulations, it is claimed, are often more complex, whereas Community legislation simply seeks to establish minimum standards. Community legislation constitutes only a minor part of the body of regulation to which companies in Europe are subject.

Despite this controversy, therefore, the Commission maintained that action was necessary to secure the enhanced level of employee commitment which present economic conditions required.[142] It thus continued along the legislative path. The key questions for British companies are: to what extent the UK will remain immune from these developments, and whether the UK's isolationist stance can be maintained?

8. CONCLUSION

The coming into force of the Maastricht Treaty on 1 November 1993 marks the beginning of a new phase in the development of what has now formally been renamed the "European Community".[143] *Inter alia*, activi-

139. TUC, *Unions after Maastricht: The challenge of Social Europe* (Trades Union Congress, 1992) at 26.

140. *ibid.*, at 27.

141. Flynn P., (Commissioner for Social Affairs and Employment), *The Future Direction of EC Social Policy* (Paper delivered at CBI Conference, London, 14 October 1993) at 8.

142. COM (94) 134 final 13 April 1994 at 4, para. 7.

143. Treaty on European Union, Title II, Article G.

ties of the Community include "the strengthening of economic and social cohesion"[144] with a view to eventual economic and monetary union.
Under the Treaty, the Community is subject to the subsidiarity principle
of Article 3b as a general constraint upon its legislative activity. Subsidiarity
requires the Community to take action "only if...the objectives...cannot
be sufficiently achieved by the Member States and can...be better
achieved by the Community". Further, any such action must not "go beyond what is necessary to achieve the objectives of [the] Treaty".[145] The
principle will apply wherever powers are held concurrently by both the
Community and member states. Social policy, as an area of shared competence, is therefore a field where subsidiarity could have a potential
impact.

The essence of the Treaty is the creation of a European Union,[146] of
which member state nationals automatically have citizenship.[147] Rights
conferred by the Treaty are to be enjoyed by all citizens of the Union.[148]
Amongst such rights is the right of a Union citizen, either individually or
in association with others, to petition the European Parliament on any
matter "which comes within the Community's fields of activity, and which
affects him directly".[149] The Treaty extends the powers of the European
Parliament, which may now both request the Commission to submit legislative proposals[150] and investigate alleged contraventions or
maladministration of Community law.[151] Given Parliament's recent pre-
disposition in favour of social legislation,[152] it is not unreasonable to sup-
pose that these powers may add a greater momentum to the formulation of social policy.

A fundamental issue arising from the Treaty, and as yet unresolved,
is the legality of the Protocol itself. Whilst the *corpus* of the Treaty provides additional powers for securing the effective enforcement — and
hence uniform application — *of* Community law, the Protocol simultaneously provides a mechanism for some states — the co-signatory eleven
— to adopt their own "Community" legislation, thus compromising that
very uniformity. This internal threat to the Community legal order may
be challenged on the grounds that it is incompatible with the principles

144. Article 3(j) EC.

145. Article 3b EC.

146. TEU, Title I, Article A.

147. Article 8(1), EC.

148. Article 8(2), EC.

149. Article 138d, EC.

150. Article 138b, EC.

151. Article 138c, EC.

152. See, for example, n.37, *supra.*

on which the Community is based. The Court previously declared that the proposed Treaty on a European Economic Area conflicted with the Community's *acquis communautaire* on precisely those grounds.[153] The Protocol may also be challenged on the grounds that it potentially distorts competition within the Community.[154] Further, to the extent that workers will not be guaranteed the same standard of rights in the UK, the Protocol may frustrate the free movement of workers within the Community,[155] and thus impede the attainment of Community objectives.[156]

Setting such considerations aside for the moment, a fundamental hurdle for the UK in the field of Community labour law is its radically different legal heritage. Almost all mainland European states are accustomed to a high degree of regulation of employment, whereas the UK is not. Most states thus have no difficulty in countenancing greater harmonisation and the setting of European standards. Indeed, such harmonisation may be welcomed, since it prevents individual states adopting lower standards in the pursuit of economic advantage. This, of course, is precisely the strategy of the UK government, which thus strikes at the principle on which the Community is founded. A genuine and effective single market requires uniformity of employment conditions, including social labour costs.

This difference in attitudes reflects, it is suggested, a deeper ideological divide. The very term "social partners" seems peculiarly "European", invoking images of shared responsibility, interdependence and alliance. It encapsulates a perception that all players in industry are essentially on the same side, and should thus make common cause where possible. Such a perspective accords closely with the Union's aim of harmonious social and economic progress.[157] It is, indeed, difficult to see how such an objective might be attained other than through closer links between economic and social policies. Interdependence between a society and its economy has long been recognised in Germany, for example, which refers not to a "free market" but to the "social market" or *soziale Marktwirtschaft*.[158] This, it is suggested, is more than mere semantics: it is an acknowledgment that part of the function of commerce is to provide not only economic success, but social stability. It reflects too, perhaps, a realisation that global competitiveness occurs not simply between individual companies but, ultimately, between socio-economic systems.

153. Opinion 1/91, *Re the Draft Treaty on a European Economic Area* [1992] 1 CMLR 245 at 272, para. 50.

154. Thus breaching Article 3(f) EC.

155. Breaching Articles 3(c) and 48 EC.

156. Thus breaching Article 5 EC.

157. Treaty on European Union, Article B.

158. Kapteyn & Verloren van Themaat, n.23, *supra*, at 665.

This *credo* sits uneasily alongside the traditionally adversarial approach between management and labour characteristic of the UK. Budd and Jones have taken the issue further, and suggested a hidden European agenda to remedy a perceived failure of such confrontational attitudes.[159] Only by the creation of a broader economic democracy, they suggest, will all states be able to participate fully in the formulation of an industrial strategy for the Community.

The ability of the UK — or indeed of any state — to remain independent of Union policy must, it is submitted, be in doubt. Of particular relevance in the field of labour law is the jurisprudence of the Court of Justice regarding individual rights. It has long been established that one of the intentions of Community law is to confer upon individuals "...rights which become part of their legal heritage",[160] a stance developed through a series of cases, culminating — in what has been seen as a "natural and logical extension" of the Court's reasoning — in the *Francovich* judgment.[161]

Such rights arise not solely from Community law, but also from a wider jurisdiction. The Court has established that fundamental rights form an integral part of the general principles of law, which the Court will take into consideration when forming its judgments. International treaties in which member states have co-operated, or to which they are parties, can also be used to interpret Community law.[162] The Protocol, it might be argued, is — at least in part — the product of international agreements to which the UK has been party.[163] Non-application of the Protocol in the UK contradicts the rights enunciated in those agreements, and is thus at odds with Community law. Further, a British worker might argue that non-application of the Protocol in the UK breaches the non-discriminatory principle of Article 6 EC, and conflicts with the right of citizenship embodied in Article 8 EC. The Court has already held that exceptions to fundamental principles of equality should be narrowly construed, and "subject to control by the institutions of the Community".[164]

---

159. Budd S. and Jones A., n.6, *supra*, at 110.

160. Case 26/62, *Van Gend & Loos* v. *Nederlandse Administratie der Belastingen* [1963] ECR at 2.

161. Steiner J., "From direct effects to *Francovich*: shifting means of enforcement of Community Law", (1993) 18 *European Law Review* 3 at 9.

162. Case 4/73, *Nold* v. *Commission* [1974] 2 CMLR 338 at 354.

163. The preamble to the Social Charter, for example, explicitly states that it has drawn inspiration from Conventions of the International Labour Organisation and from the European Charter of the Council of Europe, to both of which the UK is a signatory.

164. Case 36/75, *Roland Rutili* v. *Minister for the Interior* [1975] ECR 1219 at 1231.

The UK's inability freely to pursue its own labour law agenda is well illustrated, as Ewing observes, by the fact that European directives underpinned several provisions of the 1993 Trade Union Reform and Employment Rights Act (TURER).[165] *Inter alia*, TURER amended[166] the existing Transfer of Undertakings (Protection of Employment) Regulations, 1981.[167] The UK, in restricting application of the Regulations to commercial ventures only, was in breach of the Directive which the Regulations supposedly implemented.[168] TURER further remedied the omission from the Regulations of the requirement to consult "with a view to seeking...agreement to measures to be taken".[169] Similarly amended by TURER were provisions relating to consultation in the event of collective redundancies. These consultations, too, must now be undertaken "with a view to reaching agreement" on ways of avoiding, reducing or mitigating the consequences of redundancies.[170] No longer is the employer granted dispensation where it was not reasonably practicable for him to comply.[171]

What TURER failed to do, however, was to remove the obligation to consult only with trade union representatives, a restriction contained in neither of the relevant directives.[172] UK employers may thus circumvent their obligations simply by refusing to recognise trade unions. This defect in UK legislation, which thus failed to implement Community law, was acknowledged by the Court of Justice in its judgment of 8 June 1994.[173] It is perhaps worth noting that the Institute of Personnel Management had earlier advised British employers to apply the consultative provisions not of TURER, but of the relevant directive.[174] A similar approach was previously adopted by the British Coal Corporation, when it elected to apply the consultative requirements of Directive 75/129, rather than the relevant provisions of the Trade Union and Labour Relations (Consoli-

---

165. Ewing K., "Swimming with the Tide: Employment Protection and the Implementation of European Labour Law" (1993) 22 *Industrial Law Journal* 165.

166. Section 33(2) of the Act.

167. See n.73, *supra*.

168. Case C-29/91, *Dr. Sophie Redmond Stichting* v. *Bartol and others* [1992] IRLR 366.

169. Section 33(6).

170. Section 34(2).

171. Section 34(4).

172. Directive 187/77/EEC on the Transfer of Undertakings; Directives 75/129/EEC and 92/56/EEC on collective redundancies.

173. Case C-382/92, *Commission* v. *United Kingdom*, Notice 92/C 306/11 OJ C 306, November 24, 1992. Not yet reported.

174. Institute of Personnel Management, *Trade Union Reform and Employment Rights Act 1993: Personnel Practitioners' Checklist* (IPM, July 1993) at 2 & 3.

dation) Act, 1992.[175] This, it is suggested, evidences a growing realisation that Brussels, not London, sets the principles of employment practice in the UK.

The UK's putative isolation from the effects of the Social Protocol is further undermined by the fact that the CBI and TUC, as members of UNICE and ETUC respectively, will be involved in the social dialogue envisaged by Article 3. As Barnard points out,[176] such involvement will raise awareness in the UK of the progress of social legislation in the rest of Europe, and may well impact on UK collective bargaining. The European Works Council Directive, having advanced through the process of dialogue, may stimulate just such an awareness.

The Directive may, under Article 2(4) of the Social Policy Agreement, be implemented via collective agreements. Ironically, even this degree of flexibility could pose potential difficulties for the UK, since British law holds that collective agreements are, in general, neither binding on the parties concerned nor enforceable in the courts. Indeed, in a submission to the European Court, the UK government asserted that it was unaware of any UK collective agreement having a legally binding nature.[177]

This potential difficulty is compounded by issues concerning the scope of application of such agreements, since they will need to cover all relevant areas if full compliance is to be secured:[178] agreements having only *inter partes* effects cannot be used to ensure compliance with Community legislation.[179] Only, as Adinolfi suggests, if a collective agreement is extended *erga omnes* could it qualify as a valid Community instrument. Her observations seem to be supported by case law, which has provided that exclusion of certain workers from collective agreements constitutes failure correctly to implement a directive.[180] In any event, states must be able to guarantee the results of directives thus implemented.[181] It is perhaps apposite that the UK, in not being a signatory to the Protocol, may escape having to grasp this particular nettle. Nevertheless, such considerations constitute a latent dilemma for a future UK administration.

175. *R. v. British Coal Corporation and Secretary of State for Trade and Industry ex parte Vardy* [1993] IRLR 104 para. 129.

176. Barnard C., "A Social Policy for Europe - Politicians 1 : 0 Lawyers" (1992) 8 *International Journal of Comparative Labour Law and Industrial Relations* 15 at 28.

177. Case 165/82, *Commission* v. *UK* [1984] 1 CMLR 44 at 49.

178. Case 235/84, *Commission* v. *Italy* [1986] ECR 2291.

179. Adinolfi A., "The Implementation of Social Policy Directives through Collective Agreements" (1988) 25 *Common Market Law Review* 304.

180. Case 215/83, *Commission* v. *Belgium* [1985] 3 CMLR 624.

181. Article 2(4) Social Policy Agreement.

The difficulty in which the UK finds itself is not, however, simply a consequence of Community activity. Moves away from the traditional voluntarist approach had started even before the UK's accession to the Community. Greater regulation of health and safety, and issues raised by the Bullock enquiry,[182] for example, both preceded the concept of a Community social dimension. Towers has further observed that British voluntarist traditions were undermined by the thrust of domestic legislation introduced by the Thatcher government between 1980 and 1991.[183] The foundation of UK labour law has also been eroded by the decline of trade unions, on which the collective *laissez-faire* system was based.

The European Works Council Directive attracts particular hostility because in it are coalesced concepts both of legal regulation and industrial democracy, neither of which has been unreservedly accepted within the UK. Additionally, since the UK has the highest concentration of multinational companies, the Directive is of potentially greater domestic impact.[184] Irrespective of the UK's position, however, enactment of the Directive would require qualifying British companies to introduce a works council for their continental employees. Some companies may take the view that the UK opt-out is best ignored, rather than attempt to maintain divergent consultative practices within their workforces. Equally, is it realistic for a UK branch of a European company to refuse to send representatives to a European Works Council established elsewhere in Europe?

Yet participative ideas embodied in the Directive are not unfamiliar to the UK. Batstone has noted that such ideas, together with legislation for worker involvement, gained prominence in the UK in periods around both world wars.[185] This, he notes, was triggered by a need to ensure maximum production and efficiency, and to foster worker commitment and co-operation in the face of national crises.

The underlying hypothesis accords with current management theories, which posit that recognition of employees is important in securing their commitment: communication and participation are powerful forms of recognition. Effective social dialogue can accelerate change and help promote shared values, two critical ingredients of business success. Conversely, a perceived disinterest in employees' views can foster a sense of

182. n.64, *supra.*

183. Towers B., "Two speed ahead: social Europe and the UK after Maastricht" (*Industrial Relations Journal*, Vol. 23 No. 2) 83 at 84.

184. Sisson K., Waddington J. and Whitston C., "Company Size in the European Community", *Human Resource Management Journal*, (1991) Vol. 2, No. 1, 94 at 103.

185. Batstone E. and Davies P., *Industrial Democracy: European Experience* (HMSO, London, 1977) at 11.

helplessness and impotence in the face of change. Frustrations thus engendered can trigger a loss of enthusiasm, contributing to a decline in morale and a fall in productivity.

Arguments that worker participation can produce a conflict of interest, and impede decision making, appear unfounded. Experience in Germany, where such participation is long-established, suggests on the contrary a positive correlation between participation, high efficiency and corporate profitability. The risk of social conflict resulting from the exclusion of employees would seem to outweigh the perceived drawbacks of participation.[186]

Discussions between social partners in the area of new technology seem to have highlighted the economic benefits of a participative approach. A recent European study revealed that project participation significantly increased the acceptability of new technology to employees.[187] It improved their identification with the company, and had a positive effect on industrial relations generally. Awareness of participation as a means of enhancing corporate competitiveness and productivity was strengthened as a result.

Economic globalisation, however, injects a new urgency to the issue not just of corporate competitiveness, but to the competitiveness of the Union as a whole. Deepening of the single market, of itself and by its very nature, will disrupt national forms of practice and regulation. Trade will become more internationalised and labour markets more interdependent. Unchecked, poorer states may seek to minimise social regulation and make costs the sole vector of competition. Such an outcome would compromise the Union's strategic need to compete globally on quality in all its forms — not least in technology, production methods, marketing and technical skills. Only by supranational action can the risk of such a cost reduction war within the Union be reduced. It seems inevitable, therefore, that national structures of labour law will gradually be replaced by a *corpus* of laws at European level. The emergence of transnational bargaining, in combination with legally enforceable agreements, would significantly reinforce such a development.

The European Works Council Directive signals a new phase in the drive to realise Union objectives. Its aim of involving workers in the decision-making process fully reflects the principle of taking decisions as closely as possible to the citizen.[188] In its implication that workers are not

186. *Employee Participation and Company Structure* (Bulletin of the European Communities, Supplement 8/75) especially pp.30 -39.

187. Gill C., "The involvement of trade unions in quality: evidence from EC enterprises", *New Technology, Work and Employment*, Vol. 8, No. 2, September 1993, 122 at 132.

188. TEU, Title I, Article A.

commodities, subject to unfettered market forces, it supports the Community's task of promoting "economic and social cohesion and solidarity among Member States".[189] *Post* Maastricht, the economic and monetary road to political union has been beset with financial and recessionary upheavals. But the social route to political union, though difficult, remains open. Ideas embodied in the Directive foreshadow, it is submitted, a renewed emphasis on socio-economic concerns, as a vehicle for securing popular support for the ultimate political goal. There are wider implications too: successful resolution of the issues raised would help remove obstacles to the previously shelved proposals on a European Company Statute and the Fifth Directive.[190]

But paradigmatic change invariably engenders resistance. The UK, which foresees something of a quantum shift in its voluntarist tradition, might thus be expected to raise the most vociferous opposition — though this could change abruptly should a Labour government come to power. Paradoxically, however, Eire — which shares much of the UK legal tradition — has been more sanguine. It might, of course, be politically difficult for the Irish government to oppose a programme championed so diligently by an Irish Commissioner. Yet the Directive marks the beginning, rather than the end, of a debate. In a Green Paper on future strategy, the Social Affairs Commissioner has noted that social policy is entering a "critical" phase.[191] In the context of reinforcing social dialogue, questions such as the relative roles of national legislation, of Community standards, and of collective agreements are highlighted as issues to be clarified and agreed.[192]

The growing influence of the Community legal order, the logic of the single market, and emergent industrial practices thus all point to a growing momentum in the social sphere: a momentum, it is suggested, which the UK will be unable to withstand. Put simply, Britain faces a choice. It must choose between active participation in European political and economic life; or it must choose to remain outside, either fully or partially, in an isolation which offers few if any discernible benefits. Sooner or later, reason suggests, the UK will conform with majority practice. In the words of the Italian Foreign Minister, "...it will be like the planets — the eleven will attract the one, not the other way around."[193]

---

189. TEU Title II, Article 2.

190. See n.17 and n.16 respectively, *supra*.

191. *European Social Policy: Options for the Union* (Consultative document issued by Mr. Padraig Flynn, 15 November 1993) at 6.

192. *ibid.*, at 71.

193. Quoted in *European Community Survey*, Editor Alan Griffiths (Longman, 1992) at 169.

9. POSTSCRIPT

On 22 September 1994, the Council of the European Union agreed the final text of the Directive.[194] The principal changes and additions with regard to the text discussed in this paper are:

- For the purposes of this Directive, the term "Member States" is taken to include only the eleven co-signatory states of the Maastricht Social Protocol.[195]

- The decision may be taken not to set up a European Works Council at all, but to establish instead a "procedure for informing and consulting employees".[196]

- The threshold number of employees needed to trigger application of the Directive in an undertaking is increased to 150 in at least two member states.[197]

- Threshold workforce sizes includes part-time employees, and is based upon the average number of employees during the previous two-year period.[198]

- Central management is responsible for creating the "conditions and means" necessary for setting up a European Works Council or alternative procedure.[199] If central management is not located in one of the eleven co-signatory states then either a local representative, or the management of its largest establishment in those states, assumes responsibility for obligations arising from the Directive.[200]

- Negotiations to establish a European Works Council may be initiated either by management, or at the written request of at least 100 employees or their representatives in two or more member states.[201]

194. Directive 94/45/EC of 22 September 1994, OJ L 254 of 30 September 1994.

195. Preamble, para. 5.

196. Article 1 (2).

197. Article 2 (1)(a).

198. Article 2 (2).

199. Article 4 (1).

200. Article 4 (2).

201. Article 5 (1).

- The special negotiating body, once convened, may decide by at least a two-thirds majority not to open or proceed with negotiations.[202]

- Member states may lay down budgetary rules regarding operation of the special negotiating body, and may limit funding to cover one expert only.[203]

- The previously entitled "minimum requirements" have been re-named "subsidiary requirements". They will apply only where so agreed, or when no agreement can be reached.[204]

- Obligations arising from the Directive will not apply where an agreement for trans-national information and consultation is already in force by the date required for implementation of the Directive.[205]

These textual amendments reflect a desire to minimise unnecessary burdens on organisations,[206] and also to incorporate expressed views of the social partners.[207] The Directive clearly reflects a view that progress in this area is an essential step towards attaining broader economic objectives.[208] Imminent accession of the Nordic countries to the European Union seems likely to extend the ambit of the Directive, thereby further highlighting UK isolation in this key area.

---

202. Article 5 (5).

203. Article 5 (6).

204. Article 7.

205. Article 13.

206. COM (94) 134 final, 13 April 1994, para. 17.

207. *ibid.*, para. 18.

208. *ibid.*, para. 41.

4. Application of the Right of Free Movement for Workers under the European Economic Area Agreement

Ingeborg Borgerud

1. INTRODUCTION

The European Community and its Member States and the countries of the European Free Trade Association (EFTA) concluded an Agreement on 2 May 1992 which created the European Economic Area (EEA).[1] The aim of the EEA Agreement, expressed in Article 1, is "to promote a continuous and balanced strengthening of trade and economic relations between the Contracting Parties with equal conditions of competition, and the respect of the same rules, with a view to creating a homogeneous European Economic Area". To attain these objectives the Agreement entails six essential elements specified in Article 1(2) EEA, including free movement of goods, persons, services and capital.

The purpose of the Agreement is to extend the internal market of the Community to include also the EFTA States. Such an aim can only be realised if the same legal rules essential for the proper functioning of the internal market are applied in a uniform manner throughout all the countries concerned.[2] The acceptance by the EFTA States of the *acquis communautaire* as regards the four freedoms and the competition rules, was therefore an important issue during the negotiations.

---

1. On the same day the Ministers from the EFTA States also signed two Agreements creating among themselves the necessary institutions and structures required by the EEA Agreement. One of the separate EFTA Agreements provides for the establishment of a Standing Committee of the EFTA States. The other Agreement contains provisions for the establishment of a Surveillance Authority and a Court of Justice (hereafter called the ESA-EFTA Court Agreement).

2. Sven Norberg, "The Agreement on a European Economic Area", (1992) 29 *Common Market Law Review* 1171 at p.1171.

The provisions of the EEA Agreement on free movement of workers are based on the relevant provisions of the EEC[3] Treaty. According to Article 28 EEA free movement of workers shall be secured among EC Member States and EFTA States. Secondary Community legislation is integrated into the Agreement through references to Annexes listing the relevant regulations and directives in Community law concerning free movement of workers. A special emphasis should be made of Council Regulation 1612/68 which is the primary legal act detailing free movement of labour in the Community. The Regulation has become part of the EEA Agreement, and the principles of the Regulation now apply to most workers living within the area.

Article 28 EEA must be read in conjunction with Article 4 EEA which prohibits any discrimination on grounds of nationality. The Agreement does not only forbid direct discrimination but applies as well to all other activities which in effect could lead to the same result. The principle of non-discrimination between workers in the European Economic Area gives the nationals of any EEA State the same access and priority with regard to employment as workers in the host State. The right of freedom of movement shall entitle workers from an EEA State to engage in any occupation or profession in another State in the Area in accordance with the principle of equal treatment as regards access to employment, working conditions, and social protection. The equality of treatment implies that the migrant worker shall enjoy the same social and tax advantages as national workers. He shall also have access to vocational schools and retraining centres under the same conditions as national workers.

Free movement of workers within the EEA is certainly not without restrictions. There are limitations justified on grounds of public policy, public security or public health. Furthermore there are restrictions regarding employment in the public service. Those restrictions are worded in the same way in Article 28 EEA as in Article 48 EC. Several limitations of practical as well as legal nature may also be encountered when the worker attempts to carry out his occupation throughout the Area. For instance the recognition of professional qualifications may cause problems. The scope of this essay will therefore include limitations which are more or less directly tied up to the possibilities for the worker to carry out his profession. Highlighting the different legal and practical limita-

---

3.   The Treaty on European Union amended the European Economic Community Treaty (EEC) and renamed the revised Treaty as the European Community (EC) Treaty with effect from 1 November 1993. Hereafter EEC is used in a historical context and references to EC Treaty provisions refer to both those parts of the EC Treaty which remain unamended and to new provisions where applicable.

tions concerning free movement of workers, I shall address the question
whether the limitations encountered are the same in the EEA as in the
Community.

It is surely not sufficient in order to secure free movement of workers that the rules are worded in the same way in the EEA Agreement as
in the Community legislation. It is far more important that the individuals can be guaranteed that the provisions will be applied in the same way
throughout the whole area. Creating a homog*eneous* European Economic
Area does not only concern homogeneity as to the application of the
EEA rules as such, but also homogeneity between these rules and the
corresponding EC rules.[4]

The legal systems of the Community and the EEA differ tremendously. The Community legal system is based on transfer of competence
from the Member States to the Community with a corresponding limitation in the competence of the Member States. The essential characteristics of the Community legal order are in particular its primacy over the
law of the Member States and the principle of direct effect. Article 48 EC
as well as the Council Regulation 1612/68 have direct effect on the legal
order of the Member States and confer rights on the individuals which
the national courts must protect. The EEA Agreement does not entail
any transfer of sovereign rights to any EEA organ. The EEA is established on the basis of an international treaty obliging the Contracting
Parties to fulfil the provisions of the Treaty. The Agreement does not
confer rights directly on the nationals. The legal rights of the workers
thus fully depend on to what extent the provisions are implemented in a
proper way in the internal legal orders of the EFTA States.

The Member States of the Community will continue to apply the EC
rules among themselves, while in relation to the EEA countries they will
have to apply the corresponding rules from the EEA Agreement. Hence,
if the provisions, which intentionally should have the same effect, are
being practised differently, it may be possible that workers who are nationals of an EFTA State, may be treated less favourably in the Community than EC nationals.

In so far as the provisions of the Agreement are identical in substance to corresponding rules of the EEC Treaty and to acts adopted in
application of this Treaty, the question may be raised whether the provisions are to be interpreted in conformity with the relevant rulings of the
European Court of Justice.

The objectives of the Community have a considerably wider political
aim compared with the objectives in the Agreement establishing the EEA.
This is even more clear after the Treaty on European Union entered

4.   *ibid.*, at p.1172

into force on 1 November 1993. The question may therefore be addressed as to whether the differences of objectives of the EEA Agreement and the Treaties establishing the European Community could lead to different interpretations of the rules, and thereby influence the exercise of the right of free movement of workers.

The determination of the Contracting Parties to establish a dynamic European Economic Area means that the Agreement is supposed to develop in a dynamic way, in step with the adoption of new regulations and directives in the Community. It should therefore be examined whether the Agreement has a structure and mechanisms which are able to secure such a dynamic development of the Agreement. It should further be examined how and to what extent future development of the case-law of the European Court of Justice and new EC legislation will be taken into account or incorporated in EEA law. In answering these questions attention must be paid to the fundamental objectives and principles of the EEA Agreement, its decision-making procedures, the court systems and how the co-operation between the EC and the EFTA countries is expected to be carried out in the future.

2.   THE EEA AGREEMENT — STRUCTURE, OBJECTIVES AND PRINCIPLES

(i) *A Brief Historical Background to the EEA Agreement*

In the Preamble of the Agreement the Contracting Parties reaffirm the high priority attached to the "privileged relationship between the European Community, its Member States and the EFTA States which is based on proximity, long-standing common values and European identity". For a good understanding of the Agreement establishing the EEA, it is therefore important to have in mind the history of its creation and the development of the relationship between EFTA States and the European Community and its Member States.

The Convention establishing the European Free Trade Association (EFTA) was signed on 4 January 1960 in Stockholm by the United Kingdom, Denmark, Norway, Sweden, Austria, Switzerland and Portugal.[5] The Stockholm Convention contained first and foremost provisions concern-

---

5.   In March 1961 Finland and the Member States of EFTA concluded an Agreement, which in practice provided the same treatment for trade with Finland as for trade between the other Member States of the EFTA. Finland became a member of the EFTA on 1 January 1986. Iceland joined EFTA in 1970. So did Liechtenstein in 1991. Earlier the interests of Lichtenstein were carried out by Switzerland on the formal basis of a Protocol of the EFTA Convention. Denmark and the United Kingdom left EFTA in 1973, and became members of the EEC. So did Portugal in 1986.

ing free trade of industrial goods between the Contracting Parties, but contained no provisions concerning free movement of persons. In 1972 and 1973 bilateral Free Trade Agreements (FTAs) were concluded between the European Community and the EFTA States.

The first Ministerial meeting between EFTA and EC Ministers and the Commission took place in 1984 in Luxembourg. The Ministers signed a Declaration stating that they all had decided to strengthen their cooperation in order to create a dynamic European Economic Space (EES). About 25 working groups were established to deal not only with trade problems, but also with the participation of the EFTA States in Community programmes.[6] The process seemed insufficient, however, both from a political and an economic point of view considering the dynamic process within the Community, which, *inter alia,* resulted in signing the Single European Act in 1986 and the later efforts aiming at the completion of the internal market.

On 17 January 1989 the President of the European Commission, Mr. Jacques Delors, presented his view on the Community's relations with the other European countries, and launched the idea of a far-reaching discussion with the EFTA countries on the possibility of a broader cooperation between the European Community and the EFTA States. At a Summit Meeting in Oslo on March 1989 the EFTA countries declared their appreciation regarding the initiative taken by Jacques Delors, and gave their positive response thereto. The formal negotiations between the seven EFTA States and the Community started in Brussels on 20 June 1990 and finished by signing the EEA Agreement in Oporto on 2 May 1992. The entry into force of the Agreement was presupposed to be on 1 January 1993. Constituting a multilateral agreement under public international law, it required ratification or approval by all the Contracting Parties. The result of the referendum in Switzerland was that a majority of the voters[7] rejected ratification of the EEA Agreement. The remaining Contracting Parties decided to bring the Agreement into force between themselves in spite of the non-ratification of Switzerland, resulting in an Adjusting Protocol to the EEA Agreement of 17 March 1993.[8] The EEA Agreement entered into force on 1 January 1994.

---

6.   Armando Toledano Laredo, "The EEA Agreement: An overall view", (1992) 29 *Common Market Law Review* 1199 at p.1199.

7.   50.3 % of the voters and 18 out of 26 of the cantons.

8.   Corresponding Adjusting Protocols were also concluded as regards the three EFTA Agreements on a Surveillance Authority and a Court of Justice, on a Standing Committee, and on a Committee of parliamentarians.

(ii) The Structure of the EEA Agreement

The EEA Agreement is an Agreement between the Community and its twelve Member States and five[9] EFTA States applicable not only in the relations between the EC and EFTA countries but also among the EFTA countries themselves.[10]

Due to its dynamic character and its close relation to the legal system of the Community, the EEA Agreement is an international Agreement of quite a special character. It is no doubt the most advanced and most complete association agreement ever concluded by the Community with third countries.[11] Never have any of the EFTA countries concluded an agreement of such an extensive character.

The Agreement consists of a main part and 48 Protocols and 22 Annexes. It should be noted that the Protocols as well as the Annexes and the acts referred to therein form an integral part of the Agreement, see Article 119 EEA.[12] The main part of the Agreement lays down the foundation in general for a homogeneous and dynamic EEA. In structure and content the main part of the EEA Agreement follows the EEC Treaty. The provisions of the Agreement have been drafted identically or as closely as possible to the corresponding provisions of the EC Treaties. Thus the primary legislation of the EC with regard to the four freedoms and the competition rules, is reflected in the main part of the EEA Agreement.

EC secondary legislation in the areas covered by the Agreement, is brought into the Agreement by references to the EC law listed in the Annexes. Thus the Annexes constitute a substantial source of law, inte-

---

9.   Austria, Sweden, Norway, Finland and Iceland. Lichtenstein has not yet ratified the EEA Agreement. Special provisions are required for the entry into force of the Agreement in Lichtenstein.

10. It follows from Article 2 EEA that both the EEC, ECSC and their Member States are Contracting Parties. With regard to the Community side the notion "Contracting Parties" could mean the Community as such, the Member States only or the Community and the Member States together. The execution of the Agreement is not affected. It follows from Article 228(2) EEC that the execution of international agreements is an obligation both for the Community institutions and the Member States. It should be noted that EFTA as such is not one of the Contracting Parties.

11. Since the creation of the European Community, the Community has signed a number of association agreements with third states or groups of states. There are considerable differences between the various association agreements. The degree of participation and areas covered varies considerably, reflecting the political will of the parties to have a more or less deep association.

12. See also Article 2(a) EEA providing that for the purposes of this Agreement the term "Agreement" means the main Agreement, its Protocols, and Annexes as well as the acts referred to therein.

grating through references about 1600 EC legal acts, made up of 160 regulations, 950 directives, 120 decisions and 300 non-binding instruments.

The identification of the relevant *acquis* was carried out jointly by EC and EFTA experts during the negotiations by drawing up lists of EC acts on each specific sector. As several EC acts contain references to EC institutions not applicable within the EEA, it was necessary with some general adaptations of horizontal nature. These are laid down in Protocol 1.[13]

The continuous development of Community law made it impossible to include all the relevant *acquis* into the Agreement. For practical reasons the Contracting Parties agreed upon a cut-off day of 31 July 1991. New EC legislation relevant for the EEA, which has been adopted or published in the Official Journal of the EC after that date, are not included in the Agreement. Instead new Community legislation will be taken up by the EEA Joint Committee as soon as possible after entry into force of the Agreement. A "package" containing the additional relevant *acquis* has already been prepared, covering hundreds of EC acts adopted after the cut-off day.[14]

(iii) The Objectives and General Principles of the EEA Agreement

The aims of the EEA Agreement laid down in the Preamble, are also expressed in a more specific way in Part 1 of the Agreement under the heading "Objectives and Principles". In the Preamble the Contracting Parties emphasise the objective to establish a dynamic and homogeneous EEA based on common rules and equal conditions of competition. The Contracting Parties also express their determination to provide for the fullest possible realisation of the four freedoms and underline the important role that individuals will play in the EEA through the exercise of the rights conferred on them by the Agreement and through the judicial defence of these rights.

The fact that the provisions of the EEA Agreement and the corresponding Community rules are worded as identically as possible does

---

13. In order to have the full picture of which EEA rules are to be applied within a specific field, three different documents should be consulted;

— the EEA Agreement;

— the Annex where the EC acts are referred to with the specific adaption therein, if any, and;

— Protocol 1 EEA.

14. The EEA Joint Committee adopted these acts as EEA law during the spring of 1994. The EFTA countries must thereafter implement the acts in their national legal orders.

not ensure that the provisions necessarily will be interpreted the same way. An international treaty is to be interpreted not only on the basis of its wording, but also in the light of its objectives.[15]

With regard to the comparison of the objectives of the Agreement and those of the EEC Treaty, it must be observed that the EEA Agreement is concerned with the application of the rules on the four freedoms and the competition rules in economic and commercial relations between the Contracting Parties. The objectives of the European Community Treaties are much wider. It followed, *inter alia*, from Articles 2, 8a,[16] and 102a EEC that the amended EC Treaty aimed to achieve economic integration leading to the establishment of an internal market and to make concrete progress towards European union. The provisions of the EEC Treaty on free movement of persons were only a means for attaining those objectives. At the time when the Agreement was concluded, the main substantive difference between the scope of the EEA and the Community referred to the absence in the EEA of the four common EC policies — there is no common external trade policy, no custom union, no common agricultural and fisheries policies, and no common policy on taxation. In addition the Treaty on European Union marks a new stage in the process of creating an ever closer union among the Member States and the people of Europe,[17] leading to even further distance between the objectives of the EEA Agreement and the EC Treaties.

The general principles of loyalty and non-discrimination, which are corner-stones in Community law, are reproduced in the EEA Agreement. According to Article 3 EEA the Contracting Parties shall *take all appropriate measures*, whether general or particular, to ensure fulfilment of the obligations arising from the Agreement. Further on they shall *abstain from any measure* which could jeopardise the attainment of the objectives. Moreover, the Contracting Parties shall *facilitate co-operation* within the framework of the Agreement.[18] This provision corresponds to Article 5

---

15. Article 31 of the Vienna Convention of 23 May 1969 on the law of treaties stipulates in this respect that a treaty is to be interpreted in good faith in accordance with the ordinary meaning to be given to its terms in their context and in the light of its object and purpose.

16. Now Article 7a EC.

17. See Article A of the Treaty on European Union signed in Maastricht on 7 February 1992. The objectives of the Union are stated in Article B.

18. The principle of loyalty, stated in Article 3 EEA, applies to all authorities and institutions of an EEA State. The Principle is defined in Protocol 1 no. 7 of the Agreement stating that "Rights conferred and obligations imposed upon the EC Member States or their public entities, undertakings or individuals in relation to each other, shall be understood to be conferred or imposed upon Contracting Parties, the latter also being understood, as the case may be, as their competent authorities, public entities, undertakings or individuals".

EC, often referred to as the principle of loyalty or the principle of co-operation. Article 5 EC has been given a far-reaching scope through several rulings by the European Court of Justice (ECJ).

Article 4 EEA, reproducing the wording of Article 6 EC,[19] contains a general prohibition of discrimination on grounds of nationality. Thus the EEA Agreement lays down the general principle of equal treatment of nationals of any country within the EEA. Any EEA State is prohibited from passing any law, regulation or taking any administrative action which would involve treating nationals of another EEA State differently from its own nationals.[20] This non-discrimination principle is further elaborated in several Articles in the main part of the Agreement containing specific prohibitions such as Articles 28, 31, 34, and 36 EEA. Expressions of the principle are also found in many of the acts referred to in the Annexes of the Agreement, *e.g.* in the Council Regulation 1612/68. It should be mentioned that Article 6 EC has played an important role in the development of the case-law by the ECJ. The principle of non-discrimination has been particularly important for the application of Community law in the field of free movement of workers.

(iv) Legal effects of the EEA Agreement in the legal orders of the Contracting Parties

In order to ensure a homogeneous EEA it is essential that the legal effects of the rules in practice will be the same in the whole area. It is, therefore, necessary to recall the legal effects of Community law in the national legal orders of the EC Member States.

In *Van Gend en Loos*,[21] the ECJ laid down the foundation for two fundamental doctrines of Community law, the *primacy* and *direct effect* of Community law. As regards direct effect the Court held that the general scheme and the wording of the Treaty "must be interpreted as producing direct effects and creating individual rights which national courts must protect". The principle of direct effect together with the principle that Community law takes precedence over national law, are two cornerstones in the legal system of the Community.

According to Article 228 EEC the international treaties concluded by the Community are binding upon the Member States. Such treaties constitute an integral part of EC law, and can have a direct effect within

---

19.   As renumerated after the Treaty on European Union. (Previously Article 7 EEC).

20.   S. Norberg *et al*, *EEA Law — A Commentary on the EEA Agreement*, Stockholm, Fritzes, 1993, p.103.

21.   Case 26/62 *Van Gend en Loos v. Nederlandse Administratie der Belastingen* [1963] ECR 1.

the Community if the criteria for direct effect in EC law are fulfilled.[22]

The effects of international treaties in the legal orders of the EFTA States differs in a significant manner.[23] In Austria, international treaties can have direct effect if, *inter alia*, the provisions are sufficiently clear and precise. The Nordic countries follow a dualistic tradition whereafter international treaties do not automatically become part of national legal orders without further national legislation. These differences regarding legal effects of international treaties in national legal orders also apply in relation to the EEA Agreement.

The EEA Agreement does not expressly provide how the main part and the Protocols of the Agreement are to be implemented. The EFTA States have, however, made the main part of the Agreement part of their national legal orders by specific national legislation.[24]

As regards the provisions listed in the Annexes, which in the Community are either directives or regulations, it follows from Article 7 EEA that the Contracting Parties are obliged to implement these acts in their internal legal order.[25] Article 7 EEA which is modelled on Article 189 EEC, aims to ensure legal homogeneity as far as possible within the EEA and to secure that the acts referred to in the Annexes will have the same legal effects in the EFTA States as they have in the Community. It follows directly from Article 189 EEC that a Regulation will be directly applicable in the EC Member States. As far as the Annexes of the Agreement refer to a Regulation in Community law, the EFTA countries which follow a dualistic tradition, are obliged to incorporate that Regulation as such in their national legal order. According to Article 7(b) EEA the Contracting Parties are free to choose the form and method of implementation of an act referred to in the Annexes if the act corresponds to an EC Directive. Also this provision corresponds to Article 189 EEC, and puts as such no further obligations on the EC Member States.

Further on, Protocol 35 EEA obliges the Contracting Parties to ensure that EEA rules prevail over conflicting national provisions.[26] The

22. Case 87/75 *Bresciani v. Amministrazione Italiana delle Finanze* [1976] ECR 129.

23. Norberg et al, *op.cit.* n.20, at p. 202.

24. The Norwegian Parliament adopted on 17 November 1992 an act on the implementation of the EEA Agreement, stating that the main part of the Agreement shall constitute Norwegian law.

25. Article 7 EEA reads:

(a) an act corresponding to an EEC Regulation shall as such be made part of the internal legal order of the Contracting Parties.

(b) an act corresponding to an EEC directive shall leave to the authorities of the Contracting Parties the choice of form and method of implementation.

26. According to § 2 of the Norwegian Act of 17 November 1992 on the implementation of the main part of the EEA Agreement, legislation which aims to fulfil the obligation according to the Agreement shall prevail over conflicting national provisions.

Protocol underlines the aim of the Agreement to achieve a homogeneous European Economic Area based on common rules.[27]

(v) Supervision and Judicial Control

An effective system for preventing discrimination on grounds of nationality will depend on several factors. There must be a supervision and
control system with a capability to detect possible infringements of the
provisions relating to free movement of workers. Furthermore it is essential to react when infringements have been detected and the measures applied must be sufficient to discourage further malpractice.

The institutional structure of the Agreement consists of a political
organ, the *EEA Council*,[28] a management organ, *the Joint Committee of the
EEA*,[29] and two consultative organs including the Members of Parliament,
the EEA Joint Parliamentary Committee,[30] and social partners of the Contracting Parties, *the EEA Consultative Committee*.[31] The Agreement also provides within the EFTA for the creation of a Surveillance Authority and
an EFTA Court, analogous with the Commission and the Court of Justice.[32]

Both politically and institutionally it was important to create an EEA
surveillance system which was both efficient and independent to avoid
the risk of a "legal imbalance".[33] This resulted in a two pillar system in
which the Commission monitors the concrete implementation, application and interpretation of the EEA rules as far as the EC Member States
are concerned while the EFTA Surveillance Authority (ESA) has a corresponding task with regard to the EFTA States.[34] In other words the role
exercised within the Community by the Commission in its surveillance
capacity is mirrored by the role of the ESA in relation to the EFTA States.[35]

Questions related to the judicial system and the mechanism for settlement of disputes turned out to be among the most difficult issues in

27. In a Joint Declaration on Protocol 35 the Contracting Parties state that it is their under-
     standing that Protocol 35 does not restrict the effects of those existing internal rules
     which provide for direct effect and primacy of international agreements.

28. EEA Agreement Articles 89 - 91.

29. EEA Agreement Articles 92 - 94.

30. EEA Agreement Article 95.

31. EEA Agreement Article 96.

32. EEA Agreement Article 108.

33. Norberg *et al.*, *op.cit.* n.20, at p. 214.

34. The general rules regarding the surveillance procedure under the EEA Agreement are
     laid down in Articles 108 -110.

35. Norberg *et al.*, *op.cit.* n.20, at p.216.

the negotiations.[36] It was essential for the Contracting Parties to create a system which would provide legal security and ensure an interpretation and application of rules as uniform as possible within the whole area.[37]

During the negotiations it was proposed to establish an EEA Court which should have the competence to give preliminary rulings on questions of interpretation of EEA rules and to decide on disputes between the Contracting Parties concerning the interpretation and application of such rules. The Ministers from the EFTA and the EC States adopted a resolution on 14 May 1991 in which they agreed to create an independent EEA Court composed of five judges from the ECJ and three EFTA judges. The Commission requested the ECJ to give an opinion under Article 228 EEC on the compatibility of the proposed system with the EEC Treaty. The ECJ criticised the drafted system heavily.[38] It was therefore necessary to renegotiate the judicial system, which resulted in the establishment of the EFTA Court.

The main competencies of the EFTA Court[39] are as follows;

— cases brought by the ESA against an EFTA State for infringement of obligations laid down in the EEA Agreement,[40]

— appeals against decisions taken by ESA,

— settlement of disputes between the EFTA States regarding the interpretation and application of the EEA Agreement,[41]

— advisory opinions on the interpretation of the EEA rules upon request from national courts of the EFTA States.[42]

The procedures of the Court have been modelled on the procedures of the ECJ. There are, however, some important differences. The ESA/EFTA Court Agreement does not impose any obligations on the EFTA

---

36. The creation of a judicial system is a sensitive question from a political point of view both in the Community and in the EFTA States, affecting their sovereignty as well as the independence of their courts.

37. Leif Sevon, "The EEA Judicial System and the Supreme Courts of the EFTA States", (1992) *European Journal of International Law*, at p.603.

38. See *Opinion* 1/91, [1991] ECR I - 6079.

39. The EFTA Court consists of five judges appointed by common accord of the Governments of the EFTA States for a term of six years.

40. See the ESA- EFTA Court Agreement, Article 31.

41. See the ESA - EFTA Court Agreement, Article 32.

42. See the ESA - EFTA Court Agreement, Article 34.

States to raise a matter before the ESA before raising it with the EFTA Court. In this way the system differs from that of the Community, which requires in Article 170 EC that a Member State must bring the matter before the Commission before the matter is taken before the ECJ. Furthermore, the EFTA Court does not have the competence to give its opinion on the validity of acts of bodies established according to the Agreement except on the legality of decisions by the ESA. Furthermore, the EFTA Court does not have the competence to give its opinion on the validity of acts of bodies established according to the Agreement except on the legality of decisions by the ESA.

As pointed out by Leif Sevon the EEA Agreement does not "establish any judicial body which, from a hierarchical point of view, would be superior to the supreme courts of the EFTA States".[43] As concerns preliminary rulings there is no obligation on national courts to seek an advisory opinion from the EFTA Court, even where there is no judicial remedy under national law against the decisions of the national court. Secondly, the opinion of the EFTA Court is not binding on the requesting court. On the other hand there is reason to believe that national courts which have submitted a question of interpretation of the EEA rules before the EFTA Court, in practice will base their decisions on the interpretation made by that Court.

According to the EEA Agreement the courts and tribunals of the EFTA States may, on certain conditions, request the ECJ to decide on the interpretation of EEA rules corresponding to EC rules (see Protocol 34 EEA). An EFTA State which intends to make use of this possibility shall notify the Depository and the ECJ to what extent and according to what modalities the Protocol will apply to its courts and tribunals. For political reasons it is unlikely that the EFTA States will allow the national courts to use this opportunity.

In a case of discrimination the migrant has a legal right to carry the question before the national court which then has to decide whether the host State or an employer has behaved in a manner incompatible with the EEA Agreement. The national courts of an EC Member State are, under certain conditions, obliged to bring the actual legal question before the European Court of Justice.[44] Such an obligation is not conferred upon the national courts of the EFTA States. It may be asked what implications the different systems of courts may have for migrant workers. A migrant worker from an EFTA State who works in a Member State of the Community may get an interpretation of the relevant rules from

43. Leif Sevon, *op.cit.* n.37, at p.613.

44. See Article 177 EC, according to which a court or tribunal against whose decisions there is no judicial remedy under national law, shall bring the matter before the Court of Justice.

the ECJ, if the national court decides to ask for a preliminary ruling. A Community national working in one of the EFTA States, on the other hand, must accept that the national court in the host state gives a binding ruling in an issue concerning the provisions in the EEA Agreement for free movement of workers without asking either the ECJ or the EFTA Court.

(vi) The Significance of the Rulings of the European Court of Justice in the Interpretation of Corresponding Provisions in the EEA Agreement

The ECJ has delivered several important rulings on the provisions of free movement of workers. It is therefore essential to ask whether the interpretation of the provisions in the EEA Agreement, which in substance are identical to provisions in EC law, should be in conformity with the relevant rulings of the ECJ. Article 6 EEA, concerning the case-law of the ECJ prior to the signature of the Agreement on 2 May 1992, aims to ensure the fullest possible homogeneity by providing that:

> "Without prejudice to future developments of case-law, the provisions of this Agreement, in so far as they are identical in substance to corresponding rules of the Treaty establishing the European Economic Community and the Treaty establishing the European Coal and Steel Community and to acts adopted in application of these two Treaties, shall, in their implementation and application be interpreted in conformity with the relevant rulings of the Court of Justice of the European Communities given prior to the date of signature of this Agreement".

The rulings of the ECJ thus constitute a source of EEA law in so far as the provisions in substance[45] are identical to provisions of EC law.[46] According to Article 6 EEA the Agreement must be read in conjunction with the EC Treaties in order to ascertain whether the provision in question is specific to the EEA Agreement or whether the provision is identical in substance to a provision of the EC Treaties or acts adopted in application of the Treaties. In the latter event the provisions of the EEA Agreement must be read in the light of the case-law of the ECJ.[47]

45. The formulation "identically in substance" was chosen because the negotiators wanted to express that identity with regard to the precise wording cannot always be required. It is sufficient that the substance is identical. See Norberg *et al, op.cit.* n.20, at p.190.

46. Taking over the case law of the ECJ is nothing fundamentally new in the co-operation between the Community and the EFTA States. The Lugano Convention of 1988 on Jurisdiction and Enforcement of Judgments in Civil and Commercial Matters between the Member States of the EFTA and the EC includes a similar mechanism.

47. Norberg *et al., op.cit.* n.20, at p.189.

How will the EEA provisions be interpreted "in conformity" with the relevant rulings of the ECJ? The rulings of the ECJ are not binding upon the national courts of the EFTA countries. A national court may therefore theoretically interpret an EEA provision, albeit identically worded as the corresponding EC act, in a different way than the ECJ because the general objectives of the EEA are not the same as the objectives of the Communities. It is also unclear what the term *relevant* rulings of the ECJ means. The case-law of ECJ as a whole is certainly not relevant recalling that the EEA Agreement has a more narrow scope than the Treaties establishing the Communities. In the field of social policy and free movement of workers the case-law of ECJ on the direct effect and primacy of Community law constitutes important rights for individuals. The EEA Agreement does not include the principle of direct effect, and hence, an important part of the case-law of the ECJ may be excluded depending on the interpretation of the EFTA court.

The ECJ will also in the future continue to give rulings on provisions of Community law which in substance are identical to provisions of the EEA Agreement. In order to create a homogeneous EEA it is necessary to take into account also future rulings of the European Court of Justice. For constitutional as well as political reasons it was necessary to set a time limit for the relevant rulings of the ECJ which were "binding" for the Contracting Parties. However, the Contracting Parties expected that future rulings of the ECJ should also be taken into account.[48] Article 3(2) of the ESA/EFTA Court Agreement obliges the EFTA Court to *pay due account to* the principles laid down by the relevant rulings of the ECJ given after the signature of the EEA Agreement. The future case-law of the ECJ thus will play an important role when the EFTA Court is interpreting EEA provisions which in substance are identical to provisions in Community law. Recalling the independence of the courts and the differences of objectives of the EEA Agreement and the EC Treaties, there is, however, no legal guarantee for a uniform interpretation and application of the provisions concerning free movement of workers in the future.

Article 105 EEA provides that the EEA Joint Committee shall keep under constant review the development of the case-law of the Court of

---

48. See the Preamble of the Agreement stating that:

"Whereas, in full deference to the independence of the courts, the objective of the Contracting Parties is to arrive at, and maintain, a uniform interpretation and application of this Agreement and those provisions of Community legislation which are substantially reproduced in this Agreement and to arrive at an equal treatment of individuals and economic operators as regards the four freedoms and the conditions of competition".

Justice and the EFTA Court. Judgments of these courts and the supreme courts of the EFTA States shall be transmitted to the EEA Joint Committee which shall act so as to preserve the homogeneous interpretation of the Agreement. In order to ensure as uniform an interpretation as possible, the EEA Joint Committee shall set up a system of exchange of information concerning judgments by the Courts. Article 106 EEA underlines the political will of the Contracting Parties to do what is possible, without prejudicing the independence of the courts, to ascertain a homogeneous interpretation of the Agreement. The Contracting Parties may also intervene in cases before both the ECJ and the EFTA Court and submit written statements or observations to the courts.[49] The possibility of intervention may turn out to be very important in supporting uniformity in the application of EEA law.

(vii) Harmonisation of New Legislation

Chapter II of the EEA Agreement deals with the decision-making procedure, in particular regarding the future development of the Agreement in parallel to developments in the Community. It has been a major challenge for the Contracting Parties to establish a system capable of achieving a joint, parallel development of the legal orders of the Community and the EEA in order to fulfil the requirement of a homogeneous EEA. When setting up the decision-making procedure the Contracting Parties had to take into account the requirement of autonomy concerning the development of Community law as well as the autonomy of the EFTA States.

As soon as new legislation is being drawn up by the Commission in a field which is covered by the Agreement, the Commission shall informally seek advice from experts from the EFTA States in the same way as the Commission seeks advice from experts from its own Member States.[50] This is of utmost importance since it obviously is easier to influence the outcome of a matter the earlier the views are made known. Throughout the decision-making procedure in the Community, there will be a parallel information and consultation process between the EC and the EFTA States.

The EEA Joint Committee will meet regularly to take the formal decisions regarding the implementation and the operation of the Agreement. It follows from Article 93 (2) EEA that the decisions shall be taken by agreement between the Community, on the one hand, and the EFTA States speaking with one voice, on the other. The EEA Joint Committee

---

49. Article 20 and 36 of the EFTA Court Statute and Article 20 and 37 of the ECJ Statute.

50. See Article 99 (1) EEA.

shall take decisions concerning amendments of the Annexes of the Agreement adopting as closely as possible the corresponding new Community legislation with a view to realising a simultaneous application of the latter and of the amendments of the Annexes of the Agreement.[51] The ideal situation is when there is no delay in relation to the entry into force of an amended provision under the EEA Agreement and the entry into force of the corresponding Community rule.

Since no legislative competence is transferred to any EEA organ, the Parliament in each EFTA country will maintain its legislative power and thereby the formal right to accept or not accept amendments of the Agreement.

With regard to dispute settlement in general between the Contracting Parties, the EEA Committee is competent to settle the disputes. In so doing the Committee shall examine all possibilities to maintain the good functioning of the Agreement. It will also be possible to raise a matter of concern at the Ministerial level of the EEA Council; see Articles 5 and 89(2) EEA.

3. The Scope of Application of Article 28 EEA

(i) General Remarks

The right of free movement for workers within the EEA is laid down in Article 28 EEA, which reproduces the wording of Article 48 EC. Article 28(5) EEA refers to Annex V of the Agreement containing the specific provisions from the secondary legislation of the Community.[52]

Article 28 EEA must be read in conjunction with Article 4 EEA which prohibits any discrimination on grounds of nationality. These Articles

---

51. Article 102(1) EEA lays down certain principles regarding the adoption and the entry into force of amendments.

52. The following Community acts have thus become a part of EEA law:

   1) Council Directive 64/221/EEC of 25 February 1964 on the coordination of special measures concerning the movement and residence of foreign nationals which are justified on grounds of public policy, public security or public health;

   2) Council Regulation (EEC) No.1612/68 of 15 October 1968 on freedom of movement for workers within the Community with later amendments;

   3) Council Directive 68/360/EEC of 15 October 1968 on the abolition of restrictions on movement and residence within the Community for workers of Member States and their families;

   4) Commission Regulation (EEC) No. 1251/70 of 29 June 1970 on the right of workers to remain in the territory of a Member State after having been employed in that State;

do not only forbid direct discrimination, but apply as well to all other activities which in effect could lead to the same result. The principle of non-discrimination means that nationals of any EFTA and EC Member State shall have the same access and priority with regard to employment as national workers in the host State. The right of freedom of movement shall entitle any worker to engage in any occupation or profession in the European Economic Area in accordance with the principle of equal treatment as regards access to employment, working conditions, and social protection in the host country. Equality of treatment implies that the migrant shall enjoy the same social advantages as national workers. He shall also have access to vocational training and retraining centres under the same conditions as national workers.[53] Besides the right to work in a host EEA State on the same conditions as nationals, free movement of workers also includes the right to move freely within the EEA and to stay in a host state for a limited period while seeking employment and further to remain in the territory after the employment has come to an end.[54]

In the Community Article 48 EC, as well as Regulation 1612/68, have direct effect on the legal order of the Member States and confer rights on the individuals which the national courts must protect.[55] Article 28 EEA, however, has no such direct effect in itself. The rights of the workers therefore depend on a proper implementation of the provisions in the legal order of the EFTA States.

The principle of free movement for workers entails two types of restrictions on national legislation. Firstly, the principle implies consequences on public law limiting the right of an EEA State to regulate what criteria should be satisfied by nationals of another EEA State in order to stay and find employment in that country. Secondly, if the principle of

5) Council Directive 72/194/EEC of 18 May 1972 extending to workers exercising the right to remain in the territory of a Member State after having been employed in that State;

6) Council Directive 77/486/EEC of 25 July 1977 on the education of the children of migrant workers.

53. See Article 7 of Regulation 1612/68.

54. Regulation 1612/68, *cfr.* Regulation 1251/70. Further provisions on the rights of residence have been introduced by Directives 68/360, 90/364, and 90/365.

55. See Case 41/74, *Van Duyn v. Home Office* [1974] ECR 1337.

56. In comparison with the long-established Nordic labour market which exists between Denmark, Finland, Iceland, Sweden, and Norway the provisions of Article 48 EC differ with respect to certain aspects of private law. The Nordic convention does not regulate the implications of free movement of workers on private law. The Nordic labour mar-

free movement for workers is correctly implemented in the EFTA States, it implies restrictions on the contract autonomy insofar as Article 28 EEA prohibits direct and indirect discrimination based on nationality with respect to employment, remuneration, and other conditions of work and employment.[56]

(ii) Persons Covered

The EEA Agreement contains provisions concerning free movement of workers as well as of persons having the right of establishment and providers of services; see Articles 28, 31 and 36. As a common feature these groups of persons all pursue an economic activity. Other categories of persons are also, on certain conditions, enjoying the right of entry and residence; *inter alia*, students, retired persons, and receivers of services. As a main rule persons not able to support themselves are excluded. Excluded are also nationals from non-EEA countries even if they have residence and work permits in one of the EEA States.

(a) The Notion of a "Worker"

The right of freedom of movement contained in Article 28 EEA applies to workers only. It is therefore necessary to analyse what criteria should be satisfied in order to consider a person to be a worker in the sense of the Agreement. Neither the EEA Agreement nor the EC Treaty provide a definition of "worker". The notion of a "worker" in Article 28 EEA has, however, to be interpreted in conformity with the rulings of the ECJ prior to 2 May 1992.

In Community law the notion of a "worker" in Article 48 EC has a Community meaning which is not up to the discretion of a Member State to define. This has been ascertained by the European Court of Justice in *Levin* and *Hoekstra*.[57] If the definition of the term "worker" was a matter within the competence of national law, it would be possible for each Member State to modify the meaning of the concept and thereby eliminate the protection granted by the Treaty to certain categories of persons. The content of the notion of a "worker" should be subject to control by Community institutions to avoid the risk of excluding certain categories of persons from the benefits secured by the Treaty.[58] It has to be stressed that the notion of a "worker" defines the field of application

ket comprises only the public law aspect. See further details in, Ruth Nielsen, *EF arbeidsrett*, Gylling, Jurist-og Økonomi-forbundets Forlag, 1989, p.93.

57. Case 53/81, *Levin v. Staatssecretaris van Justitie* [1982] ECR 1035, and Case 75/63, *Hoekstra v. Bedrijfsvereiniging Detailhandel* [1964] ECR 177.

58. See also Roger Blanpain, *Labour Law and Industrial Relations of the European Community*, Deventer, Kluwer Law and Taxation Publishers, 1991, p.88.

of one of the fundamental freedoms guaranteed by the Treaty. For that reason the notion should not be interpreted restrictively.

In the *Lawrie-Blum* case[59] the European Court of Justice ruled that the concept of a worker must be defined in accordance with three objective criteria which distinguish the employment relationship by reference to the rights and duties of the persons concerned. The three criteria which should be satisfied are:

— the person concerned has to perform a service;

— the work has to be done under the power of instruction by an employer (in subordination);[60]

— there has to be remuneration for performance of a service.

To be considered as a worker the person must pursue an effective and genuine economic activity.[61] The motives which may have prompted the worker to seek employment in the host State are not decisive.[62] The job should have, however, an economic nature within the meaning of Article 2 EEC.[63] It follows from *Levin* and *Kempf*[64] that no specific wage level should be established as a minimum before the receiving person may be regarded as a worker. In *Levin* the Court ruled that the notion of a "worker" also applies to employed persons even if they get an income less than the minimum required for subsistence. In the same case the Court ruled that the freedom of movement for workers also includes persons working *part time*. There are no agreed limits to the extent of work in relation to minimum working hours or payment.

---

59. Case 66/85, *Lawrie-Blum v. Land Baden-Württemberg* [1986] ECR 2121.

60. The fact that a person is working under the direction and supervision of an employer is one of the criteria which distinguishes a worker from persons that are self-employed or supplying services.

61. See Case 53/81, *op.cit.* n.57.

62. *ibid.*

63. In Case 36/74, *Walrave and Koch v. Association Cycliste Internationale et al.* [1974] ECR 1405, the Court ruled that parties in sports are subject to Article 48 only so far as it constitutes an economic activity within the meaning of Article 2 EEC.

64. Case 139/85, *Kempf v. Staatssecretaris van Justitie* [1987] ECR 1741, dealt with a situation where a person conducted twelve music lessons per week which did not provide enough for his own support. He applied for and received social security payment which was a necessary supplement to his income. The Court stated that the fact that a person is not able to support himself through a paid job cannot be sufficient reason to exclude him from the right of free movement.

Concerning employees working with non-standard conditions, *e.g.* persons on time restricted contracts, seasonal workers *etc.*, special rules have been issued. It is worth noting that workers with non-standard conditions are predominently women. It is therefore necessary to keep a wide definition of Article 48 EC as well as Article 28 EEA to avoid an application which could lead to practices that might become indirectly discriminatory on grounds of sex.[65]

In a legal context there is no precise interpretation of whether a person pursues an effective and genuine economic activity. Due to the wide definition of "worker" settled by the European Court of Justice it will not be a major problem in practice to decide whether a person can be considered a worker within the meaning of Article 28 EEA. Despite falling outside of Article 28 EEA, a person may still be entitled to reside and work as self-employed or providing services according to Articles 31 or 36 EEA.

The Norwegian Immigration Act has been amended to be in conformity with the EEA Agreement. According to Norwegian law it is a condition for obtaining a residence permit that the EEA worker presents confirmation from an employer of appointment to a position which "shall normally be equivalent to no less than a half-time post in the occupation concerned".[66] The question may be addressed as to whether such an implementation is in conformity with Article 28 EEA, taken into account the relevant rulings of the ECJ on the notion of a "worker". As mentioned above there are no agreed limits to the extent of work in relation to minimum working hours or payment. It is clear, however, that a person who works less than a half-time post may be regarded as a "worker" in the sense of Article 28 EEA. Recalling that it is not an absolute condition in the Norwegian legislation that the occupation concerned shall be no less than a half-time post, the application of the provision will decide whether this is an acceptable implementation of Article 28 EEA.

According to Norwegian law migrant workers who are not going to work full-time, must provide proof that the employment is "real and of a certain extent". In assessing whether this condition is fulfilled, account shall be taken of whether the pay is adequate for the migrants subsistence. According to the ECJ ruling in *Levin* the term "worker" also applies to employed persons even if they get an income less than the minimum required for subsistence. As a consequence a migrant worker cannot automatically be denied a residence permit in Norway just because the "pay" is not considered to be adequate for the subsistence of the applicants.

65. *Cf.* Article 119 EC and Article 70 EEA.

66. See Article § 161 of the Royal Decree of 18 December 1992 pursuant to the Immigration Act of 24 June 1988.

(b) Unemployed Persons

It follows from the EEA Agreement that the protected "worker" is not exclusively a person who is currently employed. Article 28(3) EEA applies also to persons who remain in the territory of an EEA State after having been employed in that State. The right of a worker and the members of his family to remain in the territory after having been employed is further laid down in Council Regulations 1251/70 and 1612/68, which form a part of the Agreement under Annex V EEA. The right to remain permanently is linked to the length of residence and employment.

Article 28 EEA does not mention directly the right of labour to move freely in *search* of employment. As freedom of movement entails the abolition of any discrimination based on nationality between workers of the EEA States, it appears from the secondary legislation that this right also applies to persons who are in search of employment in the host State. The concept of a worker also extends to those who have become unemployed involuntarily. If a worker has become unemployed through circumstances beyond his control it may be essential for him to reside in the host State when trying to get a new job. In some cases it may even be necessary for practical reasons that the unemployed worker remains in the country in order to claim his right of re-employment in an efficient way.

The right to remain in the country also applies to an unemployed worker who currently does not seek a job. In the *Sylvie Lair* case[67] the ECJ ruled that a migrant worker who has begun to study at a university, with the aim of acquiring vocational training, should still be considered a worker.

(c) Citizenship

Only persons who are *nationals* of an EEA State are covered by Article 28 EEA. This is pointed out clearly in Article 1 of Council Regulation 1612/68 which is a part of the EEA Agreement.

It is up to each State to determine who is and who is not a national. The criteria on how to obtain citizenship may therefore differ from one EEA State to another. Acceptance as a citizen by one State, however, enables the person to be protected by Article 28 throughout the Area.

Within an EEA State we may find third-country nationals who legally have the right to stay in the country and whose work permits are limited

---

67. Case 39/86, *Sylvie Lair v. Hannover Universität* [1988] ECR 3161.

to the country of issue only. These persons do not enjoy the protection of Article 28 EEA.

On an inter-governmental basis co-operation exists concerning migration policy. A common immigration policy will undoubtedly have several advantages. On the Community side the framework of such a common immigration policy is laid down in the Treaty on European Union. The implementation of the provisions presupposes that all Member States agree. Even if the Member States should agree on enforcing the provisions, there would be considerable resistance to proposals to allow free movement of non-nationals within the Community bearing in mind that the issue is considered to be a delicate and sensitive political question. The Member States have traditionally been reluctant to give up their prerogatives in the field of home affairs and internal security.

(d) Family Members

The right of a worker to move freely within the EEA cannot be considered real if the person in question is not allowed to bring his family along regardless of the nationality of the family members and whether they are able to support themselves.

It is necessary to distinguish between independents who enjoy their rights directly according to the Agreement, and the dependants who enjoy their rights because of their relationship with the worker. The difference between the two categories is that the dependants cannot exercise their rights if the independent (*i.e.* the worker) loses his rights. If a member of the worker's family is a national of one of the EEA States and works or applies for work in the host State he or she will have the same right of free movement as the worker himself.

The status of a member of a worker's family is stated by Regulation 1612/68. Members of the worker's family are, in this context, restricted to his spouse, children under the age of 21, or descendants who are dependants and dependent relatives in the ascending line of the worker or of his spouse. It is no requirement that the family members mentioned should be nationals of one of the EEA States. The notion "family" as used in the EEA and the Community law is based on marriage. "Modern" families fall outside of the notion. As regards the notion of "spouse" it only includes a marital relationship.[68] Any other companion in a stable relationship with a migrant worker may not enjoy the same rights as a spouse. The question may be raised as to how appropriate this is from a legislative and practical point of view — as in many relationships the tendency in national legislation is to equalise stable partnerships with

68.   Case 59/85, *State of the Netherlands v. Reed* [1986] ECR 1283.

matrimony. The restriction of the concept of spouse to only include married people can also cause several other problems. According to Danish and Norwegian law there are legal possibilities to conclude a lesbian or homosexual marriage. The question therefore will arise whether, as a consequence of such civil marriage, the couple involved may move freely in the EEA as a worker and his family. In the *Reed* case[69] the ECJ interestingly enough extended family relationships to include an unmarried cohabitant, ruling that a host State which permits cohabitation between unmarried persons for its own nationals, cannot refuse to grant such rights to persons who are nationals of other Member States without being guilty of discrimination on grounds of nationality. The Contracting Parties are anyhow obliged to facilitate the admission of any member of the family if dependent on the worker or living under his roof in the country whence he comes.[70]

The migrant worker is obliged to provide housing for his family which is considered normal for national workers in the region where he is employed.[71] The question is, however, which criteria must be satisfied to consider the housing as *normal*. In most of the EEA countries the housing standard differs tremendously even in the same region. The requirement of proper housing thus cannot be applied strictly because a strict interpretation and application may give rise to discrimination between migrants and national workers.

(iii) The Rule of "ordre publique"

Free movement of workers within the EEA is not without restrictions. To a large extent these restrictions are similar for the freedom of establishment and free movement of services. Article 28(3) EEA, reproducing Article 48(3) EEC, contains limitations justified on grounds of public policy, public security or public health.

The particular circumstances determining what actually falls under the notion *"public policy"* may, however, vary from one country to another and from one period to another. In Community law it has been considered necessary to allow the competent national authorities an area of discretion within the limits imposed by the EC Treaty.[72] Article 28(3) EEA has to be interpreted in the same way. The European Court of Justice has given several rulings which are relevant for the interpretation of Article 28 EEA.

---

69. *ibid.*

70. Regulation 1612/68, Article 10(2).

71. Regulation 1612/68, Articles 9 and 10(3).

In the *Van Duyn* case[73] the Court ruled that a Member State for reasons of public policy can "…where it deems necessary, refuse a national of another Member State the benefit of the principle of freedom of movement for workers in a case where such a national proposes to take up a particular offer of employment even though the Member State does not place a similar restriction upon its own nationals".

Measures taken on grounds of public policy or public security have to be justified on the grounds of individual conduct of the person concerned.[74] As concerns previous criminal convictions it should be noted that the convictions in themselves do not constitute grounds for taking measures to limit the free movement of workers. Convictions are relevant only so far as the circumstances which the judgment was based on can be considered as evidence of personal conduct constituting a *present* threat to the public policy.[75]

It should also be mentioned that the Court in *Rutili*[76] placed limitations upon the freedom of action of Member States. A Member State may not expel a national of another Member State from its territory or deny him access for reasons which would not equally give rise to measures aimed at combating such conduct among its own nationals. The same principle has to be taken into account when interpreting Article 28 EEA by virtue of Article 6 EEA.

In the Community the concept of public policy and public security is recognised by the case-law as being primarily defined by national law. It is, however, clear that Community law limits the possibility for the Member States to interpret freely the grounds which can be taken into ac-

72. See Blanpain, *op.cit.* n.58, at p. 96, *Van Duyn, op.cit.* n.55,and Case 30/77, *Regina v Pierre Bouchereau* [1977] ECR 1999.

73. *Van Duyn v. Home Office, op.cit.* n.55.

74. See case 30/77, *Regina v. Pierre Bouchereau* [1977] ECR 1999. See also Article 3 of Directive 64/221 which impose on Member States the duty to base their decision on individual circumstances of any person and their protection under Community law and not on general considerations.

75. According to the Norwegian Immigration Act § 58(b), a worker from another EEA country may be expelled if he, during the previous period of 5 years, has been sentenced abroad for an offence which, according to Norwegian law, is punishable with more than three months imprisonment. Likewise expulsion may be the result if the worker has been sentenced in Norway, or placed under preventive supervision, for such an offence. Where the sentence has been imposed abroad, it shall be taken into consideration whether there are circumstances that may indicate that the migrant will commit criminal offences in Norway. This wording may lead to misunderstandings, because a host state may not expel an EEA worker unless the conviction can be considered as evidence of personal conduct constituting a present threat to the public policy.

76. Case 36/75, *Roland Rutili v. Minister for the Interior* [1975] ECR 1219. The Court ruled that the expression "subject to limitations justified on grounds of public policy" in Article 48(3) concerns not only the legislative provisions adopted by each Member State to limit within its territory freedom of movement and residence for nationals of other Member States but relates also to decisions concerning individuals.

count. The ECJ has ruled in the *Bouchereau* case[77] that the measures taken must be proportionate to the nature of the offence committed against a public order provision and the procedural aspects must be guaranteed.

The EEA State is obliged to inform the person concerned of the grounds of public policy upon which the decision taken in his case is based, unless this is contrary to the interests of the security of the State involved.[78] The person concerned shall also be officially notified of any decision to refuse the issue or renewal of a residence permit or to expel him from the territory.[79]

The EEA States may not freely decide whether a disease gives reasons for refusing a migrant worker is justified on grounds of public health. Only the diseases listed in Directive 64/221[80] may be referred to by the EEA States. Diseases occurring after a first residence permit has been issued do not justify a refusal to renew a residence permit or expel a migrant worker.

(iv) Employment in the Public Sector

Article 28(4) EEA states that "the provisions of this Article shall not apply to employment in the public service". The so-called "public service exemption" constitutes an important exception to the principle of free movement of workers. In the public sector it is — on certain conditions — legitimate for the Contracting Parties to reserve access to employment for their own nationals. The posts which are covered by the exemption clause in Article 28(4) presume on the part of those occupying them the existence of a special relationship of allegiance to the state and reciprocity of rights and duties which form the foundation of the bond of nationality.[81] The public service exemption is designed to safeguard the general interest of the state or of other public authorities, and is based on the idea of national loyalty.

The provision does not apply to all employment in the public service, nor does it allow discrimination under terms and conditions of employment once appointed.[82] It is of particular interest to study the rel-

---

77. *R. v Bouchereau, op.cit.* n.74.

78. Directive 64/221, Article 6.

79. Directive 64/221, Article 7.

80. Directive 64/221, Article 4 and its Annex.

81. Case 149/79, *Commission v. Belgium* [1980] ECR 3881.

82. See D. Wyatt and A. Dashwood, *The Substantive Law of the EEC*, London, Sweet & Maxwell Ltd., 1987, 2nd ed. p.195.

evant case-law of ECJ when interpreting the exemption clause in Article 28 EEA. In *Commission v Belgium* the European Court of Justice ruled that the exception only applies to those posts which:

> ...involve direct or indirect participation in the exercise of powers conferred by public law and duties designed to safeguard the general interest of the state and of other public authority.[83]

The formulation in the *Belgium* case is now generally accepted as the key statement of the scope of the public service exemption.[84] However, it can be said that the formulation still raises several questions. The meaning of the *exercise of powers* is not defined by objective criteria. Further on it must be mentioned that the concept of *indirect* participation in the exercise of such powers is not clear.[85] There is also an issue of exempting such functions where the exercise of power is only marginal to the duties of the post.

The concept of "public service" is a matter of Community law, and is not to be left to the discretion of Member States. Article 28 EEA must be interpreted in the same light. The term "employment in the public sector" requires uniform interpretation and application throughout the area. Article 28(4) EEA must be construed in such a way that its scope is limited to what is strictly necessary for safeguarding the interests which that provision allows the Contracting Parties to protect.

Although the ECJ has developed restrictive criteria for the exception concerning employment in the public sector one may question whether the criteria are restrictive enough. With regard to the classical public services of diplomacy and defence no issues are likely to arise. These posts have additional entry rules which may even exclude nationals from serving. However, there are public service posts, for instance in a police department, which should not be automatically blocked for foreign nationals. It can hardly be argued that a police detective qualified to investigate crime in one country could run into a loyalty conflict and not be accepted in another EEA State. In the long run it will be difficult to exclude nationals of other EEA States from obtaining public service posts even if they may exercise authority conferred by national law.

Current political trends of deregulation and reductions of state ownership in industry and business leave, in principle, more posts open to

---

83. Case 149/79 *Commission v. Belgium* [1980] ECR 3881.

84. See Gillian Morris, Sandra Fredman & Jon Hayes, "Free Movement and the Public Sector", (1990) 19 *Industrial Law Journal* 20.

85. See J. Handoll, "Article 48(4) EEC and Non-National Access to Public Employment", (1988) 13 *European Law Review* 223.

EEA workers in a host country. However, during periods of economic recession, the public will call for intervention by governments to stimulate employment. Such political actions by a State would most likely be motivated by an intention to indirectly stimulate or create alternative job opportunities for its own nationals.

4. QUALIFICATIONS FOR EMPLOYMENT

(i) Recognition of Qualifications and Diplomas

Any employer should choose the candidate considered to be best qualified for the actual job. In evaluating the criteria of the applicants, factors like formal qualifications, vocational training, experience and personal ability all count. It is therefore important to create systems which make it easy to assess and recognise diplomas and certificates obtained by a worker in an EEA country.

Free movement of workers can only become a reality if diplomas obtained in one State are valid in the others. In the Community the EC Council has adopted a number of Directives concerning the mutual recognition of diplomas, certificates and other formal qualifications on the legal bases of Article 57 EC. After a period in which mutual recognition was pursued on the basis of directives for specific professions, the Community adopted two horizontal directives which extended recognition to all regulated professions.

Article 30 EEA reproduces, to a large extent, the wording of Article 57 EC. The placing of Article 30 EEA under the heading "Workers and self-employed persons" does not indicate any difference in substance between the Community and EEA legislation, but rather reflects the legal situation within the Community in the field of mutual recognition of qualifications at the time of the conclusion of the EEA Agreement.[86]

Article 30 EEA refers to Annex VII EEA which contains the relevant Community acts in the field of mutual recognition of qualifications. Annex VII includes Council Directive 89/48 of 21 December 1988 on a general system for the recognition of higher education diplomas awarded on completion of professional education and training of at least three years duration. The Directive is not, however, applicable to regulated professions which are covered by specific directives.

The EC Council has also adopted another horizontal directive on a

86. See S. Norberg *et al.*, *op.cit.* n.20, *EEA law — A Commentary on the EEA Agreement*, Fritzes, 1993, p.422.

general system for the recognition of professional education and training.[87] This Directive was not part of the original EEA Agreement because of the cut-off date of 31 July 1991 and had to be included in the 1994 "package". The fact that this Directive did not immediately become part of EEA law illustrates, however, that for some periods there may exist different rules within the Community and the EFTA States, concerning the right of free movement of workers.

There are no provisions, neither in the Community nor the EEA, covering mutual recognition of all types of professions or education. If the education of a migrant worker is not covered by a specific Directive, or one of the horizontal Directives mentioned above, the migrant must request the host State to assess whether or not his qualifications correspond to the qualifications normally required in the Member State. If the qualifications are not accepted, the worker may bring the case before the Court. In the meantime, however, he will not be able to pursue the profession for which he is qualified.

It will be a complex but important issue for the future to ensure the equivalence of qualifications for non-regulated professions and skills. In the Green Paper on European Social Policy[88] it is emphasised that the "establishment of real and effective mutual recognition and equivalence of qualifications at all levels throughout the territory of the Union has to be an urgent political priority". Achieving a good and effective system on mutual recognition will no doubt contribute to the removal of practical barriers concerning free movement of workers.

(ii) Vocational Training

A trend in the labour markets in Europe today is a requirement for high flexibility within the work force and less opportunities for low-skilled workers. Besides high unemployment rates, there is a political challenge concerning long-term unemployment and the impact of industrial changes on poorly skilled workers. If the European countries are unable to meet these challenges, the right of free movement of workers may turn out to be a mere academic right or a right reserved for the well skilled and highly educated part of the working population.

There are close links between freedom of movement for workers, employment and vocational training. Vocational training which aims to put workers in a position to take up offers of employment from other

---

87. Council Directive 92/51/EEC of 18 June 1992 on a second general system on the recognition of professional education and training.

88. Green Paper, *European Social Policy — Options for the Union* of 17 November 1993, COM (93) 551 at p.51.

regions of Europe is necessary for realising the goal of the internal market. In the Community the Commission has the task of promoting close co-operation between the Member States regarding basic and advanced vocational training. According to Article 128 EEC the Council lays down general principles for implementing a common vocational training policy capable of contributing to the harmonious development of both the national economies and the common market.[89] There are no corresponding provisions in the EEA Agreement. As long as Council Regulation 1612/68 is a part of the EEA Agreement, however, any discrimination based on nationality regarding access to training in vocational schools and retraining centres is forbidden throughout the Area.[90]

In order to promote the movement of young people within the EEA, the Contracting Parties agree, Under Protocol 29 EEA, to strengthen their co-operation in the field of vocational training. The Protocol thus has the same aim as Article 50 EC.

5.   SOCIAL SECURITY FOR MIGRANT WORKERS AND THEIR FAMILIES

The territorial limitations of the national social security systems are capable of constructing obstacles to the free movement of workers in several respects.[91]

To secure free movement of workers it is essential that the differences between national social security systems do not create negative effects on the mobility of individual workers. Co-ordination of national social security systems is important because it concerns the potential mobility of workers, and ensures that a migrant worker will not be in a less favourable social security position than workers staying in one and the same country throughout their working lives. One of the principal objectives of co-ordination is to avoid conflicts between the various na-

---

89. The amended provisions concerning education and vocational training are now contained in Articles 126 and 127 EC.

90. According to the Community Charter of the Fundamental Social Rights of Workers "every worker of the European Community must be able to have access to vocational training and to benefit therefrom throughout his working life". In the conditions governing access to such training there must be no discrimination on grounds of nationality. The Community's "Social Charter Action Programme" reaffirms that vocational training is "at the forefront of the priorities", and that Community-level actions are needed as an impetus and a complement to the different actions being undertaken by and within the Member States. The governments of the EFTA States have made a Declaration on the Charter of the Fundamental Social Rights of Workers endorsing the principles and basis of rights laid down in the Charter.

91. D.Wyatt, "The Social Security Rights of Migrant Workers and their Families", (1977) 14 *Common Market Law Review* 411.

tional laws so as to ensure that no migrant worker is doubly insured or not insured at all. Co-ordination is, however, a dynamic, complex and open-ended process.

In order to provide free movement for workers and self-employed persons, Article 29 EEA, reproducing the relevant parts of Article 51 EC, requires that the Contracting Parties in the field of social security shall secure for migrant workers and their dependants payment of benefits, in particular:

> aggregation, for the purpose of acquiring and retaining the right to benefit and of calculating the amount of benefit, of all periods taken into account under the laws of the several countries;

> payment of benefits to persons resident in the territories of Contracting Parties.

Annex VI EEA contains references to the relevant Community secondary legislation in the field of social security. References are made to Regulations 1408/71 and 574/72 which are both of considerable importance in the social security field. These Regulations do not aim to alter or to harmonise the diverse national social security systems, but rather to co-ordinate them to provide the migrant worker with constant social security protection wherever the worker moves within the area. In other words, EEA law on social security for migrant workers aims to ensure that migrants working in two or more EC Member States or EFTA States will be able to combine the social security contributions paid in each state in order to get these benefits in whichever EEA State they are living. There are, however, several problems of co-ordinating the different types of benefits. Further on there are limitations which are of essential importance for the workers concerned. Article 2(1) of Regulation 1408/71 provides that the Regulation shall apply to:

> employed or self-employed persons who are or have been subject to the legislation of one or more Member States and who are nationals of one of the Member States...

The notion of "employed persons" does not precisely cover the same group of persons referred to by the notion of "worker" in Article 28 EEA /48 EC. The ECJ has ruled in *Hoekstra*[92] that the words "employed persons or persons treated as such" within the meaning of Article 4 of Regu-

---

92. Case 75/63, *Hoekstra v. Bedrijfsvereniging Detailhandel* [1964] ECR 177, Case 31/64 *Bertholet* [1965] ECR 81.

lation 3/58/EEC referred to all those who as such, and however they are described, are covered by the various national social security systems. The ECJ ruling in the *Hoekstra* case was later consolidated by Regulation 1408/71, in which Article 1(a) defines employed and self-employed persons by referring only to the social security scheme covering them.[93] There are no grounds for excluding certain categories of persons by virtue of the time worked. It should be emphasised that the conditions for insurance under various social security schemes are determined by national legislation alone. There are several specific categories of workers who come under special provisions, derogating from the Regulations, essentially with regard to the determination of the legislation applicable. These include frontier workers, seasonal workers, seamen, and persons employed by diplomatic missions.

Several categories of persons fall outside the defined scope of persons covered by the Regulations on social security, *i.e.* civil servants or persons treated as such with regard to the special social security scheme for these categories.

The limitations of social protection for civil servants must be regarded in the light of Article 28(4) EEA which excludes "employment in the public service" from the application of free movement of workers within the EEA. However, this is a serious obstacle to the persons concerned.

Article 4(1) of Regulation 1408/71, which has become a part of the EEA Agreement, applies to all national legislation concerning a wide range of branches of social security.[94] Three categories of benefits are excluded from the scope of the Regulation by Article 4(4); namely social and medical assistance, benefit schemes for victims of war or its consequences, and special schemes for civil servants and persons treated as such. The differences between "social security" and "social assistance" are not simple. The ECJ has, however, ruled on the matter on several occasions. To a large extent the problems which have arisen in the past due to the exclusion of social assistance now have been resolved in the Community by the adoption of Regulation 1247/92 which covers a wide range of non-contributory social security benefits.

The rules and procedures are different for each benefit. It certainly may be difficult for the migrant worker to get an overview of the benefits he is entitled to claim. Both linguistic problems and lack of information

---

93. Annex VI EEA states, *inter alia*, that concerning Norway "any person who is employed or self-employed in the meaning of the National Insurance Act shall be considered respectively as employed or self employed within the meaning of Article 1(a)(ii) of the Regulation".

94. Sickness and maternity benefits, invalidity benefits, old-age benefits, survivor's benefits, benefits in respect of accidents at work and occupational diseases, death grants, unemployment benefits, family benefits.

may lead to difficulties when applying for social security benefits.

The social security field is an extremely complex field to co-ordinate both at Community and EEA level, involving national laws that are greatly divergent and based on long-standing social traditions deeply rooted in national culture. For many reasons it would have been easier to replace the various national social security systems with a common Community or EEA system on social security. For political reasons this cannot be realised for a long time. There is a wide divergence in the standard of living among the different EC and EFTA countries, which makes it impossible to establish social security schemes with the same qualifying conditions and coverage.[95]

6.   OTHER BARRIERS TO THE FREE MOVEMENT OF WORKERS

(i)   *The Machinery for Vacancy Clearance*

Europe is faced with unacceptable levels of unemployment. Only 60% of the working-age population is currently employed in the Community. In the EFTA countries the average rate is somewhat over 70%.[96] Under such circumstances there will naturally be tough competition for the jobs available.

It is important for persons seeking jobs to get information on job offers in the various EEA countries. It is therefore necessary to strengthen the machinery for vacancy clearance in particular by developing direct co-operation between the central employment services and also between the regional services.[97] This co-operation was established by Council Regulation 1612/68 in order to ensure greater transparency on the employment market and thereby promote free movement of workers. As mentioned before, Council Regulation 1612/68 is a part of the EEA Agreement, and the co-operation mechanism regarding clearing of vacancies also applies to the EFTA States.

Today the European Employment Service (EURES)[98] network, formed by the national employment services and the Commission, is established for exchanging information on job supply and demand with

95.   *Social Europe* — 3/92, Social Security for persons moving within the Community, p.11.

96.   Commission of the European Communities, Green Paper — *European Social Policy — Options for the Union*, of 17 November 1993, COM (93) 551, p.17.

97.   See the preamble of Council Regulation 1612/68, which also is a part of the EEA Agreement.

98.   The EURES network system established by Regulation 2434/92 and Commission Decision 93/569 of 22 October 1993, OJ L/274, replaces the SEDOC system which has existed since 1972.

a view to developing free movement for migrant workers throughout the Community. EURES consists of two parts; a data bank of the supply and demand for jobs, and a human network of specially trained experts who can give an applicant key information about living and working conditions in a host area. The network aims to provide a more transparent labour market and to enable workers and their families to make decisions with better knowledge of what to expect. For all practical purposes EURES is already in operation in the EEA. However, only a small portion of the vacant jobs are actually registered by the national employment services, and an even smaller number will be available through the EURES data bank.

(ii) Border Crossing

Free movement of persons implies that frontiers will no longer constitute a hindrance. Considering the importance of the abolition of border controls for the free movement of persons, it is worth noting that the EEA Agreement does not provide for abolition of such controls. To assess what this means for the free movement of workers within the EEA, I will first examine the rules and practice concerning border crossing within the Community.

According to Article 8a EEC,[99] which was introduced by the Single European Act, the internal market shall comprise an area without internal frontiers in which the free movement of persons will be ensured. According to the Single European Act this includes "the removal of physical controls at the internal borders". The problem still remains, however, to determine precisely what should be done to achieve the results sought by Article 8a EEC. In a Communication of May 1992 to the Council and Parliament, the Commission gave an extensive interpretation of Article 8a EEC.[100] The Commission considered that the internal market could not operate under conditions equivalent to those in a national market if the movements of individuals within this market were hindered by controls at the internal frontiers.

For practical, political and legal reasons the full implementation of the objective laid down in Article 8a EEC depends on the implementation of compensatory measures regarded as essential to counter threats to security; in*ter alia,* drug trafficking, terrorism, organised crime, and illegal immigration.[101] In the Palma document of June 1989, the EC Coun-

---

99. Now Article 7a EC.

100. Commission Communication to the Council and the Parliament (SEC (92) 877 fin.) p.10.

101. The need for compensatory measures was already established in a declaration annexed to the Final Act of the Single European Act.

cil emphasised that the creation of an area without internal frontiers in accordance with Article 8a EEC required the application of certain essential measures enabling joint organisation and reinforcement of checks at external frontiers and co-operation in other fields. Special attention has to be drawn to three instruments:

- the draft convention on the crossing of external borders,

- the Dublin Convention on the determination of the State responsible for examining an asylum application lodged in one of the Member States,

- an instrument setting up a European Information System (EIS).

There are several Conventions concluded at inter-governmental level relating to border crossings between some of the Member States.[102] Of special interest, however, is the Schengen Convention concluded by nine of the twelve EC Member States.[103] The Schengen Convention provides for a series of measures such as the abolition of checks at internal frontiers, the introduction of systematic controls at the external borders, modalities of co-operation *etc.* Although the Schengen process took place outside the Community framework, it has received the approval of the Commission and the European Parliament as a dynamic element in the completion of the internal market.

The EFTA Convention[104] does not regulate issues concerning border-crossing nor control of persons crossing the borders between the EFTA States. There are, however, special arrangements between some of these States. In June 1957, Denmark, Finland, Norway and Sweden signed an Agreement, the Nordic Passport Control Agreement, on the abolition of passport controls at the common Nordic borders.[105] Accordingly, the Nordic external frontiers function as the point of passport and entry

---

102. See *e.g.* the Benelux Convention signed in Brussels on 11 April 1960.

103. The Schengen Agreement was signed on 14 June 1985 between Belgium, the Netherlands, Luxembourg, Germany and France. The same countries concluded the Schengen Convention of 19 June 1990. The other EC Member States — except Denmark, the United Kingdom and Ireland — have acceded to the Convention.

104. The Convention establishing the European Free Trade Association (EFTA), signed on 4 January 1960 in Stockholm.

105. Iceland acceded to the Agreement in 1965. The Agreement was amended in 1973 in order to enable Denmark to meet its obligations as a new member of the Community.

106. Schermers, H. G. *et al.*, "Free Movement of Persons in Europe", T.M.C. Asser Intituut, 1991, p. 63.

control for the entire Nordic region.[106]

There is no provision in the EEA Agreement which corresponds to Article 8a EEC. The checks at the borders between the Community and the EFTA countries will continue despite the fact that free movement of persons is covered in the EEA Agreement. It may therefore be asked what practical consequences border controls have for the free movement of workers? In most cases control of EEA-nationals at border crossings remains just a symbolic act.

The Governments of the EC Member States and the EFTA States have agreed on a Declaration, which is annexed to the EEA Agreement, on the facilitation of border controls. In order to promote the free movement of persons, the Contracting Parties will co-operate with a view to the facilitation of controls for each other's citizens and the members of their families at the borders between their territories.

(iii) Fiscal Barriers

Fiscal barriers like indirect and direct taxation play an important role in restricting the freedom of movement of persons. Large national differences in VAT and tax rates may result in a form of "tax competition" in which high-tax jurisdictions would lose revenue to low-tax jurisdictions.[107] There is no harmonisation of national income tax rules either in the Community or in the EEA.

Persons who work in a host EEA country are generally taxed in the country where they are employed. Current tax systems differentiate between resident and non-resident workers applying different rates of taxation to their income. Under these arrangements only income from sources within the country of employment is taxed, with no provision being made for tax relief on grounds of family circumstances or for the various deductions for which residents are eligible.[108] At the same time, migrant workers are often precluded from the benefit of such relief in their country of residence since they have insufficient taxable income in that country. These disparities may result in tax barriers to the free movement of workers. Some bilateral agreements have been concluded in order to avoid certain types of discrimination as regards the tax treatment of the income of certain frontier workers. The benefits of these agreements apply only to a small number of situations.[109]

The EC Commission adopted, on the 21 December 1993, a Recommendation on the taxation of the income of non-residents in the Mem-

---

107. *ibid.*, p. 117.

108. Press release by Christiane Scrivener, Member of the Commission, Ref: P/93/63 of 21.12.1993.

109. *ibid.*, p. 1.

ber States where they are employed. According to the Recommendation the migrant worker should enjoy the same tax treatment as residents provided they derive at least 75% of their income in that State. Commissioner Scrivener stated that "It is unacceptable that in 1993 European taxpayers have to pay more tax only because they are working in a Member State other than in which they reside". Scrivener underlined the importance of establishing minimum conditions guaranteeing non-discriminatory taxation in the country in which the taxpayers are carrying out their activity since the free movement of persons is one of the cornerstones of the European Union.

The EEA Agreement carries no provisions for a common taxation policy or co-ordinating measures. Traditionally, the matter has been dealt with by a series of bilateral taxation agreements between proper authorities of each country and in some instances even joint Conventions of co-operative projects entered into by several states. As the example on frontier workers shows, the lack of co-ordination may easily lead to obstacles to free movement. To avoid tax discrimination of migrant workers throughout the EEA it is therefore important that the Member States of the Union, as well as the EFTA States, amend their taxation rules to avoid tax barriers to free movement of workers.

(iv) Exercising Democratic Rights

Article 8 EC, as amended by the Treaty on European Union, establishes a citizenship for nationals of the EU countries whereby every person holding the nationality of an EU State shall be a citizen of the Union. This includes the right to vote and to stand as a candidate at municipal elections in the Member States in which the citizen resides under the same conditions as nationals of that State.

The EEA Agreement has no provision regarding the democratic rights to vote and stand as a candidate at municipal elections. This implies that there will be two categories of migrant workers exercising different democratic rights. This can be illustrated by an example where migrants from Denmark and Norway work and reside in the Netherlands, and only the worker from Denmark is allowed to vote and stand as a candidate at the municipal election, and thus being the only one of the two workers who is capable of influencing the social and living conditions in the town where they live. It may, of course, be argued that the situation for the Norwegian worker is just as it has been for all the Community migrants during previous years, and that the differences in executing the democratic rights only reflect the fact of being a member of the Union. The question remains, however, whether being unable to participate at municipal elections is an acceptable limitation for migrant workers within the EEA.

7. CONCLUSION

The right of free movement of workers is as essential in the EEA as it is in the Community. The provisions of the EEA Agreement on free movement of workers are almost identical in substance to those in the Community adopted before 31 July 1991. Assessing whether the right of free movement of workers within the EEA is a right hedged with unacceptable practical or legal limitations, I will first make some comments on the provisions which are "taken over" from the Community law.

In Community law provisions concerning free movement of workers have been given a wider and wider applicability through a more liberal interpretation of the notion of a worker and a more restrictive interpretation of the rule of *ordre publique* and the exemption concerning employment in the public sector. Article 28 EEA has to be interpreted in the same way.

Although the EEA Agreement seeks to establish equal treatment in a broad sense between migrant workers from an EEA State and persons in the host country, areas remain where migrant workers are not on a fully equal footing with nationals. Migrants are not eligible for certain posts in the public service. The right of residence is not absolute. Non-EEA nationals who work in one of the EEA countries are excluded from the scope of Article 28 EEA. There are areas of uncertainty with regard to family reunification. Workers may be faced with problems regarding mutual recognition of diplomas and qualifications. A special category of migrants, the frontier workers, may in certain circumstances be discriminated due to the inadequate taxation rules.

Both separately, and as a whole, these limitations complicate free movement of labour in a way that appears unacceptable to the persons concerned. Any obstacle that, in fact or in law, reduces the possibility of a worker to move freely within the European Economic Area should be reviewed in order to find acceptable solutions for the benefit of workers. Solutions to these problems have to be found in the Community, however, since the EEA decision-making system and institutions are created for the main purpose of incorporating legislation which has already been adopted in the Community.

In addition to the legal limitations, people who exercise the right of free movement are often confronted with cumbersome administrative procedures. Local administrations are not always aware of the rights enjoyed by workers. In some areas, like the social security field, it may be difficult for the migrant to get an overview of the benefits he is entitled to claim. It may also be difficult to get relevant information about available jobs. Although the new EURES network system is a step in the right direction, we must bear in mind that only a small percentage of the vacancies are advertised through national employment services, and even fewer through the EURES network.

There will, however, always be circumstances in practical life which disfavour migrants in comparison with national workers. Linguistic problems, family and cultural bonds *etc.* imply factual and psychological barriers which the legal systems of the Community or the EEA cannot solve.

Most of the limitations on free movement of workers so far described are common for the migrant workers in the Community and in the EEA. There are differences, however, in the legal frameworks which may have an important impact on the free movement of persons. The most obvious obstacle to free movement of persons is physical barriers such as border controls. The EEA Agreement has, however, no provision on the removal of physical controls at the internal borders corresponding to Article 8a EEC. The removal of controls of persons at the internal borders has been a hot political issue within the Community. Obviously Denmark has had special problems trying to fulfil its obligations according to the EC Treaty as well as the Nordic Passport Control Agreement; the latter including four of the five EFTA countries of the EEA. Taking into account the considerations by the Commission that the internal market can not operate under conditions equivalent to those in the national markets unless internal border controls are abolished, it is difficult to see how the EC and EFTA countries in the long run can maintain border controls between their territories. The Declaration annexed to the Agreement is important, stating that the Contracting Parties will co-operate with a view to the facilitation of border controls for each other's citizens in order to promote the free movement of persons.

The crucial question is, however, whether the EEA system provides for a mechanism ensuring homogeneous interpretation and application of EEA provisions which are identical in substance with those of the Community? The EEA Agreement provides for several means of guaranteeing that homogeneity. In all areas where it has been possible, the provisions of the Agreement have been formulated as closely as possible to the corresponding provisions of the EC Treaties as one of the means of securing that the interpretation will be the same. As pointed out by Sven Norberg, a primary objective behind the EEA Agreement would be jeopardised if individuals and economic operators cannot be guaranteed that the result shall be the same in principle and in practice whether Community rules or EEA rules are applied in the areas covered by the Agreement.

It is clear, however, that the homogeneity of the rules throughout the EEA is not secured merely by the fact that the provisions are identical in their content or wording. It is important that the rules are also interpreted in the same way. Article 6 EEA pursues that objective by stipulating that the rules of the Agreement must be interpreted in conformity with relevant case-law of the European Court of Justice on the corre-

228 *Free Movement for Workers under the EEA*

sponding provisions of Community law. In its *Opinion 1/91*[110] the ECJ held that this interpretation mechanism is not sufficient to enable the desired legal homogeneity to be achieved. Article 6 EEA is concerned only with rulings of the European Court of Justice given prior to the date of signature of the Agreement. Since the Community case-law will evolve, it will be difficult to distinguish the new case-law from the old, and hence the past from the future. Furthermore, Article 6 EEA does not clearly specify whether it refers to the case-law of the ECJ as a whole, and in particular how one should take account of the case-law on the direct effect and primacy of Community law.

Taking an overall view of the EEA Agreement, there is a set of measures in addition to Article 6 EEA which calls for achieving as uniform an interpretation as possible of the provisions of the Agreement and those of the Community legislation which are substantially reproduced therein. There is an obligation for the EEA Joint Committee to act to achieve that goal. According to the principle of loyalty, all the EEA States are obliged to take all appropriate measures to ensure fulfilment of the objective of homogeneity arising from the Agreement. The EFTA Court shall pay due account to the principles laid down by the relevant rulings of the ECJ given after the signature date of the Agreement. The possibilities for the EEA States to intervene in cases before the EFTA Court and the ECJ may also turn out to be of utmost importance in order to achieve homogeneity of the rules. As concerns the principle of primacy, it follows from Protocol 35 EEA that the Contracting Parties will introduce into their respective legal orders a statutory provision to the effect that EEA rules are to prevail over contrary legislative provisions. Further on, Article 7 EEA aims to ensure legal homogeneity as far as possible within the EEA by securing that legal acts, which in the Community are either directives or regulations, have the same legal effects in the EEA States as they have in the Community.

It may also be alleged that the discrepancies which exist between the aims and context of the Agreement, on the one hand, and the aims and context of Community law, on the other, stand in the way of the achievement of the objective of homogeneity in the interpretation and application of the law in the EEA. The integration process and the legislative programme in the Community will evolve to realise the internal market and the aims of the Treaty on European Union. Such a development may lead to a gap between the rules governing free movement of workers within the Union compared to those within the scope of the EEA. On the other hand, the Contracting Parties of the EEA Agreement are certainly determined not only to create, but also to develop, a dynamic

110. 1/91 *Opinion* [1991] ECR I-6079.

and homogeneous European Economic Area, in step with the developments in the Community as far as the four freedoms are concerned. Political will is an absolute condition to achieve such an ambitious aim. In spite of the clearly expressed political will of all the Contracting Parties, nobody can, however, foresee whether the EEA will stand up to its intentions.

The EEA Agreement is in many ways an unprecedented construction which may be of a temporary nature. Before the EEA Agreement entered into force four of the five EFTA countries had applied for membership of the European Union. The negotiations on membership concluded in 1994 for membership from 1 January 1995 subject to the outcome of national referenda. The results of these applications may in the future lead to considerable alterations concerning the composition of the EFTA. At the time of writing it is difficult to foresee whether a membership of the European Union will be attained, taking into account the political situation in the applicant EFTA States as well as in the Community. The EEA Agreement may, therefore, have a longer life than is generally believed. On the other hand, if several EFTA countries become members of the European Union, the EEA Agreement risks being transformed into bilateral agreements between the European Union and the few remaining countries.

5. Balancing Protection and Equal Treatment: The Relationship between the ILO's Nightwork (Women) Convention and the Principle of Equality between Men and Women in the EC's Equal Treatment Directive

Paul Cullen

1. INTRODUCTION

In February 1992, six Member States of the European Community registered with the International Labour Office their denunciation of the Nightwork (Women) Convention (Revised), 1948 (No 89).[1] As a consequence of this concerted pattern of denunciation on the part of those Member States, no Member State of the European Union is currently bound by the terms of ILO Convention No.89 which prohibits nightwork for women in industry. As grounds for their denunciation of ILO Convention No.89, most of the Member States involved cited the need to harmonise their national legal order and European Community law as interpreted by the Court of Justice of the European Communities. National legislation which had prohibited the employment of women on nightwork reflected a concern for protection which had outlived the circumstances in which it had been conceived. Notwithstanding the duty placed on Member States to respect the supremacy of European Community law and the guardianship of the Treaties entrusted to the European Commission, it was eventually necessary to secure a clear ruling from the Court of Justice to prompt national governments to confront the fact that a widespread prohibition on nightwork for women in na-

1. General Report to the 69th Session of the International Labour Conference by the Committee of Experts on the Application of Conventions and Recommendations. Geneva, 1992, pp. 10 and 11.

tional legislation was in breach of Community law.

The circumstances in which the prohibition on nightwork for women in Convention No.89 was ultimately deemed to be incompatible with European Community law and, in particular, the Equal Treatment Directive are reviewed in this Chapter.[2] Although a capacity to legislate for the improvement of working conditions on a universal basis is probably essential in order to address a complex subject in a sufficiently all-encompassing way, it is argued that the sharply focused decision of the Court of Justice in *Stoeckel* has helped to uphold fundamental rights and to inject the stimulus which may ultimately be required to enable the Commission and the Council to develop a realistic framework of regulation on working hours. The examination of this topic requires a review of the background to the establishment of ILO standards on the prohibition of nightwork for women, consideration of developments in the interpretation of the substantive character of the principle of equal treatment in European Community law, and an assessment of what the process which led to the denunciation by Member States of ILO Convention No.89 reveals about the effectiveness of the obligation placed on Member States under the Equal Treatment Directive to revise protection which is no longer justified.[3]

The contradictions which emerged between the application of the Community law principle of equal treatment and the obligations enshrined in ILO Convention No.89, have highlighted some critical issues for the direction of social policy which have not been adequately addressed in the Commission's Green and White Papers on European Social Policy. Four issues, in particular, have been highlighted in this context:

(a) the extent to which the removal of blanket prohibitions might accelerate progress in labour market reform and changes in work organisation to the advantage of women or merely stimulate opportunistic behaviour by employers;[4]

(b) the capacity of the administrative, legislative and judicial machinery at National and Community levels to develop methods of analysing situations involving the differential treatment of men

2.   Council Directive 76/207/EEC of 9 February, 1976 on the implementation of the principle of equal treatment for men and women as regards access to employment, vocational training and promotion and working conditions, OJ L 39 of 14.2.1976.

3.   *ibid.*, Article 5(2)(c).

4.   *cf.* European Commission, Forward Studies Unit and Strategic Planning Group GDV *"Labour Market, Fundamental Rights and Social Policy in the Community"*, (unpublished) May, 1993.

and women and to evaluate the alleged biological and functional differences advanced as justification for exceptions to the principle of equal treatment;

(c) the current questioning of the priorities and effectiveness of the International Labour Organisation and, in particular, of the role of international labour standards and their impact on job creation;[5]

(d) the extent to which the problems encountered by Community Member States in relation to possible approaches to the revision of Convention No.89 reflects the asymmetrical pattern of relations between the ILO and the European Community which stems from the different principles on which the two organisations are based and the different legal contexts in which they operate.[6]

Historically, the rationale for special protective measures to safeguard women from working at night was based on medical, social, political and economic grounds.[7] While the effects of nightwork were deemed to be harmful to both men and women, they were considered to be doubly problematic for the latter because they also carried the double social role of wife and mother as well as worker. Concern for women's safety when travelling to and from work and at their consorting with men at night reflected a practical concern for protection from the risks of assault as well as a strong traditional conception of the proper sphere for women. A woman's place was deemed to be in the home caring for home and family; prohibiting women from undertaking nightwork was usually justified by reference to the additional burdens which women bore in attending to housework and child care.

Protective measures designed to cut down the hours and restrict the nature of women's work have traditionally had a two-edged aspect.[8] Where trade unions were unable to secure a total prohibition on nightwork, they took the pragmatic step of supporting a ban on nightwork

5.   See F. Williams, "Soft Bark and Not Much of a Bite", *Financial Times*, 2 June, 1993.

6.   See Request for an Opinion presented to the Court of Justice by the Commission of the European Communities under Article 228(1) EEC concerning the compatibility of ILO Convention No.170, Brussels, 26 July 1991. Jur(91) 04508; pp. 26-27. Also comments by the Director of the ILO London Office, Mr P. Brannen at University of Leicester European Management and Employment Law Seminar, 9 July 1993.

7.   International Labour Office Conference Report, 76th Session (1989) Nightwork Report V(1), Chapter II.

8.   S. Rowbotham, *Women, Resistance and Revolution*, London, Pelican Books (1975) at p.115.

for women with a view to securing sufficient leverage to extend such protection to all workers.

Suspicion and hostility was also reflected in concern on the part of male trade unionists to preserve jobs from female competition, as reflected in the statement of an official of the American Cigar Makers' Union:

> We cannot drive the females out of the trade, but we can restrict their daily quota of labour through factory laws.[9]

In the industrialised market economy countries, the option of greater recourse to nightwork was identified by employers following the Second World War as a means of maximising the use of existing productive capacity. Employer organisations were increasingly prepared to question the harmful effects of recourse to shiftwork on family and social life and to highlight how progress in technology had opened to question differences in the legal treatment of women in industrial and service-type employment. In such circumstances employer interests either called for neutral regulatory measurers which would apply to wage earners of either sex or, alternatively and, with greater emphasis through the 1970's and 1980's, voiced their support for a generally deregulative approach. The traditional orientation of the trade union movement has been to hold fast to statutory prohibitions which owed their origins to concern for the protection of particular categories of workers and to use them as a platform for improving working conditions generally. This stance has sometimes been maintained in the face of the contention by women workers that attention to equity issues and the removal of the nightwork prohibition could secure efficiency gains by making better use of women's experience and skills.[10]

The promotion of basic workers' rights through agreed international labour standards has been actively pursued by the International Labour Organisation since it was established under the Treaty of Versailles in 1919. In that year the effects of nightwork on women was selected as one of the first subjects for protective international labour legislation. Paradoxically, in view of the later controversies, the subject was apparently chosen on the grounds that considerable agreement already existed on the need for protection in this area. It was also considered unlikely that any controversy would arise in deciding on the form and content of such regulation![11]

9.   *ibid.*, at page 115.

10. M. Jones, *These Obstreperous Lassies: A History of the Irish Women Workers Union*, Dublin, Gill and Macmillan (1988) Ch.8.

11. A. Alcock, *History of the International Labour Organisation*, London (1971), pp. 11 and 12.

2.   ESTABLISHING INTERNATIONAL PROTECTIVE STANDARDS ON NIGHTWORK FOR WOMEN: THE INFLUENCE OF THE ILO

(i)   *The Role of the ILO in Standard-Setting*

The unique structure and standard-setting procedure of the ILO is briefly considered here along with a review of the main provisions of the ILO Convention on Nightwork of Women No.89 (1948), which had its origins in the original Convention adopted in 1919. The influence which the ILO's long established protective standards in this area have had on the standard-setting role of such other inter-governmental bodies as the Council of Europe and the European Communities is also considered.

The International Labour Organisation (ILO) is a special institution of the United Nations. It was founded in 1919 with the aim of improving the conditions of labour and promoting social justice. Only States which are members of the United Nations may belong to the organisation. All the Member States of the European Community belong to the ILO. The main organs of the ILO consist of the Governing Body, the International Labour Office and the International Labour Conference which meets on an annual basis.[12] The operation of the ILO and its Conference is uniquely based on a tripartite composition. Member States are entitled to send four representatives to the Annual Conference; two from Government, one from employers' organisations and one from trade unions. The principal task of the Conference, which is the supreme body of the ILO, is to adopt proposals in the form of international Conventions or Recommendations, these require a majority of two-thirds of the votes cast by the delegates present.[13] Conventions are comparable to multilateral international treaties, they are open for ratification and, once ratified, create specific binding obligations on States. Recommendations offer non-binding guidance and often elaborate on the provisions of a Convention on the same subject.

The ILO Governing Body decides whether to include a discussion of the definition of standards in a specific area on the agenda of the International Conference. Consideration of proposed new standards is undertaken through two consecutive annual conferences. Following a consultative exercise, which in the case of the obligations which eleven EC Member States have entered upon, must embrace dialogue at national level with employer and workers organisations,[14] a report compiled by

---

12.   Article 2 of the ILO Constitution.

13.   Article 19(1) and (2) of the ILO Constitution.

14.   Article 39(1) of the Standing Orders of the Conference and Article 5(1) of Convention No.144 — concerning Tripartite Consultations to Promote the Implementation of In-

the International Labour Office is considered at the "first reading" which consists of a general discussion during the annual session of the Conference.[15] The Conference usually considers the form and content of proposed instruments, and decides whether to continue discussion of these matters at the next Conference. Once adopted, a Convention is communicated to Member States for ratification. The Member States are required to report on their intention to ratify the new instrument. ILO Conventions contain no provisions for abolition or repeal other than provisions for denunciation by ratifying States. Withdrawal from a Convention following denunciation is permitted once every ten years.

(ii) *The ILO Prohibition on Nightwork*

Historically, the standard-setting activities of the ILO with regard to women have been guided by two distinct themes — protection and equality.[16] The two themes have emerged sequentially. In its preamble, the ILO Constitution of 1919 affirmed the need to provide protection for women. In 1944, the Declaration of Philadelphia, adopted at the ILO's 26th Conference, introduced the principle of equal opportunity emphasising that:

> All human beings, irrespective of...sex, have the right to pursue both their material well-being and their spiritual development in conditions of freedom and dignity, of economic security and equal opportunity.

These two themes are reflected in standards which have been adopted *(i)* to protect women workers from exploitation at work, from arduous working conditions and from risks to their health with reference to their roles as child-bearers and mothers; and *(ii)* to promote equal rights and treatment between men and women in employment.[17]

The first ILO Convention prohibiting nightwork for women, the Nightwork (Women) Convention (No.4), 1919, was revised in 1934 by

ternational Labour Standards. ILO Convention No.114 has been ratified by all the Member States of the European Community with the exception of Luxembourg.

15. Article 39(3) and (4) of the Standing Orders of the Conference.

16. International Labour Organisation; Special Protective Measures for Women and Equality of Opportunity and Treatment, Geneva, 1989, p.41.

17. The adoption of the ILO Equal Remuneration Convention (No.100), 1950, constituted the most significant advance by the ILO in this direction. The Discrimination (Employment and Occupation) Convention (No.111), 1958, has a much broader scope than the field of equality between men and women.

Convention No.41. In these circumstances, the original instruments remain binding on those countries which decline to ratify any revision thereof. This reflects the fact that there is no provision under the ILO Constitution for the repeal of an existing Convention. The ILO Secretariat has provided an explanation of the nature of ILO Conventions as follows:

> Each ILO Convention has been treated as a separate self-contained treaty, binding on those countries that have ratified it, but unaffected by subsequent Conventions, even where a different obligation is formulated in the later instrument.[18]

Both the 1919 and 1934 ILO Conventions were subsequently revised in 1948 by Convention No.89. The purpose of these revisions was to render the standards more flexible, especially to ensure that women in management and technical posts would not be precluded from nightwork, although the provisions of all three instruments remain basically similar to each other. These Conventions apply only to industry, and there is no Convention on nightwork for women in non-industrial sectors. The Conventions prohibiting nightwork by women in industry provide that "women without distinction of age shall not be employed during the night in any public or private industrial undertaking, or in any branch thereof".

Although there is no standard definition of "night", all three of these Conventions prescribe a night rest period of at least 11 consecutive hours, which must include a shorter interval during which the employment of women is strictly forbidden.[19]

Of the three original Conventions, the one containing the greatest number of exceptions to the prohibition of nightwork is Convention No.89.[20] These exceptions extend to: family enterprises; women engaged in white-collar work, and in particular positions of a managerial or technical character; women employed in health and welfare services who are not ordinarily engaged in manual work; cases of *force majeure*, (*e.g.* where an unforeseen and non-recurring interruption of work occurs); or in cases where nightwork is necessary to preserve perishable materials from certain loss. Furthermore, governments may suspend the prohibition, after consultation with employers' and workers' organisations, "when in case of serious emergency the national interest demands it".

18.   J. Wood, "International Labour Organisation Conventions - Labour Code or Treaties", (1991) 40 *International and Comparative Law Quarterly* 656.

19.   International Labour Conference, 1989, *Nightwork Report* (v)(i) Chapter IV.

20.   *ibid.*, Twenty States — none of them European — which have not ratified Convention No.89, remained bound by at least one of the two earlier Conventions in 1989.

(iii) *The Influence of ILO Standards on the Development of EC Social Policy*

The corpus of ILO Conventions and Recommendations, which had been developed by the late 1950s provided the main inspiration for the rights proclaimed by the European Social Charter, drawn up by the Council of Europe in 1961. The rights proclaimed by the Charter coincide broadly with the range of obligations which had been laid upon States under ILO regulations. The Charter guarantees the right of employed women to protection. The provisions of ILO Convention No.89 are echoed in Article 8 (4)(a) of the Charter.[21] Compared with the extensive corpus of ILO regulations, the social and labour legislation of the European Community is limited in scope. The social provisions Chapter at Title III of Part 3 of the Rome Treaty. 1957, restricted the scope for *legislative* activity as distinct from other forms of inter-governmental co-operation in this field. The key social provisions of the Rome Treaty at Articles 117, 118 and 119 did not confer any express power on Community institutions to legislate to achieve the objectives they proclaim.

Following the ratification of the Single European Act, 1987, the European Commission set out to explore the social dimension of the internal market and identify the essential components of the social policy norms and practices already established within the Community. In looking forward to the possibility of establishing a body of minimum social provisions, which might constitute the bedrock of the Community's social policy, a Commission working party[22] drew attention to the contents of the European Social Charter and "a list of ILO Conventions likely to be relevant in the context of a body of minimum social provisions". Convention No.89 did not, however, feature on the Commission's list! In November 1988, the Commission requested the Community's Economic and Social Committee (ESC) to undertake a general appraisal of the possible components of a "Community Charter of Basic Social Rights".[23] The ESC, in an opinion adopted by a large majority, noted that governments and the social partners had reached consensus on the definition of basic social rights within a number of international organisations.[24] Although the ESC identified up to twelve ILO Conventions featuring basic social rights, it did not list Convention No.89 among them. Both

21. O. Kahn-Freund, "The European Social Charter", Chapter 10 of *"European Law and the Individual"*, Ed. F.G. Jacobs, North-Holland, (1976).

22. Interim Report on the Commission's Interdepartmental Working Party on the Social Dimension of the Internal Market, (Special Edition) 1988.

23. See Communication of 9 November, 1988 in *Social Europe* 1/90 at page 80.

24. Opinion of the Economic and Social Committee on "The Fundamental Social Community Rights", *Social Europe* 1/90.

the ESC and the European Parliament had urged formal recognition by the Community of, *inter alia*, ILO Conventions as the basis for Community policy in the social sphere rather than the adoption of a Charter in the form of a "solemn declaration". Both the ESC and the European Parliament had tended, however, to adopt an *à la carte* approach to the selection of those international social legal instruments which might serve as a basis for "a coherent, interdependent set of rules".[25] The ban on nightwork for women in industrial employment did not feature in their citation of generally applicable standards which should be endorsed at Community level. The assumption that a consensus on the definition of basic social rights already existed may have reflected a misplaced faith in International Labour Conventions as constituting a code rather than merely a collection of separate and sometimes internally conflicting legal instruments.[26] In the event, the text of the Community Charter adopted by the Heads of State or Government of eleven Member States in Strasbourg, on 9 December 1989, merely refers in the preamble to the "solemn declaration" that:

> inspiration should be drawn from Conventions of the International Labour Organisation and from the European Social Charter of the Council of Europe.

The European Community is not a member of the ILO but it is afforded observer status at the ILO and may take part in the deliberations of the Annual Conference.[27] Three agreements have been concluded between the ILO and the European Communities since the latter were established.[28] These agreements are essentially about administrative co-operation and provide for mutual consultation, exchange of information and joint co-operation in a range of areas. The original agreements concluded between the ILO and the European Communities have been supplemented by the exchange of letters between the ILO and the Commission which have sought to establish arrangements for direct consultation.[29] The possibility of achieving even greater co-operation between the two organisations has been identified with particular regard to, *inter alia*, the following areas: the social aspects of development and promo-

25. *ibid.*

26. J. Wood, *op.cit.* n.18, pp.649-657.

27. ILO Constitution, Article 12: Article 56(7) of the Standing Orders of the Conference.

28. 1953 Agreement between ILO and ECSC, OJ No.11. 1953 Agreement between ILO and EEC, OJ No.27 (27/4/1959). 1961 Agreement between ILO and EAEC, OJ No.18.

29. See Exchange of Letters between the European Communities and the International Labour Organisation, OJ C-24/8, 1 February 1990.

tion of human resources; working conditions; health and safety; and the promotion of equal opportunities and equal treatment.

3.   BALANCING PROTECTION AND EQUAL TREATMENT

(i)   *The Influence of EC Equality Law*

The 1976 Equal Treatment Directive is not only concerned to secure the incorporation of the principle of equal treatment into the law of each Member State, it also requires the revision of regulatory measures which run counter to that principle.[30] The interplay between actors at the level of both the Community Institutions and the EC Member States is considered here in terms of their scrutiny of the conformity of national legislation with this Community law principle. The record of ratification of ILO Nightwork Convention No.89 on the part of EC Member States in the period 1976 to 1989 is reviewed, with particular regard to how the provisions of national legislation in Ireland (which owed their origin to the ILO Convention) were scrutinised for conformity with the requirements of Community law.

For the purposes of implementing the Directive, Member States were required to revise laws, regulations and administrative provisions contrary to the principle of equal treatment when the concern for protection which originally inspired them is no longer well founded.[31] An initial four year timetable was set from the commencement of the Directive during which Member States were to undertake this revision exercise, the timetable for the initial revision exercise was scheduled to expire on 14 February 1980. In that year, the Commission reviewed the relationship between Article 2(3) and paragraph 2(c) of Articles 3 and 5 in a Report on the application of the Equal Treatment Directive.[32] It took the view that Article 2(3) refers only to pregnancy and maternity and should be strictly interpreted as such, since in practice provisions con-

---

30. Article 1, Equal Treatment Directive, *op.cit.* n.2, states: "there shall be no discrimination whatsoever on grounds of sex either directly or indirectly as regards access to employment, including promotion and to vocational training, and as regards working conditions". Article 2(3) specifically provides that this principle is without prejudice to provisions concerning the protection of women, particularly as regards pregnancy and maternity.

31. Equal Treatment Directive; Articles 3(2) and 5(2)(c).

32. Report from the Commission to the Council on the situation at 12 August, 1980, with regard to the implementation of the principle of equal treatment for men and women as regards access to employment and promotion, access to vocational guidance and training, working conditions. COM (80) 832 final, 11 February, 1981.

cerning differential treatment relating to other matters were provided for in paragraph 2(c) of Article 3 and 5 of the Directive. The Report identified the absence of any uniform pattern of application of protective regulations across the Member States. It concluded that:

> there are no common permanent requirements concerning the specific protection of women which have proved imperative in all countries in identical circumstances but, on the contrary, that a mosaic of extremely varied and highly specific regulations exists, the reasons for which are not clearly defined. [33]

(ii) *The Geography of Equal Treatment on Nightwork*

During the 1970s and 1980s, increasing concern with equality of opportunity and a growing awareness that the ban on nightwork for women could result in excluding women from jobs led a number of EC Member States to conclude that their continued adherence to international regulations prohibiting nightwork for women was inconsistent with the provision of equal treatment in employment. The 1976 Directive had obliged Member States to ensure that the principle of equal treatment applies for men and women as regards access to employment, vocational training, and promotion and working conditions. These concerns had previously prompted the Netherlands, and were to compel Ireland and Luxembourg, to denounce the ILO Nightwork Convention No.89. However, six Member States were to remain bound by Convention No.89 until February 1992 when their denunciations were registered by the International Labour Office.[34]

The majority of West European countries had ratified Convention No.89 in the years following 1948, in most cases enacting legislation to transpose its provisions into national law. There were, however, important exceptions, with Denmark, West Germany and the UK having declined to ratify Convention No.89.[35] In the case of Denmark, the question of banning nightwork for women had historically been rejected on grounds of equality.

Notwithstanding their failure to ratify Convention No.89, the Federal Republic of Germany and the UK still maintained national provisions in the mid 1980s which prohibited nightwork for women employed in industry on manual work. The UK had originally ratified Convention No.41 (1934) which preceded Convention No.89. Although the UK had

---

33. *ibid.*, p.161.

34. These six states were Belgium, France, Greece, Italy, Portugal and Spain (see Table A at Appendix 3).

35. 219 *European Industrial Relations Review*, April 1992.

denounced Convention No.41 by 1947, it did not, however, proceed to ratify Convention No.89. The ban on nightwork for women remained in force in the UK through the provisions of statutes dating from 1936, 1954 and 1961,[36] which had been influenced by the original ILO Conventions Nos.4 and 41, and were restricted in application to factories and mines. The Sex Discrimination Act, 1986, provided a mechanism enabling these provisions to be repealed in accordance with the requirements of the 1976 Directive. In the case of the Federal Republic of Germany, Article 19.1 of the *Arbeitszeitordnung* (AZO) (regulations concerning Working Time) Law of 1938, had placed a prohibition on the employment of women manual workers between 20.00 hours and 06.00 hours and after 17.00 hours on Saturday/day before holidays. Female shift workers were permitted to work until 23.00 hours (Article 19(2) AZO).[37] These provisions remained operative until the German Constitutional Court, in a decision of 28 January 1992, declared the prohibition of nightwork for women to be unconstitutional.[38]

(iii) *The Conformity of National Legislation with Community Law: Ireland — A Case Study*

The Irish Government's response to the requirement to undertake an examination of protective legislation at Article 9(1) of the 1976 Directive was to request the newly established Employment Equality Agency to undertake a review of the relevant sections of the Conditions of Employment Act, 1936, which prohibited the employment of women in industrial work at night. The Agency was requested in November 1977 to undertake this review under the terms of its foundation statute which empowers it to review the operation or effect of existing legislative provisions which are:

> likely to affect or impede the elimination of discrimination in relation to employment or the promotion of equality of opportunity between men and women in relation to employment.[39]

---

36. The prohibition on nightwork in industrial undertakings and in mines was implemented in the UK by the Hours of Employment (Conventions) Act, 1936, the Mines and Quarries Act, 1954, and the Factories Act, 1961 (Part VI).

37. Commission of the European Communities: *Protective legislation for women in the Member States of the European Community* (Brussels, 1987 COM (87) 105 final, especially Annex, pp. 27-29). See also R. A. Harvey "Equal Treatment of Men and Women in the Implementation of the European Communities Equal Treatment Legislation in the Federal Republic of Germany", (1990) 8 *American Journal of Comparative Law* 31.

38. See below part 5.

39. Section 38 of the Employment Equality Act, 1977.

The Agency found that the prohibition in the Conditions of Employment Act, 1936, on the employment of women in industrial work constituted a discrimination against women in employment.[40] It decided that women were being denied jobs, losing out on promotional opportunities and taking home less money because they could not be employed on nightwork rosters.

The Agency found that the 1936 Act, which was based on ILO Convention No.41 (1934), actually imposed more severe restrictions on the right of women to work at night than those laid down in Convention No.89. The Agency was not satisfied that medical reasons justified the different treatment of males and females (other than in the special circumstances of pregnancy). In recommending the repeal of Irish legislation which imposed special restrictions on women working at night which did not apply to men, the Agency suggested that new provisions take into account the studies of shiftwork and nightwork which were being undertaken by the ILO and the European Community's Foundation for the Improvement of Living and Working Conditions. It is noteworthy that Irish employers did not argue for change from a deregulatory standpoint but argued only for the removal of discriminatory provisions. They fully accepted that "close supervision should be exercised on the issue of shift licences so as to ensure that appropriate standards are being observed".[41]

The Agency recommended that new legislative standards governing nightwork arrangements on a non-discriminatory basis should build upon the provisions in the Irish 1936 Act in which arrangements for licensing shiftwork required prior consultation with employer and worker representatives. Accordingly, the Agency proposed that:

> A licensing arrangement incorporating a consultative process in respect of all forms of shift working, including nightwork and continuous process shift work, should take account of local conditions affecting hours of work, transport and rest periods. This would take account of child-care facilities outside the home and school which may limit the availability and mobility of parents. Special provisions would also have to be made to ensure that pregnant women would not be forced to do shift work against their own wishes or medical advice nor that they would be forced to leave their employment.[42]

40. *Review of the Ban on Industrial Nightwork for Women*, Employment Equality Agency, November 1978, pp. 36-38.

41. *ibid.*, pp. 27-28.

42. *ibid.*, pp. 36-37.

The Agency noted that, under Article 15 of Convention No.89, Ireland was formally precluded from denouncing the ILO Convention until the current ten year cycle ended in 1981. It called upon the Irish Government, however, to serve notice on the ILO of Ireland's intention to denounce the Convention at the next opportunity which should coincide with the introduction of legislation to equalise the conditions under which men and women may work at night under protective provisions.

The Irish Government's denunciation of ILO Convention No.89 was registered by the ILO in February 1982. In support of its denunciation, the Irish Government stated that the ban on nightwork for women had come to be perceived as an inadmissible form of discrimination against women.[43] It repealed the offending provisions in the 1936 Act but did not proceed to introduce new legislation on working hours. It did, however, undertake to attach recommendations on good practice to all shift work licences. It is unlikely that a further general revision of legislation on working hours will be considered prior to the coming into effect of the EC Working Time Directive.

(iv) The European Commission's Monitoring and Guidance Activity

The Commission followed up its 1981 report on the implementation of the 1976 Directive with a special report on the revision of protective legislation which was presented as a Communication addressed to the Member States.[44] Although the Commission's Communication noted the denunciation of Convention No.89 by Ireland, the Netherlands and Luxembourg, it did not call on the six Member States which continued to be bound by the Convention to do likewise. The Commission appears instead to have been concerned to avoid a situation in which the removal of a prohibition originally introduced for protective reasons might be viewed as bringing about a *de facto* worsening of women's working conditions. It argued that the obligation to ensure equal treatment should be seen within the context of the objective of improving working conditions set out in Article 117 of the Rome Treaty. The Commission revealed its preference for "levelling upwards" by questioning, in effect, the legitimacy and necessity of all nightwork. It cautiously recommended therefore that Member States consider three options in descending order of preference:

43. *ILO Official Bulletin* Vol.LXV, Series A, 1982, p.32.

44. Commission of the European Communities: *Protective legislation for women in the Member States of the European Community* (1987).

(a) a ban on night work for all men and women, coupled with equal derogations for both sexes, with the exception of pregnant or nursing mothers;

(b) removal of the ban for women in the context of a general improvement in working conditions agreed with the Social Partners, *e.g.* by a general reduction of nightwork, where possible;

(c) failing attempts to reach such an agreement, there should neither be a perpetuation of the ban, nor a worsening of women's working conditions.

The Commission sought to build upon the Court of Justice's strict interpretation of the text of the Directive:

> the Equal Treatment Directive has provided a narrow exception to this principle which authorises measures strictly necessary to protect the special biological condition of women. The Commission regards this physiological test as the touchstone for legislation protecting women, a rigorous approach which has been confirmed by the Court of Justice. It may be concluded that many of the protective measures discussed…will have to be extended to both sexes or repealed.[45]

The Commission was also seeking, however, to supplement the Court's approach by tackling areas into which the Court was not inclined to reach. By arguing that it might be insufficient for Member States to simply remove special protective measures which were originally limited to one sex, the Commission was, at that time, intent upon pursuing a social policy agenda which was markedly at variance with the deregulatory agenda, reflected in the stance of the United Kingdom Government in particular, and the concern on the part of governments and employers to avoid damage to competitiveness and the imposition of additional costs upon businesses.

(v) *The Judicial Treatment of the Exceptions to the Equal Treatment Principle*

From the late 1970s, the European Court of Justice was called upon in several cases to examine the validity of exceptions to the prohibition of different treatment. In its landmark judgment in *Defrenne III*, the Court had established that the principle of equal treatment formed part of

---

45. *ibid.*, p.23.

"fundamental personal human rights" which must be respected under Community Law.[46] It drew the inspiration for this declaration from both the European Social Charter and ILO Convention No.111. The subsequent case law established the Court's concern to ensure a narrow construction of the scope of the permissible exceptions. Three cases which illustrate the approach adopted by the Court are cited below.

The Court of Justice confirmed its adherence to a strict interpretation of the 1976 Directive in its ruling in *Johnston* which concerned the exclusion of women from the armed police force in Northern Ireland.[47] The principal issue in the case — which related to the circumstances in which the Directive permitted Member States to exclude sex discrimination complaints on grounds of national security — is not of concern here. In its judgment, however, the Court specifically related its conclusions to Article 2(3) of the Directive. The Court considered that it was clear from the express reference in that Article to pregnancy and maternity, that the Directive's purpose was to allow protection of a women's biological condition and the special relationship which exists between a woman and her child.[48] Women should not be excluded from a certain type of employment:

> on the grounds that public opinion demands that women be given greater protection than men against risks which affect women and men in the same way and which are distinct from women's specific needs of protection.

The Court's decision in *Johnston* appeared therefore to indicate that women may lawfully only be granted special protection where their condition as women specifically requires it.

The ECJ had also addressed the interpretation of Article 2(3) of the Directive in its judgment in *Hofmann*.[49] This ruling had concerned a father's entitlement to claim an equivalent State allowance to that which German law provides for the mother of a new born child who may avail of an extended period of maternity leave until her child reaches the age

---

46. Case C-149/77, *Defrenne v Sabena* [1978] ECR 1365. Note Advocate General Darmon had emphasised that: "a derogation from a human right as fundamental as that of equal treatment must be appraised in a restrictive manner".

47. Case 222/84, *Johnston v Royal Ulster Constabulary* [1986] ECR 1651.

48. *ibid.*, Point 44 of judgment of 15 May, 1986. See also point 13 of judgment in *Stoeckel*, Case C-345/89 [1991] ECR I-4047.

49. Judgment of 12 July, 1984 in Case 184/83, *Hofmann v Barmer Ersatzkasse* [1984] ECR 3047. See also discussion of *Hofmann* ruling in Ninon Colneric, "The Prohibitions of Discrimination against Women under Community Law", (1992) 8 *International Journal of Comparative Labour Law and Industrial Relations* 191.

of six months. The Court ruled that the Equal Treatment Directive was not designed to settle questions concerned with the organisation of the family, or to alter the division of responsibility between parents.[50] In relation to Article 2(3), it said that the Directive permits two kinds of protection of women:

(a) protection of a woman's biological condition during pregnancy and thereafter until all her functions have returned to normal; and

(b) protection of the special relationship between a woman and her child over the period which follows pregnancy and childbirth, in order to prevent that relationship from being disturbed by the multiple burdens which would result from the simultaneous pursuit of employment.

The Court's ruling reflected its view that a protective measure can only be justified if it corresponds to a specific condition of womanhood. By focusing on the special needs of a woman as a mother, the Court rejected the Commission's preferred remedy in the form of a non-discriminatory measure which would have provided for "levelling upwards" by enabling both parents to have an entitlement to leave for looking after young children.

The Court of Justice again confirmed its strict interpretation of the 1976 Directive when the Commission brought infringement proceedings against France under Article 169 EEC, for failure to ensure complete application of the principle of equal opportunity between men and women.[51] The French law in question enabled both sides of industry to proceed to bring the terms of collective agreements which conferred special rights on women into conformity with the equal treatment principle through collective bargaining.[52] According to the Court this legislation was unacceptable because it had failed to lay down any time limit for compliance with the obligation to remove special rights for women for which no justification was provided in Article 2(3) of the Directive. This case highlighted the difficulty of reliance on a process of negotiation between the two sides of industry as a basis for removing certain instances of inequality. The Court's commitment to scrutinising arrangements involving recourse to collective agreements to ensure that they conform to the requirements of the Directive, provided a clear sig-

---

50. *Hofmann*, point 24 of judgment. See also citation at point 17 of judgment in *Stoeckel* .

51. Case 312/86, *Commission v French Republic* [1988] ECR 6315

52. French Law No.83-635 of 13 July, 1983.

nal to those Member States such as France and Italy which had shown a tendency to fall back on agreements between the social partners, in the form of collective accords or agreements at sectoral or branch level, as a basis for derogation from a continuing prohibition on nightwork for women.

The three cases referred to above, provide examples of the Court's adoption of a consistently firm line on the need to be especially vigilant about provisions in national law or national procedures which jeopardise the exercise of the fundamental right to equal treatment. The Court's strict approach in these cases established the grounds on which it based its decision in the S*toeckel* case (which will be considered in Section 5). In contrast to the Court's restrictive focus, the Commission's more ambitious aim of "levelling upwards" to be achieved through, for instance, recommending a universal ban on nightwork may have served to deflect Member States from contemplating the straightforward action recommended by the Irish Employment Equality Agency (*i.e.* a commitment to the denunciation of ILO Convention No.89 as a prelude to developing new regulations having regard to the special needs of pregnant women and the shared child care responsibilities of working parents). The scope for designing a new regulatory framework for the organisation of nightwork as an alternative to outdated protective standards and the differences between employers and trade unions (and within their respective constituencies at national and international levels) in this regard, were subsequently brought into sharper focus when the 1989 International Labour Conference debated the revision of ILO Convention No.89.

4. **THE ILO's REVISION OF NIGHTWORK STANDARDS: THE STANCE ADOPTED BY EC MEMBER STATES**

In 1987, the Governing Body of the International Labour Office decided to place the question of nightwork on the agenda of the 76th Session (1989) of the International Labour Conference. The idea of revising Convention No.89 had developed from the early 1970s in response to concern that considerable technological and social changes had occurred since its adoption in 1948. A working party on international labour standards established in 1984 by the Governing Body, had classified Convention No.89 among those to be revised.[53] In 1985, the International Labour Conference adopted a Resolution on Equality of Op-

---

53. International Labour Conference 76th Session Report V(1) *Nightwork* Geneva, 1988, Chapter IV. The discussion at the 1985 Conference also drew on the "ILO Plan of Action" adopted in 1975 which called for measures to review all protective legislation applying to women in the light of up-to-date scientific knowledge and technological

portunity and Equal Treatment between men and women in employment which called for regular examination of ILO instruments containing special protective measures for women, including in particular Convention No.89, to determine their continuing appropriateness.[54]

In 1987, the ILO study of Protective Legislation for Women had identified two categories among the wide range of ILO standards which afforded special protection to women.[55]

First, those measures aimed at protecting "women's reproductive and
maternal functions" — such as Conventions and Recommendations on
maternity leave or on special protection for pregnant or breast feeding
workers.

Second, those measures aimed at "protecting women generally because of their sex, based on attitudes toward their capabilities and appropriate role in society".

The prohibition of nightwork by women in industry, once a widely
accepted feature of national and international labour standards, was
considered to fall into the second of the two categories comprising measures based on the alleged functional rather than biological differences
between men and women. The ILO Study had highlighted the sharply
divergent approaches between those, on the one hand, who viewed protective legislation, such as prohibitions on nightwork, as interfering with
equality through hindering women's access to certain jobs, and others,
who considered that it represented a platform from which to extend the
benefit of protection to all workers, seeing nightwork as equally deleterious for both men and women.

The 1989 International Labour Conference set up a Committee on
nightwork with a mandate to consider a Protocol revising Convention
No.89 and proposed new standards on nightwork which would apply to
workers of either sex. The proceedings of the Tripartite Committee were
controversial and widely divergent views were expressed on the part of
the Employer and Worker groups and within the Government group.[56]
The main options facing the Committee were:

> advances and to revise, supplement, extend to all workers, retain or repeal such legisla-
> tion according to national circumstances, these measures being aimed at the improve-
> ment of the quality of life (paragraph 6). Resolution concerning a plan of action with
> a view to promoting equality of opportunity and treatment for women workers, 1975.,
> (International Labour Conference, 60th Session), in Official Bulletin Vol.LVIII, 1975,
> Series A, No.1 p.88.

54.   Resolution of 27 June, 1985.

55.   International Labour Office, *Women Workers: Protection or Equality?* Conditions of Work
Digest, Volume 6, 2/1987.

56.   International Labour Conference 1989, Provisional Record 30; Report of the Committee on Nightwork, para. 300, pp. 30-34.

(a) to approve a partial revision of Convention No.89, by means of a Protocol, which would replace one or more articles of the existing Convention by a revised text or the insertion of additional articles. (This type of revision procedure would maximise the ability of the States which remained bound by Convention No.89 to diminish the impact of its restrictions on the nightwork of women in industry);

(b) to approve new standards such as a Convention and/or Recommendation covering the improvement of the working conditions of all nightworkers and to provide equal opportunities for all men and women;

(c) to decline to revise the existing standards or to adopt any new instruments on nightwork. (If the only means of disposing of Convention No.89 was through denunciation then, according to the Employers' group and some Governments, the preferred option was to leave it to wither away rather than to attempt to add greater flexibility to a discriminatory prohibition).

The Employers' Group maintained, however, that the prohibition on nightwork for women in industry was discriminatory and represented an obstacle to social and economic progress. They maintained that there was a direct conflict between the provisions of Convention No.89 and Convention No.111, concerning discrimination in respect of employment and occupation. Throughout the "first reading" procedure, the Employers' Group remained unconvinced of the need to regulate nightwork through the adoption of new instruments, in particular a Convention. They argued that the extremely varied nature of nightwork, its complexity and the variety of circumstances under which it was carried out, made it unsuitable for international regulation. The proposed instruments were considered to be insufficiently flexible and likely to reduce the scope for job creation, particularly in small enterprises and in the service sector.[57]

The Workers' Group argued that recourse to nightwork should be reduced to the minimum possible level and that it could not be justified purely for economic reasons. Nightwork was "unnatural" work which had a negative impact on the health of workers and was detrimental to their social and family life. It was necessary to recognise Convention No.89 as one obstacle to the spread of nightwork which should be built upon. In

57. International Labour Conference 1989, Provisional Record 30; Report of the Committee on Nightwork, June 1989, Geneva.

their spirited defence of the existing Convention, the Workers' Group opposed its dilution through a more flexible Protocol. The Workers' Group favoured tighter protection extended through new instruments which would apply to men and women in the service sector and in industry. New international rules were required to improve the situation of all nightworkers and to compensate them as far as possible for the drawbacks of nightwork.

There was no consensus among the EC Member Governments regarding either the status of Convention No.89 or the preferred form of any new instrument. The EC Governments were split between those who favoured a new Convention supplemented by a Recommendation, and those who preferred to settle, if necessary, for a Recommendation (see Table B). It is normal practice for the representatives of the EC Governments on the relevant Conference Committee to meet together as a group to co-ordinate their negotiating positions. These group meetings are held on the fringe of the tripartite committee meetings and are chaired by a representative of the EC State which holds the Presidency of the Council of Ministers. These arrangements stem from the commitment by EC Member States to strive to adopt a common attitude in view of the obligations arising from Articles 5 and 116 of the EC Treaty. In the case of the Committee on Nightwork, its activities were monitored during the 1989 Conference by an EC working group chaired by the Spanish delegate whose Government occupied the EC Presidency at that time. The EC working group was chaired by the Irish delegate in the following year as the 1990 Conference coincided with the Irish Presidency in the first half of 1990. Each group is assisted by the Council Secretariat and may draw on advice from the Commission during the course of the annual conference in Geneva.[58]

The deliberations of the Committee on Nightwork, established by the 1990 International Labour Conference, proceeded more smoothly than in the "first stage" reading with the result that the three instruments were adopted on the basis of what was described as almost a "model of tripartite consensus".[59] This view was not, however, universally shared among Government representatives. The U.S. Government representa-

---

58. The author is aware of the dissatisfaction of Irish Presidency officials at the Commission's response to its request for the attendance of Commission experts to assist and advise the EC delegates working group co-ordinating their contribution to the Committee on Nightwork at the 1990 International Labour Conference. A senior Commission official told the author that DGV was internally divided about whether the Conference theme was appropriate to its working conditions or equal opportunities unit.

59. Convention No.171; a non-binding Recommendation and a Protocol to the Nightwork Convention No.89; see also comments at Plenary Debate by the Chairman of Committee on Nightwork, International Labour Conference, 1990, Provisional Record 31/32, 25 June, 1990.

tive on the Committee on Nightwork, while welcoming some signs of positive progress achieved through the two-stage discussion process, protested that progress had been achieved on the basis of only a "two-party" consensus between Workers' and Employers' Groups which had effectively excluded the governments who alone are empowered to ratify and implement Conventions:

> Accordingly, too little consideration was given to whether the agreements entered into by the Workers and Employers could be implemented under current or reasonable foreseeable national conditions by a broad cross-section of member states in varying stages of economic development.[60]

At the beginning of the proceedings of the Committee on Nightwork, Government members had emphasised the need for flexibility in the instruments under consideration to ensure wide ratification and application in practice having regard to the great diversity of economic and legal situations. The Irish Government representative, speaking on behalf of the EC Member States, stated that the subject matter of the deliberations was particularly relevant for the European Community in the light of prospective proposals dealing with the adaptation of working time, atypical forms of employment and maternity protection. In the event, all the EC Member States viewed the new Convention, which was the subject of agreement at the Committee on Nightwork, as a considerable advance on their initial pessimistic expectations about the likely content of any instrument emerging from tripartite discussions.

The new Convention provides that "special measures required by the nature of nightwork" must be taken for *all* nightworkers in order to protect their health, assist them to meet their family and social responsibilities, provide opportunities for occupational advancement and compensate them properly. It is also interesting in the light of the development of social dialogue at European level and the role afforded to the social partners in the preparation and the implementation of legislation under the Treaty on European Union, that the Convention requires the exclusion of "limited categories" to be preceded by consultations with the representative organisations of employers and workers concerned. Such exclusions are permissible only if the application to them of the Convention would raise "special problems of a substantial nature". The EC Member States welcomed the deletion from the preamble of contro-

---

60. Contribution by Bill Belt, US Government representative Plenary Debate on report of Committee on Nightwork, International Labour Conference, 1990, Provisional Record, 25 June, 1990, pp. 30-37; see also contribution of Rapporteur to the Committee at 31/3.

versial paragraphs about the alleged negative effects of nightwork. They succeeded in inserting a reference to the Discrimination (Employment and Occupation) Convention No.111, (1958), in the Preamble. The provision at Article 3(2) enabling measures to be implemented progressively was regarded as an aid to flexibility. The treatment of such complex issues as the duration of nightwork (Article 1); health assessments (Article 4); access to first aid (Article 5); maternity protection (Article 7); and compensation for nightwork, were considered to have been handled in a realistic manner through the establishment of general principles rather than over-prescriptive rules.[61]

Eleven EC Member States confirmed their support for the proposed new Convention. The United Kingdom was isolated in its opposition in principle to the new Convention. The UK, alone among the EC Member States, made its own statement on the outcome of the Committee on Nightwork:[62]

> We would have preferred this Conference not to adopt any instruments on nightwork, or failing that, simply to adopt a Recommendation for the guidance of Member States and not a binding Convention. Having said that, the text of the proposed Convention that the Committee has presented to us is less objectionable than it might have been ... The trend of the discussions has been encouraging. The text of the proposed Convention contains a welcome flexibility. Some of the principles laid down are eminently sensible... [But] because we do not believe that international instruments have any part to play in determining working time arrangements, the United Kingdom Government will not vote in favour of the proposed Convention and Recommendation.[63]

The adoption of ILO Convention No.171 showed that the ILO system had the capability, albeit after more than a decade of internal controversy and debate, to establish sufficient common ground between its tripartite constituencies in order to reach agreement on the adoption of new, universal standards as an alternative to protective measures apply-

61.   See report of contents of the 1990 Convention (No.171) in "Nightwork for Women", (1992) 8 *International Journal of Comparative Labour Law and Industrial Relations*, pp. 181-182.

62.   The Irish Presidency's proposal, supported by all the other EC Member States, to present an agreed statement welcoming the adoption of the new instruments on behalf of the EC Member States, was vetoed by the UK.

63.   Contribution by Peter Brannen, UK Government Delegate, 1990 International Labour Conference, Plenary Debate, Provisional Record, 31/16-17, 25 June 1990.

ing only to women. By the close of the 1990 Conference the support confirmed by eleven EC Member States for the adoption of the new Convention marked a significant shift compared with the hesitant supportive stance of only five Member States at the commencement of negotiations in 1989. The manner in which steps towards greater flexibility and decentralisation of decision-making to the parties to collective agreements are balanced in the provisions of ILO Convention No.171 also served to signal the direction the European Commission would seek to pursue in its draft Directive on the organisation of working time which was published in October 1990. Following the adoption of an ILO Convention, however, the main focus of attention shifts from the negotiation process to the process of ratification. The reluctance of States to ratify new ILO Conventions has been noteworthy in recent years.[64] The decision of the European Court of Justice in the *Stoeckel* case in 1991, which is considered below, has already significantly altered the way in which most Member States view the possible ratification of Convention No.171.

5.   **THE JUDICIAL INTERPRETATION OF THE RELATIONSHIP BETWEEN EC LAW AND INTERNATIONAL LABOUR CONVENTIONS**

The development of a strict approach by the Court of Justice to the scope of the exceptions to the principle of equality has been outlined above with reference to three key rulings. None of these cases, however, concerned national legislation on the prohibition of nightwork for women. In 1989, the ECJ was faced for the first time with a direct question about whether such a general prohibition could be deemed compatible with the Equal Treatment Directive. The Court's case-law had already established that derogations, and exceptions from the principle of equality, had to be limited to what is expressly permitted by the Directive or implicitly permitted in the light of general principles of Community Law.[65] In the *Stoeckel* and *Levy* cases, references which arose from criminal proceedings taken by the French authorities between 1989 and 1991 against employers for employing women on nightwork, the Court was faced with similar cases which raised the thorny problem of balanc-

---

64.   The seventeen new ILO Conventions adopted between 1980 and 1990 have received an average of only twelve ratifications each; see David Goodhart, *Financial Times*, 15 November, 1993. Article 228 EEC has prompted concerns that its apparent restriction upon the possibilities of Member States in their relations with the ILO will further curtail their propensity to ratify Conventions.

65.   C. Docksey, "The Principle of Equality Between Women and Men as a Fundamental Right under Community Law", (1991) 20 *Industrial Law Journal* 258, at pp. 267-273.

ing different rights where a national law may be contrary to a Community requirement, but in conformity with, and necessitated by an obligation arising from another International Convention. The two cases are considered together with the response on the part of the Community Institutions and the Member States.

(i) The Stoeckel Case

In the first case, the European Court of Justice ruled on an issue referred to it for preliminary ruling by a French Court, concerning the interpretation of Article 5 of the Equal Treatment Directive.[66] The question arose in the course of criminal proceedings brought against Mr Stoeckel, the director of an undertaking, who was charged with having employed 77 women on nightwork in violation of Article L-213-1 of the French Labour Code.[67] Mr Stoeckel's defence was that the Code's prohibition was contrary to Article 5 of the 1976 Directive and the judgment of the Court in *Commission v France* whereby the French Republic was found not to have fulfilled its obligations by failing to adopt all measures necessary to secure the full implementation of that Directive.[68]

Economic difficulties affecting Mr Stoeckel's undertaking, as a consequence of foreign competition, had forced it to consider making up to 200 employees redundant. In order to limit the number of collective dismissals, the employer had secured the agreement of the trade unions concerned to the introduction of continuous shiftwork on condition that this would apply exceptionally and solely for the period of economic difficulty. It was agreed to give all employees, regardless of sex, an equal chance of retaining employment under the new regime, subject to agreement to the shiftwork system by majority vote of the women themselves; that agreement was obtained.

In the course of the ECJ proceedings, the French and Italian Governments had argued in their submissions that — "the prohibition of nightwork for women, qualified by numerous derogations, was in keeping with the general aims of protecting female employees and with special considerations of a social nature, such as the risks of assault and the greater burden of household work borne by women". The Court did not, however, find this line of argument compelling. As regards the aims of protecting female employees, the Court held that it was not evident

---

66. Case C-345/89, *Ministere Public v Stoeckel* [1991] ECR I-4047.

67. The action by Mr Stoeckel's Company was found to be in violation of the French Labour Code notwithstanding the relaxation of the prohibition of nightwork by women in 1987 in certain circumstances through collective agreements, (Act No.87-423 of 19 June, 1987).

68. See n.51 above.

that, except in case of pregnancy and maternity, the risks incurred by women in such work were broadly different in kind from the risks incurred by men.[69] As far as risks of assault were concerned, the Court ruled that, on the assumption that such risks were greater at night than by day, suitable measures could be adopted to deal with them without jeopardising the fundamental principle of equal treatment for men and women.[70] With regard to family responsibilities, the Court reiterated that the Directive did not seek to settle questions about the organisation of the family or to alter the allocation of responsibilities between partners.[71] As regards the various legislative derogations from the prohibition on nightwork for women, the Court held that these were not sufficient to meet the aims of the Directive since it did not, as a general principle, permit the prohibition of nightwork; the derogations could, indeed, be a source of discrimination.[72] In its ruling the Court found that Article 5 of the Equal Treatment Directive was "sufficiently precise to impose on the Member States the obligation not to lay down by legislation the principle that nightwork by women is prohibited, even if that obligation is subject to exceptions, where nightwork for men is not prohibited".[73]

In the light of this judgment, the Commission took the view that any Member States which still maintained a prohibition on nightwork for women, had to amend their legislation to eliminate discrimination. At the time of the judgment, six Member States (Belgium, France, Spain, Greece, Italy and Portugal) were bound by ILO Convention No.89. The Commission, in a letter of 18 December 1991, requested the six Member States concerned to denounce this Convention, which they did in February 1992. At the same time the Commission recommended the Member States to ratify ILO Convention No.171 of 6 June 1990, which defines common standards for nightwork conditions for workers of both sexes.[74]

(ii) The Jean-Claude Levy Case

Before the Court had delivered its judgment in the *Stoeckel* case, the *Tribunal de Police* in Metz had already referred a similar case for a preliminary ruling.[75] Whereas in the former case, the Ilkirch Police Tribu-

---

69. Case C-345/89, *Stoeckel* at point 15 of judgment of 25 July, 1991.

70. *ibid.*, at point 16.

71. *ibid.*, at point 17; see also *Hofman op.cit.* n.49.

72. *ibid.*, at point 19.

73. *ibid.*, English language text from (1992) 219 *European Industrial Relations Review*, at p.17.

74. Unpublished report by former Director General Degimbe to Informal Social Affairs Council meeting in Bruges in September 1993.

nal had only raised the question of the compatibility of French Law with
the 1976 Directive, the Metz Tribunal focused directly on whether Community rules could supersede the obligations of Member States if such
obligations arise from international treaties with other third countries
concluded before the entry into force of the EC Treaties. In this regard,
it is noteworthy that the Commission had in its submissions in *Stoeckel*
already highlighted the significance of Article 234(1) EEC.[76] The Metz
Tribunal addressed a more precise question than its counterpart in Ilkirch
by asking the Court of Justice whether the French Labour Code should
be put to one side, if in adopting it, France had only fulfilled its obligations under the ILO Nightwork (Women) Convention No.89 (1948).
The Court's ruling in the *Levy* case replied in the negative allowing the
application of an obligation arising from an international treaty concluded with other third countries.[77] While a national court is obliged to
interpret national law so far as possible in accordance with the rules laid
down in the Directive, a contrary provision in a national law remains
applicable if it is necessary in order to ensure that the Member State
discharges its obligations under an International Convention concluded
with non-member countries prior to the entry into force of the Rome
Treaty.

The Court's decision, coming two years after its *Stoeckel* decision appeared to make impossible the continued application of ILO Convention No.89, marked a reversal of direction as the Court belatedly acknowledged that Member States could continue to adhere to such Conventions having regard to the first paragraph of Article 234 EEC. Barely six
months after the Metz Tribunal had referred the proceedings concerning *Jean-Claude Levy* to the Court, France, followed by Belgium, Spain,
Greece, Italy and Portugal, denounced Convention No.89. The Court's
response to the Metz Tribunal thus proved to be of no avail since by the
time the ruling was made no Community Member State remained bound
by the Convention.

(iii) The Consequences of the Judicial Decisions

No EC Member State has so far ratified ILO Convention No.171,
despite the fact that the Commission urged this course of action on the
six Member States which had remained bound by ILO Convention No.89

75. Case C-158/91, (reference for a preliminary ruling made by the *Tribunal de Police, Tra-
     vail et de l'Emploi v Jean-Claude Levy*).

76. *Stoeckel op.cit.* n.66, p.12. See also Docksey *op.cit.* n.65.

77. Case C-158/91, Judgment of the Court of 2 August, 1993, OJ C 240/7 of 4 September,
     1993. The Court has re-affirmed its decision in the *Levy* Case in another preliminary
     ruling in a nightwork case from Belgium, Case C-13/93, *Office National de l'Emploi v M.
     Mienne*, Judgment of 3 February, 1994, (nyr).

at the time of the *Stoeckel* decision. In the light of the *Stoeckel* judgment, Member States which still had legislation with different provisions in respect of nightwork were required to amend their legislation to make it non-discriminatory.[78] In the absence of appropriate national legislation, however, national judges in France and Italy have already used the *Stoeckel* ruling to refrain from applying national legislation banning nightwork for women.[79] In both Belgium and France, moves by successive governments to repeal discriminatory legislation based on ILO Convention No.89 and to introduce new legislation broadly in conformity with the provisions of ILO Convention No.171 have either encountered resistance at the level of the social partners or have faltered for lack of a parliamentary majority.[80] The Court of Justice's ruling in *Stoeckel* was taken into consideration by the German Constitutional Court in its judgment of 28 January 1992, which declared the prohibition of nightwork for women to be unconstitutional.[81] The Court also found the prohibition to be in conflict with the directly effective requirements of the Equal Treatment Directive. The Constitutional Court's decision reversed previous caselaw which had upheld the nightwork prohibition for female blue collar workers on the grounds that the biological qualities of women necessitated differential treatment in this regard.[82]

The concerted action by six EC Member States in denouncing ILO convention No.89 has met with a mixed response from the social partners at national level, with trade unions opposing the action taken by the Governments concerned. The European Parliament reacted by asserting that night working should on principle be banned, and called upon Member States to ratify ILO Convention No.171. The issue was debated in April 1992 following a series of written questions addressed to the Commission. The Parliament expressed concerns that the denunciation of the ILO Convention could open the way to deregulating nightwork. The Parliament's Resolution deplored:

the carelessness of the Commission in permitting a situation to

78.   Spain is the only one of these six Member States to have adopted legislative measures to abolish all discrimination between men and women in respect of nightwork. (Information reported to Informal Social Affairs Council, September 1993).

79.   (1992) *European Industrial Relations Review* 219

80.   *ibid.*, also unpublished reports circulated at Belgian Presidency's Informal Social Affairs Council in Bruges, September 1993.

81.   "Nightwork of Women", caselaw commentary in (1992) 8 *International Journal of Comparative Labour Law and Industrial Relations* 180.

82.   R.A. Harvey, *op.cit.* n.37, p.42 discusses the 1956 decision of the Federal Constitutional Court.

arise in which no night working legislation exists at Community level, thus incurring the risk of deregulation of night working, since Member States are no longer required to respect minimum international standards.[83]

The Parliament condemned the vacuum in international protective standards which had emerged as a result of the denunciation by EC Member States of ILO Convention No.89 in the absence of any Community legislation in this area. It called on the Social Affairs Council to adopt the Working Time Directive restoring amendments originally put forward by the Parliament but rejected by the Commission after the "first reading".[84] The Parliament wanted to ensure that the Directive would "not infringe Member States, right to maintain, apply or introduce legislation more favourable to workers". The Directive, as ultimately adopted, incorporates definitions of "night-time" and "nightwork" inserted by the Commission to closely reflect the definitions in ILO Convention No.171. Under this Directive normal hours of work for nightworkers must not exceed an average of eight hours in any 24 hour period. In addition, there are special provisions for health assessments for nightworkers, and for the transfer to day work of nightworkers suffering health problems. The Directive, which does not enter into force until 23 November 1996, will also require information about the regular use of nightwork to be given to the competent authorities and for particular attention to be given to the safety and health protection of night workers.

The thrust of the concerns which the Court of Justice's judgment in the St*oeckel* case evoked in the European Parliament was also echoed in an opinion which the Commission's Advisory Committee on Equal Opportunities delivered on 21 January 1992.[85] The Advisory Committee was established in December 1981, as a forum in which national equality bodies established by Government, or equivalent bodies, could discuss equality issues and advise the Commission. It drew attention in particular to the qualitative aspects to be taken into consideration with regard to nightwork conditions. The Advisory Committee called upon the Commission to examine what measures might be taken with a view to regulating nightwork conditions in the same way for both men and women.

The European Commission does not contemplate any positive inter-

---

83. See Resolution of 9 April, 1992 on nightworking and the denunciation of ILO Convention No.89. PE Resolution B3-0588/92.

84. COM (90) final, 20 September, 1990. The Council of Ministers adopted a "common position" on this proposal on 30th June, 1993. The Working Time Directive 93/104/EC was adopted by the Council of Ministers on 23 November, 1993.

85. Commission Decision 82/43/EEC of 9 December, 1981, relating to the setting up of an Advisory Committee on Equal Opportunities for women and men, OJ L 20 of 28.1.92.

vention focused specifically on the regulation of the conditions of nightworkers. The subject is addressed in the Maternity Protection Directive[86] and in the Directive on the Organisation of Working Time. In its communication in 1991 to six EC Member States calling for the denunciation of ILO Convention No.89, the Commission confirmed its positive support for their ratification of ILO Convention No.171 on nightwork. The Commission did not, however, address a similar recommendation to the six other Member States which were no longer bound by ILO Convention No.89 in 1991. At the meeting of the Informal Social Affairs Council convened in Bruges, in September 1993 under the Belgian Presidency, the Commission tentatively suggested that a Recommendation — a non-binding Community instrument — might be brought forward on the subject of nightwork in order to emphasise the principle of non-discrimination and to highlight certain essential points relating to the working conditions of nightworkers of both sexes, such as medical surveillance, maternity protection, young people, adequate social services, and transfer to daytime work.[87] Commissioner Flynn warned, however, that the somewhat remote possibility of pursuing a Community initiative on nightwork conditions covering both sexes, was not a prospect to be used by any Member State as an excuse for further delaying compliance with the terms of the 1976 Directive.[88] The Commission's advice in this regard would appear to have become sharper and more decisive in the light of the *Stoeckel* decision.

6. CONCLUSIONS

The formulation of new universal standards on nightwork at the International Labour Conferences in 1980-1990 may yet prove to be a milestone in the improvement of relationships between the ILO and the European Union and in convincing the institutions of the Union of the desirability of acknowledging the specificity of the ILO system. Significant variations have been highlighted in the way in which the two systems responded to the contradiction between the equal treatment principle and the restrictive protective focus of the historic international prohibition on nightwork for women. By adopting the new Nightwork Convention No.171 the International Labour Organisation showed its

86. Directive 92/85/EEC on the Protection of Pregnant Women at Work, OJ L 348 of 28.11.92.

87. How tentative that suggestion proved to be is underscored by the absence of any reference to nightwork (other than one in the context of the Working Time Directive) in the White Paper on Social Policy (COM (94) 333 of 27 July, 1994)!

88. Unpublished text of statement by Commissioner Flynn at Informal Social Affairs Council.

capacity to grapple with complex issues within a "legislative" framework which directly involves the social partners. The achievement of the ILO in advancing new standards on the basis of tripartite consensus contrasts sharply with the difficulties experienced within the European Community in its efforts to legislate on issues such as working time, and may offer important lessons for the future of social dialogue, particularly in the context of the new role for the social partners in the formulation of legislation under Articles 3 and 4 of the Agreement on Social Policy annexed to the amended EC Treaty.[89]

The ILO's approach to the revision of Convention No.89 did not encroach upon the sensitive area of the Community's external competence as the regulation of nightwork was acknowledged as remaining within the sphere of competence of Member States. The European Commission was, however, involved in trenchant arguments on health and safety issues where it maintained, in relation to the preparation of ILO Convention No.162 (Safety in the use of asbestos), and ILO Convention No.170 (Safety in the use of chemicals), that these instruments involved areas already covered by Community law and therefore fell within the exclusive competence of the Community rather than the Member States.[90] Institutional rivalries between the Commission and the ILO, which had served to exacerbate relations in the late 1980s, may also reflect differences in the institutional structure and mandates of the two organisations. Social policy concerns have never been as central to the driving objectives of the European Community as they have for the work of the ILO. The Commission had shown little positive interest in the proceedings of the ILO revision exercise. It seemed more preoccupied in 1989 and 1990 in adopting a confrontational stance *vis-à-vis* the ILO machinery over the negotiation of Convention No.170 than in workivng constructively with Member States during the process of negotiation of the new Convention No.171 on Nightwork.

In requiring six Member States to repeal national legislation which necessitated the denunciation of ILO Convention No.89, the Court of Justice's decision in *Stoeckel* proved to be both timely and necessary. The Court of Justice had grasped a nettle which the Commission, the Council of Ministers, and most of the Member States, had declined to grasp. The Court's action resolved a fundamental contradiction which, given

89. See M. Weiss, "The Significance of Maastricht for European Community Social Policy", (1992) 8 *International Journal of Comparative Labour Law and Industrial Relations*, pp. 13-14.

90. See *Opinion 2/91* of the Court of Justice delivered on 19 March, 1993, on the compatibility with the EC Treaty of Convention No.170. The Court's Opinion in response to the Commission's reference under Article 228(1) EEC may also contribute to an improvement in relations between the EU and the ILO.

the nature of ILO Conventions as separate treaties, could not be satisfactorily resolved within the ILO itself.[91] The *Stoeckel* decision pointed the way to Member States which might possibly have been left off the hook if the Court had opted for the less peremptory approach it appears to have adopted in *Levy*. In an intervention which Morgenstern considers may have involved "excessively brusque change" the Court of Justice effectively denied Member States scope for further prevarication and ensured that, on an issue of fundamental rights, they could no longer have recourse to the kind of dilatory action which it had so sharply criticised in *Defrenne v Sabena*.[92]

In contrast to the Court of Justice ruling in *Stoeckel*, the Commission's failure to seriously question the discriminatory impact of ILO Convention No.89 is noteworthy, particularly in the light of the equal treatment rationale originally advanced by the Netherlands, Ireland and Luxembourg when denouncing it. The process of deciding whether to launch an infringement action is, of course, a highly political one.[93] The Commission, as guardian of the Treaties, has to have regard to the supremacy of European Community law. It has consistently maintained that inconsistent laws should be changed if they conflict with the requirements of Community law — and that Member States might in consequence be required to denounce international obligations inconsistent with Community law. It had also upheld equality between men and women as a fundamental human right and insisted that derogations must be interpreted narrowly. Yet the Commission declined to confront France, Italy, and the other Member States where ILO Convention No.89 was still held to justify national legislation prohibiting nightwork for women. It may have baulked at the prospect of an unsuccessful Court challenge to Member States which defended their rights in adhering to international obli-

91. The Committee of Experts on the Application of Conventions and Recommendations has ruled that ratification of the Discrimination Convention No.111 "is not to come into conflict with the ratification or implementation of other instruments adopted by the International Labour Conference providing for special measures of protection of assistance". With regard to the status of protective measures, the Convention in Article 5(1), provides that "special measures of protection or assistance provided for in other Conventions or Recommendations adopted by the International Labour Conference shall not be deemed to be discrimination". ILO Committee of Experts on the application of Conventions and Recommendations, *Equality in Employment and Occupation*, General Survey (1988) ILO Geneva.

92. Case 43/75, *Defrenne v Sabena* [1976] ECR 1365. See F. Morgenstern, "From the particular to the general. Limitations of the judicial treatment of social policy issues", (1991) 130 *International Labour Review*, pp. 559-567.

93. C. McCrudden, "The Effectiveness of European Equality Law: National Mechanisms for Enforcing Gender Equality Law in the Light of EuropeanRequirements", (1993) 13 *Oxford Journal of Legal Studies* 320, at p.358.

gations *vis-à-vis* non-member countries. The first paragraph of Article 234 EEC states that the provisions of the Treaty do not affect rights and obligations arising from agreements such as ILO Convention No.89 concluded before the entry into force of the Rome Treaty.[94] The Commission may also have been wary of instituting an Article 169 EEC infringement action in view of the strong trade union lobby in support of retaining special protection measures and the political uncertainty over the prospects for its own proposals on the regulation of working time. Since the Commission failed to utilise its strategic power under Article 169 EEC over this issue, it eventually came before the Court of Justice ultimately as the result of an Article 177 EEC reference arising from an employer's defence against prosecution under domestic law in France.

The denunciation of ILO Convention No.89, in the aftermath of the *Stoeckel* ruling, has not yet resulted in the repeal of national legislation in France and Belgium which still retains the discriminatory prohibition. It is possible that some of the Member States involved might even welcome an infringement action under Article 169 EC targeted upon their national legislation as a form of external pressure to remove the domestic obstruction they have encountered in seeking to bring about change following the *Stoeckel* ruling. Neither France nor Belgium have an independent enforcement agency along the lines of the Employment Equality Agency (EEA) in Ireland or the Equal Opportunities Commission in the UK. The Irish case study has illustrated how the contribution of the EEA, through its authoritative status and monitoring role, enabled conclusions on the relevance of protective provisions affecting women's employment opportunities to be reached in Ireland on the basis of tripartite consensus. The independent monitoring role of the UK and Irish enforcement agencies also suggests a means of harnessing some of the lessons from the operation of the specialist ILO Committee of Experts on the Application of Conventions and Recommendations in order to strengthen the implementation of equality law at national level. The independent activity of these public bodies might also serve to strengthen the hand of the Commission and the Court of Justice in scrutinising the effectiveness of the domestic enforcement of European equality law.[95]

Notwithstanding the "in principle" opposition of the United Kingdom, it is likely that a number of EU Member States will soon ratify Convention No.171. Some States, such as Ireland, may only do so after they have legislated or otherwise implemented the Working Time Directive, which is due to come into effect in November 1996. This slow pattern of

---

94. See discussion of Case 158/91, *Levy* above; also Case 13/93, *Office National de l'Emploi v M. Minne,* Judgment of 3 February, 1994.

95. C. McCrudden. *op.cit.* n.93, pp. 332-335.

accommodation to a new international standard arises partly from the practice of States which seek to ensure that implementing legislation is in place before proceeding with formal ratification. If this involves a process of consensus building at national level, it may also serve to counteract the limitations which Morgenstern identified in the nature of decisions of the Court of Justice in cases like *Stoeckel*, where in her view: *"judicial treatment, through an individual case, of wide issues of social or labour policy may result in depriving others of a protection ... for which they feel a need"*.[96]

The achievement of the ILO machinery in negotiating and concluding Convention No.171 may yet provide the European Union with the inspiration to develop the political will and the means to devise a new framework for the re-regulation of working time in order to reconcile three basic objectives:

- the demands of employers for economic flexibility;
- the demands of trade unions for a reduction in working time;
- the demands by individuals, regardless of their sex, for autonomy in fixing their working time so as to enable them to meet their family responsibilities and to have time for education, personal development and leisure.[97]

---

96. F. Morgenstern. *op.cit.* n.92, p.567; also R.A. Harvey, *op.cit.* n.37, p.70.

97. See B. Hepple, "Working Time: A New Legal Framework", IPPR, 1990, p.26.

TABLE A

Nightwork (Women) Convention (Revised) 1948

Date of Entry into Force: 27.02.1951

States	Ratification Registered	Ratification Denounced
Belgium	1 April 1952	27 February 1992
France	21 September 1953	26 February 1992
Greece	27 April 1959	25 February 1992
Ireland	14 January 1952	26 February 1982
Italy	22 October 1952	27 February 1992
Luxembourg	3 March 1958	19 February 1982
Netherlands	22 October 1954	26 February 1972
Portugal	2 June 1964	27 February 1992

TABLE B

Preliminary Stance of EC Member States
on Preferred Form of New Instruments in advance of
1989 International Labour Conference*

Member State	Form of New Instruments
Belgium	Convention and Recommendation
Denmark	Unenthusiastic about any new instruments
France	Convention and Recommendation
Germany	Recommendation only
Greece	Convention and Recommendation
Ireland	Recommendation only
Italy	Recommendation only
Luxembourg	——
Netherlands	Convention and Recommendation
Portugal	Convention and Recommendation
Spain	Recommendation only
United Kingdom	Opposed to any new instruments

* Table is based on replies to ILO questionnaire recorded in Nightwork Report V(2) prepared for the 1989 Conference.

TABLE C

The Changing International Regulation of Nightwork

	ILO Convention No 89	ILO Convention No 171
Main Purpose	Prohibition of nightwork for a specific category of workers	Improvement of conditions of work of nightwork
Scope	Women in Industry	Both men and women. All branches and occupations with a few limited exceptions
Definition of Night	At least 11 consecutive hours including at least 7 consecutive hours between 10 p.m. and 7 a.m.	At least 7 consecutive hours including the interval between midnight and 5 a.m.
Focus of attention	Any work during the prohibited periods	Workers performing a substantial amount of nightwork

6. What Options are now open to Regulate Atypical Employment in the post-Maastricht Period of Social Policy?

Nick Rahtz

1. INTRODUCTION

Since the early 1970s there has been a steady increase in atypical employment across the European Union,[1] although the pattern has varied between Member States depending on the prevailing economic, political and cultural conditions. The term "atypical employment" has become the usual way of describing work where the contractual conditions are in some way different from standard forms of employment. It has been defined by the European Commission in various draft Directives as including part-time, temporary, agency, seasonal and on-call work, homeworking and teleworking but each Member State has its own legal approach to work of this nature.[2] The political debate in Europe has normally focused on part-time and temporary employment which has been estimated by the Commission to now account for around 13.6% and 10% respectively of the labour market or at least 20% of the European Union workforce.[3] This development is a challenge to widely held assumptions about labour market regulation which have been predominantly based on the premise that work is "full-time" and that contracts are "open-ended". It has also become a testing ground in the wider po-

---

1. The term European Community (EC) will also be used in this discussion when referring to pre-November 1993 events or the EC institutions that remain responsible for social policy.

2. For a quick comparison of legal definitions see Eurostat Labour Force Survey 1991.

3. Bearing in mind that 15% of part-time employees are employed on a temporary basis. Other estimates put "non-standard" employment in Europe at about 30%, including the self-employed (Bronstein AS, in *International Labour Review*, Vol.130, No.3, 1991, p.296).

litical debate in Europe about job creation and the costs of equalising employment rights for all types of work. So far, attempts by the Commission to legislate in this field have been strongly disputed and it remains one of the unresolved areas of the 1989 Social Action Programme.

It is now widely recognised that increased labour market labour market flexibility can make an important contribution to economic competitiveness, even that it meets certain social needs but, as one source puts it, there has been a "hesitant and even vacillating attitude" towards the regulation of these new forms of employment.[4] Some Member States have extended legal protection to equalise employment rights for atypical workers[5] while others have reduced protection in the belief that this will stimulate employment growth.[6] This situation is regarded with some alarm by those who fear a spiral of worsening employment conditions for all workers because of the knock-on effects of deregulation in the Single Market sometimes referred to as "social dumping". There is no doubt in the view of the Commission (and this is underlined in their document) that "in no circumstances can the need for these specific forms of employment relationship be called into question" because they form part of a basic strategy for growth and employment.[7] However, the question of equal protection with standard forms of employment has become a focus of fierce debate between the so-called "regulationists" and "deregulationists". On the one hand, it has been repeatedly stated at European Summit meetings that the social dimension of the Community, including employment rights, is equally important as economic policy;[8] on the other, it is persistently argued that further labour market regulation will increase employment costs and stifle job creation to the further detriment of global competitiveness.[9]

Early attempts in 1981 and 1982 by the Commission to introduce legislation for part-time and temporary workers at Community level[10] were strongly opposed by employers and vetoed by the UK because of the need, at that time, for unanimity in the Council of Ministers. The

4.   European Foundation for the Improvement of Living and Working Conditions (EFILWC), *Part-time Work in the EC,* 1993, p.50.

5.   France has recently revised its regulation of part-time work to make it more attractive to employees (*European Industrial Relations Review* 230, March 1993).

6.   The UK has been foremost in this view, see Employment Department, *The United Kingdom in Europe,* 1992, p.1.

7.   COM(90) 228 final, p.4.

8.   Starting at the Hague Summit in 1969 (Gold M (ed.) *The Social Dimension - Employment Policy in the European Community,* 1993, p.21).

9.   The Community has the lowest employment rates and the highest level of unemployment compared to the USA, Japan and EFTA (*Employment in Europe* 1993, pp.17-20).

10.   OJ C 128/2, 19/5/82 (temporary work) and (part-time work).

case for regulation was reaffirmed in the Community Charter of the Fundamental Social Rights of Workers[11] (the Social Charter) and the subsequent Social Action Programme in 1989 contained three proposals for new Directives for atypical workers, each based on a different Treaty provision, namely Articles 100, 100a and 118a covering certain working conditions, distortions of competition and health and safety, respectively. However, there was such disagreement over the interpretation of Articles 100 and 100a, that the two Directives concerned did not get past the consultation stage. The health and safety Directive for temporary workers, on the other hand, did proceed under the qualified majority provisions of Article 118a and was eventually implemented in 1992. More recently, a revised proposal, incorporating both working conditions and distortions of competition under Article 100, was submitted for discussion by the Belgian Presidency towards the end of 1993 with "sharp disagreements reported",[12] but this initiative signalled a renewed desire to legislate on equal treatment for atypical workers. The German Presidency is (at the time of writing) presenting a new version of the proposals, based on Article 100, which stresses the role of equality in the promotion of new forms of employment.[13]

This new wave of enthusiasm can be associated with two areas of development in European law. Firstly, there have been a number of equal treatment cases in the Court of Justice under Article 119 concerning part-time workers which give legal support to some aspects of the contested proposals. Recent Directives on contractual information and working time have also recognised equal protection for all forms of employment. Secondly, the Social Protocol and Agreement which are attached to the revised EC Treaty allow the Eleven (not including the UK) to extend the use of qualified majority voting, according to criteria that seem to include atypical work. The subsequent Green Paper on Social Policy[14] makes a clear attempt to reframe the debate about labour market regulation and find some middle ground which can be developed by the social partners and accords with the principle of subsidiarity. The more recent White Paper stresses that the highest priority must be given to outstanding proposals under the 1989 Social Action Programme, including those on non-standard employment.[15] It emphasises that if agree-

---

11. Title I, para.7 (there is also reference in para.5 to an equitable wage for atypical workers but this was not pursued in the Action Programme).

12. *European Industrial Relations Review* 238, 1993, p.2.

13. IDS European Report 395, November 1994, p.9.

14. Green Paper on *European Social Policy — Options for the Union*, 26 October 1993.

15. *European Social Policy — A Way Forward for the Union*, COM(94) 338 final, Brussels, 27.7.94, p.9.

ment cannot be reached by the Twelve by the end of 1994 then consultations will begin with the social partners under the Agreement on Social Policy by the Eleven.[16] If this happens the German proposal may be legally enacted by qualified majority voting under Article 2(1) of the Agreement on Social Policy during 1995.

The following discussion begins by outlining the pattern of development of atypical work in the Community and then examines in more detail the arguments surrounding the Commission's proposals for legal intervention in 1990, particularly the confusion over the meaning of "distortions of competition". The progress of this debate is used to highlight the inherent tension in the legal bases that were used in these attempts at legislation and how this was exploited by opponents of the regulation of atypical employment. The dispute is then situated in the wider context of the debate surrounding the social dimension and its ambivalent status in the legal framework of the Community. The new climate of post-Maastricht social policy is considered firstly in the light of developments in equal treatment arising from legal activism around Article 119 and related legislation. Secondly, the status of the Social Protocol and Agreement under the Maastricht Treaty is critically examined together with the implications of the Green and White Papers for future developments in employment regulation. It is concluded that although there now seems to be a real possibility of progress by the 11 (excluding the UK), it is likely to be in the spirit of a "minimalist" approach to regulation to satisfy the demands for flexibility and job creation.

2.   The Pattern of Atypical Work in the EU

Explanations for the spread of non-standard forms of employment in the European Union usually refer to both economic and social factors. The preamble to the 1990 proposals for the regulation of atypical work mentions international competitiveness, technological innovation, radical changes in the organisation of production, and changes in individual needs.[17] The economic rationale is that greater labour flexibility is needed by employers to meet rapidly changing market demands and fiercer competition both within European and world markets. It is also claimed that changes in family responsibilities and new attitudes to work, especially from the younger and older elements of the labour force, have contributed to new demands for contractual diversity. Finally, there is the common political view, now enshrined in the White Paper on Growth,

16.   *ibid.*

17.   COM(90) 228 final, p.4.

Competitiveness and Employment,[18] that the encouragement of atypical work will contribute to the process of job creation.

However, these broad assumptions do not adequately account for the whole range of factors that influence the use of atypical contracts. Rubery and Horrell argue that the analysis of new forms of work often assumes that competition is a "black box" and that employers simply have to respond to market and technological demands. They consider that this deterministic approach does not account for the wide range of responses to competitive pressures which relate to custom and practice, labour market regulation, social status and management control strategies.[19] On this last point there is the suspicion that some employers may be more interested in exploiting the advantages of a more passive labour force; higher productivity from reduced rest periods; extended probationary periods; and less trade union attachment, than the usual reasons given of fitting the labour force more exactly to operational requirements. This can be associated with the variation in legal protection of atypical workers and the efforts of some Member States, notably the UK, in trying to reduce unemployment by deregulating the labour market and reducing social costs.[20]

The claim that the growth in atypical work is somehow compatible with changes in social aspirations also needs to be examined carefully. There is no doubt that part-time work can be attractive to those with family responsibilities or other sources of income, and that temporary work meets the need of some young people, especially students, and older workers. However, the question remains of what proportion of those employed are coerced into atypical work because there is no alternative. A survey by the Commission of worker's attitudes in 1989[21] reveals that 37% of part-time workers in the Community would prefer to work full-time and, paradoxically, that 22% of full-time workers would prefer part-time work. This is recognised as only a rough indicator because definitions of part-time work and cultural expectations will vary considerably between Member States. However, it appears from these calculations that there is actually considerable scope for more part-time work, particularly in Italy and Portugal.[22] It is estimated that temporary workers tend to fall into three groups with about one third preferring temporary contracts for a number of reasons; another third using it as a means of transferring to permanent work; and the remaining third, mainly older, un-

18. COM(93) 700 final, 5.12.93.

19. Rubery J and Horrell S, in *HRM Journal*, Vol.3, No.2, 1992/93, p.11.

20. Cordova E in *International Labour Review*, Vol.125, No.6, 1986, p.646.

21. *Social Europe*, Supplement 4/91.

22. Green Paper, p.14.

skilled workers and immigrants unable to find any alternative.[23] However, the Commission found that 60% of temporary women workers would prefer permanent employment, with this proportion rising to 85% in Spain where 28% of female employment is temporary.[24]

However, there are clearly a number of negative implications to atypical work including; increased labour market segmentation, job insecurity, irregular earnings and lowering of standards in the labour market, which could have an adverse effect on employee commitment and productivity as well as creating distortions of competition.[25] There is also likely to be less access to training and promotion opportunities and restricted access to fringe benefits, in particular, sick pay and pension schemes. These adverse social effects were clearly seen by the Commission as a diminution in working conditions which can be considered as separate from the "distortions in competition" argument, thus providing a justification for the two separate proposals under Articles 100 and 100a EEC. It is hardly surprising, given these social implications, that the trade union response to atypical work, at national and Community level, tends to be defensive or even hostile. There is a fear that trade union power is being seriously damaged by a segmentation of the labour market into two, or even three, if the informal sector is included, competing sectors which will undermine the rights of the mainstream of their membership.[26] Despite being generally in favour of shorter working hours,[27] part-time work is seen as slowing down the negotiating process because it undermines the recognition of equivalent pay for less hours.[28] Temporary work is seen as an employer's strategy to promote insecurity and thereby lessen bargaining power and increase managerial prerogative.

Turning to the actual distribution of atypical employment, there is a remarkable variation between Member States of both part-time and temporary work, with a clear divide between North and South. The Commission's statistics show that the growth of part-time work, by 28% between 1983 and 1988 (compared to 2.4% growth in full-time employment), has not been evenly spread between Member States. The average part-time figure was 13.6% of all employees (14m. in total) but with a wide variation between nearly 30% (up by 30%) in the Netherlands and

23. Bronstein AS (*supra* FN 3), p.300.

24. *Employment in Europe* 1992, p.161.

25. COM(90) 228 final, pp. 4-5.

26. Delsen L, in *Industrial Relations Journal*, Vol.21,No.4, 1990, p.263.

27. A firm ETUC principle since the Munich Summit of 1979.

28. Recent agreements on reduction in working hours have tended to be based on a partial reduction in earnings; e.g. Volkswagen and Sheffield City Council in 1993.

4% (down by 0.9%) in Greece.[29] There is a marked division between the
south of Europe, where Portugal, Spain, Italy and Greece, have 5% part-
time employees or less, and the north of Europe, where the Netherlands,
Denmark and the UK all have more than 20% and Germany, France and
Belgium, have in the region of 12%. It can also be noted that part-time
work has grown most rapidly in countries such as Italy, Ireland, Belgium
and France (45%, 39%, 36% and 36% respectively), where there has
been a negligible increase or reduction in full-time employment. More
recent figures show that where the numbers employed have risen most,
they are accounted for mainly by part-time employment which means
that the actual increase in the volume of work is less than it seems.[30]

The Cranfield survey tries to identify the reasons for these national
differences and divides them into five categories.[31] Firstly, those countries with the highest share of service sector employment, like the UK,
Netherlands and Denmark, tend to have the most part-time employment;
secondly, the higher participation of women in the labour market in
Denmark and the UK correlates with high part-time numbers, albeit for
different reasons,[32] while in Greece and Spain there are low levels of
both; thirdly, some countries, notably Belgium and France, have encouraged employment creation since 1983 through job-splitting; fourthly,
demographic factors resulting in local labour shortages have encouraged part-time recruitment; and fifthly, the provision of comprehensive
child care, particularly in France, may be a reason for less part-time employment.

Two of these reasons draw particular attention to the role of women
in the part-time labour market. According to the Commission,[33] 28% of
women in employment work part-time in the Community (compared to
4% of men), although this average disguises vast differences between
just over 60% in the Netherlands and less than 10% in Greece and Italy.
What is even more striking is that 82% of the European part-time
workforce are women with Belgium, the UK and Germany nearing 90%
and Italy and Greece around 65%.[34] Also, there are significant patterns
of increased female part-time work related to family size[35] and age,[36] the

29. COM(90) 228 final, pp. 9-10.

30. *Employment in Europe* 1992, p.32.

31. Brewster *et al*, Flexible Working Patterns in Europe, 1993, pp. 13-18.

32. In Denmark there is much greater support from the welfare state.

33. *Employment in Europe* 1992, p.159.

34. Brewster *et al*, (*supra* FN 31), p.15.

35. *Women in the Community*, Ch.9, 1992.

36. *Employment in Europe* 1992, p.145.

latter showing that more women work part-time as they get older compared to part-time men who are mainly concentrated in the under 20
and over 65 age-groups.

As far as temporary work is concerned, the Commission's statistics[37]
show that the overall figure for the Community had risen by 1988 to
9.6% (10m. employees). Later figures for 1991[38] indicate that the highest proportion by far is in Spain where temporary work has doubled
between 1983 and 1991 from 16 to 32 % of the labour force. Greece and
Portugal have a fairly stable rate of about 17% and the UK, Italy and
Belgium only have around 5% on temporary contracts. This North/South
divide (the reverse of that for part-time work) is even more marked if
male and female temporary employment levels are separated. This reveals that only 3.1% of male workers in Belgium are employed on a temporary basis compared to 24.5% in Spain (where it is 31% for female
workers).[39] The profile of the temporary labour force shows that young
people are highly represented with 70% of temporary workers under
the age of 30 in Belgium, the Netherlands and France.[40] Women are also
more likely to be on temporary contracts in all Member States, with these
more likely to be part-time (74% in the UK) in northern Europe and
full-time in southern Europe.[41] The balance of men and women tends to
be reflected in the relative demand for white collar (mainly women) and
blue collar (mainly men) which can vary according to employer's strategies and economic circumstances.[42]

Apart from Spain, the largest increase in temporary employment
has occurred in the France where the percentage has risen from 3 to
10% in the 1983-91 period. In both these countries this dramatic increase seems to be associated with the relaxation of restrictions on fixed-
term contracts as a measure to stimulate employment creation. In other
Member States, the numbers have remained fairly static in the same period, although the Cranfield survey notes that use of temporary work
has increased significantly in the UK's public sector, presumably due to
the uncertainty involved in privatisation and "market testing".[43] The other
reason for national differences appears to be relative levels of unemployment, particularly if there is a higher dependence on agriculture

37. COM(90) 228 final, pp. 9-10.

38. *Employment in Europe* 1992, p.181.

39. Brewster *et al*, (*supra* FN 31), p.22.

40. Bronstein AS (*supra* FN 3), p.299.

41. Brewster *et al*, (*supra* FN 31), p.26.

42. Bronstein AS (*supra* FN 3), p.299.

43. Brewster *et al*, (*supra* FN 31), pp. 24-25.

and tourism. The Commission estimate[44] that about half of all temporary work in Northern Europe is accounted for by employment agencies that are most prevalent in the Netherlands, Germany, the UK and France, but not permitted by law in Greece, Spain and Italy. According to Bronstein,[45] there are 2500 agencies with 10,000 branches in the UK alone, although in other Member States there is a greater tendency for professional concentration, especially where agency activities are more highly regulated, as in the Netherlands and Belgium. It is also noted by the Commission that a remarkable 70% of new recruitment in France, and about a third in Germany, was by fixed-term contract. The difference between the use of fixed-term contracts and more uncertain periods of temporary work, is related to national variations in legal regulation. In Denmark, the Netherlands and Germany, for example, the strong influence of collective bargaining and stricter control of temporary agencies encourages a greater use of fixed-term contracts, whereas the UK and Ireland have a higher incidence of temporary/casual employment.[46]

The incidence of part-time and temporary work have been covered in some detail because they are the areas of atypical employment included in the proposed legislation. However, there is some concern that these two categories do not represent a true picture of the whole range of non-standard forms of employment and there is a danger that other forms will be excluded such as homeworking and teleworking; self-employment; and the informal sector.

Accurate evidence of homeworking is difficult to find because it overlaps with other employment categories but the Commission estimates that numbers vary between 0.7m in Italy and 60,000 in France and that, overall, 80-90% of these workers are women.[47] There is little evidence so far of the predicted explosion in teleworking although there are reports of systematic use in the UK, Germany, Italy and Belgium.[48] It is usual to distinguish traditional homeworking, with its nineteenth century origins in the textile industry, and teleworking, which is office related and may be carried out partly or fully at home or elsewhere. The former is covered by some sort of regulation in each Member State, but the latter has not yet acquired a separate legal status. This means that the problems of traditional homeworkers in terms of low pay, health and safety, working

44. COM(90) 228 final, p.11.

45. Bronstein AS (*supra* FN 3), p.301.

46. Brewster *et al*, (*supra* FN 31), p.23.

47. *Employment in Europe*, COM(89) 339 final.

48. EFILWC, New Forms of Work, 1988, p.85.

hours and employment protection, are in danger of being extended to teleworking.[49]

Self-employment is a category of work that is often excluded from discussions about atypical work because of its separate legal status as a contract for services rather than employment. However, it is an important element of the labour market, accounting for about 50% of the agricultural workforce and 13% of workers in industry and services (16% overall).[50] As in the case of temporary work self-employment is highest in the southern countries of Greece (28%), Italy (22%), Portugal and Spain (17%), and lowest in Denmark and Luxembourg (7%), and Germany and the Netherlands (8%). This can partly be explained by the relative importance of agriculture but this sector is declining and numbers in other sectors are steadily growing. Unemployment levels are also important, especially as it seems that the vast majority of self-employed workers have been forced into a sub-contracting relationship with employers because of policies to externalise services.[51] This can be illustrated by the growth in self-employment in the UK from 7% to 13% between 1979 and 1986 when unemployment rates more than doubled.[52] This is also related to the rate at which people become self-employed with new entrants of 15-20% in the UK and the Netherlands but 10% going out of business every year.[53]

Informal sector work, by its very nature, evades statistical investigation but it is estimated to be widespread either as "moonlighting", family labour, or clandestine work. The first is said to be most highly developed in Italy, Greece, Spain and Portugal, and the last more associated with the northern Member States.[54] However, the rates of illegal immigration suggest that the latter is rapidly growing throughout the Community. Apart from the total lack of employment protection, this category of work is important because of its relationship to self-employed labour, homeworking, part-time and temporary work. Some will experience a variety of these forms of employment according to their legal status and the availability of alternative sources of income. There is also the question of social security and taxation provisions in each Member State which will influence the development of the informal sector.

So the uneven pattern of atypical employment across the European Union can be attributed to a range of factors including: levels of unem-

49. EFILWC (*supra* FN 48), p.86.

50. *Employment in Europe* 1992, p.32.

51. EFILWC (*supra* FN 48), pp. 88-89.

52. *Employment in Europe* 1991, p.39.

53. *Employment in Europe* 1992, pp. 9-10.

54. EFILWC (*supra* FN 48), p.90.

ployment; female participation in the labour force; demographic factors; the relative size of the service sector; the strength of collective bargaining; job creation initiatives; employment agency regulation; and restructuring or privatisation of particular industries. The match between employer demands for more flexible forms of labour and new attitudes to work clearly needs to be examined more critically if we are to understand the balance of forces for and against regulating to achieve equality between standard and non-standard forms of employment. The distinct North/South divide in the incidence of part-time and temporary work means that there will be different priorities between Member States on the form such regulation should take and, for those preferring the minimalist approach, whether it should be considered at all. Then, of course, there is the wider issue of the relative attraction to employers of atypical employment contracts with regard to employment costs in each Member State. This in turn is linked to their economic policies concerning job creation, international competition and attraction of inward investment. These matters form the background to the next part of the discussion covering the legal debate in the European Community about the grounds upon which such regulation can be justified under the Treaty of Rome and its subsequent amendment by the Single European Act and the Maastricht Treaty.

3.   The Attempts at Community Regulation

(i)   Community Initiatives on Atypical Employment

The need to regulate atypical employment has been on the Community agenda since the 1974 Social Action Programme referred to the need to protect temporary agency workers, extend social protection to those not covered, and provide social security for the self-employed.[55] In December 1979, a Resolution by the Council of Ministers on a variety of issues concerned with the adaptation of working time[56] included the need for clarification of part-time conditions of employment, particularly as they affected women. This led to the Commission eventually submitting a proposal for a Directive on part-time work in December 1981.[57] Strong differences of opinion between Member States[58] resulted in this proposal

---

55. Byre A, *Leading Cases and Materials on the Social Policy of the EEC*, 1989, pp. 8-9.

56. OJ C 1980 C2/1.

57. COM(81) 775 final.

58. The UK, Germany and Denmark argued against legal intervention and France, Italy and Belgium argued in favour (Disney R and Szyszczak E, in *Industrial Law Journal*, Vol.18, 1989).

being referred to two further meetings of the Council in May and December 1982 and, despite an amended draft in January 1983, no further progress being made because of the need for unanimity under Article 100 EEC. A second proposal, for a draft Directive on temporary work, was submitted to the Council in May 1982, but was also opposed and, despite a more flexible redrafting in April 1984, also effectively dropped from the Council's agenda until the revival of social policy under the Single Market Programme. All these proposals required unanimity because, at that time, the only legal base available was Article 100 EEC.

The Single European Act, 1987, provided for the scope of legal intervention to be extended by the addition to the Treaty of Rome of Articles 100a and 118a EEC, both of which were designed to facilitate progress towards a Single European Market in 1992. Article 100, requiring unanimous agreement by the Council, was directed at the harmonisation of national provisions that affected the establishing or functioning of the common market. Article 100a, only needing a qualified majority vote (QMV) by the Council, allowed for derogation from Article 100 if action was required to promote the establishment or functioning of the internal market. However, under Article 100a (para. 2), this new legal base did not apply to "the rights and interests of employed persons", the clause which is central to later discussion of the atypical employment proposals. It is said that Mrs Thatcher personally insisted on this as a condition of the UK's acceptance of the Single Market legislation. Article 118a, also based on QMV, was limited to "improvements, especially in the working environment, as regards the health and safety of workers" but here again there is controversy over the breadth of interpretation.[59]

The impetus for exploiting these new legal possibilities came in the form of a Community Charter of Fundamental Social Rights of Workers. This "solemn declaration" by eleven Member States (not including the UK), at the Strasbourg Summit in December 1989, formally recognised the principle that "the completion of the internal market must lead to an improvement of the living and working conditions of workers in the European Community". In this context, particular reference was made[60] to the duration and organisation of working time, and forms of employment other than open-ended contracts, such as fixed-term contracts, part-time working, temporary work and seasonal work. This "Social Charter"[61] had been shortly preceded by a Commission proposal for a Social

59. The UK government are currently challenging the Working Time Directive because its content is considered to be beyond the scope of Article 118a.

60. Title 1, point 7.

61. Not to be confused with the 1960 European Social Charter of the Council of Europe, although there is, intentionally, some similarity between the two.

Action Programme[62] which contained detailed proposals for the implementation of many of the Charter's objectives, including three draft Directives on atypical employment and one each on working time and contracts of employment. In the explanatory memorandum[63] which accompanied the Commission's proposals in August 1990, it was recognised that non-standard forms of employment included a wide range of work including part-time, temporary, seasonal, on-call, homeworking and teleworking.[64] However, it was thought to be most practical to concentrate on part-time and temporary employment, the former defined as "working hours shorter than normal working hours" and the latter defined as a fixed-term contract or work done through an employment agency.[65]

The need for legislation was justified in the Social Action Programme by the fact that atypical employment had grown considerably in recent years, "often in a quite anarchical manner", and was open to "the development of terms of employment such as to cause problems of social dumping, or even distortions of competition, at Community level".[66] However, the legal basis in the revised Treaty of Rome for measures needed to complete the single market was complicated by the exclusion in Article 100a of provisions that relate to "the rights and interests of employed persons", mentioned earlier, and the problem, discussed later, of whether this excludes *all* employment issues. In the event, the Commission decided to divide its proposals on atypical employment into three separate Directives: working conditions under Article 100; distortions in competition under Article 100a; and health and safety of temporary workers under Article 118a.[67]

(ii) The Commission's Proposals

The *first draft Directive* on "certain employment relationships with regard to working conditions" was first submitted by the Commission on

---

62. Published eleven days before the "Social Charter" was signed indicating that the Commission had already decided to pursue an alternative line of action.

63. COM(90) 228 final.

64. It did not seem to be acknowledged that these "non-standard" forms of work overlap into self-employment estimated at 16% of Community employment overall (*Social Europe* 4/91).

65. COM(90) 228 final, pp. 7-8.

66. Byre A (*supra* FN 55), p.26.

67. It is interesting to note that a prior proposal for a Directive on atypical employment from the European Parliament to the Commission is a composite of all three areas and is based on Articles 8a, 8b, 100a, and 118a (EP doc.A3-134/90).

29 June 1990,[68] based primarily on Article 100, but also referring to Article 117 at the end of the preamble. It concerns part-time and temporary employment relationships in public and private undertakings (not including those of less than eight hours per week) and makes provision for equality with regard to vocational training and social welfare;[69] informing temporary workers of the grounds for their employment relationship; protection of agency workers; access to internal labour markets; and rights of employee representation including requirements for information.[70] In the explanatory memorandum from the Commission,[71] dated 13 August, there was some attempt to expand on the content of the Directive but no explanation of why these particular issues should appear under Article 100.

The *second draft Directive* on "certain employment relationships with regard to distortions of competition" was submitted at the same time as the first, on the legal basis of Article 100a. It uses the same definition of part-time and temporary employment and provides for equal treatment under statutory and occupational social security schemes; the same entitlement to annual holidays, dismissal allowances and seniority allowances; limitations on the length of temporary contracts; and coverage of seasonal workers.[72] This content is subject to a much more detailed explanation in the Commission's memorandum about why these measures are necessary to prevent distortions of competition in the European Community, and are not simply an attempt to improve employment conditions. It is argued that differences in wages, benefits and working conditions between atypical workers in different Member States, do not affect comparative unit costs to any great extent because of similar patterns of productivity and infrastructural advantage.[73] However, there are other, indirect, labour costs which derive from a variety of rules within Member States which differentiate between atypical employment and open-ended, full-time employment, and it is these that can result in dis-

---

68. OJ C 224/4.

69. Equality with workers employed in full-time employment of an indefinite duration (Articles 2(1), 3 and 4).

70. But not consultation or negotiation (Articles 2(2/3)).

71. COM(90) 228 final. The timing of this memorandum is interesting because between 29 June when the Directives were first submitted and 13 August, an alternative draft covering all aspects of atypical employment was proposed by the European Parliament. However, there is no mention of this in the memorandum.

72. Articles 2 to 5 of the second draft directive.

73. Which, it is assumed, will even out when less developed regions "catch up" as a result of greater economic and social cohesion.

tortions of competition.[74] This will occur when employers choose to use atypical labour not because it is more "flexible" but because cheaper indirect costs give them a competitive advantage over employers in other Member States. These distortions are seen as most likely to occur in frontier areas where production using atypical labour is relocated in more favourable areas or agency workers carrying lower labour costs are used across the border.

The Commission's analysis of a range of indirect employment costs, including social security contributions for part-time workers; entitlements to sick pay; pension rights; annual leave; redundancy pay; unfair dismissal; restrictions on fixed-term employment contracts; and the regulation of temporary contracts through employment agencies, reveals that there are some major discrepancies between national systems in the Community. As far as part-time work is concerned, for the majority of Member States (two-thirds), employment rights do not depend on the number of hours worked, but in four of them[75] there are limitations based on hours thresholds. The most extreme case cited was the UK where protection against unfair dismissal and redundancy did not exist if hours worked are less than 8 per week, and required a longer period of service, 5 years rather than 2, if between 8 and 16 hours per week.[76] However, the House of Lords ruled, in February 1994, that the five year qualifying period was a form of indirect discrimination against women in part-time work affected by unfair dismissal and redundancy.[77] It was decided that the job creation justification used by the government could not be sustained and that the Secretary of State was in breach of the Equal Treatment Directive.[78] It now seems inevitable that UK law will be amended to remove this particular form of discrimination. Another differentiating factor is the limit of earnings below which part-time workers cannot participate in national insurance, which thereby excludes them from state pension and sick pay schemes.[79] This appears to be most advantageous in Germany where 36% of gross wages is not paid by the employer if incomes are below DM 470 per month. The Commission estimate that no social security contributions are made on 2.4 million part-time contracts in the UK and 0.45 million in Germany. The savings

---

74. Although it is noted that these rules must be considered in the wider context of economic policy, tax systems *etc*. (COM(90) 228 final, p.14).

75. The UK, Ireland and, to a lesser extent, in Germany and the Netherlands.

76. See debate between Hakim and Disney and Szyszczak on the extent of legal discrimination against part-time workers in the UK (*supra* FN 58).

77. *R v Secretary of State for Employment ex parte EOC*, House of Lords, 3.3.94 .

78. Council Directive 75/117/EEC.

79. Found in the UK, Denmark, Germany and Ireland.

on reduced legal protection in the UK and Ireland are harder to measure but are clearly seen as a significant advantage to employers.[80]

The situation with regard to temporary work is a little more complicated because of the distinction between fixed-term contracts and work
done through temporary work agencies. There is some legal regulation
of fixed-term contracts in all Member States except Denmark where they
are covered in collective agreements. In over half of these countries[81]
their use has to be justified by law, although these conditions vary considerably, and there is some limitation on their length and possibility of
renewal. These conditions are most stringent in Italy, Greece and Luxembourg,[82] but in Denmark, Ireland and the UK, regulation is minimal.
There is normally standard protection if the contract is terminated before its completion date although, as in the case of the UK and Ireland,
there may be a service qualification which disadvantages temporary workers. There are also restrictions on sick pay for short contracts in the UK
and Germany[83] and limitations on unemployment benefit for seasonal
workers in France. Again, it is hard to estimate the comparative savings
to employers but a Dublin Foundation survey, quoted by the Commission,[84] found that in Spain 34% of temporary contracts involved lower
social security contributions, compared to 11% in the UK and 3% in
Germany. Only in Belgium and Greece is there any additional compensation for premature termination, and only in Spain and France is there
any requirement for a bonus to be paid at the end of the contract.[85]

With regards to temporary agencies all Member States have some
degree of regulation but, as previously mentioned, they are not permitted at all in Italy, Greece and Spain. The agencies themselves in the other
nine Member States are subject to the same regulations as any other
employer, as in the preceding paragraph, with some additional requirements. In Belgium, Denmark, Germany and the Netherlands, there are
some restrictions on the use of agency staff; only in the UK, Ireland and
Portugal, is there no limit on the length and renewal of this kind of
contract; and in Belgium, France, the Netherlands and Portugal, there
must be comparable pay and conditions with the user company. This
variation in practice can result in considerable differences in the availability and cost of temporary labour, which, as the Commission point

80. COM(90) 228 final, pp. 18-19.

81. Denmark, Greece, Spain, France, Italy, Luxembourg and Portugal.

82. Comprehensively revised in 1989 (EIRR Dec.1989).

83. Less than 3 months in the UK and 4 weeks in Germany.

84. COM(90) 228 final, p.24.

85. 12 days pay per year worked in Spain and 5% of wages in France (COM(90) 228 final,
    p.24).

out, may be particularly prevalent in border areas where unemployment is higher than average.[86]

The *third draft Directive* is concerned with the health and safety at work of temporary workers only, including both fixed-term contracts and agency workers, and is based on Article 118a EEC. It is accepted that the framework Health and Safety Directive 89/391, and subsequent "daughter" Directives, were intended to cover all workers but that additional regulation was necessary in: specifying the occupational requirements of agency contracts, particularly the risks involved; making sure that user organisations take full responsibility for agency workers; providing proper training and health assessment for all temporary workers; and not using temporary labour on contracts requiring long-term medical supervision.[87] The justification given in the preamble of the draft Directive for this additional regulation is that temporary workers can be demonstrated to be more exposed to accidents at work and occupational diseases than other workers. The Commission's memorandum gives figures for France, Belgium and Germany, of two to three times the accident rate for temporary work and attributes this to lack of familiarity and proper training, especially for agency workers.[88] The underlying theme is that employers may be avoiding their responsibilities for health and safety, and implicitly additional costs, by using temporary labour and, although distortion of competition is not mentioned in this context, there is a link.

Overall, the separation of protection of atypical workers into three different proposals is seen as necessary by the Commission because "a full, effective, flexible response at Community level demands a varied approach as regards the legal basis to be used".[89] However, the response of other parties to these proposals indicates that it is far from clear to them why the first two draft Directives should be defined as they are and whether they have gone too far or not far enough in their scope and application. The third proposal has been relatively uncontroversial, although it needed to be re-drafted before it could proceed, ultimately, to be implemented.

(iii) Parliament's Response

As mentioned previously, Parliament had already submitted a proposal for a Directive on atypical work that relied entirely on Articles 100a

---

86. COM(90) 228 final, p.26.

87. Articles 2 to 6 of the first draft of the directive.

88. COM(90) 228 final, pp. 29-30.

89. COM(90) 228 final, p.31.

and 118a.[90] Their reaction in September 1990 to being consulted by the Council on the three draft Directives was therefore fairly predictable. The first proposal was rejected completely[91] and a call was made for various amendments (37 in all) to the second which incorporated some of the provisions that had appeared in the first.[92] For example, training and social welfare schemes reappear under revised Articles 1, 2 and 3; co-operation with representative bodies and recruitment to full-time, permanent employment is included in revised Articles 1,3 and 6e.[93] The other amendments are concerned with widening the definition of atypical work covered by the legislation; providing for written contractual details; compensation for atypical employment; guarantees of overtime pay. The third proposal was also amended (22 changes) to include all kinds of atypical work; a strengthening of the provisions for information and training; and a system of accountability.

This rejection of Article 100 as a legal base, and the amendments to the Article 100a proposal, are clearly related to a difference of legal philosophy between Parliament and the Commission. In the revised Recital to the second proposal, Amendment No.14 states that "Article 100a allows such measures to be taken if they are connected with an economic need and do not relate exclusively to the rights and interests of employed persons".[94] In an explanatory statement, it is argued that the Commission is, by separating the social and economic aspects, effectively removing the social aspect from Article 100a and giving it an extremely restrictive interpretation. These particular social measures are seen as directly in support of the objectives of Article 8a and are therefore not subject to the Article 100a(2) restriction. The assumption is that labour is a factor of production and the completion and smooth running of the internal market are bound to affect the rights and interests of employed persons. Therefore "Article 100a(2) does not require Article 100 to be invoked in respect of social measures with economic consequences".[95] The Article 118a proposal is not questioned with regard to its legal base and is treated as a separate component of Parliament's response.

These attempts to reshape the legislative framework for atypical

---

90. It was stated in a subsequent memorandum that this new departure was prompted because the Parliament was "disturbed at the Commission's slowness in drawing up the directive on atypical employment". (EP doc.A3-0241/90, p.30).

91. EP doc.A3 0241/90, p.4.

92. Using the co-operation procedure under Article 149(3) EEC.

93. See Amendments 24 to 34 in the Parliament's revised version of the directive on distortions of competition.

94. EP doc.A3-0241/90, p.8.

95. EPdoc.A3-0241/90, pp. 32-33.

employment were formulated for discussion by the Committee on Social Affairs, Employment and the Working Environment. There were, however, additional points made in the Opinion of the Committee on Women's Rights which are a reminder of the relationship between equality for atypical employment (which the Committee refers to as more "typical" for women), and sexual equality because of the predominance of women in part-time and temporary work. This Opinion supported the foregoing argument and proposed, in addition, that the threshold for protection should be reduced to two hours; that maternity leave should be included in equality for social security schemes; and that the maximum length of temporary contracts should be reduced to 12 months.[96] The first two amendments were not adopted in Parliament's response but the third was covered by the entire deletion of that clause.

(iv) The Economic and Social Committee's Opinion

In their Opinion to the Council, also in September 1990, the Economic and Social Committee were in general agreement with Parliament on a broad interpretation of Article 100a, although it was thought that wider use could also be made to the clause in Article 118a which refers to improvements in the working environment.[97] Other comments included the need to include sub-contracted employment; a stress on collective bargaining and consensus management in the achievement of labour flexibility; the link between atypical employment and the "black" labour market; the need to ban temporary labour to replace striking workers; the dubious nature of the link between atypical work and job creation; and the apparent omission of "cultural workers".[98]

There was, however, a lack of unanimity on the Committee which can be seen in the split vote,[99] and a minority declaration by the employer's group, which made a number of objections to the report. These included, a complete rejection of all the proposals for legislation on atypical work; disagreement that employment costs for atypical workers are significantly different from all other employees; the risk of such legislation reducing employment levels overall; the need for detailed provision on employment protection to be left to Member States; and opposi-

96. EPdoc.A3-0241/90, pp. 36-37.

97. OJ C 332/168 and 169.

98. OJ C 167-169.

99. 72 in favour, 59 against, 9 abstentions (OJ C 332/167).

tion to the idea of lumping together all forms of non-standard employment.[100] These appear to be common themes in the perspective of European employers as the next section illustrates.

(v) The Employer's View (UNICE)

A memorandum submitted by UNICE, in August 1990,[101] takes up most of the points raised above in more detail. It argues that the proposals are anti-competitive because they will increase costs, especially for small and medium-sized enterprises (SMEs), and prejudice the Communities' position in world markets. The differences in regulation between Member States are said to "express different traditions and customary practice as well as different labour market requirements"[102] which, if disturbed, could be counter productive, and in any case, are comparable with other labour costs as a normal factor of competition. So details such as thresholds for social security and legal protection, which are "tailor-made" by each Member State, need remain under national control, with the Community's role, if any, limited to general principles.

Other matters raised in the UNICE memorandum deal with the need for clarification on a number of points, many of which amount to a call for a more accurate redrafting. However, this should not be taken as a sign of a conciliatory approach judging by the statement that the detailed proposals are "without prejudice to UNICE fundamental opposition in principle"[103] and that the draft on distortions of competition clearly falls within the scope of Article 100a(2). The Article 118a proposal is also subjected to a range of fundamental criticisms including doubts about the evidence for different health and safety risks for atypical workers and the assertion that the content is already in Directive 89/391 which covers all types of employment.

(vi) The Trade Union View (ETUC)

There does not appear to be on record a specific response from ETUC to the proposed atypical work directives other than that represented by the majority report from the Economic and Social Committee referred to above. However, at the seventh Annual Congress held in Luxembourg in May 1991,[104] there were several references to the prob-

---

100. OJ C 332/171 and 172.

101. House of Lords Select Committee, HL Paper 7, 107-111.

102. UNICE memorandum, point 4.

103. HL Paper 7, p.108.

104. ETUC, *Confederation Europeenne des Syndicats, 7ieme Congres Statutaire*, Luxembourg 13-17 May 1991.

lems associated with the dual labour market and the lack of comprehensive legislation. A "specific resolution" was made to the effect (according to my French), that much of atypical employment is not really necessary and demanding that this kind of work should be limited by collective agreement at enterprise level wherever possible.[105]

Further comment was made by the then General Secretary of ETUC, Jean Lapeyre, to the effect that social and economic cohesion can only be achieved if workers can be given social guarantees against social dumping, mentioning atypical employment as a priority in this respect.[106] This seems to imply support for the Commission's tactics in separating out the "distortions of competition" under Article 100a EEC because he also recognises that improvements in working conditions can only be sustained if economic and social cohesion is successful. A later statement from the next General Secretary of ETUC, Emilio Gabaglio, in 1992, expressed great dissatisfaction that the most important proposals in the Social Action Programme had been blocked, again referring specifically to the rights of non-standard workers. He sees some way forward in the pursuit of social dialogue but says that this must go hand-in-hand with minimum levels of social protection.[107]

(vii) The Commission's Revised Proposals

In October 1990, in accordance with Article 149(3) EEC, the Commission submitted amended proposals to the Council on, firstly, atypical workers with regard to distortions of competition and, secondly, on safety and health at work for temporary workers, having clearly decided not to pursue the third proposal on improvements in working conditions at this time. The concessions made to Parliament's Opinion are limited, in the former proposal, to allowing for across-the-board measures to improve protection of workers and putting the Article 1 threshold in more precise terms. The moves to redefine the meaning of atypical workers were resisted as were other amendments which were considered to come under Article 100 EEC. There are also additional clauses relating to involving the two sides of industry;[108] abandonment of the maximum period for temporary contracts in favour of more general measures to avoid temporary work replacing permanent jobs;[109] and a requirement for a report on implementation of the Directive. In the latter proposal, the

---

105. ETUC (*supra* FN 104), pp. 40-41.

106. *Social Europe* 1/90, p.26.

107. *Social Europe* 2/92, pp. 13-14.

108. New Recital 19.

109. Revised Article 4.

Commission accepted some stronger wording, on equal treatment of temporary workers and compulsory training for dangerous work, but rejected calls for extending the scope of the Directive beyond temporary employment.[110]

A common position was adopted by the Council on the redrafted proposal on health and safety of temporary workers but not the one on distortions of competition, presumably because of the level of disagreement about the scope of Article 100a. The Parliament, in its second reading,[111] made some further amendments to try and maintain the wider inclusion of all types of atypical workers; extend the responsibilities of employers for the conditions of work; to prolong special medical supervision beyond the termination of the contract; and require the public authorisation of temporary agencies.[112] In its re-examined proposal,[113] (according to Article 149(2) EEC), the Commission rejected all these amendments, except the one relating to medical supervision, and the Directive was finally adopted on 25 January 1991 with a view to implementation on 31 December 1992.[114]

These attempts to legislate for the equal treatment of atypical workers at Community level were therefore largely frustrated, with the exception of health and safety, by arguments over the scope of Articles 100, 100a and 118a, the detailed content of the draft Directives, and the effects that legal regulation will have on employment creation. Some Member States, mainly the UK and Denmark (though for different reasons),[115] and employers' representatives, oppose regulation in principle arguing that variations in legal protection of atypical workers in the Community cannot be divorced from other differences in employment costs. Most other Member States, the left of centre European Parliament, and trade union interests, are in favour of regulation to correct distortions of competition caused by unequal treatment of atypical workers and differences in the costs of their employment. Among the two main interest groups, there are differences in emphasis concerning, for example, the definition of atypical work, the role of collective bargaining, and the principle of subsidiarity. However, the consultation process seemed to involve more political horse trading than logical argument.

110. COM(90) 533 final, p.2.

111. According to the co-operation procedure introduced by the SEA.

112. OJ C 158/82.

113. COM(91) 211 final.

114. Directive 91/383/EEC.

115. Denmark has an alternative system of employment regulation through national collective agreements, the UK does not.

The sequence of the debate over the proposed legislation suggests that the Commission, in adopting a three-way strategy, failed to convincingly delimit the case for distortions of competition under Article 100a, or the reasons for distinguishing between Articles 100 and 100a in terms of "certain" conditions that do not contribute to differences in employment costs and those that do. This strategy was clearly aimed at trying to maximise the balance in favour of qualified majority voting but, in doing so, left an area of uncertainty which allowed one side to argue that the Commission had not gone far enough and the other side to argue that it had gone too far. The health and safety proposal was questioned in terms of detailed content but its legal base was not seriously challenged. In fact the only real objection, from the UK, was whether another Directive was necessary, given the comprehensive coverage of the "framework" Directive recently passed.

(viii) Recent Proposals

The more recent attempts by the Belgian and German Presidencies to present revised proposals on atypical employment have clearly tried to side-step this impasse by going back to Article 100 as a legal base. The Belgian version, discussed towards the end of 1993, was reported to represent a merger of the two blocked Directives and although little progress was made, the Council now seems to be giving the matter a higher degree of priority.[116] The revised German text stresses that greater adaptability of labour can only be achieved where employees are entitled to the same basic rights irrespective of employment status or working hours. The recognition in the White Paper on Growth, Competitiveness and Employment,[117] that job creation is linked to the growth of atypical work is reflected in the new title of the draft Directive "on the promotion of employment and the protection of part-time and fixed-term relationships". It is reported that the proposed Directive refers to a simplified range of rights:[118] all part-time and temporary contracts are entitled to equal treatment with full-time and permanent staff, with no lower limit on weekly hours (however, different treatment is possible if it is "objectively justified"); all employees wanting to change contract hours or length must be informed of suitable vacancies; employee representation should be based on all types of employment; representative bodies should be informed of workforce composition before recruiting more atypical workers; and fixed-term contracts should only be used where there are

116. *European Industrial Relations Review* 248, September 1994, p.2.

117. *supra* FN 18.

118. IDS Report (*supra* FN 13), p.11.

objective grounds, with a national maximum for contract length. There is no reference to subcontracted employment relationships (including agency work) or equivalent social security coverage.

It seems very unlikely that a "common position" will be agreed between all 12 Member States by the end of 1994 because of the UK's strong resistance to any regulation in this area. So, at the time of writing, it is expected that the proposal will be switched to the Social Protocol mechanism in 1995. It is interesting to note that the recent revival of the atypical employment issue coincides with an ILO Convention on part-time work which focuses on collective bargaining rights of part-timers and equal treatment for health and safety, social security rights and employment benefits.[119] It would clearly be invidious for the European Union to have lower standards of employment protection than the ILO.

4.   PERSPECTIVES ON FUTURE DEVELOPMENT

(i)   *The Wider Debate about Legal Intervention*

The previous discussion about the disagreements between the Commission, Parliament, and the social partners, over the use of Article 100a as a legal base for regulating atypical employment conditions, can be seen to be a reflection of the wider debate about the development of a social dimension to European integration. It is generally accepted that, since the 1970s, the *laissez-faire* assumptions of the original Treaty no longer hold because social conditions are under increasing pressure from the need for economic restructuring. However, it has been difficult to achieve a consensus on social policy at European level with a very limited Treaty base to work from[120] and resistance from employers and some Member States (primarily the UK). Despite a stronger legal base in the Single European Act, and now in the amended EC Treaty, there are still fundamental disagreements about the role of labour market regulation in Community integration which go back to original intentions of the Treaty of Rome.

The approach to social policy in the original Treaty was contained in Article 2 which states that the objectives of the EEC were "a harmonious development of economic activities, a continuous and balanced expansion, an increase in stability, an accelerated raising of the standard of living and closer relations between Member States". The implication is that the economic benefits of the common market will lead to improved

---

119. *supra* FN 117.

120. Articles 117 to 121 EEC had limited scope so recourse has also been made to the wider Treaty provisions in Articles 100 and 235.

living and working conditions because competition in the European labour market will force those Member States with weaker levels of social protection to raise their standards. This was based on a *laissez-faire* assumption of sustained economic growth, which was realised during the 1950s and 1960s, and the gradual harmonisation of social policy through the mechanism of the market.[121] However, as Gold points out,[122] in the second paragraph of Article 117 EEC there was an ambiguity between improvements in standards of living which "will ensue from the functioning of the common market" and, on the other hand, that "law regulation and administrative action" may be required to achieve this end. This has been at the root of the argument about Community competence in the social field which is reflected in the atypical employment impasse.

The importance of this issue was realised when worsening economic conditions and higher unemployment in the early 1970s created the reverse effect in which Member States were under pressure to reduce their social costs to remain competitive. This problem has since been defined as "social dumping" which can either involve lower cost labour being used in high labour cost countries or if companies relocate their production facilities to Member States with lower labour costs. The term is derived from the effect of exporting unemployment to the Member State with the higher labour costs. The first meaning is particularly relevant, as previously discussed, to temporary workers who are employed across national boundaries. The second meaning can apply to all instances where atypical employment is created as a result of relative labour costs which give one employer a competitive edge over a rival in another Member State, previously discussed as a distortion of competition.

The fear that social dumping would lead to a downward spiral in social conditions in the Community was recognised at the Paris Summit of 1972 in the declaration that "economic expansion is not an end in itself but should result in an improvement in the quality of life as well as of the standard of living".[123] This principle has been repeatedly reiterated at European Summits and provides the basis of social policy initiatives since then which can be described as the "maximalist approach"[124] to legal intervention at a European level. This was expressed by Jacques Delors in 1986 as the development of European social space and the

---

121. Hepple describes the overall approach, confirmed in the wording of Art.117, as "neo-liberal" (*Industrial Law Journal*, Vol.16, 1987, p.77).

122. Gold M (ed.) (*supra* FN 8), p.13.

123. This became the third recital of the first Social Action Programme in 1974 OJ (74/ C13/01).

124. Mainly the Commission, the Parliament, trade unions, and some Member States, notably France.

preamble to the Single European Act (1987), stated that Member States were "determined to work together to promote democracy on the basis of ... freedom, equality and social justice". The basiş for supranational intervention is theoretically explained by the "Regulationist School" as the need to create a new institutional structure across the whole of Europe (a federal system) because the old national arrangements that were appropriate to "Fordist" conditions of production[125] could no longer be sustained in the new global market place with the need for more flexible forms of production. This has a direct bearing on the atypical employment discussion because the rapid increase in relatively unregulated non-standard forms of work is one of the main indicators used to demonstrate the need for a new social order and a new approach to labour market regulation.

However, the view that the Community should take a positive and active role in social policy to further collective welfare as well as collective economic interests is not shared, as we have seen in the case of atypical work, by all the parties concerned. Opposing views are of two kinds which are based on different interpretations of the prevailing philosophy of the early days of the Community. One is that action in the social field is only necessary insofar as it prevents distortions of competition due to differences in national social standards.[126] The other is that the Community has no role to play in social policy because any differences in labour market standards are offset by variations in productivity levels which will even out as the Single Market develops.[127] This tension between welfare and free market competition is not peculiar to the Community. The International Labour Organisation has been trying to get consensus on labour standards for 75 years and each Member State has its own political history of social policy and market regulation. As Watson says, the debate about Community competence in social affairs has a more fundamental undercurrent of division on the management of the capitalist system.[128]

This tension was clearly evident in the controversy surrounding the 1989 Social Charter where there was fierce dispute over the content of the measures and how they could be enacted.[129] The substance of the Charter was disputed because it was too restricted or because it did not

---

125. Mass production, large enterprises, standardised consumption patterns, Keynsian economic policies, national collective bargaining, the welfare state (Teague P in *International Journal of HRM*, 1993, p.350).

126. This view has been strongly held by the Court since the 1970s e.g. in redundancy cases.

127. This relates back to the original views in the Spaak Report.

128. Watson P in *Common Market Law Review*, Vol.28, 1991, p.41.

129. The result being that the UK opted-out and the programme only being given the status of a "solemn declaration".

go far enough, and the limited use of majority voting was either opposed in principle or demands made to extend it to all social areas. This became a focus for a wider attack from both sides on the need to reform the Community's social policy in the face of renewed recession and high unemployment and formed the background to the Maastricht negotiations. It is not surprising, therefore, that the 1989 Social Action Programme was seen either as stretching the boundaries of Community competence, particularly in relation to majority voting, or as a weak and confused approach to social reform. The pragmatic nature of the proposals seem to reflect the Commission's attempt to satisfy all the competing interests by adopting a "bolt on" approach as opposed to the definition of a systematic set of social rights. Gold sees this as a signal to the "minimalists" that social policy is an optional extra.[130]

So the arguments about Community competence around the use, in particular of Articles 100a and 118a, have been heavily loaded with conflicting ideological overtones about the basic objectives of the European Community. The wording of Article 100a(2) concerning the exclusion of the "rights and interests of employed persons" seems to be sufficiently ambiguous to allow for quite different interpretations. Vogel-Polsky has identified three possibilities:[131] firstly, that a proposal that has *any bearing* on the rights and interests of employed persons is excluded from majority voting; secondly, that only those proposals which were *predominantly* concerned would be excluded; and thirdly, that only those proposals concerned *solely* with this issue would be affected. The first option would have the effect of excluding most Community measures from majority voting because it is difficult to imagine an area of economic policy that does not in some way affect the rights and interests of employed persons. The second option is not considered to be viable because of the difficulty in defining predominance, so Vogel-Polsky argues that only the third interpretation is clear and unambiguous.[132] She reasons that "labour law is concerned not only with the reconciliation and compatibility of the respective rights and interests of employers and employees, but also with the guiding object of fixing common rules for enterprises which have resort to the labour market, so as to ward off unfair competition".[133] Therefore, most employment regulation should be enacted by qualified majority voting and the Commission has got itself into an unnecessary tangle by trying to separate out those aspects of policy on, for example, atypical workers, that are covered by Article 100, and those

---

130. Gold M (*supra* FN 8), p.28.

131. Vogel-Polsky E in *Industrial Law Journal*, Vol.19, 1990, pp. 70-72.

132. This view is shared by Hepple (*supra* FN 121)

133. Vogel-Polsky E (*supra* FN 131), p.72.

that are covered by Article 100a.

The opposing view, that any measure affecting employment rights requires unanimity, seems to be less concerned with the argument about Community competence to enact legislation, than the wider question of the desirability of labour market regulation at all. The "neo-liberal" approach that was adopted by employers, and the UK government in particular, during the 1980s, argued that the European labour market was suffering from inflexibility and rigidity in wages, employment protection and social security.[134] The cure for this was seen in less emphasis on institutional integration at Community level and a more active role in labour market policies[135] which would encourage higher levels of employment. Although this approach was originally resisted by the Commission it has now enthusiastically endorsed it in the White Paper on Growth, Competitiveness and Employment, the principles of which have also been incorporated into the White Paper on Social Policy.[136] This confirms the view that a drift has occurred since the Single European Act to accommodate the minimalist approach. The Social Action Programme emphasised the need for a wide range of policy options, only some of which would take the form of legislation, and that there should be maximum freedom for Member States to implement social policy in ways that were compatible with national systems.[137] This meant, in practice, dropping some of the more controversial elements of the Social Charter such as acceptable pay levels, bargaining rights and participation, and including a number of voluntary measures. It is also relevant to note the clause in Article 118a which says that an undue administrative burden on small and medium-sized enterprises (SMEs) should be avoided.

However, it would be mistaken to assume that this political compromise has had a neutralising effect on social policy because many of the measures proposed under the Social Action Programme have now been enacted and the "Social Chapter" of the Maastricht Treaty had the support of eleven Member States to extend the application of majority voting to other areas. The Commission has recently stated that "the premise at the heart of this Green Paper is that the next phase in the develop-

---

134. This theme of "Euroscleurosis" is linked by Teague to the growth of new management practices which emphasise a loosening of ties to institutional labour market regulation (*HRM Journal*, Vol.2, No.1, 1991, p.4).

135. The 1986 Action Programme for Employment Growth, initiated by the UK, included the encouragement of entrepreneurship and small business and the limitation of employment regulation.

136. *supra* FN 15, p.3

137. Reference is made in point 3 of the General Introduction to the Action Programme to the principle of "subsidiarity" (Byre A, *supra* FN 55, p.14) which would later be central to the Maastricht debate.

ment of European social policy cannot be based on the idea that social progress must go into retreat in order for economic competitiveness to recover. Much of Europe's influence and power has come precisely from its capacity to combine wealth creation with enhanced benefits and freedoms for its people".[138] So there appears to be a determination not to give in to free market demands for employment "flexibility".[139]

However, it can still be argued that the Commission is holding back on the more contentious areas of social policy, as illustrated in the previous discussion on the failure of two of the atypical employment directives. The confusion created by trying to satisfy opposing interests by dividing the proposals into those that were related to distortions of competition and those that were not is indicative of a wider problem. This is related partly to the issue of Community competence in enacting legislation but also stems from the polarisation of views between those wanting to protect atypical workers from market forces and those that see legislation as a restriction on economic activity *per se*.

(ii) The Possibilities of Related Legal Developments

The lack of movement on two of the three atypical work directives needs to also be considered in relation to other developments in social legislation and case law at European level which have had the effect of complementing or extending the protection of part-time and temporary workers by other means. This is particularly evident in some Court of Justice judgments on equal treatment for men and women, but also occurs in the areas of social security; contractual information; working time; and provision of services. The issues covered by these alternative sources of law often overlap with the same concerns of the proposed directives but can be argued to be very patchy and inadequate sources of protection. However, they may provide a framework of rules which can be consolidated in subsequent legislation.

As far as equal treatment is concerned there are a range of cases based on Article 119 and subsequent Directives[140] which extend protection to part-time workers in such matters as sick pay; severance pay; social security; seniority pay; occupational pension schemes; training facilities; and thresholds for employment rights. Because the vast majority of part-time workers are women, many of whom have dependent chil-

---

138. *supra* FN 14, p.8.

139. The Delors II package for employment regeneration in Europe argues the case for high levels of protection being compatible with different methods of employment creation.

140. Directives 75/117 on equal pay; 76/207 on equal treatment; and 79/7 on social security.

dren, it has been consistently argued by the Court that discrimination against part-time workers constitutes unlawful sex discrimination. The principle has usually been that an employment condition that only applies to part-time workers is a form of indirect discrimination if, in practice, it works to the disadvantage of women.

The key case in recent years is *Bilka-Kaufhaus GmbH v Weber von Hartz*,[141] in which a German department store excluded part-timers from its occupational pension scheme unless they had worked 15 years full-time during 20 years service. The Court ruled that, as this policy disproportionately affected more women than men and counted as "pay" it was contrary to Article 119, but that there would be no breach "if the employer was able to show that its pay practice was explained by objectively justified factors unrelated to any discrimination on the ground of sex". This derogation is explained, in the details of the judgment, as a matter for the national court to decide whether the policy adopted corresponded to a genuine requirement of the undertaking, that they were appropriate for obtaining the objective being pursued and necessary for that purpose.[142]

Two other cases, both involving collective agreements with the *Freie und Hansestadt Hamburg*,[143] followed the same logic with regard to employment policies. In the *Kowalska* case, severance pay on retirement was not given to part-timers because it was contended that "part-time workers do not provide for their needs and those of their family exclusively out of the income from their employment".[144] So the policy was only in breach of Article 119 and the Equal Pay Directive 75/117, if the national court decides that this is not an objective economic reason. In the *Nimz* case, the rules on upgrading after a prescribed period of service which disadvantaged part-timers were also found to be in breach of Article 119. The reason given, that upgrading was based on experience which depended on cumulative hours, was not considered by the Court to be sufficient as a general condition and it was ruled that such circumstances need to be considered on a case by case basis. A third case, *Arbeiterwohlfahrt der Stadt Berlin (ASWB) v Botel*,[145] concerned the right of part-timers to attend full-time training courses and receive full pay. This clearly demonstrates that the principle of indirect discrimination for part-time work-

---

141. Case 170/84 [1986] ECR 1607. See also *Jenkins v Kingsgate*, Case 96/80 [1981] ECR 911.

142. Point 36 of the Decision. In the *Bilka* case the employer claimed that the policy was necessary to discourage part-timers.

143. *Maria Kowalska v FHH*, Case 33/89 [1990] ECR I-2591 and *Nimz v FHH*, Case 184/89 [1991] ECR I-297.

144. Decision in *Kowalska*, point 14.

145. Case C-360/90 [1992] I-3589.

ers goes beyond "pay" into other areas of employment conditions covered by Directive 76/207 on equal treatment.

The principle of allowing objective grounds for exemption from Article 119 has also been applied to national legislation. In the case of *Ingrid Rinner-Kuhn v FWW Spezial-Gebaudereinigung GmbH*,[146] the exclusion of part-timers working 10 hours or less a week from sick pay provisions under German law was ruled as incompatible with Article 119 and Directive 75/117, because far more women were affected than men. Here it was argued by the German Government that those affected "were not as integrated in, or as dependent on, the undertaking employing them".[147] The ruling allowed for exceptions to be made if the Member State can demonstrate that the provision was necessary to meet a social policy aim with objective factors unrelated to discrimination on grounds of sex.[148] This principle was also applied in the case of *ML Ruzius-Wilbrink v Bestuur van de Bedrijfsvereniging voor Overheidsdiensten*,[149] where national provisions for social security (incapacity to work) discriminated against part-timers and it was ruled that a breach of Article 119 depended on the absence of "objective reasons" for the policy.

The *Rinner* judgment, in particular, opens up the question of whether any legal thresholds which discriminate against part-timers are in breach of Article 119, if objective reasons which did not involve sex discrimination could not be found. The House of Lords case, previously referred to,[150] found that the Department of Employment could not justify unequal treatment of part-time workers with regard to qualifying periods for statutory redundancy pay and unfair dismissal compensation on the grounds that it encouraged job creation. In any event, Dickens argues, that even if the state were able to justify social policy on these grounds this "does not mean that individual employers who ape the statutory thresholds (or impose others) in barring access to part-time workers to various benefits cannot be successfully challenged under European law".[151]

So on the one hand, there is the prospect that any employment provision that discriminates against part-time workers, assuming that the majority are women, may be in breach of Article 119 and subsequent Directives. The issues already covered in the cases discussed above represent important elements of the two remaining proposed directives on

146. Case 171/88 [1989] ECR 2743.

147. Decision in *Rinner-Kuhn*, point 13.

148. Decision in *Rinner-Kuhn*, point 14.

149. Case 102/88 [1989] ECR 4311.

150. *supra* FN 77.

151. Dickens L, in *Employee Relations*, Vol.14, No.2, 1992, p.9.

atypical employment with regard to part-time employment. The Article 100a draft's approach to statutory and occupational social security schemes is supported by the rulings in *Bilka, Rinner* and *Wilbrink* and the reference to various allowances relate to the rulings in *Kowalska* and *Nimz*. The Article 100 issues are also partly covered in more than one aspect in *Botel* with references to both training and employee representation. On the other hand, it could be argued that progress of this sort is rather haphazard because it depends on taking up individual cases, waiting for years for cases to be heard, and being subject to the interpretation of national courts about what constitutes objective grounds for discrimination against part-time workers.

The rights of part-time workers have also been considered by the Court in relation to freedom of movement. In *Levin v Staatssecretaris van Justitie*,[152] the Dutch definition of "favoured worker", with regard to the application of Article 48 EEC, excluded those who were below the national minimum wage. The Court ruled that the Community meaning of work included any activity as an employed person, including part-time work "provided that he there pursues an effective and genuine activity".[153] Specific reference was made to the possibility of discrimination against women, the disabled and the elderly, which makes a link with the equal treatment cases but without the qualification of "objectively justified factors unrelated to any discrimination on the grounds of sex". However, this ruling only applies to the equal rights of migrant part-time workers (Member State nationals) with regard to national employment and employment conditions and does not affect the inequalities that may exist with full-time employment rights.

The same argument applies to the rights of migrant temporary workers under Regulation 1612/68 and subsequent legislation and to the protection for atypical migrant workers in Regulation 1408/71[154] on social security, based on Article 51 EEC. However, in the latter case, an exception is made for temporary workers whose contracts are for 12 months or less, meaning that their social security entitlements remain with their country of origin. In the case of *Manpower Sarl v Caisse Primaire d'Assurance Maladie de Strasbourg*,[155] it was ruled that temporary agency workers being posted to another Member State, in this instance from Germany to France, fell within this provision. However, this exception

152. Case 53/81 [1982] ECR 1035.

153. The judgment was based on the Recitals in Regulation 1612/68 and Directive 68/360, Article 4.

154. Extended to include the self-employed in Regulations 1390/81 and 3795/81.

155. Case 35/70 [1970] ECR 1251.

156. This proposal is still subject to "sharp disagreement" according to EIRR (Dec.1993).

will no longer apply if the current proposal on the posting of workers is agreed.[156]

Another recent piece of legislation which complements the atypical employment proposals is Directive 91/533 on an employer's obligation to inform employees of the conditions applicable to their contract or employment relationship. This was an element of the Social Charter Action Programme which was unanimously agreed by the Council on the basis of Article 100 and makes an interesting comparison with the atypical version. It covers all employees with the exception of those on temporary contracts of less than one month; contracts of 8 hours or less; and certain types of casual work, so it includes similar categories of non-standard work as the atypical proposals. In fact, the preamble of the Directive specifically refers to the development of new forms of work which have led to an increase in the number of types of employment relationship, and the subsequent need for improved protection against possible infringement of their rights and "transparency" in the labour market.[157] It obliges employers to give certain details of the employment contract, in writing, within two months of commencing employment; when working abroad; and within one month if a contract is modified. Contract terms are hardly referred to in the atypical drafts but in the response from the European Parliament there was a concern for more precise details of terms of employment.[158] There is a clause in the Article 100 version that temporary workers should be informed of the reasons for their contract,[159] but otherwise the legislation is clearly drafted with separate if complementary purposes.

It might be asked whether Directive 91/533 was so innocuous in its provisions that it was not regarded as a threat by those who oppose the improvement of working conditions because they are presumed to lead to increased labour costs.[160] Apparently there was minimal comment from the press and Jacques Delors is quoted at the time as saying that nothing of importance had been achieved by the Social Charter Action programme.[161] Clark and Hall argue that, on the contrary, it is a "Cinderella Directive" which has much wider implications for reform, particularly in the UK where a number of interested parties, notably the right-wing Institute of Directors, thought the requirements did not go far enough.[162]

157. The first and second "whereas" of Directive 91/533.

158. Revised Article 1b in the amended text. OJ C 295/102.

159. Article 2(4).

160. However, the UK did abstain from the vote and disputed the appropriateness of Article 100 as a legal base (Clark J. and Hall M. in *Industrial Law Journal*, Vol.21, No.2, 1992, p.109).

161. Quoted by Clark and Hall (*supra* FN 160), p.106.

162. Clark and Hall (*supra* FN 160), p.112.

This view does not necessarily coincide with the objective of worker protection because it also contains an implicit suggestion of individualisation of employment relations at the expense of collective bargaining. However, it does recognise, in the interests of promoting greater labour flexibility, the equal legal existence of all kinds of employment contract. Furthermore, the Directive actually benefits part-time workers in the UK by reducing the threshold from 16 to 8 hours for the receipt of written details of their contract. This might not seem a great advance but it can be argued that it represents a break in the UK legal practice of setting a five year threshold for part-timers which can be exploited further.[163]

As far as temporary workers are concerned there might be some additional benefit from Directive 91/533 in the closer regulation of contractual details (if employed for one month or more), but two other pieces of recent Community legislation are likely to have greater implications. These are Directive 93/104 on the organisation of working time and the proposed directive on the posting of workers in the framework of provision of services.[164] The first, based on Article 118a EC, applies to minimum daily, weekly and yearly rest periods, and to certain aspects of night and shift work. As it is highly likely that temporary (and part-time) workers will be used during unsocial hours, and are less likely to be guaranteed paid holidays and rest breaks, this appears to be an important addition to their legal protection which is complementary to the atypical proposal under Article 100a. The second, based on Articles 57(2) and 66 EC, and still at the proposal stage, applies to the transfer of workers to other Member States either as part of a contract for work or services, employed by a temporary work agency, or outplacement provision. Although this includes open-ended contracts it is highly likely that the first two instances will involve a temporary employment relationship. This draft directive is clearly related to the concerns of the Article 100a atypical proposal because it aims to ensure that these workers are entitled to the same employment rights[165] as those that apply in the host Member State. The issue of cross border postings is specifically referred to in the Article 100a proposal with a claim in the 5th recital that "dangers of distortions of competition are particularly great in frontier areas". In the Commission's explanatory memorandum, previously discussed, the activities of temporary agencies were specifically mentioned as taking advantage of different employment costs between Member States. However, the three month limitation means that this danger is

163. Clark and Hall (*supra* FN 160), p.109.

164. COM(93) 225 final - SYN 346.

165. With the important proviso that contracts of less than three months are not covered by minimum pay and holidays - Article 3(2) of the draft Directive.

still there.

In conclusion, the greatest potential for alternative forms of protection for part-time workers seems to lie in the broad interpretation by the Court of Justice of Article 119 and related legislation. The principle that unequal treatment of part-timers, who are predominantly female, amounts to sex discrimination has been well established in a number of cases and leaves the door open to further legal claims around the issues that are covered by the proposed directives on atypical employment. Furthermore, these examples of the Court's approach might be setting a general climate for reform which can be exploited within national legal and collective bargaining systems. However, it may not be that easy to counter the determination of employers or governments to justify unequal treatment on grounds that are unrelated to sex, as the UK has tried to do. The acceptance of part-time work under freedom of movement provisions, and the lower threshold for part-timers in the contractual terms Directive, might not seem to be a great advance in employment protection, but at least this category of employment is being formally recognised and being brought into the mainstream of legal developments. The same can be said of the draft directive on posting of workers although, like the other freedom of movement provisions, the law only applies in practice to a very limited proportion of temporary employment.

(iii) The Treaty on European Union — A Way Forward?

The adoption of the Protocol and Agreement on Social Policy, which is annexed to the Maastricht Agreement,[166] raises a number of questions about the future development of European social policy in general and legal protection for atypical workers in particular. Now that the Treaty on European Union has been finally implemented there are two main routes by which social legislation may be pursued. Firstly, there is the continuation of the original Treaty base[167] which requires all twelve Member States to participate in Council decisions on legal measures which affect all of them equally. Secondly, there is the agreement by all Member States, referred to above, that eleven of them, excluding the UK, may pass social legislation which only applies to those eleven. The prospect of any progress on the atypical employment proposals under the former route has already been discussed so this final section will concentrate on the debate surrounding the latter. This will include a consideration of the legal status of the Social Protocol; the implications for atypi-

166. OJ C 191/1992.

167. This is rewritten in the Maastricht Treaty with very few amendments but perhaps with greater precision.

cal employment in the content of the Agreement on Social Policy; the tone of the 1993 Green Paper and 1994 White Paper on Social Policy; and the possibilities of the increased role envisaged for the social partners.

The Social Protocol and the Agreement on Social Policy came into being as a last ditch attempt to get the UK to sign the Maastricht Treaty in November 1991 and, as a completely new departure in Community law, has generated fierce legal debate. The case for the Agreement being part of the Treaty is based on the argument that all twelve Member States signed the Protocol (to which the Agreement is attached) and therefore any provisions agreed by the Eleven will be subject to the same rules as the rest of the Treaty. Watson supports this view by referring to Article 239 of the Treaty which states that Protocols annexed to it "by common accord of the Member States shall form an integral part thereof" and by virtue of Article 236 of the Treaty of Rome it is valid as Community law.[168] However, the status of the Agreement can also be interpreted as an independent arrangement between the Eleven with the status of an intergovernmental treaty. If this view is taken, the institutional framework of the EC Treaty would not be available and Member States would have to take primary responsibility for implementing legislation. The grounds for this interpretation are that the wording of the Social Protocol (No.14) does not explicitly suspend the UK's voting rights (compared to Protocol 11 that does) and refers to "among themselves" and "applying as far as they are concerned" which seems to suggest a separate agreement by the Eleven.[169]

Perhaps a more fundamental criticism of the UK opt-out of the "Social Chapter" is that it creates two systems of law on social policy which can be argued to be contrary to the principle of unity of Community law and potentially distortive of competition. Under this two-tier system the UK will have an unfair advantage over other Member States in terms of the social costs of employment and, furthermore, British workers will have a lower level of social protection than their continental counterparts. Barnard lists a number of legal bases in the Treaty which would allow any legislation passed by the Eleven to be contested in the Court. These include the restriction of freedom of movement under Article 48 EC; being potentially in breach of Articles 2 and 5 EC regarding approximation of economic policies and measures to fulfil the Treaty; possible legal challenges from other Member States (under Article 173 EC) and the Commission (under Article 169 EC); use of Article 236 EEC because the Agreement does not cover all twelve Member States; and

---

168. Watson P, "Social Policy after Maastricht", (1993) 30 *Common Market Law Review* 481.

169. See Vogel-Polsky E, DOC EN/CN/202155, p.3.

action on the grounds of equality of treatment under Article 6 EC.[170]

Clearly, there is plenty of scope here to question the legal challenge to the status of the Social Protocol and Agreement. Any attempt to discredit the Social Protocol as unconstitutional within the terms of the Treaty of Rome may be politically unacceptable but the actual effects of distortions of competition arising from the UK opt-out may well be pursued in individual cases. Whiteford comments that if different social costs are found to be anti-competitive then the arguments used in the Article 100a directive for atypical workers will be vindicated, which is ironic in the context of this discussion.[171] In practice, however, it seems more likely that the Commission will attempt to introduce social legislation first through the pre-Maastricht Treaty route and only resort to the Social protocol as a last resort.[172] Finally, it is open to the UK to opt-in to particular pieces of legislation after they have been agreed by the Eleven or ultimately to sign up to the "Social Chapter" of the Treaty. In the meantime, any social legislation under the Agreement will be under some doubt.

Turning to the particular case of the legal base for atypical employment protection under the Agreement on Social Policy, there appears to be some ambiguity about whether it would be covered by unanimous or majority voting procedure. In Article 2(1) of the Agreement there is reference to five main activities: health and safety; working conditions; information and consultation; equality between men and women; and integration into the labour market, all of which can be adopted by qualified majority voting.[173] If the same terminology is used as the 1989 Social Charter Action Programme "employment conditions" seem to be comparable with "employment and remuneration", the category used for the initiatives on atypical employment. However, in Article 2(3), which lists a number of other areas which can only be agreed unanimously, there is reference to "social security and social protection of workers" which also seems to include certain aspects of the atypical proposals. There is also reference in Article 2(6) to "pay" as being one area outside the competence of the Agreement altogether, which may be a source of ambiguity if pay is given a broad interpretation.[174] However, Weiss assures us that the three new demarcations override the principle underlying Article 100a(2) and give "ample scope for matters to be placed un-

---

170. Barnard C in *The International Journal of Comparative Labour Law and Industrial Relations*, Spring 1992, p.22.

171. Whiteford E in *European Law Review*, Vol.18, No.3, 1993, p.220.

172. This is the way the current proposal on atypical work is being handled - see later discussion.

173. In Article 2(2) the legal procedure is specified as Article 189(c) EEC.

174. As it is in the application of Article 119 EEC.

der the broad term "working conditions", so as to limit the principle of qualified majority voting for the few remaining subjects of employment law".[175] He thinks that there is no longer any need to discuss what tricks of interpretation might be indulged in but still foresees difficulties in the existence of two sources of law.

The Green Paper on European Social Policy, "Options for the Union", issued by the Commission in October 1993, does not give any guidance on how atypical employment rights might be pursued under the revised Treaty, but there are clear indications of it being on the agenda. For example, under "Medium Strategy",[176] a new Community-wide framework for analysis and action in the labour market has as first on its list "improved adaptability at the workplace and development of new types of employment based on innovative forms of work organisation".[177] This, and reference to reduced employer's social security contributions and work-sharing, is discussed in the context of job creation but reinforces the mainstream acceptance of atypical work and implies the involvement of Community institutions in the construction of common policies. Later, under "Labour standards and working conditions",[178] there is a strong indication that this will include legislative action in the assertion that, in the context of increased labour flexibility, "the Commission emphasises the need for early adoption of existing proposed directives, because on balance they will help rather than hinder the support of the workforce in the fundamental process of change".[179] There is a further comment on the need for equal social and labour standards in the different forms of labour contracts and, in the section on equal opportunities between men and women,[180] reference to discrimination in part-time work and mobility between standard and non-standard forms of employment. This reinforces the general direction of the Commission's thinking but gives no indication of the legal base that might be adopted, other than to repeat, in Section IV.D, the legal competencies outlined in the Agreement attached to the Social Protocol.

The revised approach to consultation and implementation of social legislation is discussed in the Green Paper which says that "the Maastricht Treaty opens up, for the Eleven, the possibility of both complementarity

---

175. Weiss M in *The International Journal of Comparative Labour Law and Industrial Relations*, Spring 1992, p.7.

176. Green Paper, Section IV, Part B.

177. Green Paper, p.38.

178. Green Paper, Section IV.C (2)(b).

179. Green Paper, p.43.

180. Green Paper, pp. 63-64.

and alternance between legislation and collective bargaining".[181] The desire to involve the social partners in future labour market regulation is one the main features of social policy in the Maastricht Treaty and it seems likely that the content and means adopted to protect atypical workers will not be finally decided until extensive consultation has occurred. The role of social dialogue[182] has been expanded in the Agreement on Social Policy in allowing directives to be implemented by collective agreement;[183] consulting management and labour on the possible direction of Community action and content of proposals;[184] and allowing social dialogue to lead to contractual relations at European level, if so desired, which can be implemented by national procedures or by Council decision.[185]

The subsequent White Paper on European Social Policy highlights the outstanding proposals left over from the 1989 Social Action Programme, including those on non-standard employment, and states that "the highest possible priority must be given to bring these proposals to a successful conclusion".[186] It also says that if no progress is made on the basis of current proposals by the end of 1994, consultation will start under the Agreement on Social Policy, but no reference is made to QMV or unanimity as the basis of agreement. It is suggested that a first step might be a directive on part-time work only, although the subsequent German proposal, still under Article 100, also includes temporary workers. The White Paper also introduces the principle that, if flexible forms of work are to be generally accepted, such workers should have equal treatment.[187]

This means that the latest atypical proposals from the German Presidency will be subject to the new consultation procedure with the social partners before they are resubmitted to the Council, or they may go on the agenda for European level collective bargaining. The latter route is intended to facilitate greater consensus over social issues but, as the Green Paper points out, "progress will depend on the political will of the social partners, on the capacity and functioning of the machinery of the social dialogue and on the real prospects for European-wide collective bargaining".[188] The Commission is working to develop and facilitate structures

181. Green Paper, p.56.

182. Formally introduced by the Single European Act as Article 118b EEC.

183. Agreement on Social Policy, Article 2(4).

184. Agreement on Social Policy, Article 3.

185. Agreement on Social Policy, Article 4.

186. COM(94) 333 final, p.21.

187. COM(94) 333 final, p.22.

188. Green Paper, p.69.

of consultation and negotiation although it is recognised that the variety of national industrial relations systems makes this process a difficult one.[189] A Communication has now been issued on how the new consultation procedure will operate[190] and the White Paper proposes further action on a number of points including a new role for the Standing Employment Committee; a discussion document on social dialogue; a European training centre for industrial relations; and establishment of clear links between social standards and productivity.[191]

A particular problem, discussed by Bercusson, is "bargaining in the shadow of the law"[192] by which he means that the social partners will be bargaining under the threat of legislation if they cannot agree to autonomous regulation. The problem lies in the timing of the initiation of the special procedure under Article 3(4) and the question is "which consultation of the two envisaged by Article 3 — before or after the Commission produces its envisaged proposal?". Whichever is the case, there seems to be grounds for claiming that the process of collective bargaining will be impaired. Both Bercusson and Weiss,[193] also ask what is meant by implementation "in accordance with the procedures and practices specific to management and labour in the Member States".[194] It seems to them unlikely that these agreements can be enforceable against industrial relations actors at national level who were not party to the European-level agreement. A number of other procedural difficulties are discussed by Weiss, leading him to the conclusion that "virtually every detail of the new procedure has been left unclear".[195] It is alarming to note that if European framework agreements are implemented they may only apply to one industry, opening up the possibility of another dimension of inequality for atypical workers.

So the Social Protocol and Agreement under the Maastricht Treaty does open up new possibilities for the enactment of equal rights for atypical workers. Assuming that no agreement will be reached by the Twelve before the end of 1994, the current proposal under the German Presidency will enter into the consultation procedure in 1995. It remains to be seen whether agreement can be reached in the form of a directive or whether the collective agreement route is seen as more appropriate to a

189. Green Paper, p.70.

190. COM(94) 600 final, 14.12.93.

191. COM(94) 333 final, p.43.

192. Bercusson B in *Modern Law Review*, Vol.53, 1992, p.185.

193. Weiss M (*supra* FN 175), p.11.

194. Article 4 (1) of the Agreement on Social Policy.

195. Weiss M (*supra* FN 175), p.11.

minimalist approach to legal intervention and the new spirit of subsidiarity. It is also possible that no progress will be made at all if the social partners remain in "sharp disagreement". However, the history of the Works Council Directive, now implemented by the Eleven, shows that the Social Protocol route may be more productive.

5. CONCLUSION

It should be clear from the foregoing discussion that the problems that have so far prevented the implementation of Community legislation to provide greater employment protection for atypical workers (with the exception of health and safety) will not be easily resolved by the new provisions under the Maastricht Treaty. There are a now a greater variety of possibilities for regulation which extend from the previous proposals under Articles 100 and 100a through continued legal activism by the Court under, for example, Article 119, to the new competence by the Eleven to enact this kind of legislation by qualified majority voting and the alternative of European-wide collective agreements. However, the strong opposition from employers' associations, and some Member States, to minimum standards that are seen as limiting labour flexibility and increasing labour costs is unlikely to subside. The interests that represent labour were also unhappy that the previous proposals did not go far enough, so resistance from the trade unions and the European Parliament can also be expected to any compromise between the social partners on this issue. Furthermore, the status of the Social Protocol and Agreement is open to challenge in the Court and any attempts to enact social legislation for the Eleven may be undermined by protracted legal argument. Whether the latest proposal from the German Presidency, which emphasises the potential of equality for atypical workers for job creation, will be any more acceptable remains to be seen. The tone of the White Paper on Social Policy indicates a renewed political will to legislate, for the Eleven at least, and we may see a minimal level of protection introduced in 1995.

This cautious note of optimism might be more sustainable if it were believed that employers are gradually coming round to the view that all labour is a valuable resource rather than a cost to be minimised. The 1993 Green Paper and 1994 White Paper on Social Policy both emphasise the need to build on the European tradition of a high level of labour protection and take on global competition with a highly motivated and involved labour force. This theme is also taken up in the Human Resource Management (HRM) literature which argues that competition is not just about labour costs but a wider appreciation of HRM that includes commitment and long-term development of employees. However, this approach can be seen to represent the "soft" side of HRM[196] which tends to focus on "core" employees (standard contracts) rather than atypical workers who are much more likely to come within the "hard" side of matching numbers to production requirements at the lowest possible cost. While unemployment is high and trade unions relatively weak there is no shortage of people willing to take on this kind of work and employers are largely free to restructure their labour force in ways that are most favourable to them.

The degree to which different Member States are prepared to maintain or improve protection for atypical workers varies between those who already have a reasonable floor of employment rights and might find it politically unacceptable to deregulate, like France, and those that are sympathetic with the UK approach (but do not necessarily show it) to deregulation and lower social costs. However, the problem of "social dumping", if one Member State lowers its levels of employment protection, puts a lot of pressure on those maintaining higher standards, especially if unemployment is rising. This was illustrated in the furore over the decision by Hoover to relocate production capacity from France to Scotland,[197] although it is not clear whether the decision was based primarily on lower social costs in the UK. It is ironic when this kind of dispute occurs because one of the basic objectives of the common market is the free movement of capital to even out regional disparities. All Member States are under pressure to encourage job creation by relaxing labour market regulation and many have done so, particularly in widening the scope of fixed-term employment contracts. So it is unlikely that there will be a great deal of support for any Community initiatives that have the effect of raising the cost of labour under current economic conditions.

The dispute over the atypical employment proposals under Articles 100 and 100a in 1990 encapsulates the tension between the Commission's desire to regulate to ensure social as well as economic cohesion and the opposing forces of deregulation. The attempt by the Commission to distinguish between "distortions of competition" and "certain working conditions" as a way of getting something done by qualified majority voting was clearly seen by the opposition as a way of getting in minimum levels of social protection through the back door. So the next attempt to introduce legislation will already be seen in ideological terms as further evidence of the federalist tendency. The new emphasis on subsidiarity in the Maastricht Treaty is clearly stated in the Agreement

196. See discussion of "hard" and "soft" HRM in Storey J (ed.), *New Perspectives on Human Resource Management*, 1989, pp. 8-9

197. EIRR, March 1993, pp. 14-20

attached to the Social Protocol in the wording on implementation which emphasises the need to adapt to different industrial relations systems and national traditions in labour law. Will this be enough to encourage the reluctant Member States to take a more positive attitude to social legislation?

The distortion of competition argument has a powerful resonance in the history of Community legislation and rulings by the Court, but proving that it exists purely because of different social costs between Member States is difficult in the face of counter claims concerning different levels of labour productivity and the need to encourage movement of capital to the poorer regions. However, the 1990 proposals did not actually tackle the problem of national differences because they only aim for parity between full-time open-ended contracts and atypical ones within national legal systems. The competition argument then becomes more complicated and the main protagonists in the atypical work debate seem to have fallen back on more simplistic ideological assertions about the relative merits of social regulation and free competition.

Another limitation of the 1990 proposals is that they were limited to certain categories of atypical worker by various exclusion clauses. For example, the part-time threshold was eight hours and the temporary worker threshold was three months, in some instances, with the status of casual work somewhat indeterminate. Then there was the exclusion of other forms of atypical work such as homeworking, teleworking, on-call and self-employment. The Parliament made a strong bid to extend the definition of atypical work but the Commission resisted, apparently on the grounds that "administrative costs" would go up and anyway these forms were not so widespread as mainstream part-time and temporary work. This is hardly the case with self-employment but it could be argued that this should not be covered by employment law as such despite the fact that sub-contracting may be a disguised form of direct employment. Finally, as in the case of all social legislation, there is the exclusion of third-country nationals who are a significant element of the atypical workforce either legally, or illegally as clandestine workers. This raises the important point that atypical employment represents a range of insecurity and quasi-legality in the secondary labour market that should be considered as a whole in the interests of social justice and the economic argument about unfair competition and social dumping. On the other hand, it could be said that partial regulation is better than none and the protection of some of the atypical workforce will raise expectations and political will to protect the rest. Alternatively, it may have the effect, that is feared by the trade unions, of further segmenting the labour market and weakening the position of those higher up the employment protection ladder.

So how far are the problems inherent in the 1990 draft directives being reproduced in the current round of discussion on the German proposal for atypical workers? The published details (in November 1994) only reveal a simple list of measures with little supporting argument so it is difficult to tell whether the ambiguities of "distortions of competition" are still of central concern. The process of social dialogue envisaged by the Social Protocol and Agreement may be difficult to sustain, given the apparently entrenched positions of the social partners, although the labour movement may consider it to be tactically beneficial to take a positive attitude towards this new avenue of policy-making. The trade unions have so far largely resisted the inclusion of atypical work into collective bargaining but may now feel that 20% of the labour force can no longer be ignored because of their "knock-on effect" on collective bargaining. The complications presented by the competence of the Eleven to enact social policy in future are also likely to slow things down especially if the UK opt-out is challenged in the Court or the legality of the Social Protocol and Agreement are seriously challenged. There is still the remote chance, however, that the atypical proposals will be processed under pre-Maastricht arrangements if the UK feels exposed enough to the disapproval of other Member States, and, of course, there is the real possibility that the political regime in the UK will change to one that accepts the logic of harmonisation of working conditions. The Commission seems clearly set on deepening and widening the social dimension through the Maastricht Treaty and the question of labour flexibility is central to the vision of a labour force that can compete with other world powers. So in the medium to long-term the issue of atypical work is unlikely to go away.

Another longer term consideration is the effect that judicial activism in the Court of Justice will have on the process of labour market regulation. It cannot be claimed that the range of judgments under Articles 119 and 48 provide a comprehensive alternative route for the protection of atypical workers, but there is clearly the potential for basic principles to be established. Because a large proportion of part-time workers are women, the fundamental principle of equality between men and women has become closely associated with equality between part-time and full-time workers. Temporary workers have also been given equal recognition in some aspects of freedom of movement and, as many temporary workers are also women, there is crossover of principle between temporary and part-time status. Given the other recent legislation on contracts and temporary labour services there is a range of legal competence that can be drawn upon by the Court in future litigation. The history of judgments based on Article 119 suggests that the Court has the will to develop these areas and the scope of Article 6 EC seems wide open to the cause of atypical workers. However, legal activism is a lengthy process and can only be regarded as a long term strategy.

Taken together, the above conclusions represent both threats and opportunities with regard to the protection of atypical workers. On the one hand, the forces for deregulation seem to have the potential to delay any new initiatives or at least water them down to a point where, like the Working Time Directive, it is hard to see what gains have been made. On the other hand, the Commission seems determined to extend the social dimension and the Court will probably support this process over the longer term. Not much has really changed in the political alignments on employment protection since the atypical proposals in 1990 but the relevant provisions of the Maastricht Treaty may now unblock the path to legislation although it is not certain whether the strengthening of social dialogue will help or hinder this process.

Biographical Notes on the Authors

Ingeborg Borgerud LL.M., has been the Norwegian State Secretary at the Ministry of Justice and Police since 1992 and was formerly an Attorney-at-Law with the Norwegian Federation of Trade Unions.

Paul Cullen M.A., is a civil servant in the Irish Department of Enterprise and Employment where he has worked on the preparation of industrial relations, trade union and employment equality legislation. He has also served as Labour Attaché in the Irish Embassy in London and was assigned under Ireland's Presidency of the EC Council of Ministers in 1990 to chair the co-ordination group for EC Member States participating in the Nightwork Committee at the International Labour Conference in Geneva.

Brian Jones M.A., J.D., LL.M., read mathematics at Oxford and then qualified as an actuary, opening his own consulting firm in New York. He took a U.S. law degree and became a member of the New York and District of Columbia Bars.

Philip Jones B.Sc., M.Sc., M.A., has had a 20-year career in the airline industry specialising in the business applications of information technology.

Jeff Kenner is Lecturer in Law, International Centre for Management, Law and Industrial Relations, University of Leicester.

Nick Rahtz B.A., M.A., M.I.P.D., is a Senior Lecturer in Industrial Relations at Sheffield Hallam University.